PRAISE FOR *THE NEW WO*

Peter Cheese's considerable experience in the world of HR makes this book on the future of the workplace and workforce a must-read.
Lord Mark Price, former Managing Director of Waitrose, Founder of Engaging Business and WorkL, Chairman of Fair Trade UK, and Member of the House of Lords

As a passionate advocate of equality in the workplace, it is fantastic to see this book talk about the future of work and the challenges and the opportunities it will present. Everyone in business should read this. It opened my eyes to the future we all face.
Baroness Ruby McGregor-Smith, former CEO of Mitie Group, President of British Chambers of Commerce, and Member of the House of Lords

Never has the pace of change in the world been so rapid. And while we can't be certain of the future, as Peter Cheese sets out in this book, we can shape it. *The New World of Work* is a compelling narrative of the factors at play and the principles at stake, and is a must-read for policy makers, business people, educators, indeed, for all of us, as it touches the heart of humanity and the skills we will all need to adapt and prosper in the future.
Sir Peter Estlin, former Lord Mayor of the City of London

Peter Cheese's unique perch offers readers a thoughtful perspective on the changing world of work. His observations are astute, his predictions compelling and recommendations impactful. With his insights, business and HR leaders will discover opportunity as they harness the uncertainty ahead.
Dave Ulrich, Rensis Likert Professor, Ross School of Business, University of Michigan, and Partner at The RBL Group

The New World of Work

Shaping a future that helps people, organizations and our societies to thrive

Peter Cheese

Publisher's note

Every possible effort has been made to ensure that the information contained in this book is accurate at the time of going to press, and the publishers and authors cannot accept responsibility for any errors or omissions, however caused. No responsibility for loss or damage occasioned to any person acting, or refraining from action, as a result of the material in this publication can be accepted by the editor, the publisher or the author.

First published in Great Britain and the United States in 2021 by Kogan Page Limited

Apart from any fair dealing for the purposes of research or private study, or criticism or review, as permitted under the Copyright, Designs and Patents Act 1988, this publication may only be reproduced, stored or transmitted, in any form or by any means, with the prior permission in writing of the publishers, or in the case of reprographic reproduction in accordance with the terms and licences issued by the CLA. Enquiries concerning reproduction outside these terms should be sent to the publishers at the undermentioned addresses:

2nd Floor, 45 Gee Street	122 W 27th St, 10th Floor	4737/23 Ansari Road
London	New York, NY 10001	Daryaganj
EC1V 3RS	USA	New Delhi 110002
United Kingdom		India
www.koganpage.com		

Kogan Page books are printed on paper from sustainable forests.

© Peter Cheese, 2021

The right of Peter Cheese to be identified as the author of this work has been asserted by him in accordance with the Copyright, Designs and Patents Act 1988.

ISBNs

Hardback	978 1 39860 211 3
Paperback	978 1 39860 209 0
Ebook	978 1 39860 210 6

British Library Cataloguing-in-Publication Data

A CIP record for this book is available from the British Library.

Library of Congress Cataloging-in-Publication Data

Names: Cheese, Peter, author.
Title: The new world of work: shaping a future that helps people, organizations and our societies to thrive / Peter Cheese.
Description: London, United Kingdom; New York, NY: Kogan Page Limited, 2021. | Includes bibliographical references and index.
Identifiers: LCCN 2021013745 (print) | LCCN 2021013746 (ebook) | ISBN 9781398602090 (paperback) | ISBN 9781398602113 (hardback) | ISBN 9781398602106 (ebook)
Subjects: LCSH: Personnel management. | Employees–Mental health. | Employee morale. | Organizational change. | Job satisfaction. | BISAC: BUSINESS & ECONOMICS / Human Resources & Personnel Management | BUSINESS & ECONOMICS / Organizational Development
Classification: LCC HF5549 .C4445 2021 (print) | LCC HF5549 (ebook) | DDC 658.3/14–dc23
LC record available at https://lccn.loc.gov/2021013745
LC ebook record available at https://lccn.loc.gov/2021013746

Typeset by Integra Software Services Pondicherry
Print production managed by Jellyfish
Printed and bound by 4edge Ltd, UK

CONTENTS

Foreword xi
Acknowledgements xiv

01 A new era of work 1
The fourth industrial revolution 1
It is not just about technology 3
A perfect storm? 4
Managing in an increasingly uncertain world 5
Known knowns – what we need to be addressing 8
Some of the known unknowns – looking ahead 9
Guiding principles for the future 11
A collective and collaborative effort – time to step up 13
Endnotes 14

02 Economics and the economy 15
A time of creative destruction and what crises teach us 16
The longest bull market in history 19
Short-termism and the profit motive 21
Lack of investment in the future 23
The real nature of our economies today 24
Large, medium, small and micro enterprises 27
How models of employment are changing 30
The gig economy 30
Employment and unemployment 32
How ways of working are changing 35
Understanding productivity 36
The UK productivity puzzle 39
In conclusion 41
Endnotes 42

03 Globalization and geopolitics 45
Eras of industrialization from the past to the present 47
The evolution of globalization 50
From a bipolar world to a multipolar world 53

Where is globalization headed now? 55
How global interconnection helps standards of practice 58
Populism and politics 60
Era-defining changes – accelerated by the pandemic 61
Tribalism and individual politics 64
In conclusion 66
Endnotes 67

04 Social and demographic change 69

A growing crisis of trust 70
Going beyond virtue signalling – from words to action 74
Trust what you know – importance of evidence and transparency 75
Increasing inequalities undermining trust and impacting social cohesion 76
The economics of inequality 79
Government actions and policy interventions 80
Understanding pay gaps 82
Equality of opportunity 85
The impact of demographic trends 86
Migration rates and ethnic diversity 89
The rise of the new generations – the 5G workforce 91
Rising intergenerational tensions? 95
In conclusion 97
Endnotes 97

05 Technology: Automation, AI and beyond 101

Technology powering the fourth industrial revolution 102
A new era driven by data and artificial intelligence 104
How new technologies are impacting organizations and business models 106
Are robots coming after our jobs? 108
Technology improving people's performance at work 110
Virtual reality vs real life 112
Social media – from word of mouth to world of mouth 114
Looking further out – utopia or dystopia 116
Regulation and education 120
In conclusion 122
Endnotes 122

06 Education and learning 125

Understanding skills gaps and the imperative for change 126
What skills are really needed for the future 129
Digital and technology skills 133
Will our systems of education meet the needs of the changing world of work? 134
The rise and rise of higher education 138
The payback for degree-level education – the need for a balanced debate 140
Alternative educational routes – vocational education and training 142
Do we have too many types of qualification? 146
The case for strengthening non-degree post-secondary education and learning through the FE sector 147
New models for education – the disruptors 148
Corporate universities 150
Corporate investments in skills development 152
Understanding the value of learning and training 154
In conclusion 157
Endnotes 158

07 Focusing on the right things 162

What gets measured gets done 163
Measuring the big things 164
Life satisfaction, purpose and wellbeing 166
Gross National Happiness – is it for real? 168
Gross National Wellbeing 170
Acknowledging business responsibilities to all stakeholders 173
Towards broader corporate reporting and governance 175
Progress and changes in corporate regulation and standards 177
Importance and challenge of measuring people 180
Regulatory approaches to reporting on people 182
Improving diversity and opportunity – does regulatory reporting work? 184
Representation of men and ethnic minorities at senior levels 186
What about quotas? 189
Top executive pay and reward – is this part of the problem? 191
In conclusion 193
Endnotes 194

08 Building responsible business 197

Framing corporate responsibility and intent through purpose 198
Why are values important? 202
CSR – doing well by doing good 204
People-centric cultures 209
Inclusion and diversity as drivers of good business 210
The power of empowerment 211
The importance of listening and speak-up cultures 213
Good corporate governance 215
Board constitution and diversity 218
In conclusion 219
Endnotes 220

09 Leadership for the future 222

What is leadership – is it different from management? 224
A brief history of leadership models – are they helpful? 225
What and how we learn from crises 227
What we must take forwards from here – the mindsets and capabilities leaders will really need 231
Importance of evidence and measuring the right things 233
Key metrics and the balanced scorecard 235
Leading from principles – a 21st-century model of compassion and safety 237
Developmental models of leadership – navigating the uncertain and thinking systemically 238
Building leadership capabilities 242
Talking it through – open leadership 244
Judgements and ethical decision-making 246
In conclusion 248
Endnotes 249

10 People strategy at the heart of business strategy 252

People and organizational strategy, and HR 253
People and organization strategy versus HR strategy 255
Core competencies and strategic workforce planning 257
Talent sourcing and recruitment – diversity 259
What the pandemic has changed in talent sourcing and recruitment 261
Starting recruitment with the young – working with education 262
Borrowing talent and skills 264
Crowdsourcing talent and skills 266

Acquiring capabilities through M&A 267
Productivity and performance 268
Optimizing the organization 270
Voice and empowerment as organizing principles 272
In conclusion 274
Endnotes 274

11 Good work as a goal 276

Our working lives and what is important as good work 277
Are we working harder? 278
Engagement as a way of understanding good work 279
Understanding the drivers of engagement 281
Giving people voice in the workplace 284
Seeing engagement in a wider context 286
What have been the trends in engagement? 287
The principles of job quality and movement towards good work 290
Surveying job quality and working lives in the UK 294
Use of skills at work 295
Design of jobs and work 297
Humans working together with automation 299
The issues of bias – keeping our values and ethics front and centre 300
The opportunity of flexible working 302
Giving people more choice – unlimited holidays 306
How we use our time 307
Flexible careers 309
In conclusion 310
Endnotes 311

12 The agile learning organization 314

Becoming an agile learning organization 315
Importance of a learning philosophy and vision 319
Methods of learning and how they are changing 320
Evolving learning effectiveness through evidence and the next generations of digital learning 322
The evolution of learning technologies 323
The outcomes of learning and how should they be measured 325
Making training and learning inclusive 328
Implications for corporate learning and development functions 330
In conclusion 332
Endnotes 333

13 Wellbeing as an outcome 334

What actually is wellbeing? 335
The drivers of wellbeing in the workplace 337
Physical safety and wellbeing and the outcomes of the pandemic 339
The importance of understanding stress 340
The growing mental wellbeing challenge 342
Impact of crises on mental health and wellbeing – the long shadow 344
Managing stress and supporting wellbeing in the workplace 345
Improving mental wellbeing through work 348
The importance of sleep 348
Financial wellbeing and the issue of in-work poverty 349
How organizations can support the financial wellbeing of their people 352
A broader understanding of wellbeing in an online world 354
In conclusion 355
Endnotes 355

14 #WTF: What's the future? 358

Pulling it all together 359
How do people view the future of work? 360
Principles, evidence and outcomes 362
A scenario of scenarios 365
Common themes from scenario planning 367
Different forms of our economies for the future 369
Some reasonable hopes and expectations for the future of work 370
What work should really mean to us 373
Endnotes 374

Index 375

FOREWORD

Machiavelli wrote in *The Prince*, 'It should be borne in mind that there is nothing more difficult to arrange, more doubtful of success and more dangerous to carry through than initiating change. The innovator makes enemies of all those who prospered under the old order, and only lukewarm support is forthcoming from those who would prosper under the new.'

And nothing could be more apposite than this, as we enter a new era of work. This change will be profound, given how work itself has significantly changed during the Covid-19 pandemic, but also because of political change and economic challenges with a major recession that may follow over the coming years. All these circumstances have created a perfect storm, which will transform the lives of many individuals, companies, public sector bodies and the institutions that underpin them.

So, what lessons have we learned during this pandemic, as we move forward, which will change the workplace in the future?

First, working more flexibly is not only doable but also meets working people's needs for greater autonomy and control over their job and life more generally. Prior to the pandemic the global research evidence was that if you could and wanted flexible working, it delivered enhanced job satisfaction, lower stress-related sickness absence and great productivity. It is now a reality that flexibility will survive the period of the pandemic, and, as research has been showing, should deliver to the bottom line as well as to the financial and mental wellbeing of working people.[1]

Second, we have learned how vitally important line managers are to creating purpose and value-led organizations. As we enter the hybrid era of flexible working at the same time as recession and political realignment in the post-Brexit era, how people's fears, uncertainties and skills are managed will be significant in any recovery, as well as in employee health, wellbeing and performance.[2] Many HR and occupational health professionals have for many years been advocating the need to recruit and recognize different strengths in every line manager which must include high levels of emotional intelligence, empathy and social skills. This advocacy needs to be turned into reality, with leaders from shop floor to top floor being promoted and recruited on the basis of these personal traits – in effect, where there is parity between potential leaders' technical and social skills. Vital if we are to manage the tsunami of change about to hit all organizations in all sectors in the fourth industrial revolution and next era of work.

Third, if we are to engage Generation Z and Millennials in this new era of work, we need to listen to them. They are the new generations in work who are much less willing to work in workplace cultures that don't develop, value or trust them. Their parents, on the other hand, were more accepting of intolerant attitudes and behaviours for the sake of job security. These generations want more from work. They want a strong sense of purpose, consistent and supportive values and behaviours, greater work–life integration, and challenge. These generations will lead us into this new greener world, where values count, where having a sense of purpose will drive their performance and ambition and where they will contribute to the quality of life in their personal relationships, communities and in society more generally.

This book highlights how globalization, geopolitics, technologies, demographics and economies are dramatically changing, leading to fundamental reorientation in the way we do things; in education and learning, in new forms of leadership, and in the importance of 'people' at the heart of business.

This movement toward building wellbeing cultures in our workplaces was foreseen even at the start of the Industrial Revolution by the great social reformer and thinker John Ruskin, when he wrote in 1851, 'In order that people may be happy in their work these three things are needed: they must be fit for it, they must not do too much of it and they must have a sense of success in it.' It took two major recessions and a global health crisis to get us all to understand, as the author of this book states, 'wellbeing is at the heart of productivity, of engagement and of good work itself… and we have to reverse the trends of recent years of declining wellbeing, of stress and growing concerns for mental health.'

As the author convincingly lays out in this book, the time for this change is upon us all, as we put 'people first', and business leaders as well as the HR community embrace the challenges ahead.

This book leads the way in beginning the dialogue for all of us interested in people at work, but we have to go beyond rhetoric and take the action to enable effective, humane and sustainable change. George Bernard Shaw, in his play *Mrs Warren's Profession*, summed it up nicely: 'People are always blaming their circumstances for what they are. I don't believe in circumstances. The people who get on in this world are the people who get up and look for the circumstances they want, and if they can't find them, make them!'

The New World of Work lays out the challenges and circumstances which we all have to action in the coming years.

Professor Sir Cary Cooper, CBE
ALLIANCE Manchester Business School, University of Manchester

Endnotes

1. Norgate, S and Cooper, C L (2020) *Flexible Work: Designing our heathier future lives*, Routledge, London and New York
2. Cooper, C L (2021) *Psychological Insights for Understanding COVID-19 and Work*, Routledge, London and New York

ACKNOWLEDGEMENTS

Writing a book is never an easy undertaking. It's takes a lot of time and commitment, perseverance and belief. And it takes a lot of help.

Having started on the book during the summer of 2020, the Covid-19 pandemic and the lockdowns we all had to endure unexpectedly gave me the time and space needed to write. With no social commitments and over the darkest period of the year, evenings and weekends became consumed with writing – somewhat to the dismay of my family, but to the delight of the publisher who must have been wondering if they would ever see the manuscript.

I have always enjoyed the process of writing, the discipline of trying to assemble thoughts and put them to paper, and to question, challenge and research further. Writing a book in some ways is a luxury and a bit of an indulgence as well. Usually, like many people, my writing is limited to articles or blogs, or perhaps the occasional foreword or chapter in someone else's book. Writing something short and concise is often harder than writing something long – whoever said I didn't have time to write something short, so I wrote something long had it spot on.

A book allows the opportunity to write something long. To bring together lots of ideas, experiences and interests in to one place, to look for evidence as much as possible, and to try to make some sense of it all.

But of course, a book of this kind needs real support from others. That support comes in so many forms, but for me in writing a book of this nature, it begins with the many people I have met over the last 20 years or more who have influenced me and helped to shape my thinking.

Over the last eight years or so as CEO at the CIPD, I have had the privilege of meeting many people, visiting many organizations and places, and talking on many forums and platforms. Similarly, in my time at Accenture, I always regarded it as a privilege that as a consultant I was able to meet so many people from all around the world, hear about their businesses and the challenges they faced, and explore the future.

Through all of this, I have been lucky to have a seat close enough to the action to be able to see many of the changes that have been happening, and to talk with people who are influencing or seeking to shape the future.

Politicians, business leaders, academics and thought leaders, and of course many leaders in the HR profession.

These experiences have always inspired me and excited my interest in what is happening and how we should think about the future of work.

So my first thanks go to all of them, many of whom I talk about or reference in this book.

In putting the book together, finding the themes and the structure, and in so much of the initial writing and research I owe a great debt of thanks to Josie Cox. Josie is an exceptionally talented journalist and broadcaster, having amongst other things been the Business Editor of *The Independent*, and now a freelance writer whose work appears regularly in top-notch media outlets. We worked together on this project from the outset and immediately hit it off in our shared perspectives of the world of work, what needs changing and what the future might hold.

Without her, this book wouldn't have happened and not only did she bring her insights of the business world, but also her journalistic talents in writing. Keep the sentences short, make it readable and understandable, never stop writing at a point where you are stuck or you will find it hard to return to it.

Throughout the book I have referenced research and content from the CIPD. That is not because I intend this book to be some kind of advert, but because the work of my colleagues is frequently exceptionally good, provides great insight and deserves to be referenced. The research and the collaborations that the CIPD has developed over the years focus on so many of the themes of this book, and these will be our themes for the future. So a big thanks goes to all of them and the organization which I have been proud to have had the opportunity to lead.

I particularly want to recognize Professor Sir Cary Cooper, who has been the President of the CIPD over the last six years, but also a great colleague, friend and mentor, and also Louise Fisher, who has been Chair of the CIPD over the same period. Her calm leadership and support has made my job easier as well.

Finally, and it may be a bit clichéd, but it is true, a big thanks to my family. Families see the best and the worst of all of us as it is usually the environment in which we are all at our most authentic, and raw. But if you are lucky enough to be surrounded by a supportive family, as I am, then you are blessed. I am particularly blessed by being in a very female family – my wife, and three daughters, all of whom are now forging their careers and futures in this world of work. I learn from them all, they keep me grounded, and have always helped me iron out the stresses and strains of a demanding working life.

I really do believe that work should be good for us, helping us to grow, to find our talents and interests, and hopefully for each of us to be able to make a positive contribution and difference. Now is the time to shape a better future of work for all, to focus businesses on all that they should be responsible for, and to address the issues of fairness, inclusion and wellbeing for the good of our economies and society at large.

We owe it to each other, and to the generations that follow. It is to them, in which I certainly include my own children and all the young people that I have the pleasure of spending time with, that this book is dedicated.

01

A new era of work

It's difficult to make predictions, particularly about the future.
MARK TWAIN, FROM AN OLD DANISH PROVERB

The debate about the future of work has really taken off in recent years. What jobs we might all be doing, what future careers will look like, what skills will be needed, what organizations and places of work will look like, how whole industries may be restructured.

It's not that before then, work wasn't being talked about. It was doubtless a subject that was being debated by our forebears for centuries, but as a field of research and 'science' it was more formally recognized around the early part of the last century.

But there has been a growing recognition that we are facing a new era of work, driven in particular by the extraordinary advances in information technology and automation in all its many guises.

The fourth industrial revolution

This new era has been framed as what is now widely referred to as the fourth industrial revolution, or Industry 4.0. It evolved from industrial strategy development in Germany in the early 2010s looking at how 'high-tech' would impact industry in the future, but was really popularized by Klaus Schwab, the chairman and founder of the World Economic Forum, in 2016.

As Schwab wrote at the time without any sense of hyperbole, 'We stand on the brink of a technological revolution that will fundamentally alter the way we live, work, and relate to one another. In its scale, scope, and complexity, the transformation will be unlike anything humankind has experienced before.'[1]

Five years on, most of us would agree that we are experiencing and using technology in many more ways in almost all aspects of our lives. The internet and mobile communications have grown enormously as bandwidths, speeds and processing power have enabled new services and capabilities to be accessed everywhere. Our phones have become indispensable tools for our everyday lives, we have apps for anything you can think of, and the world has been opened up through the inexorable rise of social media.

By the end of 2020 almost 4 billion people were active on social media worldwide, almost double the number in 2015.[2] And the average number of social media accounts we each have is now more than eight, which surprised me until my youngest Gen Z daughter rattled off more than ten without pausing for breath (not just the likes of Facebook, Instagram, WhatsApp or Twitter, but Vimeo, Pinterest, Reddit, YouTube, TripAdvisor, Airbnb, etc).

As an example of how technology is influencing change over the last half decade, it is as good an indicator as any.

Having started as a way for friends to connect and share – hence, social – it has grown into a communication medium that every business, business leader, politician, media personality, fund raiser or anyone who wants to influence or make change has to be part of. It is not so much social media as societal media and our new global communication system. We use it publicly, privately, at home and at work.

Whole new businesses have been developed off the back of it, and it may be the biggest source of digital disruption. It is greatly influencing how people think, allowing good, bad and sometimes positively dangerous ideas to be shared, by everyone and anyone, and whole social movements to be rapidly mobilized. Post-truth has entered our language – it was the *Oxford English Dictionary*'s word of the year in 2016 – and is part of the challenge of greater divisions, politically and, increasingly, socially.

Other technology advances that have rolled out at scale since around 2015 include facial and voice recognition – Alexa, Google Assistant and the like. Artificial intelligence is beginning to come into our lives in ways that are changing how we interact with technology, changing and humanizing the interface and shifting our relationship with it as a result.

Interconnectivity and the Internet of Things (IoT) are also growing and have been impacting logistics and distribution in particular. Other big areas being talked about, such as blockchain, are still in their early stages. Sometimes new solutions still seem to be looking for problems to solve.

The tech companies that dominate this world have grown immensely in this time. The biggest – Microsoft, Amazon, Alphabet, Apple – head the lists of the world's largest companies by market capitalization and are trillion-dollar companies – bigger than most economies of the world.

These are some of the most visible changes, but as yet, the fourth industrial revolution is still in its early stages in significant or widespread impact on the world of work and in the workplace.

It is not just about technology

Many of the changes that have been happening since the idea of the fourth industrial revolution was described are less about technology and more about other changes and crises. These will have great impact on the future of work as well.

They include social and demographic changes. Different views and expectations of younger generations in how they live and work, ageing demographics in many of the Western economies of the world, but also the sense of growing inequalities and a future of work that may not be fair and open to all. We are also in a context of significant economic fluctuations and uncertainties, and the political and geopolitical shifts of more protectionist and nationalist sentiment that has increasingly taken hold, appearing to put the handbrake on the trends towards globalization.

And let's not forget the great wake-up call about the environment. The toll that the modern era of consumerism and growth is taking on our planet. This has been dramatically forced on to the front pages over the last few years and cannot be ignored by business, any more than it can by politicians and each one of us.

One of my favourite presentations on what is happening around us is the 'Shift Happens' video. An amusing play on words, these started with a presentation from a teacher in Colorado, Karl Fisch, to colleagues to help them understand how the world was changing, and what this might mean to the futures of the students in their charge (and probably to help the teachers keep up with half the stuff many of their students already knew).

It was developed into a video that in 2007 went viral through social media and is one of the most viewed presentations of all time, with many updates and variations. A good sequence in the video says, 'We are currently preparing kids for jobs that don't yet exist, using technologies that haven't been invented, in order to solve problems we don't even know are problems yet.'[3]

Change is happening, but not everywhere and not uniformly. As the science fiction writer William Gibson observed, 'The future is here, it's just unevenly distributed.'[4]

For most of us, the world of work, our jobs and daily work lives have not changed much since the middle of the last decade. Actually, many aspects of our working lives had barely changed for many years before then.

Inequalities seem to be growing, and the many issues of poor work cultures – lack of trust, slow progress on inclusion and diversity, imbalances of opportunity, fairness of reward, stress at work and presenteeism, levels of engagement, and productivity – have plateaued or even headed in the wrong direction.

This is not to paint a dystopian view of where we are or where we are headed, but to recognize that we are still very much in the early dawn of the new era. And that the issues we need to understand and work on go way beyond just thinking about how to use clever technology to improve productivity.

We have such an opportunity, and need, to improve the world of work. To take responsibility, to think systemically and holistically, to work together and not apart. The fourth industrial revolution, or whatever we want to call this moment in time, must signal positive change. A point of inflection.

A perfect storm?

And then along came the pandemic.

The global Covid-19 pandemic that emerged in the early months of 2020 will doubtless be seen as the most significant event for the world since the great wars of the last century. It impacted the whole world, with millions suffering and dying, and it will cast a long shadow on physical and mental health and wellbeing, as well as on jobs and livelihoods, businesses in many sectors and economies as a whole.

It was a storm that everyone found themselves in, but it also became very apparent that not everyone was in the same boat.

The word 'unprecedented' was the People's Choice 2020 Word of the Year by Dictionary.com. For the *Oxford English Dictionary*, so many unprecedented things happened that it had a problem in analysing its word of the year. Instead, for the first time it decided to come up with a series of words for the year.[5] As Casper Grathwohl, the president of Oxford Dictionaries, said, 'It's both unprecedented and a little ironic – in a year that left us speechless, 2020 has been filled with new words unlike any other.'[6] Words like pandemic, lockdown, bushfires, Covid-19, WFH, circuit-breaker, support bubble, keyworkers, furlough, Black Lives Matter and moonshot.

Crises always act as a stimulus for change. By definition they cannot be ignored, we have to respond, and we can learn. They require great collaborative efforts to solve, involving all parts of our societies.

In a speech delivered in Indianapolis in April 1959, the then Senator John F. Kennedy[7] was commenting on the crises the world faced with the emergence of the Cold War and the growth of communism. But he also saw opportunity, saying, 'The space age offers the opportunity for new voyages of discovery. Atomic energy and automation can mean the opportunity for unprecedented abundance.'

He summarized his thoughts by remarking, 'When written in Chinese, the word "crisis" is composed of two characters – one represents danger and one represents opportunity.' It captured a very important construct and has been widely quoted. It turns out that he wasn't quite right on his facts of language, but at least the idea endures.

People quote Kennedy because it's human nature to want to see the upside to a grim situation. We're inherently optimistic[8] and hopeful, and much of the time that serves us well.

As neuroscientist Tali Sharot explains in her short book *The Science of Optimism*,[9] humans possess the extraordinary talent of mental time travel, that is, the ability to move back and forth through time and space in one's mind. By imagining ourselves in the future we make better decisions in the present, which, Sharot argues, is critical for our survival.

'It allows us to plan ahead, to save food and resources for times of scarcity, and to endure hard work in anticipation of a future reward,' she says. In times of crisis, our ability to scan the longer-term horizon helps us appreciate the enduring implications of any panicked, knee-jerk decision-making.

Now is the time when we need that thinking, that ability to understand the present, but also to look ahead and to work towards a positive future. As has been said before, the best way to predict the future is to shape it.

Managing in an increasingly uncertain world

The crises and the many other changes that are happening do, however, make the future harder to predict than it perhaps ever has been. The expression that we live in a VUCA world – volatile, uncertain, complex and ambiguous – has been doing the rounds for some time.

Uncertainty can even be measured. Work by the Stanford Institute for Economic Policy Research (SIEPR) led by Nick Bloom, Professor of Economics at Stanford University, and Hites Ahir and David Furceri from the IMF, developed the World Uncertainty Index, defined using the frequency of the word 'uncertainty' in the quarterly Economist Intelligence Unit country reports.[10] Starting with a baseline of 100 around the turn of the new millennium, we are now up at 200–250.

I don't think anyone expects that these levels of uncertainty won't continue for as far out as we can see.

A further difficulty for all of us is that people are not generally very good at predicting things or even understanding where the limits of our knowledge really are. Another reason why we don't generally like uncertainty.

As Israeli-American psychologist, economist and Nobel Prize winner Daniel Kahneman notes in his seminal 2011 book, *Thinking, Fast and Slow*,[11] and as has been demonstrated rather too well by the coronavirus pandemic, we're very poor at understanding just how little we actually know.

Kahneman references a 2005 study by Philip Tetlock, a psychologist at the University of Pennsylvania, on the accuracy of expert predictions. The latter collected in excess of 80,000 prognoses on a whole spectrum of issues, from political to cultural and economic to social, and evaluated whether they actually mirrored the way events turned out.

The results were humbling and no doubt a little devastating for many of the participants. The pundits' predictions proved poorer than probability dictates those of dart-throwing monkeys would have been (do they really exist?). Even in the fields in which the forecasters claimed to be most knowledgeable, their predictions were not significantly more accurate than those made by non-specialists.

Considering this, it's perhaps no surprise that making sense of everything can feel like an impossible task.

In his 2007 bestseller *The Black Swan: The impact of the highly improbable*, Nassim Nicholas Taleb argues that it's impossible to forecast certain events which he describes as outliers. But, as he says, we can develop a degree of robustness to deal with them and the deviations from the norm they cause.[12]

All of us, but particularly the leaders tasked with developing strategy and navigating the choppy waters of the present and the future, have to be able to understand paradoxes, be at least somewhat comfortable with multiple possible truths and find a way forward.

That is not easy. And it becomes harder when so many leaders have grown through their careers being encouraged or required to manage out uncertainty and create clarity. 'Don't bring me problems, bring me solutions.'

It's human even to ignore contradictions or inconvenient truths – either through our inherent confirmation bias (the tendency to interpret new evidence as confirmation of our existing beliefs) or as a wilful blindness.

In seeking more certainty, and to reduce the variables around which we have to make decisions, we have sought out simplifications, heuristics and models, and best practices. We've written lots of rules to make things predictable and to control the often more unpredictable human behaviours within our organizations. Command and control – a construct that at last seems to be on the wane.

Even if they didn't best answer the problem or the challenge we were dealing with, it gave us all very good excuses. I always remember a saying, 'Nobody ever got fired for buying IBM' – interesting when I was working for a competitor firm, but it became a proverb of the times.

Now, we cannot think like that. In times of rapid change it is imperative that we adapt and that we learn in our context. Best practice should also be removed from the lexicon. Of course we can learn from others, but it's really about best fit. What is likely to work best in this context and what evidence we are using to make that decision or choice. And then we need to reduce or take out the unnecessary rules, the barriers that constrain thinking and innovation, and seek to empower people to contribute, to challenge.

The simple answer is that we must learn to live with uncertainty. And we must learn more to adapt, to accept and manage change, and even to thrive from it. Resilience is not putting up shields to protect ourselves from change, it is learning how to understand and manage change, and to be clear on the things we do know and what can we control and influence. That is true for individuals as much as it is for organizations.

So we should start with the known knowns and the things we know we need to take forwards, fix or learn from. Then we should explore the known unknowns – things we recognize are likely to happen or change, how we can plan for them, shape them or take advantage of them. Adoption of technology is a good example. We will need to learn as we go, course correcting as necessary.

Unknown unknowns will always come and bite us, so we need to be agile to be able to respond when they happen. But in reality these are rare. Even the pandemic was predicted by many as a possible event. Bill Gates in a 2015 TED talk[13] spoke of a viral epidemic as the greatest risk of global catastrophe, and that we hadn't invested enough to stop it, in stark contrast to nuclear Armageddon which was seen to be our biggest threat in the past.

Known knowns – what we need to be addressing

As we will explore throughout this book, there are many issues in the world of work and of business that need to be understood and addressed. Trends that have been slowly happening, and of which we have not all been aware. Many of these have had a strong light shone on them by the pandemic, creating a catalyst for change.

Debates about the future of work leading up to the pandemic had increasingly focused on challenging the old order – the paradigms of work and business that have been with us for decades. From the norms of the standard working weeks even to the pillars of capitalism. The primacy of the shareholder, the absolutism of the profit motive, the reward systems of top executives, the behaviour of stock markets, and short termism that has held back longer-term investment. And the growing inequalities and unfairness, in work poverty and lack of progress on diversity and inclusion.

New business models were emerging and the disruptive force of the digital world has been increasingly felt in sectors like retail, financial services, media, manufacturing and logistics.

Businesses were starting to be held more to account. Questions about culture, purpose and values were in the minds of regulators as well as investors, and certainly in the younger generations of employees coming into the workplace. Greater transparency was being demanded, and a growing focus on environmental, social and governance issues, as well as on the people and the workforce.

Skills mismatches and gaps were appearing everywhere as the needs of jobs were changing. Education and the investments in learning development were being challenged, with the need to promote vocational routes into work, and to properly encourage and support lifelong learning.

The principles of good work and job quality have been emerging. Ways of putting people more at the heart of our organizations, supporting them better so they can be more effective and productive. Mental health and wellbeing had been moving up the corporate agenda to address the ever-increasing issues of stress, burnout, but also toxic cultures that never should have been acceptable. Flexible and agile working were being promoted as ways to support better work–life balance, but also to create opportunities for people who can't work standard hours or working days or always be in a place of work.

It has also become increasingly apparent that there are great issues of inequalities, in income, in opportunity and in how people are treated. The benefits of growth are not being fairly shared and people were reacting to that, sometimes through the ballot box where they heard political leaders talk of protecting their interests against the forces of globalization.

The plateauing of productivity since the global financial crisis has been an almost continual refrain, but solutions were appearing elusive. Focus has been put on the quality and capability of leadership and the long tail of smaller, less profitable businesses. But it was also apparent that lack of investment, slow uptake of technology, skills mismatches, and how much people were committed and engaged at their work were important drivers.

All these issues and challenges create a big agenda. We need to be able to see them in the round, the interconnections of ideas, and how we can make lasting and sustainable change for a better future of work. Leaders have to think systemically and also hold competing ideas and paradoxes, to imagine different outcomes and scenarios. The pandemic reminded us of so many of these issues and has given us that opportunity and stimulus to accelerate positive change.

Some of the known unknowns – looking ahead

The future of work also leaves many unknowns ahead of us. Each of the big macro-trends in geopolitics, in social, environmental and technological change has a long way to play out.

There are many different possible scenarios that could occur. But the essence of strategy and forward planning is to be able to think through different possible scenarios, to find the common threads and to build from those. For example, we know skills needs are going to change more rapidly, even though we don't know exactly what all those skills needs will be, because jobs and roles will change.

So within organizations, we can plan now to build better capabilities for upskilling and reskilling our workforces, and reinvent learning to be more adaptive and flexible, more digital, more embedded with work, and to build towards real learning cultures. We must also look at this from a wider education and policy perspective. How do we bring education and the world of work closer? How do we open up vocational learning in different ways and really create the systems that support lifelong learning?

We know also there are significant impacts on economies and jobs as a result of the pandemic, which will have an enduring impact on many. Unemployment rates increased significantly during 2020 and they will continue rising as job support schemes unwind, but also as companies in all sectors restructure and resize. As we saw after the global financial crisis, return to full employment could take several years. And the impacts across the workforce are never equal.

An assessment by the International Labour Organisation (ILO) reported in early 2021[14] indicates four times as many working hours were lost last year than during the previous global financial crisis. The ILO estimated that nearly 9 per cent of all working hours were lost globally in 2020, equivalent to about 255 million full-time jobs disappearing.

The ILO also reported that aggregate wages had declined by more than 8 per cent as a result, equivalent to $3.7 trillion, or 4.4 per cent of global GDP. Guy Ryder, director-general of the ILO, said: 'This has been the most severe crisis for the world of work since the Great Depression of the 1930s. Its impact is far greater than that of the global financial crisis of 2009.' He added: 'All scenarios project that working-hour losses will continue; in other words, the financial and social distress for millions of people will continue through 2021 and beyond that.'

Young people in particular suffer during downturns. Youth unemployment (18–24-year-olds) rose sharply from 2009 and peaked in 2013 at around 25 per cent across the EU27.[15] In the UK it hit 21 per cent in the same year.

Significant rises in unemployment don't get fixed overnight. But for those organizations that are hiring and building, there is also an opportunity.

Governments will need to support programmes to help young and older workers back into work. There will need to be more support on transitioning across jobs and sectors, building the basic employability and transferable skills, and on careers advice and guidance. This won't just be a short-term expedient but needs to be part of a longer-term shift in supporting an increasingly mobile workforce as they navigate a future of a life of jobs instead of the old world of a job for life.

The pandemic has also accelerated changes in working patterns that could impact the economy in other ways in the coming years. Fewer people going into offices, more networked and distributed operating models and ways of working, all could change the face of office-dominated city centres and commercial property. Transportation companies may find longer-term declines in passenger numbers as people realize they can work virtually and don't always have to hop on trains, planes or automobiles to meet up.

What the pandemic has also shown us are the levels of inequality and of unfairness of opportunity across our communities and societies. How 'essential' work is so often poorly paid. How people from different backgrounds can get such different opportunities and chances. How in work, poverty is growing at the same time those at the highest end of the pay scales pull further away.

The crisis creates that opportunity to address these wider known unknowns. They will require policy makers, business leaders, economists and others to work together with a shared intent. But if we don't address these kinds of issues, the future of work could make them worse. Automation and investments in technology can and will displace jobs, and not only at the lower skill levels. Young people could find it harder to get into work, just as much as older workers could suffer from not being supported to transition their skills. Income and wealth disparities could also grow as increasing productivity and profitability does not get shared equally.

These are great challenges to our longer-term thinking, but vital to shaping the future of work that improves lives and society at large.

Guiding principles for the future

Throughout the book I will come back to the idea of principles that should guide us. We cannot be certain of the future, but as we shape it, we should hold on to shared principles to create a better future.

We have already touched on principles such as greater equality and fairness, inclusion and diversity, and ideas of good work and job quality, and we will develop these further.

We must also look to the principles of responsible business. Public trust in big business has generally been declining, as it has for the wider 'establishment'. People not feeling that they are acting in a collective interest versus purely self-interest, particularly following the global financial crisis and subsequent recession.

During the pandemic there was further scrutiny on businesses and how they behaved, how they treated their workforces during the challenging months of 2020 and into 2021 and, for example, the extent to which they took government-funded support. Many companies recognized that it was ethically indefensible to take government support while maintaining dividend payouts or bonuses to executives, particularly in financial services where there was wide recognition that they were still living in the shadow of public perception of having been bailed out in the global financial crisis.

As reported in the *Financial Times*,[16] as pressure mounted, many companies that realized they could afford it as conditions improved and paid back money they had taken through the furlough programme in the UK. 'It would be harder to justify resuming dividends and making good missed dividends if you haven't paid back furlough money,' a senior fund manager at Jupiter was reported as rightly observing.

Responsible business, I believe, is strongly based on the principles of a multi-stakeholder perspective. Understanding all the stakeholders and responsibility towards them – the workforce, the customers, suppliers, communities of which the business is part, and the environment. There have been many movements encouraging this shift, which we will explore in greater detail, but it is founded on the reality that businesses are not just solely responsible for their financial stakeholders. Business needs to make money, but it needs to do it responsibly. As some have called it, you can do well by doing good.

In August 2019, the Business Roundtable, a CEO lobbying group based in the US and led by JPMorgan Chase's Jamie Dimon, committed to an updated definition of what the true purpose of a company should be.[17] The new definition stipulates that a business must recognize that its responsibilities to customers, employees, suppliers and the environment have to be on par with its responsibilities to shareholders. This is a positive signal. Now we need to see the action.

To drive these principles forward, there needs to be more transparency. Commitments made to change only get real when they are measured and made visible. Fundamentally our systems of measurement have to change. We have to build measures for our societies and economies as well as our businesses that give us the wider view of what is really important.

Having already observed a bit of a catalogue of known knowns which we have to address, we need to make sure we are measuring them and focusing attention and action. What gets measured does tend to get done. And we need the right measures also to point the direction ahead. A good example is wellbeing – another theme that we return to throughout the book. Individual and collective wellbeing is absolutely central to healthy society and should be seen, and measured, as one of the most important outcomes of good work and responsible business.

All these ideas of principles and outcomes we should see as important are not contradictory to profitable business. Indeed, it's the opposite. But there are still plenty of sceptics and we need to continue to build good evidence to show the connections. With that, we can start to break the cycles of short-termism, to invest smarter for the future for the good of all stakeholders.

Plenty of evidence is out there. In 2017, McKinsey conducted a study[18] to measure the financial impact of short- and long-termism at a company level, devising what it dubbed the Corporate Horizon Index. The research concluded that among the firms identified as focused on the long term, average revenue and earnings growth were significantly higher than for those companies focused on the short term, and total return to shareholders was higher, too. They also added more jobs, contributing in other ways to the overall economy and society.

None of this should really surprise us. But somehow we've needed that impetus for real and sustainable change. Now should be that time.

A collective and collaborative effort – time to step up

Shaping a better future of work requires us all to pull together. We all have agency, we can all have a voice and we can all make a difference.

The issues and opportunities we explore throughout the book are wide ranging but interconnected. They are relevant to policy makers, regulators, business leaders, finance leaders and managers everywhere. They have a strong bias to the human at work because above all, the future of work should be human. This also means it is a book about the bigger agenda and role the HR function and profession can play in business everywhere.

In Chapters 2 to 6, we lay out the major drivers of change that are impacting work, workforces and workplaces today, and the trends and direction of travel. They go from macro-economic and political shifts to technological advancement and social change. We also take a look at the issues of education and learning, and how we adapt for the rapidly changing roles and skills people will need.

In Chapters 7 to 14, the focus is on the elements of business and business thinking that need to come together. Starting with measuring the right things, going through the principles of responsible business and the challenges for leadership, and on into more strategic thinking about our workforces of the future, the principles of good work and creating agile learning organizations.

As Socrates, the great Greek philosopher, said: 'I cannot teach anyone anything, I can only make them think.'

That's not a bad positioning for this book. It is not intended as a 'how to' guide, but given the scope and context of what we are covering, it is more of a broad reflection on all that is going on around us in these times of extraordinary change, and what it might mean. Where do we put our attention now? What is important? How do the many different changes going on connect and interact? And what are the ideas and principles that might guide us into this uncertain future?

Endnotes

1. https://www.weforum.org/agenda/2016/01/the-fourth-industrial-revolution-what-it-means-and-how-to-respond/ (archived at https://perma.cc/DA7G-K9EX)
2. https://backlinko.com/social-media-users (archived at https://perma.cc/2GME-HJUW)
3. https://www.youtube.com/watch?v=u06BXgWbGvA (archived at https://perma.cc/5TDH-M2AA)
4. The Economist (2003) Cities & Health, 4 (2), p 152, 4 December, DOI: 10.1080/23748834.2020.1807704
5. https://languages.oup.com/word-of-the-year/2020/ (archived at https://perma.cc/NPW4-J2W7)
6. https://www.bbc.co.uk/news/entertainment-arts-55016543 (archived at https://perma.cc/9BP4-ETXF)
7. Papers of John F Kennedy. Pre-Presidential Papers. Senate Files. Series 12. Speeches and the Press. Box 902, Folder: 'United Negro College Fund, Indianapolis, Indiana, 12 April 1959'
8. University of Kansas (2009) People by nature are universally optimistic, study shows, *ScienceDaily*, 25 May
9. Sharot, T (2012) *The Science of Optimism*, https://www.amazon.co.uk/dp/B00A9YC7DA?linkCode=gs2&tag=braipick-21 (archived at https://perma.cc/MAQ5-R7A6)
10. https://siepr.stanford.edu/sites/default/files/publications/19-027.pdf (archived at https://perma.cc/CFJ4-YUUK)
11. Kahneman, D (2011) *Thinking, Fast and Slow*, Macmillan, New York
12. Taleb, N N (2010) *The Black Swan: The impact of the highly improbable*, Penguin Books, New York
13. https://youtu.be/6Af6b_wyiwI (archived at https://perma.cc/H4NQ-MQGL)
14. https://www.ilo.org/wcmsp5/groups/public/@dgreports/@dcomm/documents/briefingnote/wcms_767028.pdf (archived at https://perma.cc/U34B-CUTL)
15. https://ec.europa.eu/eurostat/statistics-explained/index.php/Unemployment_statistics (archived at https://perma.cc/SXH8-WBJ9)
16. https://www.ft.com/content/d9b4c815-d709-4b34-9301-47ce44ee4260 (archived at https://perma.cc/7E5U-GHDB)
17. https://www.businessroundtable.org/business-roundtable-redefines-the-purpose-of-a-corporation-to-promote-an-economy-that-serves-all-americans (archived at https://perma.cc/KDJ3-PJCF)
18. Koller, T, Manyika, J and Ramaswamy, S (2017) The case against corporate short-termism, *Milken Institute Review*, 4 August, https://www.milkenreview.org/articles/the-case-against-corporate-short-termism (archived at https://perma.cc/3PAU-CEU2)

02

Economics and the economy

We need a reset in the way the economy grows around the world.
CHRISTINE LAGARDE, FORMER MANAGING DIRECTOR,
INTERNATIONAL MONETARY FUND

Our economies and how they are performing are central to all of us. Economic performance and forecasts impact our societies, our political views, our well-being and every organization.

In this chapter, we will explore some of the ways in which our economies are changing, specifically with regard to jobs and employment, but also some of the bigger drivers that impact how organizations invest and think about the future. This helps set a context for some of the broader changes that need to be considered for the new era of work.

Economics is interesting in that it is both an art and a science. That becomes apparent particularly in times of uncertainty when economists can differ widely, or even wildly, in their views of where we are and where we are headed.

As has been observed, if you laid all the economists end to end, they would still not reach a conclusion. Throughout the book we will come back to various economists' views of the world.

Indeed, economics itself is often described more as a social science discipline than a pure science. At its core, economic theory is about understanding human actions and behaviours as they relate to production, consumption, pricing and markets. The influence of behavioural economics in business and wider economic thinking is a clear manifestation of this. It brings together the disciplines and evidence of economics with behavioural science to help understand the behaviours of people – their apparent irrationality as much as their rationality.

As structural shifts take place across our economies such as happened after the global financial crisis or following the Covid-19 pandemic, many prevailing views about what is important can be reset. Crises act as stimuli for change in our economies, which impact markets, consumers, organizations and society everywhere.

Governments and regulators have to respond to economic shifts, to help to set direction through macro-economic policy and the levers of fiscal stimulation that they have. But these policies are driven by prevailing political thought and philosophies which themselves have been challenged. The pandemic drove a right-leaning Conservative government in the UK, and indeed most other countries as well, to throw away previous views on 'fiscal rectitude'. Huge stimulus and spending plans were put in place, and rescue or loan schemes got government much more involved in business and people's lives.

Whatever happens to our economies over the next few years, these programmes will take years to unwind, if they ever do.

Other structural shifts in our economies are emerging. While the language at the outset of the pandemic in early 2020 was that we were all in this together and the virus didn't discriminate, it became very clear that wasn't true. Not only did the virus itself seem to impact different people in very different ways, but the economic impact of lockdowns had greatly differing outcomes on different sectors and parts of our economies as well as on people's livelihoods.

As we write, the collective short-term economic impacts have been dramatic. The Bank of England estimated that over the first half of 2020 in the midst of the pandemic, global GDP dropped by more than 12 per cent. For the UK, GDP was more than 20 per cent lower in 2020 Q2 relative to 2019 Q4.

So as we seek to understand the future of work and organizations, a dive into the world of economics is a critical piece of the bigger picture. But as with so many of the changes that are happening around us, the issues are complex and multidimensional, and the cause and effect linkages often hard to establish. VUCA has never been more apt in describing the world we are now in.

A time of creative destruction and what crises teach us

An economic theory that has received a lot of renewed attention as a result of these crises of the modern era is that of 'creative destruction'. It was the US economist Joseph Schumpeter who coined the term back in 1942, and what he observed as the dynamics of economics and of capitalism that created the need to adapt, to reinvent on an almost continuous basis.

Crises accelerate change, and there is a clear analogy with evolution and nature. Not all will survive these disruptions, but new opportunities are created, old inefficiencies will disappear and new ideas can flourish. Many of the world's most enduring companies were created in the midst of economic crises – IBM, General Motors, Disney, Microsoft, HP, FedEx, Netflix and many others.

Besides the economic disruption we are seeing, technology is talked of in the same way – what has become known as digital disruption, a major driver of the future of work that we will explore further in Chapter 5.

Creative destruction is not just about financial realities. It is also about long-held paradigms and ideas, prevailing norms and beliefs, or accepted givens. In Warren Buffett's 2001 letter to Berkshire Hathaway shareholders, the financier reflected on many Americans' misguided belief early on during that decade that house prices would keep rising forever. True to his style of using rather colourful metaphors to illustrate economic trends, he warned: 'You only find out who is swimming naked when the tide goes out.'[1]

It's a phrase that continues to resonate in financial circles largely because, time and time again, it's proved to be painfully accurate.

An obvious example is the dotcom boom and bust spanning the late 1990s and early 2000s, when waves of speculative money inflated valuations of new technology companies beyond reason. 'The irrational exuberance of the markets', as Alan Greenspan, Chairman of the US Federal Reserve Board, memorably described it at the time. It was far from the first time this had happened, and certainly not the last – it's human irrationality at work.

When Buffett penned that 2001 investor letter, the tide was about to go out yet again. US home prices, as Buffett referenced, had already started to fall. A few years later, two huge hedge funds, which had previously loaded up on the so-called subprime mortgage securities, collapsed.

This was the beginning of what became known as the global financial crisis, or GFC.

The spectacular and symbolic collapse of Lehman Brothers then set in motion a chain of events that would lead to a dramatic and protracted international liquidity crisis and the first global recession since the Second World War. The eurozone sovereign debt crisis would drag on for years.

The heart of the failure was not specifically one of regulation but of a whole intertwined system of cultures and beliefs. From individuals and business to the markets themselves. Reinforced by internal and external reward systems that encouraged excessive risk taking and profit making by the banks without understanding or much thought towards the consequences. Protected by a mantra that banks were 'too big to fail', that the markets would act rationally, and that debt and leverage were inherently good and allow us all to have or make more money.

Mortgage lending and a massive expansion of debt that led to houses being built in places they were not needed. People being sold financial products they didn't understand or need. The subprime mortgage market (always thought the clue was in the name) was built on sand. And a whole system of creating increasingly complex assets to trade where it became impossible to properly evaluate their integrity or what they were really based on.

This time as the tide pulled out, it exposed a terrifying landscape of lenders built on flimsy balance sheets. Individuals found themselves saddled with personal debt or assets that became almost worthless.

Its consequences really showed how irresponsible behaviours of the few and a loss of sight of purpose and other accountabilities can create huge knock-on impacts. However, although it took several years of painful recovery, that crisis has also led to a much greater degree of resilience across the banking system.

A cultural shift materialized. The pre-crisis period had been characterized by widespread hubris, greed and speculation, which many would say had been building up for some time.

The crash sobered not only investors, organizations and employees who suffered as a direct consequence but also many of the key players who had been at the heart of this system – the over-confident traders, bankers who had profited from short-term gain and the game of musical chairs, and a wider industry that began to reflect on what their real purpose should be.

While it took a bit of time to understand, the failures were not just about rules and regulation. They were as much if not more about cultures and behaviours. A recognition that too many people had lost sight of their accountabilities to their customers, or even to the wider economy of which they played an unduly large role in impacting.

In terms of its origins, the more recent 2020 global economic downturn caused by the Covid-19 pandemic was completely different from anything we'd ever seen before. The pandemic spread rapidly and indiscriminately, paralyzing great chunks of the global economy almost overnight, costing millions of lives and impacting the livelihoods of millions more, and even sending whole sectors to the brink of bankruptcy.

In other ways, though, it can legitimately be compared to previous crises. When the tide went out it once again exposed vulnerabilities and reminded us all of what really is important. It revealed the disparities in how people work and their opportunities, and the huge importance to all of us of what became called essential jobs and workers, and their relative levels of pay and security. It showed us the importance of positive cultures of trust and engagement, and that many businesses' operational infrastructure and ability to adapt and operate more digitally hadn't kept pace. In many areas of our economies, the social support infrastructure had to be rapidly ramped up, as well as revealing the systemic underinvestment in infrastructure in health and social care systems.

But the pandemic has also shown us many positive things, and many businesses have radically adapted their business models to meet the new context. The pandemic, as with any crisis, will act as a stimulus or catalyst for change, and many of the themes we explore throughout this book we believe will and should be accelerated as a result.

The longest bull market in history

To understand some of the important economic lessons we can draw from the Covid-19 crisis, it's important to appreciate what had happened in the preceding years. Just weeks before governments started imposing social distancing orders, media outlets were still marvelling over the longest global bull market in history[2] – loosely defined as a period of upwards trajectory for stock markets – and speculating when and why it might finally come to an end.

This bull market has led to some huge increases in the market value or capitalization of private sector organizations over the last few years, and some significant distortions. Today, there are five $1 trillion-valued companies – Alphabet, Apple, Amazon, Microsoft and Saudi Aramco – all of which have hit these heady heights since 2018, although PetroChina briefly had a market capitalization of $1 trillion at its IPO in November 2007. At the time of writing there are only 16 countries in the world with a GDP bigger than that, and Amazon has broken through the $2 trillion valuation, which puts it close to that of Italy's GDP.

A 2016 article in the US-based *Foreign Policy* magazine talked about 25 of the world's largest companies having possibly more power than many countries.[3] Quite sobering.

There is much to be debated about the power of corporates over our lives, their accountability and governance, and themes we will cover in other parts of the book, but it should make us all reflect on the power and responsibility large organizations have. The days when organizations saw their accountability to be only to their financial stakeholders or shareholders should be long gone, and governance takes on a much wider meaning to include all stakeholders.

The decade from 2010 had been an extraordinary one. Interest rates were initially cut in the wake of the collapse of Lehman Brothers, in order to kickstart an economic recovery, but real growth never materialized so rates stayed low. While wage growth across large parts of the western world was stagnant, corporations found themselves flooded with cash. Squeezed by those rock-bottom interest rates, investors were on a hunt for any asset – stocks, bonds, commodities, currencies – that offered any kind of yield to speak of.

Bond yields fall as prices rise. As a result of this surge in demand, more than half of outstanding government debt was by the end of 2019 offering a negative yield – that's to say that investors were paying for the privilege of lending money to countries. Even corporations, which generally have a much higher chance of defaulting than governments, were able to issue bonds with yields below zero, purely because the interest their debt offered was marginally higher – or less negative – than the interest offered by other assets.

As the universe of negative yielding bonds expanded and, elsewhere, as brand new companies started commanding huge valuations also thanks to that glut of capital, the phrase 'irrational exuberance' had started creeping back into media coverage.

In 2018 and 2019, Uber, Lyft and the owner of Snapchat became just three examples of businesses that received investments giving them multibillion-dollar price tags despite all recording operating losses. Tesla, which had around $13 billion in debt at the end of 2019, had a market capitalization of $160 billion by early 2020, which was greater than that of General Motors and Ford combined.

WeWork became perhaps the most high-profile example of a stratospheric corporate rise made possible by an abundance of investor cash. The operator of trendy co-working spaces was eventually forced to abruptly call off plans for a massive stock market listing when it emerged that the group's fundamentals were flawed and its valuation was slashed from $47 billion to around $8 billion.[4]

With stock indices across all global financial hubs hitting record highs, by the middle of 2019 some investors had started to become unnerved and cognisant that a pullback might be on the cards, but nobody expected quite such an abrupt and indiscriminate correction.

When Covid-19 sent equities tumbling and the price of oil into freefall, parallels were quickly drawn between what was happening here and the Great Depression of the 1930s.[5] Unemployment rates around the world surged, and at the time of writing were expected to be in double digits in most economies for some time. In the US, one in six people lost their job within weeks.[6] Corporates with previously resilient balance sheets and dependable cash flows were left struggling to stay afloat. Many were turning cap-in-hand to governments. Scores of small and medium-sized businesses folded before the first financial support packages were even drafted.

The human toll has been devastating and the financial damage was a brutal awakening after a decade of relative economic calm.

Short-termism and the profit motive

One of the major challenges of crises is the uncertainty they create and the not unnatural reaction of shortening our horizons. They can exacerbate a sense of risk aversion, even though what is so often needed is risk taking and innovation. However, short-term horizons and risk aversion have not been peculiar to the circumstances of a crisis. Short-termism has troubled economists and policy makers for years.

Short-termism is a mindset and behaviours that prioritize short-term results, immediate profit or projects over short time frames, over longer-term investments and strategies. It is driven by our inherent cognitive biases to favour visible and more controllable short-term outcomes over longer-term uncertainty, but is also greatly amplified by systems of reward, for example based around short-term profitability or share price movements, together with highly reactive stock markets.

Part of the challenge of short-term thinking is the long-held belief in the profit motive and the primacy of the shareholder. Half a century ago, famous US economist Milton Friedman published his seminal article in *The New York Times* arguing that the sole social responsibility of business is to increase profit.[7] This was undoubtedly the mantra that drove business for many decades through the latter part of the last century and into the new millennium. Profit was what investors looked for and by which business leaders were rewarded, too often regardless of any other outcomes.

Today, as we will discuss further in particular in Chapter 7, businesses everywhere are being held under greater scrutiny for their responsibilities to all stakeholders, and for having and demonstrating a wider purpose.

One of the most critical issues of short-termism is lack of investment in businesses for the longer term. Investments in technology and infrastructure, or in the skills and capabilities in the workforce, or in addressing pay differentials and fairness – all these areas we will highlight and explore further through the book.

In 2011, the then UK Secretary of State for Business, Innovation and Skills asked the well-respected economist John Kay to review activity in UK equity markets and its impact on the long-term performance and governance of UK-quoted companies.[8] As he stated, 'Overall we conclude that short-termism is a problem in UK equity markets, and that the principal causes are the decline of trust and the misalignment of incentives throughout the equity investment chain.'[9]

There were many recommendations, many of them relating to cultures and behaviours among investors as much as among the businesses themselves, with a particular emphasis on more shared stewardship and oversight of longer-term interests.

An example of where and how short-termism can play out is in how businesses use or invest their profits to maintain share prices. If maintaining or growing share price in the short term is the dominant incentive, then using profits to push up dividend payments to shareholders, or in share buyback programmes, has the most immediate impact.

In the 1980s, under President Ronald Reagan, a 'trust the market' deregulatory spirit gained traction across corporate America that championed share buybacks – the practice of companies using profits to buy back their own shares – and the deployment of capital to pay dividends. Up until then, the Securities Exchange Act of 1934 considered large-scale share repurchases a form of stock manipulation and it was therefore illegal. This was also the case in the UK.

Share buybacks inflate metrics like earnings per share and push up share prices. Many investors as well as the growing number of corporate executives who had reward systems based around upward share price movement benefitted. As a result, the gap between those at the top and those they employ really started to accelerate.

In many respects little has changed since then. Short-termism, or quarterly capitalism as it has been referred to, continues to dictate many management decisions. The world's largest corporations have spent hundreds of billions on dividends and share buybacks over the last few years, in many cases unnoticed.

JUST Capital, an analytics company that ranks US businesses on a range of metrics relating to pay and sustainability, found that since Trump's tax reforms, constituents of the Russell 1000 Index of the biggest US corporations spent ten times more cash on share buybacks than they did on workers.[10]

But when Covid-19 forced businesses to explore ways of tapping emergency cash to remain solvent, it shone a fresh and unflattering light on the prolific use of this strategy. Companies like Boeing found themselves in the spotlight when asking for government bailouts to meet liquidity needs[11] when in the preceding years, even as it struggled with crises like the 737 Max, it was a real champion of stock buybacks and dividend payouts.

Larry Fink, the chief executive officer of BlackRock, the world's largest-asset manager, has vocally advocated for what he calls 'long-termism' in financial markets and has criticized corporations that resort to share-boosting measures like buybacks and dividend repurchases to pacify investors.[12] Politicians also are increasingly arguing the case. Joe Biden wrote in an article for the *Wall Street Journal* back in 2016 that 'a high level of buybacks has led to significant decline in business investment'. And 'most of the harm', he concluded, is 'borne by workers'.[13]

Although US corporations have used these mechanisms more than UK companies, they had gained popularity in the years leading up the Covid-19 crisis, and buybacks and dividend payments hovered around record highs, something that many argue had stifled investment where it was needed most.

Returning to the business philosophy of Milton Friedman, we are seeing more and more leaders and commentators standing up to dismiss his polarizing view of business purpose. In August 2019, some of the US's most powerful executives, the Business Roundtable, committed publicly to a new age of corporate management which 'balances the needs of shareholders with those of customers, employees, suppliers and local communities'.[14]

It is these views that ultimately will most change what we measure, how businesses are viewed, and hopefully therefore also create the shift to a better balance of long-term investment and corporate stewardship.

Lack of investment in the future

A May 2019 report from industry group Tech Nation found that the UK was lagging behind the broader EU as well as countries like Israel, Sweden, Denmark and Finland when it comes to spending on research and development as a proportion of GDP.[15]

Similarly, a survey conducted by the Confederation of British Industry and technology giant Oracle published in June 2019 showed that a lack of spending on technology, innovation and management practices might actually lead to the 'extinction' of some companies. Allocating more cash to these areas could add over £100 billion to the economy, Oracle and the CBI argued.[16]

A stark example is how the UK lags behind much of industrialized world when it comes to using robots in manufacturing, according to data from the International Federation of Robotics. Despite the UK's advanced manufacturing economy, the 2015 survey showed there were just 71 robots per 10,000 manufacturing employees, compared with almost 500 in South Korea, about 300 in Japan and Germany, and approaching 200 in Sweden and Denmark.[17]

With AI and other applications of advanced computing, a consistent picture for the UK emerges. A 2018 study by Dell Technologies reported in *Information Age* found that only 16 per cent of UK businesses were investing in advanced AI, falling behind France (31 per cent), Germany (26 per cent), the Netherlands (17 per cent) and Italy (22 per cent), and when compared with the global average, the UK was behind on investments in other areas of emerging technologies.[18]

Beyond investments in technology, extensive research has also underscored the significant implications of employers neglecting to spend money on recruiting, retaining, and fostering talent. In too many organizations training is limited to inductions or health and safety and compliance-based exercises that are too often treated like bureaucratic tick-box exercises. As we will explore in later chapters, investment in people, in their skills and capabilities, is a strategic imperative which now more than ever will help determine those organizations that succeed over the long term.

In fact, many measures designed to enhance businesses have not succeeded in significant part because management has not sufficiently focused on longer-term goals. Developing skills is a cost or expense born in the short term but largely delivering value over the longer term. We have to recognize too that the measures of those longer-term value outcomes have typically been insufficient to sustain the case against short-term pressures to deliver on profitability goals, and that has to change as well.

The real nature of our economies today

The way in which we measure our economies is still largely based on the traditional models of employment – the production and distribution of goods which are relatively easy to measure, versus the growth of the service sectors which are harder to measure in terms of output and productivity.

Economies everywhere have dramatically changed their shape over the last few decades, however. The services industries and the growth of the so-called knowledge economy have greatly outstripped the more traditional manufacturing and industrial sectors. This 'de-industrialization' has created a huge shift in where and how people work.

According to data from Eurostat,[19] between 2008 and 2016 employment in knowledge-intensive services increased by almost 9 per cent across the EU27 countries and made up over 40 per cent of total employment. The UK had the highest percentage at almost 50 per cent by 2016. Italy by contrast had 35 per cent. These days the services industry accounts for around 80 per cent of revenues generated by the entire UK economy. According to ONS data, in 1970, manufacturing-related jobs accounted for 1 in 3 jobs; by 2010 this was down to 1 in 10, where it roughly is now.[20] Figure 2.1 shows the shifts of jobs across industry sectors in the EU between 1996 and 2016.[21]

As the figure shows, the public sector continues to make up a large proportion of work across all economies. It constitutes around 24 per cent of employment across the EU but varying from as much as one third in countries like Sweden, Denmark, Belgium and France to less than 20 per cent in Italy and Eastern European countries. These changes are reflected in the nature of jobs and skills, with the rise of what are classified as professional or associated professional and technical jobs, often regulated through certification and qualifications.

In terms of occupation, according to data from Eurostat,[22] professionals represented the largest group in the EU27 in 2019 with 19.5 per cent of employment. This was followed by technicians and associate professionals (16.9 per cent) and service and sales workers (16.3 per cent).

The UK has the highest proportion of these types of jobs, which reflects the dominance of the service sector across the economy. It is also likely to be a reflection of the high proportion of people now going to university and a corresponding drop-off in vocational and technical training. We will discuss these trends further in Chapter 6.

Over the last decade these shifts have accelerated quite quickly. Across the EU, these types of jobs grew by 2.6 million between 2011 and 2014. This contrasts with the drop-off of over 2 million skilled or semi-skilled jobs. Automation, as we discuss later, is likely to increase this direction of travel, although professional jobs themselves will also be significantly impacted.

FIGURE 2.1 Share of 10 main economic activities in EU employment, 1996 and 2016

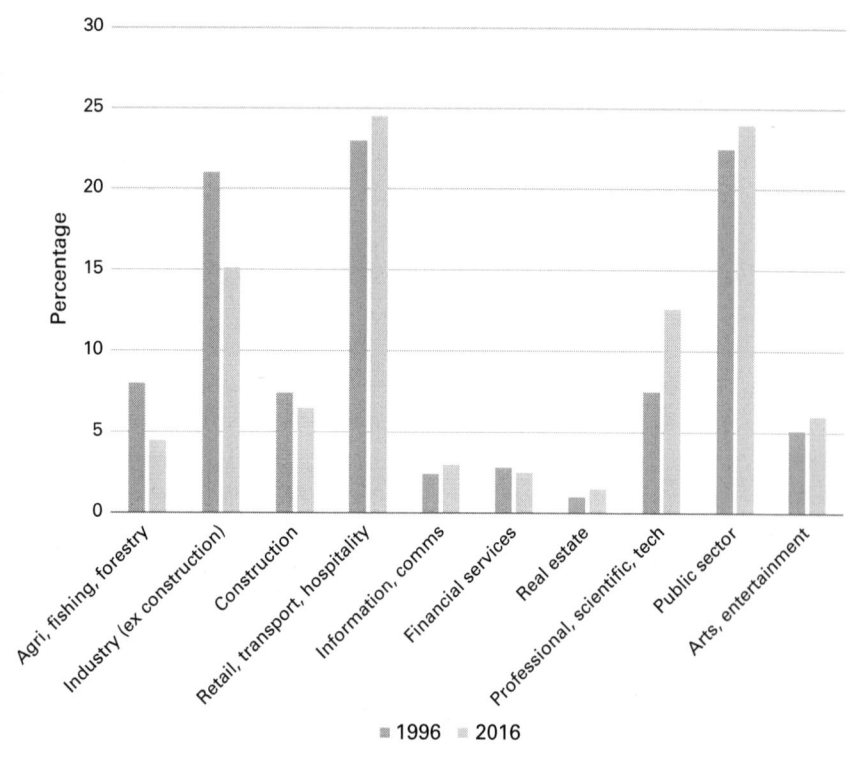

SOURCE Eurostat 2017

These changes have led to a view of the labour market as having shifted from an hour glass (higher proportions of high- and low-skill jobs vs mid-skill) to more like a cocktail glass, with the growth in higher-skill jobs accelerating vs a reduction in numbers of low-skill jobs. But this is far from a clear picture, and relative wage changes don't generally seem to reflect this pattern.

Looking at particular skill sets, it is interesting to look at the trends for information technology skills (ICT). With the prevalence of technology in the workplace, it is not surprising to see the rise of ICT-related jobs as a share of total employment. As we will explore later on, skills shortages in these areas are of significant growing concern for employers everywhere.

According to Eurostat data, the number of people employed as ICT specialists grew by 40.0 per cent during the period from 2011 to 2019.[23] This was almost six times the rate of increase for total employment. ICT jobs now make up around 4 per cent of total employment across Europe, but between 6 per cent and 7 per cent in the Nordic countries, Switzerland and the UK.

Also interesting to note is that although ICT is often perceived to be the domain of the younger worker, around 64 per cent of ICT workers across the EU were over the age of 35 in 2019. The UK was at this level, and may also be a reflection of the older average age of populations across Europe than many other parts of the world.

Large, medium, small and micro enterprises

Another feature of how economies are changing are the relative proportion and dominance of large organizations as employers versus smaller organizations.

Small and medium-sized enterprises (SMEs) constitute the backbone and the largest part of most countries' economies – typically two-thirds or more of jobs and at least half the economic output. But because smaller businesses are so numerous and diverse, our appreciation for their collective power to export, import, produce, employ and grow is limited.

In most countries, an SME is taken as an independent or non-subsidiary organization with 250 or fewer employees, although in the US it is 500 employees. Small firms are typically designated as having 50 or fewer employees, and micro-enterprises as having 10 or fewer. They can also be defined by their level of turnover, particularly as it relates to access to funding or governmental support.

The EU includes in its definition of an SME having turnover of less than €50 million, or a balance sheet total of less than €43 million. This is probably more useful given how many SMEs can have very large turnovers with the scaleability of technologies, or actually access bigger workforces through partnering or outsourcing arrangements or contractors.

In the UK, SMEs account for about three-fifths of employment and around half of turnover in the private sector.[24] At the beginning of 2019 there were 5.8 million small businesses, defined as those employing up to 49 people, accounting for 99.3 per cent of the total number of businesses. At least 99.5 per cent of all businesses in every main industry are SMEs.

Across OECD countries, the share of employment in the private sector for SMEs does vary. Where there are fewer large multinationals, not surprisingly the number of people employed in SMEs is higher. The US has more like 60 per cent of employment in large companies, whereas Italy, for example, has 20 per cent.

Given the wide and varied nature of the SME sector it is hard to clearly determine whether there is any trend in recent years of shifts of proportion of employment from large to smaller employers. In their comprehensive book *21st Century Workforces & Workplaces*,[25] Bevan et al assessed that the share of SMEs in the UK had not changed much since 1994.

Figure 2.2, based on CIPD analysis of ONS data, shows that the share of small and medium-sized firms in the UK hasn't changed in the last 10 years, but large company share of employment has been on a downward trend.

Micro enterprises appear to have lost share of employment, but the two other SME categories, small (10–49) and medium (50–249), have grown their share. 'No employees' as the biggest growth reflects the self-employed or individual businesses.

Large companies are focusing a lot of energy on restructuring, becoming more agile with delayering, or focusing more on core capabilities. Automation is also likely to take effect more strongly in the coming years in larger companies, which particularly in the UK have fallen behind in workplace investments. The pandemic has accelerated this thinking, and we think it is likely therefore that these trends will continue.

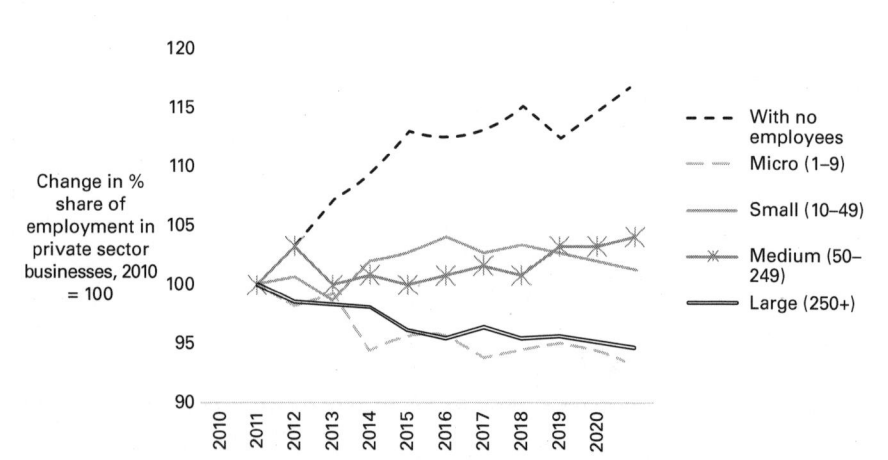

FIGURE 2.2 Relative shifts in employment in the UK across size of organization

SOURCE CIPD Research based on ONS data, https://www.cipd.co.uk/knowledge/work/trends#gref

Given the importance and scale of SMEs across economies, they are an important part of government policy and thinking. Particularly through the pandemic, there has been a response from governments to create financing or loan schemes and to encourage banks and others to lend to smaller businesses through the hard times as well as through the good. But they still also need access to critical knowledge and skills with their more limited resources, and often in fundamental areas of business operations such as financial and legal experience and people management or HR knowledge.

The CIPD ran a programme supported by the JPMorgan Chase Foundation in 2016 to assess need and provision of support to SMEs around basic people management and HR.[26] Pilots in three areas of the UK were run over a period of 18 months, which included access to a few days of free consulting support from experienced HR practitioners.

The programme highlighted among other things the challenge of reaching many small businesses. In the three pilot areas, different channels worked in different ways – for example, how local councils, or Chambers of Commerce, or Local Enterprise Partnerships connected with and engaged small businesses. It strongly reinforced that there is not one solution and that so much of the support to SMEs needs to be very localized. Furthermore, the support they needed was often basic guidance on people-related issues – so often they didn't know what they didn't know.

Even in more stable times, the issues for small businesses that cause the most concern and risk are areas such as cash flow, regulatory and compliance issues, marketing and basic people management issues. Failure rates among small businesses are very high. In the US, according to the Small Business Administration (SBA), as of 2019, startup failure rates were around 90 per cent – 21.5 per cent of startups fail in the first year, 30 per cent by the second year, 50 per cent by the fifth year and 70 per cent by their tenth year.[27] According to the UK Insolvency Service, during 2019 the rate of company insolvencies was running at 1 in 246 of all companies or about 41 per 10,000 active companies in England and Wales.[28]

When crises like the pandemic hit, life rapidly gets more complicated. In early March 2020 when authorities were beginning to urge members of the public to practise social distancing as a way of preventing the spread of infection, many small businesses discovered that the insurance they thought they had bought for an eventuality just like this was basically useless.[29]

How models of employment are changing

Besides formal employment in large and small businesses, there has been a steady growth in self-employment, including freelancers, contract and temporary work, and the gig economy – all generally classified as atypical work, which of itself indicates how much our traditional views of employment still predominate.

Self-employment and the growth of micro-businesses have played out in many economies around the world in the last decade or so. The biggest growth has been in one-person businesses, and the emergence of the gig economy powered by online platforms has provided some of the fuel.

The reasons for the growth in self-employment are various, and differing viewpoints are expressed. Some see it that lack of other formal employment opportunities has forced people to create their own work and jobs, while others see this as an active choice, possibly indicators of the growth of a more entrepreneurial society where the costs of starting and developing a business are low, and market visibility and channels to market can be established online in ways unimaginable in the past.

Having risen significantly since 2008, the proportion of self-employed in the UK seems to have plateaued in recent years at around 15 per cent of the total workforce. But the numbers in self-employment have continued to grow as a higher proportion of the population are in work – particularly among women, older workers and other groups where flexibility of work is essential and opportunities in formal work are insufficient.

Other factors that drive self-employment include tax and regulatory systems. The IR35 regulations in the UK are already challenging many people who might have had the tax benefits of self-employment but should actually be classified as workers working through contracts where their work is determined by others.

In other countries like Italy and some of the Central European countries, there is a culture and favourable tax regime that encourage a lot more people to be self-employed. In Italy, a quarter of the workforce are self-employed, whereas in Germany and France the number is around 10 per cent. The US and Canada are at less than 10 per cent, according to OECD data.[30]

The gig economy

The phrase gig economy was apparently first coined in 2009 by journalist Tina Brown, editor of *The Daily Beast*.[31] She wrote about the trend of workers pursuing 'a bunch of free-floating projects, consultancies and part-time bits and pieces while they transacted in a digital marketplace'. Not a bad definition.

These forms of work have existed forever, however. But the growth of digital platforms like UpWork, Checkatrade, TaskRabbit, Lyft, Uber and Deliveroo has created more efficient ways in which people looking for a 'gig' can find a paid-for piece of work. This creates opportunities for people to sign onto the platform when they have some spare time and find a piece of work – good for groups like students, or for those people who need some extra money and do some gig work alongside their main form of employment.

Much of the volume of work is relatively low skilled, but higher-skilled technical and professional workers, including many skilled trade workers, or self-employed accountants, solicitors and others, are also finding these platforms useful in accessing piece work.

While many of these new platforms are seen as classic disruptors, other businesses have used this model to meet particular needs of variable work across their workforces. They become connectors for people and work opportunities, particularly companies that need a large and variable workforce to meet fluctuating demand, for example in the online retail and delivery sector companies like Amazon, Ocado, Argos and DPD.

A 2016 report by McKinsey estimated that what they called the independent workforce globally was over 160 million people.[32] This included up to 30 per cent of the working-age population in the United States and most of Europe, which was much higher than the OECD reported numbers for the self-employed. For the UK, the number reported at 5 million people was much closer to the number as stated who are self-employed. The gig economy has become rather conflated with self-employment and it is hard to get reliable data. For example, many working in gig ways may have other forms of employment, as noted.

The McKinsey research also looked at reasons for working in these ways. It estimated about 30 per cent actively chose independent work and it was their primary source of income; 40 per cent used it to supplement their income and the rest were not doing it out of choice, preferring better paid stable work.

The flexibility that working in these ways can provide is offset by the support and protections people in formal employment take for granted, from investments in them in training, to holiday entitlements, sick leave, notice periods, pension contributions and insurance schemes. There are calls, particularly from unions, to provide more security for self-employed and contract workers whom they worry can be too readily exploited or taken advantage of.

Unscrupulous employers can always find ways to exploit workers and sadly there is a long history of this in workplaces everywhere. While the debate about legal rights for these different forms of employment will continue for a while, it will be important that we maintain a good balance between protections and flexibility, both for the individual and for those providing the work.

CIPD experience and research has shown there is a lot of confusion on what people's rights are in the different forms of employment, between an employee, worker and self-employed.[33] Every organization using these different ways of accessing the sources of skills and talent they need should develop its own clear guidance on atypical working, setting out principles of good work and responsible employment. It should be clear on individual rights and communicate these to all the workforce.

Looking at the impact of the pandemic on the self-employed and gig workers, at the time of writing there was some evidence of self-employed workers looking for more secure work as the economy took a significant downturn. ONS data from August 2020 reported a record drop in self-employment from the previous quarter of 238,000 people, or roughly 5 per cent.[34]

However, over the longer term, these forms of working will likely revert to an upward trend. In a future of work where skills needs change rapidly, specialist skills will be in demand for periods of time and there is the possibility of automation impacting the traditional models of employment, we could see higher proportions of people working in these flexible and agile ways.

Employment and unemployment

Employment and unemployment rates are always key measures used in understanding the health of economies. While there are some variations in how countries measure unemployment rates, the OECD describes those unemployed as people of working age who are without work, are available for work and have taken specific steps to find work.

Unemployment rates roughly doubled as a result of the GFC, but by the end of 2019, the US and the UK had unemployment rates of below 4 per cent, Japan was as low as 2 per cent and the EU countries were just below 7 per cent, having peaked at over 11 per cent around 2012.[35] These low rates of unemployment in many countries hadn't been since the 1970s.

Similarly, headline employment rates – the percentage of the working-age population in work – rose steadily. In the UK, the rate of employment had reached over 76 per cent at the beginning of 2020, up from a low of just over 70 per cent in 2012.[36] This was particularly driven by higher proportions of women and older people in work.

Economists generally regard unemployment rates of below 5 per cent as not sustainable for a healthy labour market that supports some churn and movement between jobs. As demand outstrips supply, wages tend to rise as organizations find it harder to recruit. But, as we have already observed, wages have largely stayed flat in recent years.

The real dynamics of the labour market and employment rates are a lot less straightforward than the headline numbers suggest, however. For example, there is great variability across age groups – unemployment rates for those below the age of 25 are typically 2–3 times higher. Some countries such as Spain, Greece and Italy have systemically higher youth unemployment rates – at the end of 2019 their youth unemployment rates were between 30 per cent and 40 per cent.[37]

Being 'employed' is counted as one hour or more of paid work per week together with those who had a job that they were temporarily away from. It covers employees (permanent or temporary) and those who are self-employed. This means there will be many who are working less than they want or are able to do, or those who are in more insecure work, and many other factors which indicate more flex in supply of labour than the headline numbers suggest.

Furthermore, there is a significant part of the working-age population who are described as 'inactive'. This includes people who may be willing to work but have stopped looking for work for reasons such as health issues or a disability who could work with support, those with caring responsibilities who are unable to access support, those who have taken early retirement, or just people who think there are no available jobs and have given up.

The OECD together with the Centre for Cities published a report in 2019 looking at the economically inactive in the UK.[38] They concluded that if the economically inactive who might be able to access work are included, the 'true level of unemployment rate would rise from 4.6 per cent to 13.2 per cent of the working-age population, not in education'. There was strong evidence of a significant north–south divide. In many cities in the north of the UK, such as Liverpool, Sunderland and Dundee, approximately one in five people could fall into this category.

That is a huge difference. And consider also that according to the same OECD report, the UK has a relatively lower level of inactive people of working age than many other developed countries. It creates a big call-out for the importance of more flexible working practices and the agendas for greater inclusion and diversity in our workplaces to create more opportunities for people right across our working-age population.

Not only, therefore, has the jobs economy not been working well for everyone, but quite clearly the pandemic has now had a huge impact on overall employment levels. Figure 2.3 gives a summary of where things were towards the end of 2020 in comparison with 2019.

These rates of unemployment will grow. Countries with job-retention schemes, such as the UK, may see a surge in unemployment as those schemes come to an end. The US did not have such schemes and instead focused more on support for those who were unemployed.

It is also concerning that the hardest-hit demographics will again be younger and older workers, those in less secure or lower-skill jobs. Some of the gains in recent years among these segments of the workforce, including women, will be set back.

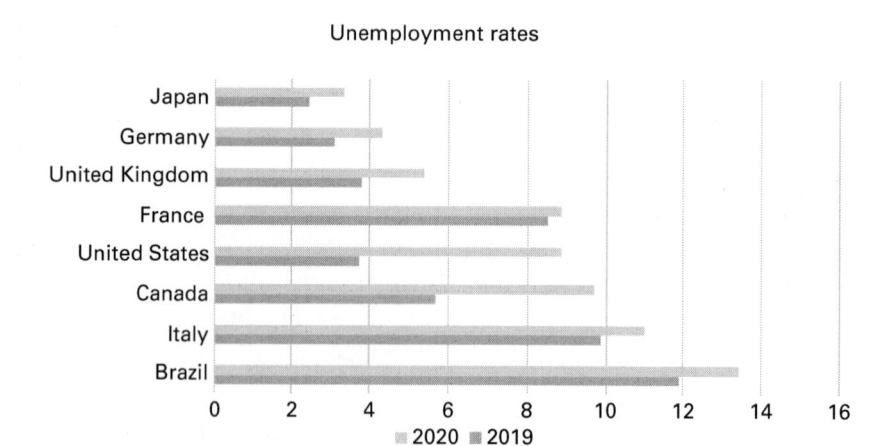

FIGURE 2.3 Yearly change in rates of unemployment 2019–2020

SOURCE International Monetary Fund, https://www.imf.org/external/datamapper/LUR@WEO/OEMDC/ADVEC/WEOWORLD/ISR

It is far from clear whether the increasing levels of unemployment will be easily reversed as the economy improves. As automation and technology really take hold in the new era of work, we could be shifting to systemically higher rates of unemployment if we don't find ways to balance out work opportunities and really understand future demand and supply. The policy and support implications become very significant, and we will review some of these as we work through the many interrelated themes in this book.

How ways of working are changing

Flexible working is an important part of engaging and supporting more people into gainful work and in supporting people's work–life balance and wellbeing. It includes working different schedules, part-time working, working from home and giving people more choice in how they work.

Across all the more developed nations in the OECD, around 17 per cent of the workforce works other than what is usually described as a 'standard' full-time job.[39] This proportion has grown over the last 20 years, though not dramatically so, but it has been a major factor in the growing proportion of national populations in work.

High female participation rates in the workforce coincide with higher rates of part-time working. This results in significant gender differences in how many people work non-standard hours. Despite the push in many countries to shift long-standing societal expectations or norms (including shared parental leave), many more women than men work part-time, balancing caring responsibilities with work.

The Netherlands is a stand-out example, with more than 60 per cent of employed women working part-time hours. In the UK, just over 40 per cent of employed women work part-time,[40] which is one of the higher figures among countries. There are significant gender differences as only just over 13 per cent of men in the UK work part-time.

Figure 2.4 shows comparisons between the UK and some other countries on both part-time and home working.

Through the pandemic close to half the working population found itself working from home. This must and should be a big catalyst to drive positive changes in the traditional paradigms of what a standard job is, regular

FIGURE 2.4 Selected country comparisons in proportions of people working part-time and working from home

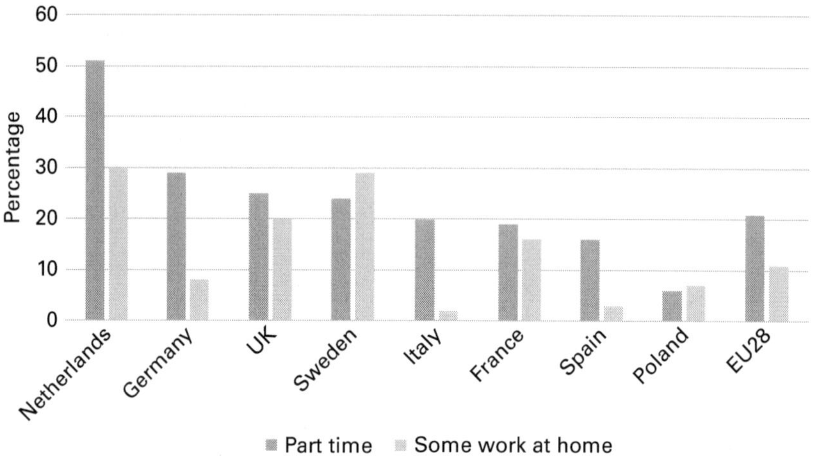

■ Part time   ■ Some work at home

SOURCE CIPD analysis from Eurostat data 2017, https://www.cipd.co.uk/Images/megatrends-report-flexible-working-1_tcm18-52769.pdf

working hours, and many of those aspects that have defined our working lives for generations. We will explore all these issues in more detail in later chapters.

Understanding productivity

The Nobel Prize-winning economist Paul Krugman famously observed in 1994 that 'productivity isn't everything, but in the long run it is almost everything. A country's ability to improve its standard of living over time depends almost entirely on its ability to raise its output per worker.'[41]

There is little doubt that productivity has long been seen as a key outcome of monetary and industrial policy and continues to dominate much government and macro-economic thinking everywhere. But with the significantly changing shape of economies as described earlier in the chapter, our measures of productivity and perhaps even the notion of its almost divine importance need challenging.

In the most simple terms, labour productivity is a measure of output divided by units of input – usually either hours worked, number of workers or cost of labour.

By dividing the units of output by the units of input, which would include all related and overhead costs such as plants and facilities, labour and raw materials, you start to address the challenge of accurate measurement – but what about when you have employees who, like the vast majority of UK workers, don't produce anything physical at all? How do you compare the value of a piece of advice, an idea or a service with the value of something tangible? What about high-quality products like Swiss watches or a luxury handbag? Does the fact that it takes weeks of craftsmanship to produce one product mean that the person making it is not being very productive?

Measuring productivity is a deeply complex and inexact science, which is becoming harder to do as the economy becomes more digital and less physical. International comparisons are also fraught with inconsistencies. As Paul Lewis from the University of Birmingham writes in his paper 'The false promise of productivity',[42] the output part of the productivity equation is generally calculated as value-added expressed as a monetary difference between what is sold and the intermediate goods used in its production.

To compare the productivity performance of the UK with that of other countries, or that of London with other parts of the UK, requires making comparisons at exactly the same point in time to essentially make sure we're comparing apples with apples. National statistics offices use prices in each country at the point of comparison, converted into a common currency, which is usually US dollars, and adjusted for what these can buy in each place – purchasing power parity (PPP).

When we say that productivity is higher in London than in Wales, for example, what we're actually saying is that the value-added at current prices produced per hour worked in those places is different, Lewis explains. This will be hugely influenced by the activities that are being performed in each place and is not necessarily indicative of how productive any single worker in a car factory in Bridgend is being relative to a single worker in a car factory in Oxford.

Productivity is also sometimes wrongly used as some kind of proxy for employee efficiency. Again, this fails to account for differences in organizational structures, the types of products produced and those constant market forces over which individual organizations do not have control.

Productivity measures are hugely important for setting policy and economic targets, for example, but we need to appreciate their shortcomings, lack of nuance and inability to highlight regional, national and even industry-specific particularities. Similarly, GDP is widely championed as the broadest gauge of economic prosperity of a country, yet it also fails to encapsulate aspects that could potentially add immense value to a nation: intangible assets, brands, talent and lived experiences, to name but a few. Something we return to at length in Chapter 7.

The principle also that Krugman described of productivity being the driver of standards of living and prosperity has proved illusory for many. It depends in large part on the distribution of the gains from productivity improvements being distributed in a balanced way and not just to the benefit of the financial stakeholder.

Figure 2.5 is a telling critique of the principle. From OECD data across 24 countries it shows the decoupling of wages growth from productivity growth over the last couple of decades. With the significant future threats to the wealth of so many, whether from ongoing recession or from impacts of automation and job losses, this is a critical issue to be understood and addressed. There is a real worry that the disconnect between improving productivity and wages growth will be further exacerbated by businesses seeing more pressure to automate, to reduce labour costs and to restructure as a result of the post-pandemic recession and economic changes.

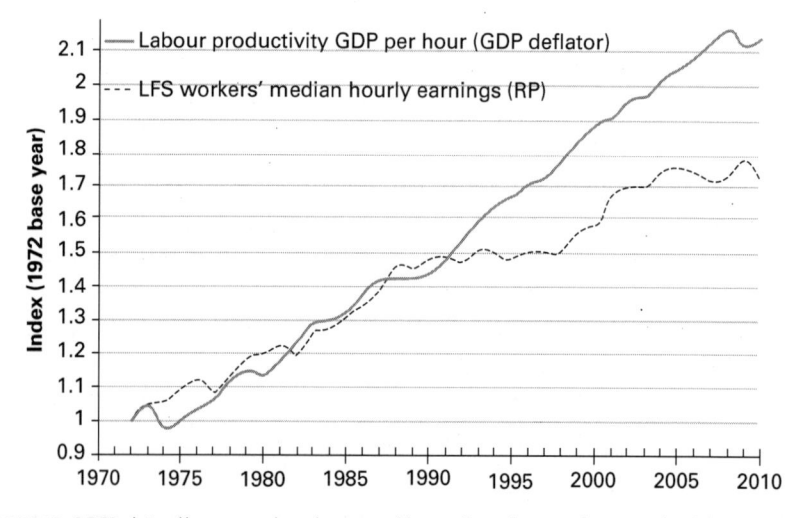

FIGURE 2.5 Productivity growth vs wages growth across 24 countries

SOURCE OECD, http://www.oecd.org/economy/decoupling-of-wages-from-productivity/

But with all that said, the productivity statistics at national levels paint some challenging pictures. According to OECD data,[43] in the years following the GFC, annual growth in labour productivity slowed to 0.9 per cent, about half the rate recorded in the 2000–2005 pre-crisis. This 'great stagnation' is a conundrum that has been challenging economists and politicians everywhere.

It is particularly seen as a big issue for the UK. The UK's productivity growth had been lagging that of other major economies for decades. But after the GFC in 2008, productivity growth plateaued from a pre-crisis rate of 2.3 per cent to only 0.4 per cent – what has become known as the UK's productivity puzzle.

The UK productivity puzzle

As so often reported and worried over, the UK productivity rates of GDP per hour worked or per worker compare very unfavourably with those of other major economies, as Figure 2.6 shows. The graph vividly shows that if French, German or American workers worked only four days a week, they would still be ahead of what apparently a British worker produces in five days.

FIGURE 2.6 Relative labour productivity comparisons across the G7 (GDP divided by labour hours)

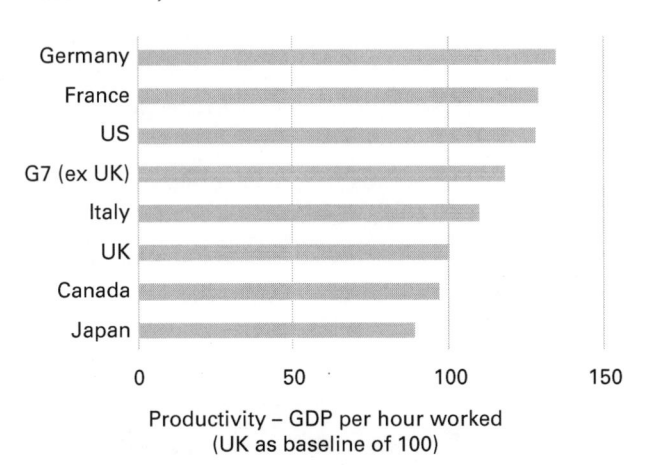

SOURCE ONS Statistical Bulletin, International comparisons of UK productivity (ICP), first estimates: 2016. 6 October 2017

These relative productivity figures are in stark contrast to how it used to be in the 1960s when the UK led Europe on this measure. The pace of productivity growth slowed in comparison with other major economies and the UK started to fall behind from the early 1970s.

Many reasons have been given for this.[44] The Bank of England talked of the 'long tail' of unproductive smaller companies in the UK relative to other nations. Also the big companies that had been leading the productivity charge fell back. According to research by the Economic Statistics Centre of Excellence,[45] particularly computer programming, energy, finance, mining, pharmaceuticals and telecoms, although accounting for one-fifth of the economy, generated three-fifths of the decline in productivity growth.

Very hard to understand the causal links and extraordinary to see these sectors called out when they are all sectors that might be expected to have higher investments in technology.

The issues we reviewed earlier on short-termism, which is particularly noted in the UK, and lack of investment must also be drivers of lack of productivity growth. Other issues relate to skills and skills gaps. CIPD research on the UK skills system carried out in 2017 highlighted a range of issues.[46]

At a national level, too many UK businesses are built around low-skilled, low-value jobs. Historic easy access to labour supply and migrant workers, and more liberal labour regulations may also be a factor. Employers taking what they may see as a lower-risk approach to employ more workers in low-skill jobs rather than invest in those jobs to use higher levels of skill more effectively.

In comparison, it's much harder to make someone in France redundant, meaning that labour costs tend to be higher across French businesses. To counteract that, businesses generally tend to invest more in infrastructure, technology and machinery, which in turn can drive higher labour productivity than in other countries.

Analysis by the OECD suggests that average labour productivity could be increased by as much as 5 per cent if the level of skills mismatch in the UK was brought into line with OECD best-practice levels.[47] The UK also suffers from poor basic skills, weakness in the vocational education system and low investment in workplace training, the report concluded.

Improving how skills are both developed and used should be at the heart of addressing the UK's low productivity levels, and indeed for any nation. The OECD and other bodies have long reported mismatches in skills usage, both at the high- and the low-skill end. This needs more investment in the workplace, in skills development, better leadership and management capabilities, and better people management practices. We will discuss all these areas in the second half of the book.

It may be also that there is another truth at play here. Economists have long recognized that working longer hours doesn't necessarily result in increased productivity. In reality, so have we all, but it doesn't stop too many of us working longer when we are not being particularly productive. The French in particular guard their working hours and their many public holidays as part of their working culture. This is reflected in their recent law barring work emails after hours.

Mexico, the least productive of the 38 countries listed by the OECD in its 2015 data, has the world's longest average work week at 41.2 hours (including full-time and part-time workers). At the other end of the spectrum, Luxembourg, the most productive country, has an average work week of just 29 hours. American workers work 33.6 per week on average, longer than all four of the European countries with higher productivity rankings.

In conclusion

We are in a new era of how we think about work and how we understand our economies. We need to truly harness the incredible progress in technology and science in recent years to drive positive growth and change.

The relative stagnation of economic growth and the fallout from the GFC have to be turned around. We have been able to learn from these crises and to stabilize our financial systems. But we can't continue to be short-term focused and risk averse if we really are to invest for the future as we must.

We also have to make sure that economic growth comes at the benefit of all. That we hold businesses to account for not just what they do but also how they do it. That political systems and regulatory oversight provide the right incentives and frameworks, and that businesses everywhere become more transparent in how they operate.

Improving productivity will remain a key metric and goal for economies everywhere. Despite the challenges of measurement and the concerns about fair distribution of gains made from productivity improvements, we should be seeking all the ways to get more out of all our resources – from raw materials to people.

Emerging from the pandemic, there will be a new era of growth and recovery. This crisis has taught us about the importance of people, of fairness and inclusion, and it has highlighted the centrality of what responsible business is about. We will take these points forward into the following chapters as we explore the other big drivers of change that are shaping the future of work.

Endnotes

1. https://www.berkshirehathaway.com/letters/2001pdf.pdf (archived at https://perma.cc/DP7V-HMBE)
2. https://www.newsweek.com/coronavirus-stock-market-correction-recession-economy-1489730 (archived at https://perma.cc/2R56-6J2W)
3. https://foreignpolicy.com/2016/03/15/these-25-companies-are-more-powerful-than-many-countries-multinational-corporate-wealth-power/ (archived at https://perma.cc/X7ZL-GLW4)
4. https://www.ft.com/content/9b3ebf28-cfe2-11e9-b018-ca4456540ea6 (archived at https://perma.cc/5Z66-CT3Q)
5. https://fortune.com/2020/04/14/coronavirus-recession-predictions-great-depression-covid-19-lockdown-crisis-imf/ (archived at https://perma.cc/L9MP-SNKW)
6. https://apnews.com/e928d091f81f75b9bc8830c7370f41fb (archived at https://perma.cc/43BN-69YQ)
7. https://www.nytimes.com/1970/09/13/archives/article-15-no-title.html (archived at https://perma.cc/UK4N-CSF5)
8. https://assets.publishing.service.gov.uk/government/uploads/system/uploads/attachment_data/file/253454/bis-12-917-kay-review-of-equity-markets-final-report.pdf (archived at https://perma.cc/CX93-GRGQ)
9. https://assets.publishing.service.gov.uk/government/uploads/system/uploads/attachment_data/file/253454/bis-12-917-kay-review-of-equity-markets-final-report.pdf (archived at https://perma.cc/CX93-GRGQ)
10. https://justcapital.com/news/looking-back-on-tax-reform-workers-arent-winning/ (archived at https://perma.cc/Q953-RWQQ)
11. https://www.washingtonpost.com/business/2020/03/17/boeing-asks-at-least-60-billion-trump-expresses-support-bailout/ (archived at https://perma.cc/R8P6-ZXXK)
12. https://www.blackrock.com/corporate/investor-relations/larry-fink-ceo-letter (archived at https://perma.cc/GR89-U5NX)
13. https://www.wsj.com/articles/how-short-termism-saps-the-economy-1475018087 (archived at https://perma.cc/TVD6-DL3J)
14. https://opportunity.businessroundtable.org/ourcommitment/ (archived at https://perma.cc/NC68-9NDY)
15. https://technation.io/report2019/ (archived at https://perma.cc/KV6V-DJRZ)
16. https://www.cbi.org.uk/media-centre/articles/technology-laggards-face-extinction-unless-they-transform-their-approach-to-innovation-cbi-oracle-report-finds/ (archived at https://perma.cc/W3BY-NCZQ)
17. https://ifr.org/news/world-robotics-survey-service-robots-are-conquering-the-world-/ (archived at https://perma.cc/J85W-LCY4)

18 https://www.information-age.com/uk-europe-technology-investment-123471202/ (archived at https://perma.cc/T2JH-CU9Z)
19 https://ec.europa.eu/eurostat/web/products-eurostat-news/-/DDN-20171024-1 (archived at https://perma.cc/FV3K-K3V2)
20 https://www.ons.gov.uk/economy/nationalaccounts/uksectoraccounts/compendium/economicreview/april2019/longtermtrendsinukemployment1861to2018 (archived at https://perma.cc/MB33-JDMD)
21 https://ec.europa.eu/eurostat/web/products-eurostat-news/-/DDN-20171024-1 (archived at https://perma.cc/W9G2-CTFH)
22 https://ec.europa.eu/eurostat/statistics-explained/index.php?title=Employment_-_annual_statistics (archived at https://perma.cc/MY7T-B4TQ)
23 https://ec.europa.eu/eurostat/statistics-explained/index.php/ICT_specialists_in_employment#Relative_share_of_ICT_specialists_in_the_total_workforce (archived at https://perma.cc/7QKS-NMXA)
24 https://www.fsb.org.uk/uk-small-business-statistics.html (archived at https://perma.cc/5JB4-REWC)
25 Bevan, S, Brinkley, I, Bajorek, Z and Cooper, C (2018) *21st Century Workforces & Workplaces*. Bloomsbury, London
26 https://www.cipd.co.uk/knowledge/strategy/hr/hr-capability-small-firms (archived at https://perma.cc/FK2T-4BND)
27 https://www.national.biz/2019-small-business-failure-rate-startup-statistics-industry/ (archived at https://perma.cc/5ZSQ-6EJ3)
28 https://assets.publishing.service.gov.uk/government/uploads/system/uploads/attachment_data/file/861187/Commentary_-_Company_Insolvency_Statistics_Q4_2019.pdf (archived at https://perma.cc/K2NZ-D84N)
29 https://www.theguardian.com/commentisfree/2020/mar/18/coronavirus-exposed-britain-insurance-industry-businesses-cover (archived at https://perma.cc/GK6S-XFRD)
30 https://data.oecd.org/emp/self-employed-rate.htm (archived at https://perma.cc/M9RN-5AGW)
31 https://www.thedailybeast.com/the-gig-economy (archived at https://perma.cc/V76U-SN45)
32 https://www.mckinsey.com/featured-insights/employment-and-growth/independent-work-choice-necessity-and-the-gig-economy (archived at https://perma.cc/W98Z-QSHQ)
33 https://www.cipd.co.uk/knowledge/work/trends/gig-economy-report (archived at https://perma.cc/G5F5-GXQU)
34 https://www.ons.gov.uk/employmentandlabourmarket/peopleinwork/employmentandemployeetypes/bulletins/employmentintheuk/august2020 (archived at https://perma.cc/XC45-UFW4)
35 https://data.oecd.org/unemp/unemployment-rate.htm (archived at https://perma.cc/LL6G-M5R7)

36 https://tradingeconomics.com/united-kingdom/employment-rate (archived at https://perma.cc/TY2N-68LA)
37 https://www.statista.com/statistics/266228/youth-unemployment-rate-in-eu-countries/ (archived at https://perma.cc/6XBS-G8YW)
38 https://www.centreforcities.org/publication/hidden-unemployment-in-uk-cities/ (archived at https://perma.cc/7SG8-2NRH)
39 https://www.oecd.org/employment/Employment-Outlook-2019-Highlight-EN.pdf (archived at https://perma.cc/68Q4-KM7F)
40 https://www.ons.gov.uk/employmentandlabourmarket/peopleinwork/employmentandemployeetypes/datasets/fulltimeparttimeandtemporaryworkersseasonallyadjustedemp01sa (archived at https://perma.cc/W5BW-5KCL)
41 Krugman, P (1994) *The Age of Diminishing Expectations*, The MIT Press, Boston
42 Lewis, P (2021) The false promise of productivity, in Berry, C, Froud, J and Barker, T (eds) *The Political Economy of Industrial Strategy in the UK: From productivity problems to development dilemmas*, Agenda Publishing, Newcastle upon Tyne
43 http://www.oecd.org/sdd/productivity-stats/ (archived at https://perma.cc/Q39C-FMLG)
44 Financial Times (2018) Britain's productivity crisis in eight charts, 13 August
45 https://www.escoe.ac.uk/publications/below-the-aggregate-a-sectoral-account-of-the-uk-productivity-puzzle/ (archived at https://perma.cc/JG8B-VX47)
46 https://www.cipd.co.uk/Images/from-inadequate-to-outstanding_2017-making-the-UK-skills-system-world-class_tcm18-19933.pdf (archived at https://perma.cc/59EX-CRNG)
47 http://www.oecd.org/economy/growth/Skill-mismatch-and-public-policy-in-OECD-countries.pdf (archived at https://perma.cc/2G4Y-479U)

03

Globalization and geopolitics

You can disagree without being disagreeable.
RUTH BADER GINSBURG, US SUPREME COURT JUSTICE

Society, politics and economics all operate together and shape the world around us and the context in which every business operates.

Politics and economics are deeply intertwined. How much state control and regulation should exist, levels of taxation, debt and financial stimulus, benefit systems. Debates have long been held over where economics or politics and ideology are more important. They of course both influence each other. Even economists such as Thomas Piketty, to whom we will return in Chapter 4, recognize that ideology can trump economics. And most modern politicians are not renowned for their economic literacy.

Advances in science and technology have greatly influenced the shape of the modern world, and there have been definable eras of change or what many see as different industrial revolutions. But societal pressures and politics also shape how these advances are used, and even who they benefit. Nation states which define our borders and different norms and cultures have historically competed. Conflicts of the past have seemingly been driven by a belief in a zero-sum game – I win, you lose.

Today, politics and geopolitics are more uncertain, more polarized than they have been for a long time. People are more aware of inequalities that are being reflected in apparent shifts away from the trends of globalization that had been driving the world over the last several decades.

In 2018, an Ipsos Mori survey on global sentiments showed some startling results.[1]

- 70 per cent agree the economy is rigged in favour of the rich and powerful.
- 66 per cent agree traditional politics ignores 'people like me'.
- 54 per cent agree their country's society is broken.
- 64 per cent want a strong leader to 'take the country back' from the rich.
- 62 per cent agree that local experts don't understand people like me.
- 49 per cent want a leader willing to break the rules to fix the country.

Disaffection appeared strongest in Latin America and Eastern Europe. Even 56 per cent of Swedes think the system is rigged. The was UK roughly mid-table, less keen on a strong leader and more positive towards globalization, but 85 per cent of Brits thought the country was divided, nine points higher than the global average across 27 countries. An echo of the divisive outcome of the Brexit referendum.

Most historians believe that since the Second World War, we have been living in what has been called the Long Peace. In his 2011 book *The Better Angels of Our Nature: Why violence has declined*,[2] well-known Harvard University psychologist Steven Pinker argues humans are now living in the most peaceful era in the history of our species.

Emerging from the awful experience of the Second World War and what preceded it, institutions including the United Nations, the World Bank, the International Monetary Fund and the General Agreement on Tariffs and Trade were set up to help define more peaceful international cooperation. The United Nations is committed to maintaining international peace and security, developing friendly relations among nations, and promoting social progress, better living standards and human rights.

Over recent decades globalization has emerged from this, with the steady opening of borders, multilateral trade and increasingly free movement of goods, services and labour. But today we are in times where many of these ideas seem to be challenged and the direction for globalization is uncertain. Modern populism is shaking up political institutions and political thought, and issues of growing inequalities and breaking down of trust in politics and politicians and the establishment more generally are big factors in these changes.

Business leaders are becoming more concerned about these issues as they seek to navigate a more uncertain future. PwC's most recent annual CEO survey highlighted how 'CEOs express increasing concern over uncertain economic growth, trade conflicts and other global disharmonies'.[3]

In this chapter we will further explore some of these shifting tides of globalization and geopolitics and of the next era of industrialization, and how they impact businesses everywhere. Predicting the future in these areas is challenging as there are many different forces at play, but we can focus on the roles of business and the principles that we hope can guide us all.

Eras of industrialization from the past to the present

Trade and commerce throughout history have been greatly accelerated by invention and innovation, leading to new eras and new opportunities for growth. Each of these eras has also brought about significant social change, and many changes in work, jobs and working lives. Looking back, it is still easy to see many aspects of the modern world of work recognizable from past eras.

The shift from more agrarian economies to industrialization and mechanical production in the late 1700s and early 1800s was powered by steam and the steam engine. Described as the first industrial revolution, it drove big shifts in society – the opening up of factories, travel and communications, and the acceleration of urbanization for large parts of the population. It became the power behind the growth of empires from the more advanced economies of Europe, and the opening up of the United States through railroads.

It was also a time of huge inequalities. Working conditions in these early factories were grim by any standards, and the ruling classes held sway over the masses of poorer workers, whether in factories or on the land. Workers had no protections and while many nations and economies grew rapidly, wealth was very unevenly distributed. This gave rise to the thinking and philosophies of people like Karl Marx – the belief in the inherent and

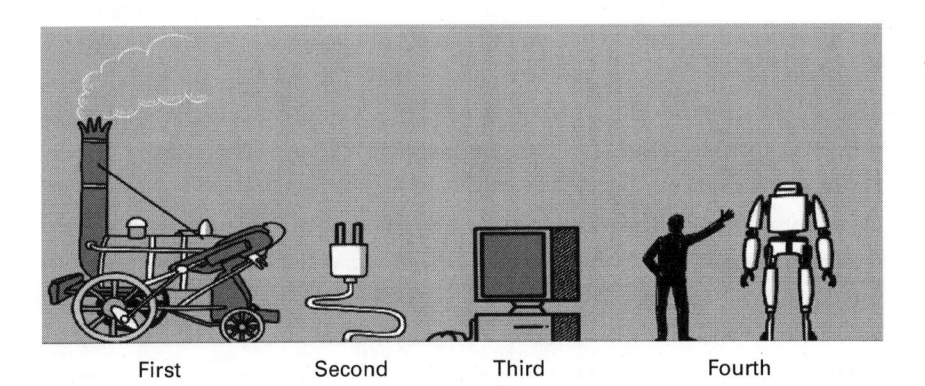

FIGURE 3.1 The four eras of industrial revolutions

First   Second   Third   Fourth

unsustainable tensions between the ruling classes that control the means of production and the working classes that enable these means by selling their labour power in return for wages.

By the early 1900s science and technology were advancing production methods and products, notably the internal combustion engine, electricity, and new forms of communications via radio and telephones. This second industrial revolution paved the way to much of what we see in today's world of work – the growth of mass production, automation and assembly line work, pioneered by people like Henry Ford and the Ford Motor Company. These developments also triggered a change in how people were treated at work.

Henry Ford has been credited with pioneering principles and ways of working that included the five-day working week. His philosophy was to challenge the prevailing view that if workers were not working, they were wasting time and money, and that they needed time to rest to help them be more productive. Also, if he paid them a proper wage, it would ultimately give them the means to afford his car.

People follow the jobs and the early 1900s saw workers leaving their rural homes to move to urban areas and factory jobs. By 1900, 40 per cent of the US population lived in cities, compared with just 6 per cent in 1800. This urbanization was repeated in the rapidly developing economies of many countries in Europe through the 1900s.

In more recent years the same effect has been seen in China and other parts of Asia as their economies have accelerated off the back of globalization and the growing wages of workers and domestic consumer markets. This era of the second industrial revolution also saw the rise of understanding of productivity and output, and of efficiency. Humans were part of the system of production, working alongside the machines.

Optimizing the efficiency and output of people at work from the theories and practices of scientific management championed by the work of Frederick Winslow Taylor became a driving force that has shaped so much of the modern world of work. Taylor was working from principles of improving productivity also to improve workers' wealth, to reduce the tensions inherent in the system as Marx had called out. His approach in breaking down work into tasks, in being able to train workers in these tasks, arguably underpinned the great gains in productivity that accelerated through the Second World War.

It's also worthy of note that the role and organization of welfare workers in the UK started around the time of Taylor.

The historical roots of the CIPD, and in many ways the HR profession, began with the Welfare Workers' Association (WWA), which was formed at a conference chaired by Seebohm Rowntree in York on 6 June 1913. Alongside his company, Rowntree's, almost 50 other companies were present, including Boots, Cadbury, Lever Brothers and Chivers and Sons. The association they founded was described as an association of employers interested in industrial betterment and of welfare workers engaged by them.

These principles of employers' responsibility in looking after the welfare of their workers led to a lot of the employment legislation that we know today. And so many of those companies are still with us and continue to espouse the wellbeing and welfare of their workforces as key principles.

As Peter Drucker, the hugely influential management thinker, noted in an interesting article on the subject of the history of work in 1993,[4] Taylor faced a lot of resistance from unions and intellectuals. They saw the undermining of the more protectionist attitudes at the time based around apprenticeships and guilds, where knowledge about work was gained over long periods.

Drucker credits the growth in productivity over the last 100 years, and therefore also the shift in the nature of work, in large measure to Taylor. In the early part of the last century, as many as 9 in 10 people's work was manual – principally making things or moving things. In the developed nations of the world, by 1990 manual work was around 1 in 5 jobs and now it accounts for around 1 in 10, as we saw in the previous chapter.

These shifts in turn have led to significant societal changes, and what has been described as the growth of the middle classes, and professional and management work. Figures compiled by Ipsos Mori from the National Readership Survey in 2016 for the UK show that in 1968, two-thirds of households were in the manual or lower-paid social grade bracket known as C2DEs. But by 2015, the proportion of C2DEs had shrunk to 45.8 per cent.[5]

As productivity grew and more people could afford products that more efficient factories were producing, exports soared. They accounted for about 6 per cent of global gross domestic product at the beginning of the 19th century, but that figure had grown to around 14 per cent before the start of the First World War. Many describe this time as the first phase of the modern era of globalization.

However, progress towards a more interconnected world came to an abrupt standstill in 1914. When the First World War broke out, trade stopped and countries shut their borders. Later, the Great Depression sent the web of global financial markets into a tailspin before the Second World

War erupted, putting any possible recovery on pause. Trade, as a proportion of global GDP, plummeted to levels not seen for generations.

Then, as a new peacetime dawned, so did a collective appetite for reconnecting. Spurred by the emergence of technologies like the aeroplane and the automobile, particularly in America, international trade resumed and expanded at an unprecedented pace. The trade organizations and agencies instituted after the Second World War gained prominence and incomes across much of the western world rose. Free trade agreements were adopted widely, although it took until 2001 for China to gain membership of the World Trade Organization.

This was the second phase of the modern era of globalization, which lasted until the early 1970s, when it was then curtailed, or at least slowed, by the oil crisis in the mid-1970s.

The third phase of globalization emerged with the expansion of computing and computer power into the world of work at scale – what has therefore also been called the era of the third industrial revolution. New forms of automation and global communication systems started to connect the world in the 1980s in new and exciting ways. The exponential growth was extraordinary. In 1993 the internet communicated 1 per cent of the information flowing through two-way telecommunications networks; by 2000 this figure had risen to 51 per cent and by 2007 it was more than 97 per cent.[6]

With great opportunities for automation of many jobs and tasks, this accelerated the move away from manual work even further. Now the focus was shifting to non-manual work and the growth of the knowledge and services economy.

As technology has advanced, we are now in the digital age. Artificial intelligence and machine learning, robotics, the Internet of Things and universal connectivity. The fourth industrial revolution. As Klaus Schwab of the World Economic Forum noted, 'We do not yet know just how it will unfold, but one thing is clear: the response to it must be integrated and comprehensive, involving all stakeholders of the global polity, from the public and private sectors to academia and civil society.'[7]

The evolution of globalization

Enabled by communications and technology, over the last 20–30 years borders were opening up around the world to encourage more movement of goods, services and labour. There are today only a few countries that would be regarded as having closed borders, North Korea being the most curious example of what has become a bygone era.

One of the best examples of open borders comes from the Schengen Agreement, first signed in 1985 and incorporating five countries at the time, which then became a cornerstone of EU law, allowing for free movement of people now across 27 EU member states.

Open borders, which were the basis for so many of the trends of globalization, don't all mean free movements, and regulations of course exist in many forms. Bilateral and multilateral trade deals underpin the regulatory frameworks of globalization where countries have tried to maintain the balance of their own interests while encouraging the ideas of open access.

The explosion in communications and borders started to enable much more distributed operations for organizations. There was an acceleration of outsourcing of manufacturing and services around the world, and from that the development of globally integrated supply chains. This was the beginning of what today we would call the multinational corporation or MNC.

This trend drove new operating models and philosophies of business which have persisted, such as the focus on core competencies and being both global and local, or 'glocal'. No longer was it good enough to be either totally global with single products, cultures and structures that all operated out of one place, or entirely decentralized and adapted to local markets, but to be able to balance global with local.

Many businesses also looked at their operating models to determine what were their real core competencies and how could they outsource or partner with others to deliver non-core activities more cheaply. Price competition and ways of reducing costs were forcing the pace, and opportunities to scale, reduce costs by operating in lower-cost parts of the world and standardizing business operations all helped.

Outsourcing really started to take off in the late 1980s. Spurred on by consultants and the growth of outsourcing providers, the era of BPO (business process outsourcing) and shared service operations started to flourish. It was exciting for me working at Accenture (or Andersen Consulting as it then was) at that time, seeing the growing market and as the firm became a global leader in this space – moving from IT outsourcing to outsourcing of much of the administrative and transactional parts of functions like finance and HR, and even call centres and areas of customer support.

Large consumer products companies were good examples of these big shifts in global operating models. Some, such as Unilever, having had a very distributed and localized model of products, looked to create more consistency and global brands, as well as outsourcing more of their manufacturing to low-cost parts of the world. P&G, having started from the other end of the spectrum as a US-centric global company, shifted more towards responding and adapting to local markets and channels.

This time was also largely characterized by a view of the world as developed vs developing, and a bipolar view of the West and the rest, where western multinationals largely dominated globalization.

Many of the developing countries sought to encourage the big western MNCs to invest through tax breaks and other incentives, giving rise to an acceleration of foreign direct investment (FDI) through the building of factories or operations, acquisition of local businesses, or joint ventures. In many ways this brought benefits to many countries in not just tax incomes but the sharing of knowledge, development of capabilities and infrastructure in support.

Eastern European countries, India, China and some of the Asean countries all benefitted from this, having not only significantly lower cost bases and costs of labour in particular, but also increasingly well-educated workforces.

Manmohan Singh, the Indian prime minister and economist, as finance minister was the architect for Indian economic reforms in the early 1990s that positioned India to take advantage of these shifts in the 2000s. In particular he sought to liberalize the economy and allow entry of private players into major sectors. He encouraged inward investment from western multinationals, launching a bold budget and strategy to the nation with the memorable words 'No power on earth can stop an idea whose time has come'. It helped transform India's economy in the succeeding years to double-digit growth rates.

Competition for talent in India in the late 1990s and early 2000s was as fierce as in any market in the world, particularly for technology skills. As the big cities like Delhi and Mumbai literally began to run out of available resources, other cities like Bangalore and Pune became the new places for international businesses to search for talent.

Similarly in Eastern Europe, other countries in Asia and even Latin America, businesses were looking for key skills and global business strategies were being determined as much by where talent and skills could be found as by local consumer markets.

As a consultant working with some of these organizations, they were heady times. All kinds of organizations were spreading areas like R&D and IT to all corners of the globe to access talent.

Today there is barely a major multinational that doesn't have operations in India, from IT and back-office functions, to call centres and manufacturing facilities. The largest western MNCs there include the big tech companies such as Microsoft, Google, IBM, HP, and firms like Accenture, many of the global consumer products companies such as P&G, Colgate-Palmolive and Coca-Cola, and financial services businesses like Citi, but also Japanese and Korean MNCs such as Sony and Samsung.

From a bipolar world to a multipolar world

However, as the first decade of the new millennium unfolded, another phase of globalization was becoming apparent. The rise of what conveniently became known as the BRICs – Brazil, Russia, India and China – challenging the economic dominance of the West. This led to a different, more multipolar view of the world and the acceleration of emerging market multinationals or EMMs or eMNCs – don't we all just love an acronym?

India, and perhaps even more so China, were never going to be content in a world where they were defined as the cheap providers of the products or services that were designed in the West. They had also been learning from the MNCs they had encouraged into their markets. They wanted to compete directly on the global stage, and investment in innovation and R&D was just as much within their grasp.

Indeed, as Manmohan Singh said in a speech in 2017 quoting the Nobel Prize winner and until recently president of the Royal Society, Venkatraman Ramakrishnan, 'If India has to solve its development problems of poverty, ignorance, disease and unemployment, more emphasis has to be there on science and innovation.'[8]

Ramakrishnan also noted, 'India currently is using a development model with cheap labour and so it can attract companies for manufacturing based on labour costs. But if we are not careful we are going to miss the boat completely — because manufacturing is going to become largely automated.'

Wipro, Tata, Infosys, Mittal, Mahindra & Mahindra are all examples of Indian companies that rose to become multinationals competing on a global stage with the long-established MNCs of the past. Many of these companies moved from back-office service provision to selling direct to organizations around the world. And rather than just providing components for end products developed in the West, they turned to producing their own end products and selling directly to consumer markets around the world. Companies like

LG of South Korea, Huawei from China and Acer from Taiwan are other good examples.

Accenture, in a research report in 2007 called the 'Rise of the emerging market multinational',[9] highlighted the innovative growth of these companies, noting how they were particularly attuned to complex variations in consumer habits brought about by differences in culture and geography. They use their own local markets and diaspora populations as springboards to global expansion, but often expanding first into other developing countries. They also understood local talent markets and rapidly became very attractive for the brightest and the best, successfully competing for talent against the MNCs in their home markets.

A seminal moment in this phase of globalization was the acquisition by Tata Steel of Corus, the old British Steel, at the end of January 2007. *The Times of India*, with some glee in reporting the event, used the wonderful headline 'The Empire Strikes Back'.[10]

This was a major event for India and its growing confidence as an international player, which has continued to this day. At the time, Corus was almost three times as big as Tata Steel, but Tata had a vision. Working as a consultant there at the time, it was fascinating to see how they thought quite differently from the often-prevailing smash-and-grab approach to acquisition in the West. Cost takeouts and 90-day plans were not the immediate drivers. Instead, they talked about creating a combined Anglo–Indian business and wanted to encourage the two businesses to work together and find a common culture and values from which to build the future business.

Tata had already begun seven years earlier with the acquisition of Tetley Tea, then followed the Corus deal with the acquisition of Jaguar and Land Rover in an all-cash deal in June 2008, buying the companies from Ford for $2.3 billion, or under half of what Ford Motor paid for both brands in 1989.[11] Other EMMs also emerged from India's historical industries, notably Mittal, which grew through many international acquisitions and then the controversial merger at the time with Arcelor in 2006.

Not only companies but also global leaders have emerged, notably from India. Some of the biggest tech companies in the world are run by Indian CEOs who themselves often learned their trade working in the Indian tech companies that grew rapidly in the early 2000s. Google, Microsoft, Nokia, Adobe, Xerox Business Services, Cognizant are all great examples.

Chinese companies, by contrast, during this phase tended to grow from their very large domestic markets. Since opening up to foreign trade and investment and implementing free-market reforms in 1979, China has been among the world's fastest-growing economies. Its annual gross domestic product growth averaged 9.5 per cent through 2018, a pace described by the World Bank as 'the fastest sustained expansion by a major economy in history'.[12] Today China has more than 100 companies counted in the Fortune 500, but around 80 per cent of their income comes from their domestic markets.

As with India, many western MNCs have found it difficult to compete back into China's domestic market, and the rules have long favoured the local, often state-owned enterprises. Chinese companies tend to remain owned and operated from China with Chinese management, and few make the shift to running MNCs or even acquiring them in the way that India grew some of its biggest companies.

But it is interesting that many of these companies that have emerged from Asia, and the national cultures behind them, are relatively still homogenous and operate in more closed ways than western companies tend to.

For example, the Korean chaebols, the mostly family-owned huge conglomerates that dominate that economy, the Chinese state-owned enterprises (SOEs), which dominate that economy – only 15 per cent of China's companies in the global Fortune 500 are privately owned. Even Japanese companies still are very Japanese dominated and Japan as a culture is not easily open to foreigners.

These will be constraints in how these companies grow in the future in a world where not only are critical skills scarcer but also companies will have to be able to adapt to a more politically complex world and understanding of local markets. As we will explore in subsequent chapters, the importance of diversity and inclusion also is essential to sustainable business success.

Looking ahead, given the growth rates of these developing countries and these multinational businesses, it is clear that an old world order has shifted to a new world order where business thinking and practices will come as much from Asia as they did in the past from the Anglo-American world.

Where is globalization headed now?

These trends of globalization, emerging over the last two or three decades, appeared to be unstoppable. The natural order of a maturing, developing and interconnected world. More than just movement of goods, it was the steadily accelerating movements and exchanges of people, goods and services, capital, technologies and even of cultural practices and norms all over the world.

Economists' projections of global growth had for long time pointed to the higher growth rates of the BRICs or emerging market economies and a subsequent shift in global economic power in the coming decades. But the real picture isn't simple.

From the 1950s to the latest global economic crisis, the growth rate of international trade was almost consistently twice that of economic activity as a whole. From 2000 to 2008 world trade increased by an average 5.4 per cent each year, while GDP increased on average by 3 per cent per annum.[13]

UNCTAD, the UN Conference on Trade and Development,[14] observed the shifts that happened around the turn of the millennium and the growth of the developing economies. Before that, as it observed, 'we clearly had colonial trade patterns where developing countries exported raw materials and imported—as marginal players—mainly consumer goods'.

It went on, 'Since 2000, the situation has changed dramatically with many developing countries being involved in primary product trades, but also major exporters and importers of finished and semi-finished products.'

These shifts in global trade echoed what we have described as the different phases of globalization. But in recent years there have been clear and growing tensions with the ideas of globalization. That globalization is not benefitting everyone equally, and that too much power is being exerted by institutions, and organizations, that are beyond people's control or understanding. That migration and movement of people are threatening social cohesion. Or that jobs are being taken either by migrant workers or by the outsourcing or movement of work elsewhere. And that growing inequalities are being caused by these things as well.

Reassertion of sovereignty, protectionism and nationalism is gaining some ground, and there have been clear increases in trade tensions.

According to the World Trade Organization, trade tensions caused a significant drop in global export trade across almost all sectors in 2019.[15] For example, world exports in iron and steel dropped by 12 per cent, having grown on average 6 per cent per year from 2000. This was before the pandemic and resulting global economic crisis, which will see much steeper declines. As a comparison, iron and steel exports dropped 45 per cent in 2009 as a result of the GFC.

Other effects of consumer behaviour on global trade are interesting to observe. WTO figures show world exports of solar energy-powered goods and related products increased by an annual average of 10 per cent between 2005 and 2019. World exports of electric and hybrid cars increased by almost 60 per cent from 2018 to 2019. And world exports of plastics, having increased on average by 6 per cent per year from 2000, saw a 5 per cent drop in 2019, declining more quickly than total merchandise exports (−3 per cent). A sign hopefully of environmental campaigns having an impact.

Questions are emerging as to whether these signs of change will change our business models too. In a world where political tensions may be higher and trade tensions or barriers create more uncertainty, will businesses naturally revert to working with suppliers closer to home or will they bring operations closer – what has been referred to as reshoring?

From the late 1980s, the trend for displacing work to lower-cost locations (offshoring or nearshoring) grew as part of managing overall business costs. Often that was done with partners, and outsourcing of different support functions and operations started to grow, as we discussed earlier.

However, in more recent years, in large part driven by the changes in globalization and geopolitics, there has been some growing evidence of retrenchment by businesses – reshoring operations to reduce risk and complexity, even where there may be some increase in unit costs. Under the Trump administration, US firms were actively encouraged to do this.

The pandemic has significantly raised these debates. Disruptions to supply chains as countries went through lockdowns showed many businesses some of the risks of their more globalized supply chains. But shifting long-outsourced or offshored operations from, say, Asia to the US is complex and involves not just building new facilities but huge challenges of knowledge transfer and capability development.

Technology development is also playing a role. Where more can be automated, then location or access to low-cost labour become much less the issue. As Venkatraman Ramakrishnan sagely observed about the future for India.

A 2020 Deloitte survey on trends in outsourcing highlighted four main effects:[16]

- Cost reduction is back on top as a key driver, particularly with the concerns of a global recession following the pandemic.
- Cloud and robotic process automation (RPA) is developing rapidly and seen to be central to most outsourcing strategies. It drives efficiencies, but also as it evolves further reduces the need for labour and can therefore also drive greater flexibility.
- Management of complex and integrated supply chains and service providers is proving difficult and capability to do this is often lacking. The many issues of regulatory compliance, security, risk, data protection and the strain of the pandemic have added to this.

- Agility is critical. Outsourcing can be part of the solution, but service providers will have to develop further capabilities, leveraging technology, and contracts and relationships will have to allow them to pivot as business priorities evolve.

As always, the debate for any organization will likely centre on risk versus unit economics but also now the need for agility.

The longer-term impact of the pandemic on sourcing strategies and globalization will take a long time to play out and there are many variables at play. A good article in Reuters in May 2020 referencing various experts considered that the globalization trend is now towards greater regionalization (nearshoring).[17] Regions from the EU to countries like Japan and India are encouraging relocation away from places like China with tax and land incentives. But in relocating any operations the emphasis will be on automation to keep unit costs down.

Companies like Nike are reported to be looking to diversify their production, to counter the issues of long lead times and large minimum order quantities that these previously globalized supply chains required.

It's also true to observe that through the pandemic, organizations have learned that physical colocation of resources is not always necessary for people to work effectively. More distributed networks of workers, maybe with smaller, more localized offices, allow firms to access talent in different ways and at different cost points.

How global interconnection helps standards of practice

Globalization has made a huge difference in accelerating economic growth, particularly as we have discussed in the developing economies of the world over the last 20–30 years. It has also allowed a great spreading of knowledge and of innovation. Some worry that this extends competition, which it does, and that is part of the political dialogue that has led to more of a sense of protectionism and nationalism in recent years.

Another very positive way in which globalization is helping is the spreading of good standards and management practices. Governments in many of the OECD nations are encouraging companies to take more responsibility for their supply chains – building on the ideas of wider stakeholder responsibility of organizations, a responsibility to support suppliers but also to encourage good practices in areas like environmental sustainability and how supplier companies treat and manage their people.

The UK Modern Slavery act published in 2015 set out to prevent modern slavery and human trafficking in the UK. Section 54 of the Act on Transparency in Supply Chain Provisions requires businesses with turnovers above £36 million to publish an annual statement confirming the steps taken to ensure that slavery and human trafficking are not taking place in the business or in any supply chain.

This was a very positive statement of intent regarding responsibilities of businesses for ensuring ethical practices extended into their supply chains. However, progress has been mixed. The Business & Human Rights Resource Centre (BHRRC) has been monitoring the quality of Modern Slavery Act annual statements since its inception, and in its 2018 update and report said that the Act had 'failed to deliver the transformational change that many of us hoped for'.[18] Too many companies either took the easy option and declared they had not evaluated modern slavery in their supply chain, or their statements of compliance were 'vague or generic'. But the BHRRC cited some good examples such as Marks & Spencer, Diageo, Morrisons, Sainsbury's, British American Tobacco, Tesco, Burberry, Vodafone, Unilever, BT, Kingfisher and National Grid.

Companies that do stand behind these principles also recognize the value in branding and marketing. Statements on products, such as being ethically or sustainably sourced, reflect also a greater consumer awareness, and pressure, for businesses to act in these ways.

Unilever has always had strong purpose and principles in its responsibilities to influence and manage good practice in its supply chains. In January 2020 Unilever announced a pledge that every worker in its global supply chain would earn the living wage by 2030, with the aim of helping 'workers to participate fully in their communities and help break the cycle of poverty'.[19]

These are tough things for organizations to do and fully ensure, with the complex nature of supply chains, and the huge number of smaller suppliers who will also need help from large corporations in addressing proper and ethical workforce practices.

Other countries like Australia are putting more force of the law behind modern slavery, and we expect to see this continue as an important part of responsible business. No organization should be minimizing its supply chain costs while turning a blind eye to issues like modern slavery. Many groups also would like to see stronger action on companies ensuring environmental sustainability through their supply chains.

Procurement approaches and supply chain management are moving in these directions in other ways as well, for example increasing expectations on suppliers to disclose much more about their principles, how they manage their workforces and support diversity, or how they invest in training and development and apprenticeships.

As we will discuss further in subsequent chapters, if we measure these things better, expect more transparency and take a multistakeholder view, we can all help to make a collective difference.

Populism and politics

As noted earlier, many of the trends of globalization have been impacted by changing political opinions in many countries. The sense people have that globalization might be good for big business but it is not good for me.

In Bevan et al's *21st Century Workforces & Workplaces*,[20] the authors explored data on migration. They recognized that the concern about migrant workers depriving the local populations of jobs has long been a fear but is not borne out by the facts. While the share of non-UK nationals in the workforce doubled from around 7 per cent to just over 11 per cent between 1996 and 2016, there is no evidence of a detrimental impact on job opportunities, wages or inequalities. As the authors noted, 'few areas illustrate the gulf between the populist view and the economic evidence than on migration'.

Nonetheless, the trends of greater localism have been reflected by growth of right-wing and so-called 'populist' parties and greater political division across the spectrum. Politics has become more divisive and polarized, old allegiances are changing and the political landscape of the future is as uncertain as it has ever been in recent times.

Alternative für Deutschland is a notable example. Only founded in 2013, it became the third largest party and largest opposition party in Germany after the federal election in 2017 and is variously described as right wing, nationalist, populist and Eurosceptic.

In 2019 in the European Parliament, nine far-right parties formed a new bloc called Identity and Democracy (ID). In Hungary, Austria and Switzerland, nationalist parties won more than 25 per cent of the vote in their most recent national elections. In the Nordic countries, Finland, Sweden, Denmark and Estonia all had nationalist parties winning more than 17 per cent of the vote, and Italy, France, Spain and the Netherlands were not far behind.

New political leaders tapped into this and were being elected because they highlighted these tensions. Donald Trump's slogans of 'America First' and 'Make America Great Again' tapped into this growing zeitgeist in the

US and got him elected in 2016. His subsequent withdrawal from or challenge to many global institutions were seemingly a key part of America's policies under his presidency.

The referendum in the United Kingdom in June 2016 about the country's continued membership of the European Union was another big signal. The vote for Brexit was fundamentally about a separation and belief that going it alone as 'Global Britain' was better, and the slogan of taking back control resonated with many, right across political, social and class divides.

While many Asian countries have been less open to the world in their more recent histories, they are at the same time now trying to represent themselves as more global. Perhaps they are sensing the changes happening in the West and seeing their opportunity differently.

The World Economic Forum has always operated under the principle of 'committed to improving the state of the world'. In 2017, President Xi Jinping was the first Chinese president to attend the annual forum in Davos. His message was that despite the uncertainties that were coming from the then new presidency of Trump, China was ready to play its part in the multilateral, pluralistic, liberal, free-market world order.

The irony of this was not lost on the audience. It was an extraordinary moment when the leader of one-party, communist China, whose economic model is based on state intervention in the economy and where freedom of the press and human rights are strictly controlled, was seeking to reassure the world about the continued progress of globalization, in contrast to an apparently retrenching United States.

Retrenchment of this kind feels at odds with the global issues we face – the pandemic itself, environment, and the many other issues expressed through the UN Sustainability Development Goals.

As John Donne noted many centuries earlier, 'no man is an island unto himself, but everyman a piece of the continent, a part of the main'.[21] We are all part of and involved with mankind, part of communities and societies where we have more in common than that which divides us.

Era-defining changes – accelerated by the pandemic

These are in many ways era-defining questions, and the pandemic has been accelerating these trends.

While Schwab was speaking primarily of the influence of technology driving a new era, social and political shifts will be no less significant. In their 1991 book *Generations*,[22] US authors William Strauss and Neil Howe laid out the foundations of the Fourth Turning theory, which prescribes that history is dictated by recurring generational personality types, or archetypes.

The duo argues that these archetypes unleash new eras – or turnings, as they call them – and that these create a new social, political and economic climate. Turnings last around 20 years and every 80–90 years a crucial 'fourth turning' occurs, which they describe as a 'crisis'. It is marked by the destruction of the social order and the creation of a new one, after which a fresh cycle begins. The authors describe the most recent fourth turning or 'crisis' as starting with the Wall Street Crash of 1929 and climaxing with the end of the Second World War. That was followed by turnings they describe as 'High', 'Awakening' and 'Unraveling'.

Almost three decades after the publication of their book, their reasoning dictates that Covid-19 might be one of their crises, not only because of direct economic consequences but also in accelerating underlying trends that are driving this uncertain next wave of globalization.

Criticism has been levelled at Strauss and Howe for being overly deterministic and generalizing too much, but the idea of eras is not unique to them. Whether we are now at a true 'turning' or not, there are many indicators of significant change. On a fundamental level, the relentless spread of the disease around the world highlighted a vulnerability of increasingly global supply chains and international integration. Dependencies on other nations to provide goods and services that each nation needs.

When restrictions and lockdowns started to take hold from early 2020 in response to the growing pandemic, supplies of many goods faltered. Early on in the pandemic, voices were raised in support of more national independence and some degree of legitimacy for restrictions of trade and even migration. Movement of people was after all how the virus spreads. Initially China, where the pandemic began, and later Italy and other countries which had high infection rates even became stigmatized.

In the days after travel bans were introduced, political economist Philippe Legrain wrote that while much of the disruption to international trade and travel would likely be temporary, the crisis could have a lasting political impact because of its potential to reinforce existing trends already undermining globalization.[23]

China-centred global supply chains that had grown through globalization were already coming under pressure. As the country had become richer and wages had risen, the cost–benefit of producing in China and other lower-cost countries had already been waning. Legrain said the coronavirus was now likely to be the tipping point that triggers businesses to revamp their supply chains and focus more on local and regional production.

Sadly, as is so often the case with fear of the unknown, there also was a rise in xenophobic incidents. As the virus spread through France, for example, Asians in the country created a Twitter hashtag, #Jenesuispasunvirus ('I am not a virus'), to signal abuse.[24]

As the pandemic rolled on across the world during 2020, China seemed to recover quickly and was able to open up its economy. Tight lockdowns, localized from the beginning to the biggest cities or regions of infection, and a fast-responding health system had an impact, all learned from previous virus epidemics such as SARS. This gave some opportunity for the Chinese government to claim that their country's response to the virus was evidence of the ruling Communist Party's superiority.[25] Recriminations from abroad, meanwhile, called to make China pay for the pandemic,[26] which in turn triggered defensiveness on the part of many Chinese.

Robert Ward, of the International Institute for Strategic Studies think tank, concluded in his analysis that over the longer term, a likely uneven recovery from the pandemic could fuel existing discontent and encourage a move towards protectionism.[27] He argued that regions with high levels of social unrest, poor growth outlooks and macroeconomic imbalances would be particularly vulnerable. At the time of writing, the patterns are unclear – while parts of Latin America have suffered badly, the Middle East, sub-Saharan Africa and Asia seem to have fared better.

Ward also said that the fragmented nature of the response to the coronavirus crisis contrasted sharply with the 'global rallying during the 2008 financial crisis' and underscored a 'weakening of international institutions'. The profound economic shock resulting from the health crisis would 'shift political attention (certainly in the EU and the US) to domestic concerns', he predicted, which in turn 'risks narrowing the political bandwidth among key players for supporting multilateralism, so feeding protectionism and nationalism, and casting a shadow over an already fragile global trade system and hence the strength of the recovery'.

But even within nations, the pandemic has created many issues and in many instances has undermined trust in governments. Trust is so essential to social cohesion and works at so many levels. If people are increasingly suspicious of the motives of the establishment and feeling that globalization is not acting in their best interests, they look closer to home and where their voice can be expressed. With social divisions already growing with a sense of disenfranchisement, inequalities and lack of fairness of opportunity, the pandemic has in most cases certainly not helped.

In Italy, for example, a delay in shutting virus hotspots in the Lombardy region enabled the virus to spread swiftly and inflamed a row between the government and La Liga (The League) party, which governed Italy in a coalition for a year until summer 2019. Each side blamed the other for failing to act quickly enough.

'If people begin to suffer seriously, rage could spread throughout the country... at which point far-right propaganda becomes very effective,' Giovanni Orsina, professor of politics at Rome's LUISS University, told AFP at the time.[28]

Tribalism and individual politics

As a consequence of all these issues, politics for each of us has probably never been more part of our lives. News channels over the last few years have been almost completely consumed by political crises and change, and the crises of the pandemic and of the environment.

People struggle to keep up and greatly conflicting views get expressed through the multiplicity of channels that people can connect through. Truth, half-truths and lies blend into each other, and conspiracy theories abound. The uncertainty and polarization of opinions and views sadly create many divisions, which impact people's relationships and mental health and even the stability of our societies.

In 2016, in the midst of the US presidential campaign, the American Psychological Association (APA) conducted a survey of a representative sample of the US workforce and concluded that a quarter of respondents felt they were negatively affected by political talk at work. Some 17 per cent admitted that as a result of political discussions, they felt tense or stressed out, while 15 per cent said that they were more cynical and negative at work. One in 10 said that political talk made it more difficult for them to get work done and the same proportion considered the work that they were doing to be of lower quality because of the political conversations that were being had.

Other research also shows a huge change in the way the public feels about someone who's politically opposed to them. As the journalist Jeremy Deaton points out, in 1960, only 5 per cent of Americans said they would be displeased if their son or daughter married someone in a different political camp. By 2010, that proportion had risen to around 40 per cent.[29]

Alarming research by political scientists Kalmoe and Mason in the US in 2019 showed that 60 per cent of voters think members of the opposing party represent a serious threat to America and its people, more than 40 per cent would call them evil and 20 per cent would describe them as animals.[30]

Simon Kuper in 2018 wrote that both the election of Trump and the Brexit referendum in Britain had created a new type of tribalism and sense of belonging,[31] but more recently signs have started to emerge that political affiliation could be weakening too, and this might also be accentuated in the long run by the public's perception of politicians' response to the Covid-19 crisis.

The tribulations of the UK's Labour Party provide an interesting example of this. In December 2019, Labour suffered one of its most catastrophic general election defeats in history. Analysis pegged the dismal outcome on everything from Corbyn's personal likability to the party's election strategy. But perhaps Labour's fate is symptomatic of a much broader shift across the political world, namely, a shift away from party politics and towards issue politics.

In a column for *The Economist* published in December 2019, Andrea Venzo and Colombe Cahen-Salvador, co-founders of activism group Now!, phrased it as such: 'Our grandparents attended party conventions teeming with balloons and bunting. Our parents took to the streets to demand radical changes from those same parties. Our generation regards political parties as a relic of an era of black-and-white television, transatlantic ocean-liners and the jitterbug. We simply don't care about them at all. We care about issues, not allegiances.'[32]

The arguments about politics and political affiliations also of course spread into our work cultures. During the Brexit referendum many of Europe's large businesses were against Brexit,[33] citing a survey by law firm KWM that showed at least two in three thought it would be bad for their organizations and business and trade. Large UK businesses were mostly against, but smaller businesses were more evenly split.[34] A number of business leaders notably let it be known to their employees, advising them to vote to remain – companies like Rolls-Royce and Airbus, and a number of the big banks. But most businesses remained steadfastly neutral, concerned that taking sides in the divisive issue could lead to a backlash from customers or their employees.

However, within organizations we can't easily ban political discussions or sharing of opinions. In the worst case it might draw even more attention to irreconcilable differences in opinion: a phenomenon that's somewhat humorously referred to as the Streisand Effect:[35] American singer Barbra Streisand in 2003 attempted to have a photograph of her home censored but in doing so actually drew far more media attention to it than it otherwise would have garnered.

Instead, David Ballard, director of the APA's Center for Organizational Excellence, recommends managers acknowledge that political conversations are going to occur but also that they ensure employees are aware of what's expected of them.[36] 'The most effective approach is to promote a workplace culture that embraces respect and trust so that difficult conversations and disagreements (political or otherwise) can take place in a civil environment. A psychologically healthy workplace is good for employees and the organization even in the best of times, but it's particularly critical during challenging and polarizing times,' he writes.

Ballard says it's particularly important that managers recognize the risk of political environments having an impact on employees. The wellbeing of workers should be the concern not just of HR departments but of every manager and supervisor within a business. It's also their responsibility to lead by example, demonstrating the types of behaviours they wish to encourage across an organization.

In conclusion

It is clear we are in times of significant change and disruption and all the issues we have explored in this chapter are part of that.

The direction of globalization will impact business strategies and thinking. How supply chains get managed, the extent to which trends in outsourcing and offshoring might change, and access to skills and talent, as well as the markets themselves.

We will all have to work hard to build or rebuild trust, connection and our abilities to listen to each other. The reactions against the establishment and the trends of globalization are fundamental issues of trust, and the attendant drivers of feelings of inequality and unfairness, which we will further explore in the next chapter.

And as we have noted throughout, agility and ability to respond to changing context and circumstance will be the critical capability for organizations for the future.

We will examine in later chapters the issues for leadership in this much more uncertain world, the issues of skills and capabilities, and other areas where business needs to respond. But now, perhaps more than ever, the role of business as part of society and as a positive force for change must be central to our agendas.

Endnotes

1 www.ipsos.com/ipsos-mori/en-uk/anti-system-sentiment-still-strong-around-world (archived at https://perma.cc/2YDV-KRKQ)
2 Pinker, S (2011) *The Better Angels of Our Nature: Why violence has declined*, Viking Books, London
3 www.pwc.com/gx/en/ceo-survey/2020/reports/pwc-23rd-global-ceo-survey.pdf (archived at https://perma.cc/ZBL2-GWZM)
4 http://archive.wilsonquarterly.com/sites/default/files/articles/WQ_VOL17_SP_1993_Article_02_1.pdf (archived at https://perma.cc/D3AM-SB4E)
5 www.theguardian.com/news/datablog/2016/feb/26/uk-more-middle-class-than-working-class-2000-data (archived at https://perma.cc/3DDU-BKE2)
6 Hilbert, M and López, P (2011) The world's technological capacity to store, communicate, and compute information, *Science*, 332(6025), pp. 60–65
7 www.foreignaffairs.com/articles/2015-12-12/fourth-industrial-revolution (archived at https://perma.cc/5AZW-ZSWV)
8 Economic Times of India, 23 September 2017
9 www.criticaleye.com/inspiring/insights-servfile.cfm?id=351 (archived at https://perma.cc/5WHN-VCST)
10 www.reuters.com/article/us-corus-tata-reaction-idUSDEL19355520070201 (archived at https://perma.cc/7QSZ-4J4K)
11 https://economictimes.indiatimes.com/industry/auto/auto-news/how-ratan-tata-brought-life-to-jaguar-land-rover/jlr-was-going-through-a-rough-patch/slideshow/63245740.cms (archived at https://perma.cc/G4XQ-GCBQ)
12 www.worldbank.org/en/country/china/overview (archived at https://perma.cc/984T-CAKZ)
13 https://worldoceanreview.com/en/wor-1/transport/global-shipping/ (archived at https://perma.cc/EG7A-LVKK)
14 https://unctad.org/system/files/official-document/dtl2018d1_en.pdf (archived at https://perma.cc/MR6G-MNKC)
15 www.wto.org/english/res_e/statis_e/wts2020_e/wts2020chapter04_e.pdf (archived at https://perma.cc/8Z5T-G9DM)
16 www2.deloitte.com/us/en/pages/operations/articles/global-outsourcing-survey.html (archived at https://perma.cc/3SL2-XFVR)
17 www.reutersevents.com/supplychain/supply-chain/reversing-globalisation-near-shoring-reshoring-or-staying-put (archived at https://perma.cc/PQ9M-8LE5)

18 https://media.business-humanrights.org/media/documents/files/FTSE_100_Briefing_2018.pdf (archived at https://perma.cc/ZP4U-85HT)
19 www.thetimes.co.uk/article/unilever-promises-living-wage-to-its-supply-chain-98jlr57kp (archived at https://perma.cc/RV7C-XRGB)
20 Bevan, S, Brinkley, I, Bajorek, Z and Cooper, C (2018) *21st Century Workforces & Workplaces*, Bloomsbury, London
21 Donne, J (1624) Meditation XVII, Devotions upon Emergent Occasions
22 Strauss, W and Howe, N (1991) *Generations*, William Morrow & Co, New York
23 https://foreignpolicy.com/2020/03/12/coronavirus-killing-globalization-nationalism-protectionism-trump/ (archived at https://perma.cc/WAA5-7FUH)
24 www.reuters.com/article/us-china-health-france-sentiment/i-am-not-a-virus-frances-asian-community-pushes-back-over-xenophobia-idUSKBN1ZU2PV (archived at https://perma.cc/7LHN-8WTK)
25 www.nytimes.com/2020/04/16/world/asia/coronavirus-china-nationalism.html (archived at https://perma.cc/K52W-TL5Q)
26 www.washingtonpost.com/business/2020/04/24/republican-coronavirus-china-xi/ (archived at https://perma.cc/2FK8-9CNF)
27 www.iiss.org/blogs/analysis/2020/04/gstrat-coronavirus-crisis-and-rising-political-risk (archived at https://perma.cc/CM4F-ED66)
28 www.france24.com/en/20200418-will-italy-s-coronavirus-epidemic-fuel-the-far-right (archived at https://perma.cc/JK6P-7VV8)
29 https://pcl.stanford.edu/research/2012/iyengar-poq-affect-not-ideology.pdf (archived at https://perma.cc/EW4E-687M)
30 www.dannyhayes.org/uploads/6/9/8/5/69858539/kalmoe___mason_ncapsa_2019_-_lethal_partisanship_-_final_lmedit.pdf (archived at https://perma.cc/VE5L-XEQY)
31 www.ft.com/content/89f16688-fb15-11e7-a492-2c9be7f3120a (archived at https://perma.cc/6SQV-7LFF)
32 www.economist.com/open-future/2019/11/01/party-politics-is-dying-so-make-citizen-movements-the-new-unifier (archived at https://perma.cc/P2MA-L6R2)
33 Cordell, J (2016) EU businesses want a hard line in any post-Brexit negotiations, *City AM*, 11 May
34 www.theguardian.com/business/2016/jun/02/uk-small-businesses-are-evenly-split-on-brexit-poll-says (archived at https://perma.cc/V4AP-6Y5H)
35 www.economist.com/the-economist-explains/2013/04/15/what-is-the-streisand-effect (archived at https://perma.cc/QH8Z-9CDK)
36 https://hbr.org/2017/03/navigating-political-talk-at-work (archived at https://perma.cc/N8GH-KFFQ)

04

Social and demographic change

If you don't like something, change it. If you can't change it, change your attitude.

MAYA ANGELOU, AMERICAN POET, PLAYWRIGHT
AND CIVIL RIGHTS ACTIVIST

We have explored many of the big changes in our economies and in the trends of globalization and political change. But we are also in an era of significant social change.

Changes in beliefs, affiliations and expectations, driven by the shifting demographics, the new generations, and the increasing diversity of our societies and communities. Social change is of course also significantly influenced by economic changes, particularly in more difficult times such as those experienced following the global financial crisis and the pandemic.

In this chapter we will explore the drivers of social change and what they mean for business. From the importance of understanding trust, fairness and equality to inclusion and diversity, and the ideas of responsible business.

Social attitudes have changed significantly in the last 20 or 30 years. The growth of populism and the 'wisdom of the crowd', less formality and hierarchy or deference, and at the same time the growing loss of trust in the establishment.

People everywhere are speaking up, and they have more channels through which to do that than ever before. But social media is also creating echo chambers for purveyors of conspiracy theories and unsubstantiated opinion, making it harder to see reality from noise or just plain hubris – look at the conspiracy theories for COVID-19, which included views that the virus was introduced so that vaccines could be produced that make people infertile in order to reduce population growth, or that it was a plot by Bill Gates to put microchips into us all.

Social attitude surveys give us a picture of changing issues and concerns on people's minds. In recent Eurobarometer surveys, Europeans mentioned the typical social concerns related to rising prices, health and social security, pensions and the financial situation of their household as the most important issues they faced at a personal level.[1] But they also raised concerns relating to environment, climate and energy issues and housing as gaining ground.

Business is itself part of society and should be a positive force for good. Not only must business understand and adapt to social change, but in turn businesses can influence positive change. More than ever before, business is expected to act responsibly, to have clear and positive purpose, and to act in the interests of all stakeholders, not just the financial shareholders.

Crises raise the stakes significantly. As Boin et al write in the 2012 book *Comparative Political Leadership*,[2] crises tend to place the deeds, personalities, styles and competencies of office holders in focus and are highly public affairs which are often followed by 'a spate of no-holds-barred post-mortem investigations'.

Through the recent crises, spotlights are more focused on leaders everywhere, and they exaggerate underlying divisions and issues of equality and fairness. The impact of crises is never evenly spread. The pandemic, both from a health and from an economic perspective, impacted countries, regions, localities, sectors, organizations and segments of our populations and workforces differently.

Over the last decade, not only have crises affected social change but the voices and expectations of younger generations everywhere have shone the spotlight even deeper. Increasing diversity of our populations driven by globalization and greater movement of people has also sharpened the questions of fairness and inclusion. These issues cannot be ignored by politicians and they cannot be ignored by business.

A growing crisis of trust

One of the most visible signs of change and the expectations of people across all levels of society is the issue of trust. Trust is fundamental to effective functioning of societies as well as businesses. Trust in businesses, their leadership, their behaviours and actions is central to brand and reputation.

Which in turn influences consumer behaviour as well as employee performance, attraction and retention.

Understanding and addressing trust is therefore a theme we will be coming back to in subsequent chapters on leadership, transparency and corporate governance.

Edelman, the global public relations and marketing consultancy, has for 20 years researched the issues of trust. Their Trust Barometer,[3] based on surveys of people's attitudes and beliefs around the world, has for a number of years been showing the erosion in trust in what might be called 'the establishment' – our political leaders, large corporations, the rich and powerful, the media, or even the intellectual elite.

The introduction to the 2020 version of the Trust Barometer summarizes the issues: 'The 2020 Edelman Trust Barometer reveals that despite a strong global economy and near full employment, none of the four societal institutions that the study measures—government, business, NGOs and media—is trusted. The cause of this paradox can be found in people's fears about the future and their role in it, which are a wake-up call for our institutions to embrace a new way of effectively building trust: balancing competence with ethical behaviour.'

FIGURE 4.1 How institutions are trusted on ethical behaviours and competence

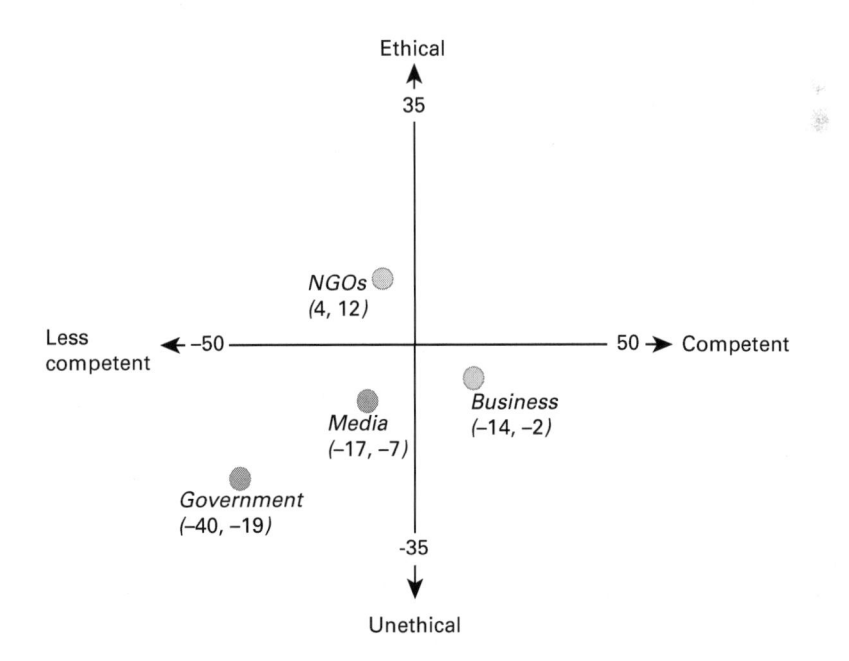

Ethical
35

NGOs (4, 12)

Less competent ← –50

50 → Competent

Media (–17, –7)

Business (–14, –2)

Government (–40, –19)

-35

Unethical

SOURCE Edelman Trust Barometer 2020

In the 2020 survey, more than half of people globally said they now believed capitalism in its current form was doing more harm than good. This picture is more noticeable in the West and the developed markets where the majority in these parts of the world do not believe they will be better off in five years' time.

Figure 4.1 shows that no institutions are viewed as both competent and ethical.

These issues of trust have also altered traditional senses of belonging. At an individual level, we all need to feel we belong to something. We are inherently tribal – from football team affiliations to local community and national pride. Tribal identities and affiliations are built on shared and common purpose, identity, beliefs and trust. But as trust has been eroding in the establishment, allegiances and what people identify with have been changing. People are more likely to trust those closest to them or most like them. Within an organization, that might be close colleagues or line managers, before it reaches up into senior leadership.

As summarized in the CIPD's March 2012 report 'Where has all the trust gone?',[4] trust in an organization stems from the behaviour of direct managers as well as that of the organization's leaders, but organizations with high trust are those where staff feel their trust is reciprocated and that they are themselves trusted by their managers.

For leaders to be trusted, CIPD's research and others show that they need to demonstrate some key characteristics, namely:

- **ability** – demonstrable competence at doing their job;
- **benevolence** – a concern for others beyond their own needs and having benign motives;
- **integrity** – adherence to a set of principles acceptable to others, encompassing fairness and honesty;
- **predictability** – a regularity of behaviour over time.

These characteristics are as true for political leaders as they are for business leaders, as well as for institutions and organizations.

Research published in 2020 by Accenture[5] showed that 72 per cent of global CEOs surveyed believed that trust would be critical to their competitiveness in the next five years. Frankly, we would worry about the other 28 per cent who didn't seem to think it was critical.

Edelman's research also highlighted how much trust is linked to meeting people's expectations, as show in Figure 4.2.

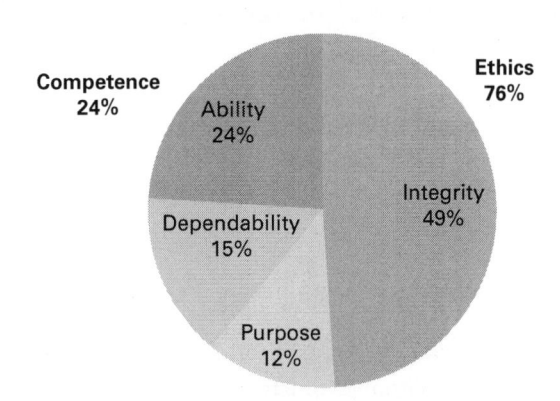

FIGURE 4.2 Importance of meeting employee expectations

Competence 24%
Ability 24%
Ethics 76%
Integrity 49%
Dependability 15%
Purpose 12%

SOURCE Edelman 2020 (US, UK and German general population data, collected between January and December 2019, based on 40 major companies)

Through crises, as uncertainty grows, for many people the notion of benevolence takes on greater meaning and importance. Do the organization, or my leaders, or my direct line manager and colleagues care about me? Furthermore, do I believe I am being treated fairly, have fair opportunity, that people around me are behaving with integrity?

There is a memorable proverb in Dutch – *Vertrouwen komt te voet en vertrekt te paard*. Trust arrives on foot and leaves on horseback. Trust is famously hard to build, and in an age of social media and fast news it's perhaps never been easier to destroy.

Employees, like consumers, expect a degree of transparency from the brands and companies they give their money, time and energy to. They also demand a certain degree of moral and ethical alignment, at which point politics can actually re-enter the picture.

In the wake of President Trump's 2017 executive order banning immigrants and refugees from seven Muslim-majority countries, ride-sharing company Uber faced a viral boycott tied to its chief executive officer's role on the president's economic advisory council. Uber CEO Travis Kalanick eventually stepped down from the council,[6] yielding to pressure from disgruntled customers as well as frustrated employees. More broadly across Silicon Valley, where scores of executives and founders – but also rank-and-file workers – are immigrants, Trump's policy became an issue that corporations found themselves unable not to take a stand on.

Trust is closely tied to brand reputation. From Edelman's June 2019 survey[7] across eight countries, the vast majority of consumers, regardless of age, income and gender, agreed that their ability to trust a brand was central to any buying decision. Some 81 per cent of respondents said they would only consider purchasing a particular product from a brand if they were able to trust it to 'do what is right', and 53 per cent agreed that every brand has a responsibility to get involved in at least one social issue that does not directly impact its business.

Going beyond virtue signalling – from words to action

Understanding what 'the right thing' is can be difficult though, and the cost of getting it wrong substantial. Numerous brands have faced media backlash or ridicule and some have been accused of trying to reap commercial value from what many see as virtue signalling.

The most basic rule companies can follow is to consider authenticity. Does it make rational sense in the eye of the public for me to align with this particular cause or campaign? Does this cause echo the values that I've previously displayed, or is this just PR spin?

In 2017, German car maker Audi showed an advert during the US Super Bowl depicting a father wistfully watching his daughter driving a go-kart as he dwelled on all the hurdles she might face during her life on account of her gender.[8] The intention of the ad was to draw attention to Audi's commitment to providing equal opportunities regardless of gender. Inconveniently for the car maker, viewers and the media were quick to point out that Audi's six-person board at the time didn't include a single woman.[9]

The same year, US bank State Street unveiled the Fearless Girl statue, which it had commissioned for display near Wall Street with a plaque engraved with the words 'Know the power of women in leadership'.[10] Also in 2017, State Street agreed to pay $5 million to settle charges that it had discriminated against female senior executives by paying them less than male colleagues.[11]

More recently, in mid-2020, as protests erupted across US cities in the wake of the violent deaths of George Floyd, Ahmaud Arbery, Breonna Taylor and other black people, many global corporations publicly condemned racism. As journalist David Gelles of *The New York Times* noted, however, 'many of the same companies expressing solidarity have contributed to systemic inequality, targeted the black community with unhealthy products and services, and failed to hire, promote and fairly compensate black men and women'.[12]

One example he pointed to was that the commissioner of the US National Football League, Roger Goodell, had issued a statement saying that the protests expressed 'the pain, anger and frustration that so many of us feel'. But the NFL had previously banned players – the majority of whom are black – from kneeling to protest police brutality.

Likewise beauty brand L'Oréal published a social media post in response to the protests that read 'Speaking out is worth it', a play on its long-time corporate slogan. Many were quick to point out that three years earlier, in 2017, the group had dropped its first ever transgender model, Munroe Bergdorf, from a campaign after she had spoken out publicly about racism following white nationalist violence in Charlottesville, Virginia.[13]

Gelles notes that 'generations of well-intentioned pledges by businesses have resulted in only marginal advancement for the black community' and that the coronavirus pandemic has exacerbated grim employment trends, one example of which is that fewer than half of black adults in America had a job at the time of writing.

Trust what you know – importance of evidence and transparency

It's well documented that humans fear the unknown,[14] so one of the greatest barriers to the public trusting a corporation – even one they work for – might be a lack of understanding of how that corporation actually works.

Business and finance is often dismissed as a specialist subject, reflected in the fact that national newspapers will mostly allocate more resources to general news and political coverage than to business and economic reporting. Most people have little knowledge of who runs the country's largest corporations because even the publicly traded ones are considered opaque. Balance sheets and company statements, even if they can be sourced, can be intimidating and hard to decipher. It can be tricky to interpret what individual facts and figures actually mean in real terms. Greater transparency, built on clear evidence, data and narrative, must be key to the solution and we will explore this in more detail in later chapters.

It's easy to create an impression of a company based on a few factually questionable headlines, and many individual businesses suffer reputational damage because of a preconception about the broader industry.

After the 2008 financial crisis, banks fought hard to recover their tarnished reputation for causing a massive economic downturn. Many have still not succeeded. Big pharmaceutical companies have battled public accusations of being intent on profiting from other people's suffering. Short-termism and shareholder primacy across the corporate sphere, as we detailed in the previous chapter, have also contributed to large corporations' public image as potentially reckless and amoral.

If companies were able to become more accessible, and if the public were able to develop a keener interest in understanding truly how businesses work, trust might be enhanced too. An important step is for corporations to demonstrate plausibly that they are purpose-driven, with clearly stated purpose beyond just making money.

Countless surveys conducted by both professional service firms[15] and consultancies[16] in recent years have shown a trend towards CEOs championing businesses that are driven by purpose as much as profit. We follow that up in much more detail in Chapter 8. But as we've seen, many of the companies run by those individuals still spend more money on dividends and share buybacks – which primarily benefit shareholders – than on research and development or recruitment and training.

Once companies are able to match their actions to their narrative, they are likely to be rewarded with employee and consumer trust and loyalty.

Increasing inequalities undermining trust and impacting social cohesion

Many of the wider societal issue of trust are driven by issues of fairness and equality.

Contemporary movements of protest from the Occupy Wall Street movement, the Yellow Vest protests in France, the Black Lives Matter movement, and even movements like #metoo, all reflect issues of inequalities, lack of trust and discontent with the establishment. And as noted in the previous chapter, even the advances of globalization are seen by many to be compromising their opportunities.

Advances in technology and the potential acceleration of the displacement of labour through capital could cause yet more concern as we look to the future. According to data from the World Economic Forum, the average income level in high-income countries is more than 70 times higher than in low-income countries.[17]

At the same time, while high-income countries face the challenge of an aging population, many lower-income countries have rapidly growing working-age and younger populations.

However, as we noted in Chapter 2, while economic inequalities between countries are falling, those within countries are rising. The gap between the haves and the have-nots is growing. Gaps in wealth, income and opportunity.

So what are the facts about inequalities? Branko Milanovic, the Serbian-American economist, summarized the changes in income in his popular book *The Haves and the Have-Nots*[18] (see Figure 4.3). Yet even families on middle incomes are feeling a lot less secure than they have in the past. At EU level, more than half (53 per cent) of people in the middle classes report a feeling of vulnerability and difficulty in making ends meet financially. And while there has been growth from eastern member states in the middle classes, in western member states there have been declines.[19]

The picture is unquestionably complex. Research by the Institute for Fiscal Studies in the UK[20] showed that while the very top of the income distribution 'raced away' from the 1980s, and continued steadily until the onset of the Great Recession, in recent years the trend is less clear. There has been more volatility in top incomes, in part caused by high-income individuals responding to changes in top income tax rates.

The researchers stripped out the extremes of the income distribution and found that inequalities had reduced over time. They took the 90:10 ratio, which measures how many times higher incomes are 90 per cent of the way up the distribution compared with 10 per cent of the way up. They found

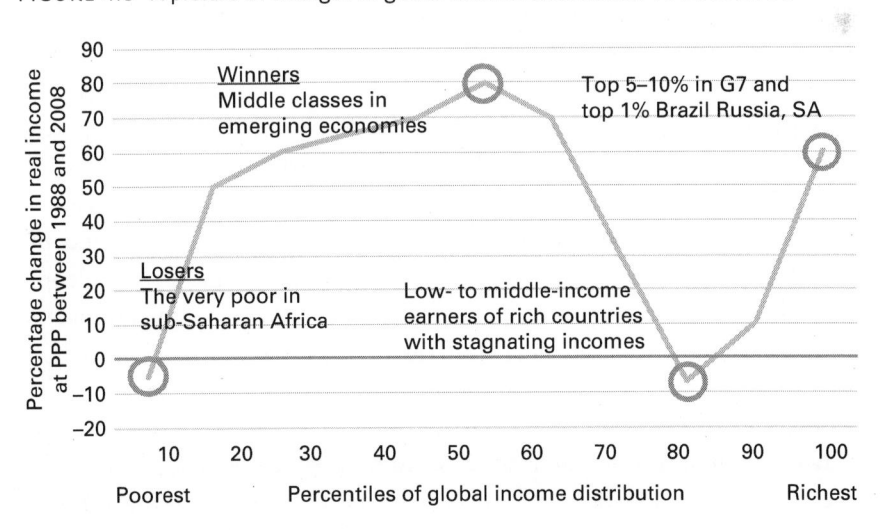

FIGURE 4.3 A picture of changes in global income distribution 1998 to 2008

SOURCE Branko Milanovic

the large increase in inequality during the 1980s was again evident, but since then the 90:10 ratio has generally been falling and at the time of writing is lower than it was 20 years ago.

Income inequalities, not surprisingly, have a real impact on how people feel. A 2016 paper by Richard Burkhauser, Jan-Emmanuel De Neve and Nattavudh Powdthavee[21] examined data from the Gallup World Poll and the World Top Incomes Database and found that the more income is concentrated in the hands of a few, the more likely individuals are to report lower levels of life satisfaction and more negative daily emotional experiences.

In other words, the greater the share of national income that is held by the top 1 per cent, the lower the overall perceived wellbeing of the general population. The academics specifically found that a 1 per cent increase in the share of taxable income held by the top 1 per cent hurts life satisfaction by the same rate as a 1.4 per cent increase in the country-level unemployment rate would.

As the rich get richer, you might consider your chances of ever belonging to the elite class of the wealthiest top 1 per cent to be diminishing.

This research adds to earlier work by Daniel Kahneman and economist Angus Deaton. In their 2010 paper, the Nobel laureates found that happiness peaks at an annual income level of $75,000, which at the time of data collection was about $26,000 above the median US yearly household income and about $7,000 above the mean.

Kahneman and Deaton's research made an important distinction between what they call life satisfaction – or how people generally evaluate their lives – and day-to-day emotions or the way we feel immediately in that moment. The former, they found, was sensitive to socioeconomic factors like income, but the latter were influenced far more by other things, such as how a person spends their day or whether they have caring duties.

Burkhauser et al's research from 2016 echoes these results. They found that while life satisfaction was negatively related to increased income inequality, the same was not consistently true of emotional wellbeing. People didn't necessarily report more positive emotional wellbeing when income inequality was lower, but individuals in countries where the richest hold most of the country's income were more likely to admit to feeling 'stressed', 'worried' or 'angry'.

Both the pieces of research we refer to here were conducted at country level, but we can nonetheless draw conclusions that are important for individual businesses. It's clear that excessive income inequalities and perceptions of unfairness impact people's satisfaction and engagement.

Between 2015 and 2016, PayScale, a US-based company that collects data on salary profiles, surveyed more than 500,000 employees to examine the relationship between pay and employee engagement.[22] The study revealed that one of the most reliable predictors of employee sentiment, which refers to both 'satisfaction' and 'intent to leave', was an organization's ability to communicate clearly and openly about compensation.

But it also revealed other interesting things. The perception of being underpaid, the survey found, dramatically increases the chance of an employee leaving an organization. Yet how much employees are paid relative to the market for their position matters relatively little in terms of employee satisfaction. What does matter is how they feel about how they're paid, which has 5.4 times as much impact.

The economics of inequality

As a result of all these trends, there is no doubt that the politics and economics of inequality have become central issues. 'Rock star' economists like Yanis Varoufakis and Thomas Piketty have become the poster boys in recent years.

Both have been described as successors to Marx in that they focus on the inequalities that they believe are inherent in the system of capitalism and how they are growing. However, they clearly differ in their interpretations and remedies. While Marx focused on the misery of labour and its commoditization, Varoufakis points out the other side of labour, which is about value creation, and he highlights the dangers of the commoditization of labour.

I would similarly argue that work and labour should now focus more on value – for individuals, for organizations and for society. Not least because commoditized labour can be displaced ever more easily by capital – through automation. However, as we discussed in Chapter 2, higher-skilled work and value output are harder to measure and hence, quantifying labour hours and productivity in a more commoditized way is easier to fit to economic models.

Piketty's book *Capital in the Twenty-First Century*, published in 2013, focused on wealth and income inequality in Europe and the US since the 18th century.[23] His view is that inequality is not an accident but rather a feature of capitalism that can be reversed only through state intervention and the possible remedy of a global tax on wealth. He describes a simple formula – R>G (return is greater than growth) – as a distillation of how wealth grows faster than income and why inequality therefore increases over time.

These gaps are creating social issues in many different ways. The Princeton University husband and wife economists Anne Case and Sir Angus Deaton wrote in their much acclaimed book *Deaths of Despair*[24] about what they describe as the flaws in capitalism, which are literally fatal for America's working class. Life expectancy in the United States has recently fallen for three years in a row – something not seen in any other developed economy since the end of the First World War. In the past two decades, deaths of despair from suicide, drug overdose and alcoholism have risen dramatically, most notably among the working classes.

In their view they demonstrate why, for those who used to prosper in America, capitalism is no longer delivering and they point to the deep unfairness of American society. A century ago the richest 10 per cent of Americans were taking home 41 per cent of all domestic income; today, they take 48 per cent.

We're not even capturing the full picture through our traditional measures of economies.

Data in 2016 from the US public policy think tank The Brookings Institution found that 7 million American men between the ages of 25 and 54 – who are mostly too old to be at school but too young to retire – are neither working nor looking for work.[25] Those individuals aren't looking after children or ageing relatives either. Though many would like to be employed, they have struggled to find adequately paid work and as a result have given up looking, which means that they are not counted towards the official unemployment rate.

The pandemic will have made troubling statistics like this even worse. In late 2020 the Institute of Fiscal Studies in the UK launched a review of inequality in the UK led by Angus Deaton to understand more about the impact of the pandemic.[26] As noted in the report, the coronavirus pandemic has underlined the many deep social and economic fractures within countries – divides of race, class, education and income.

Government actions and policy interventions

As awareness of inequalities has grown, so have expectations about how inequalities should be addressed. Many economists have historically preferred the arguments that the markets should determine wealth and income distribution. The disparity of CEO pay, for example, is explainable as being driven by what the market expects and pays for top talent, and that overall the markets function reasonably well in rewarding talent and merit accurately.[27]

But as differences in income and opportunity have become a lot more visible in recent years, in response, regulators, investors and other stakeholders are demanding more. Regulators have increasingly focused attention on areas they expect responsible organizations to address, and on helping to ensure there is no discrimination in the workplace, giving fair opportunity to all and helping to close gaps in income.

Diversity covers many different dimensions, most of which are recognized and protected under law in countries around the world. Through the United Nations, the international human rights legal framework aims to combat specific forms of discrimination – against indigenous peoples, migrants, minorities, people with disabilities, women, race and religion, sexual orientation and gender identity.

The Equality Act in the UK is a good example of this legislation at a national level. It covers age, sex, sexual orientation and gender reassignment, race, religion or belief, disability, pregnancy and maternity, and marriage and civil partnership.

Discrimination is generally recognized in particular ways. The UK Equality Act calls out four different forms of discrimintation.[28]

DISCRIMINATION DEFINED IN UK EQUALITY ACT

- Direct discrimination – treating one person worse than another because of a protected characteristic.
- Indirect discrimination – when an organization puts in place a rule or a policy or a way of doing things which has a worse impact on someone with a protected characteristic than on someone without one.
- Harassment – being treated in ways that violate your dignity, or create a hostile, degrading, humiliating or offensive environment.
- Victimization – being treated unfairly if you are making a complaint of discrimination or supporting someone else in doing so.

All these forms of discrimination are easily recognizable in too many parts of our societies and our workplaces. While progress is being made, every responsible organization should see these as immutable principles to create fairer and more trusting cultures that are good for all, regardless of background.

Other forms of legislation have been emerging more recently, notably pay gap reporting and demands for greater diversity at the tops of organizations. Mandates to increase gender diversity on corporate boards are common in a growing number of countries. Norway, Spain, France and Iceland all have laws requiring that women make up at least 40 per cent of boards at publicly listed companies. Recent legislation in California is proposing similar requirements. Mostly, however, countries such as the UK are encouraging change through greater transparency and reporting rather than through specific legislation.

Still, the World Economic Forum projects that it will take more than a century to close the current gender gap in the countries it covers.[29] But there are positive trends in many countries showing increasing gender equality. According to research by the Pew Research Centre in the US, majorities in 23 of the 27 countries surveyed believed that equality between men and women in their country had increased in the past two decades.[30]

Understanding pay gaps

It is apparent, however, that we still have much to do. Gender pay gap reporting, which has been required in the UK since 2018, still shows great variability across organizations and sectors. A quarter of companies and public sector bodies have a pay gap of more than 20 per cent in favour of men. Sectors such as professional services and financial services have among the biggest gaps. International law firm Allen & Overy reported a 59.9 per cent mean gender pay gap as at April 2020 and an ethnic pay gap of 22.4 per cent for their UK workforce.[31] Transparency and reporting is an important step forwards.

Ethnicity pay gaps and opportunities are less visible or researched, yet are significant indicators of inequality of opportunity and progression within the labour market and organizations everywhere. It is important to see ethnic equality in the context of demographics, but the central issue is always one of fair opportunity and recognition.

According to 2019 UK data from the ONS,[32] the ethnicity pay gap was largest in London (which has a very diverse population) at 23.8 per cent, and smallest in Wales at 1.4 per cent, and even −8.6 per cent in the East of England region where there is much less diversity in the populations.

Beyond raising demands on organizations everywhere to better understand and address inequalities, key areas of government policy can have a huge impact.

Taxation is the main policy instrument for wealth distribution. It also lies at the heart of political thinking and dogma. It is more than a simple idea of spreading wealth from the rich to give to the poor, but rather also about the level of state intervention in the economy. Should we tax more and have the politicians decide how to spend the income on running parts of the economy that support us all (health, education, utilities, public transport, etc) or let more be run by the private sector and let market forces determine more where the money gets spent?

Public spending also creates jobs and opportunities and is therefore also argued to be a form of income distribution, alongside benefit systems that support those at the lowest levels of income or opportunity.

Hence taxation policy is highly politicized and one of the most central philosophies that differ between the traditional left and right, and almost as old as civilization itself.

Minimum pay legislation is another instrument. According to the International Labour Organization,[33] more than 90 per cent of the 186 ILO member states have one or more minimum wages set through legislation or binding collective agreements. But it does not mean that in all these countries minimum wages cover a majority of workers or that they are regularly adjusted.

Policy debates therefore tend to focus not so much on whether to have a minimum wage but on how to make one work effectively. However, minimum wage is a low floor and of itself not enough to address the bigger inequality questions. The highest levels of hourly minimum wage in 2019 were in Australia at just over $14, followed by most northern European countries at from around $10–13. But the hourly rate in the United States yields the equivalent of US$6.63 of purchasing power, and that of Russia is worth only $1.87 in purchasing power terms.[34]

In September 2020 in the Swiss canton of Geneva there was a referendum to increase the minimum wage to the equivalent of $25 per hour or around $4,300 per month.[35] It was passed with support from 58 per cent of voters and driven in part because of the economic impact of the pandemic. Geneva is an expensive place to live, but this is now the highest minimum wage in the world and will be a challenge for the many small businesses, restaurants and others that employ so many of the lower-paid workers.

The Swiss democratic process and fondness for referenda in 2013 led to a national referendum on CEO pay ratios. Campaigners pointed to how the ratio of the average employee's wage to the salary among Swiss CEOs had leapt from 1 to 6 in 1984 to 1 to 43 in 2011. The proposal was to cap the ratio at 1 to 12, but in the end this was rejected by about two-thirds to one-third. However, earlier that year, voters had approved a measure that increased shareholders' power over top executive salaries and banned one-off golden hello and golden goodbye bonuses.

In most countries, as indeed the Swiss challenge showed, there is wariness about too much 'interference' from policy makers in the running of businesses. Greater reporting and strengthening corporate accountabilities are the primary mechanisms.

Movements such as the Living Wage Foundation in the UK challenge businesses to do more to ensure their workers are at least paid enough to live on. As its website[36] states, 'The real Living Wage is based on the cost of living and is voluntarily paid by over 6,000 UK employers who believe a hard day's work deserves a fair day's pay. The rate in 2020 was £10.85 in London and £9.50 across the rest of the UK, versus the UK national minimum wage of £8.72 for over 25 year olds.'

Around 7,000 employers in the UK are signed up to the living wage, and there was a positive increase during the pandemic. However, according to research from the Living Wage Foundation, in 2020 there were still 5.5 million jobs in the UK – 20 per cent of all employees – that paid less than the living wage.[37]

At these minimum levels of pay, though, many would be in the zone of what is known as in-work poverty. In the UK, according to the Institute for Fiscal Studies, the number of people living in relative poverty – defined as having incomes of less than 60 per cent of the average – has fluctuated between 21 per cent and 23 per cent over the last 20 years. But for those in working households, the level of in-work poverty increased from 13 per cent to 18 per cent from mid-1990s to 2017.[38]

The Institute for Fiscal Studies cites the causes as higher housing costs and reductions in benefits and tax credits since 2010, but also the higher levels of employment driven off the back of the highest levels of employment since the 1970s. Too many of these jobs, though, were low skilled and low paid, and wage increases stagnated during this period.

Across the EU, it is good to see that generally there has been improvement, driven by record high levels of employment in the years leading up to the pandemic and as the standards in eastern member states have improved. By 2017, 4.2 million fewer people were at risk of poverty and social exclusion than in 2008 pre the financial crisis.[39] That could now change as we enter the post-pandemic era with significant economic slowdown and sector-level restructuring.

These issues of in-work poverty are something that responsible business must help solve. The push-back from paying proper wages is always the short-term argument about absorbing an increase in people costs. The reality, however, is looked at through a longer-term lens, that if paid at least a living wage level, people will stay longer, it will be easier (more cost-efficient) to recruit people and reputationally the organization will be seen to be a responsible employer in an area that will be receiving a lot more attention.

Equality of opportunity

While I am supportive of living wage principles, progression and opportunity to grow income alongside skills will be the biggest levers of substantive change.

Although jobs and employment grew in most economies in the years leading up to the pandemic, many of the jobs were low skilled. Conversely, employers were increasingly citing lack of available specific skills as holding them back. As we will explore further in Chapter 6, the mismatches between education and work and the unevenness of educational opportunity have led to significant skills gaps that have been hampering many organizations. But they have also exacerbated the issues of equality and opportunity.

Data from the United States shows that in more than one-third of the fastest-growing 20 occupations in the United States,[40] the wages being paid are less than the average income for workers across the country.[41] As highlighted in a recent report by the Brookings Institute,[42] the issues are not just about skills training but also about equity in workforce development.

A report by the Center for American Progress,[43] an independent policy institute, highlighted the fact that even completing a training programme that focuses on one of those occupations would not necessarily lead to a job that provides adequate pay or leads to career progression. The report further highlighted the data that shows women and people of colour at all education levels 'overwhelmingly make up most of the workforce in lower-paying jobs'.[44]

In the UK, there have been some more positive average trends in ethnic pay gaps in recent years, although as we discuss further in Chapter 7, there remain much more significant gaps in ethnic representation at top levels.

Overall, as data from the Office for National Statistics shows,[45] the pay gap between white and ethnic minority employees in 2019 was at its lowest level since 2012. Further, those in the Chinese, White Irish, White and Asian, and Asian groups all had higher hourly earnings than White British, which surprises many.

It will be important to maintain the focus and momentum, particularly as job demands change following the pandemic and economic downturn, and there is more to be done particularly in support of black, Asian and ethnic minority communities. We will discuss this more in the context of good work principles in Chapter 11.

The impact of demographic trends

Changing demographics are of themselves significant drivers of social change. Younger generations with different expectations and viewpoints, alongside ageing populations and increasing ethnic diversity in many countries, all have an influence.

The workforce across the OECD countries numbers almost 600 million people. The trends in globalization we discussed in the last chapter have opened up a truly global workforce. The global workforce numbers over 3 billion people including the BRIC countries with their huge populations.[46]

But populations across different parts of the world are at different stages of development. In many of the developing countries not only are people's skills less developed, but their mobility and access to work are usually more limited. Work for many in the poorer countries is still made up of some form of self-employment or informal family-based work. The International Labour Organization estimates that over 80 per cent of workers in low-income countries work in these ways, and even in mid-income countries the figure is still 50 per cent, whereas for OECD countries it is only 10 per cent.[47]

So while we may talk about a great expansion of the global markets for labour and the opportunities this can provide to pull people out of poverty and give them other beneficial societal impacts, it will likely take a very long time.

Demographics are important in other ways, such as the different age profiles of OECD countries versus more developing countries. The median age across the continent of Africa is just under 20 years. In the EU countries it is over 43 years. By UN classifications, the more developed countries' median age is 42, the less developed countries' is 29 and the least developed countries' is 20. In 1960, these numbers were 29, 20 and 19.[48]

FIGURE 4.4 Population changes for different regions of the world of people over the age of 60

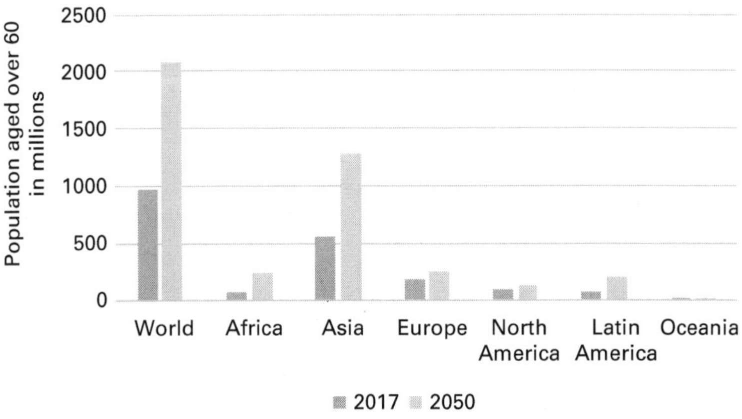

[Bar chart showing population aged over 60 in millions for 2017 and 2050 across World, Africa, Asia, Europe, North America, Latin America, and Oceania]

SOURCE UN 2017 World Population Prospects

As the world's population ages and people live longer, projections for the numbers of over-60-year-olds show how the world's demographics will change in the next 30 years, as Figure 4.4 shows.

Working-age populations in the higher-income OECD countries are projected to fall from around 67 per cent of the total population in 2000 to 60 per cent by 2040, while the rest of the world is at around 65 per cent and likely to stay at around that level.[49]

Developed countries' populations have been steadily ageing over recent decades, as the UN numbers so starkly show. Declining birthrates over the last 40–50 years along with longer life expectancy are catching up with many countries. As populations age, there are increasing economic and social impacts which will place greater demands on health and social care, and pensions and benefits support, along with growing questions of fairness across generations.

Ageing populations also impact business in a variety of ways. As reported in the CIPD's October 2019 MegaTrends report on aging workforces,[50] there is a range of age profiles in UK industries. The youngest industry – hospitality – has an average age of 34, while the oldest – primary industries (including agriculture and mining) – has an average age of 47. The four industries with the largest number of 50+ workers (health, retail, education and manufacturing) account for approximately half (47 per cent) of all 50+ workers in the economy.

In part the response has been for older workers to be encouraged to work longer. Workers in the UK now exit the workforce at an average age of 65 for men and 64 for women. This is up from a low point of 63 and 60 in the 1990s, which marked the end of a long shift from the 1950s when it was 67 and 64. It has been reflective of the workforce itself where the proportion of over-50s increased from 21 per cent to 32 per cent between 1992 and 2019.

Internationally, there are some countries that really stand out and are even seeing their total populations decline in number.

According to World Bank data,[51] South Korea has the lowest birth rate at about 1.0 child per woman – 2.1 is seen as the rate to maintain population size. At the other end of the spectrum are the countries in sub-Saharan Africa at 4.7. The rate across the Euro area is 1.5, with Italy and Spain the lowest at 1.3 and others like Finland and Greece only at 1.4.

Across Europe between today and 2060, the number of people aged over 65 is expected to increase from 30.5 to 51.6 per 100 people of working age (15–64).[52] That translates to fewer than two workers per person over 65 years of age by 2060 as opposed to over three today.

Japan, China and South Korea are standout countries where declining birth rates are seen as real threats to sustained economic growth.

South Korea for the first time in 2020 recorded more deaths than births, and the birth rate dropped 10 per cent from 2019. The figures prompted the Interior Ministry to call for 'fundamental changes' to its policies. One of the schemes is to provide cash incentives to families for support for babies in their early years.[53]

In Japan, the birth rate in 2019 was around 1.4; it has been low for many years and declined again from 2018 by 53,000 births. The country had just 865,000 births in 2019 compared with 1.38 million deaths, resulting in a natural population decrease of more than 500,000.[54] It now means that more than 20 per cent of Japan's population is over 65 years old, the highest proportion in the world. By 2030, one in every three people will be 65 or older and one in five people 75-plus years old. Apparently already more adult diapers than infant ones are sold in Japan.

The declining birth rates in Japan are attributed to the reluctance to marry or have children because of shrinking employment opportunities for young men. In 1960, 97 per cent of men aged 25–29 were employed, but by 2010 this number had dropped to 86 per cent.

As a result, Japan and South Korea now have the highest average ages of their working populations and effective retirement ages for men are over 70. Besides the pressure from employers to retain older workers, access to pensions and savings is another factor which influences the difference between effective retirement ages and state pension ages. The difference in

South Korea is more than 10 years and in Japan more than 5 years, but countries like Mexico and Chile and even New Zealand also have a big disparity, according to OECD data.[55]

China similarly has a declining and ageing population, driven in large part by the one-child-per-family policy introduced in 1980. In 2017, around 17 per cent or just over 240 million were above 60 years old. It is expected that by 2030 there will be 330 million Chinese over the age of 65, and that will reach 487 million, or nearly 35 per cent, by 2050. If current trends continue, China's population will peak at 1.44 billion in 2029 before entering 'unstoppable' decline, according to a Chinese Academy of Social Sciences study released in January.[56] Fewer people means a smaller workforce and less domestic consumption, and the ageing population will create significant economic as well as social challenges.

It appears that the Baby Boomer cohort will be the first to work to a later age en masse. This will increase pressure on employers for workplace adaptations and more flexible working, which we explore further in Chapter 10. Sometimes it takes a large cohort to pave the way.

However, the trends for ageing populations and longevity are showing other signs that again illustrate issues of inequality. As noted by Case and Deaton, average life expectancy in the US has fallen three years running, and there is evidence that these deaths are also on the rise in the UK. There has always been a divergence in the longevity of the richest and the poorest, but that could increase with the growing gaps in wealth and income previously noted.

All stark signals of how economics and social change work together.

Migration rates and ethnic diversity

For the past five years in a row in the UK migration has been a bigger driver of population change than births and deaths. Immigrants are younger and have higher fertility rates on average. Changes to immigration will thus affect the age, cultural and ethnic diversity structure of the population.

The UK has long been a destination for migrant workers and families. As for most countries with a colonial past, over many generations, people have moved to the UK as a preferred destination and that has increased in the modern era with migration from across the EU to the UK. Relatively liberal labour markets and a more multicultural society as well as the English language have all been positive attractors.

TABLE 4.1 UK change in employment share by region of birth

	Employment share 2004 Q4 (%)	Employment share 2019 Q4 (%)
UK	90.2	82.4
EU	2.9	7.4
Non-EU	6.9	10.2

SOURCE ONS Labour Force Survey

Migration trends in the UK over the last 15 years show how quickly the makeup of the workforce has been changing. According to the ONS Labour Force Survey,[57] between 2004 and 2019 the employment share of those born outside the UK increased from 9.8 per cent to 17.6 per cent, as shown in Table 4.1.

According to the 2019 Q4 data, the transport and communication (25.1 per cent) and the distribution, hotels and restaurants (20.5 per cent) sectors had the highest proportion of non-UK-born in employment. The manufacturing (11 per cent) and the transport and communication (10 per cent) sectors had the highest proportion of EU-born in employment. By comparison, transport and communication (15.1 per cent), distribution, hotels and restaurants (11.4 per cent) and banking and finance (11.3 per cent) had the highest proportion of non-EU workers.

Brexit will change that for migration from within the EU. At the time of writing, leading up to the end of the transition period at the end of 2020, the number of EU-born workers in the UK fell by 20 per cent or almost half a million people between January–March and July–September. That reversed more than five years of growth among this part of the UK workforce.[58]

The data also showed a fall in non-EU-born workers in the UK by an estimated 227,000. Not surprising, then, that sectors which had become particularly dependent on migrant workers, such as hospitality, agriculture, construction, and health and social care, have been vocal in their concerns about future immigration policies.

This has to be factored into longer-term workforce planning, as we will explore in Chapter 10, in particular for sectors like hospitality, which is the only sector that has a majority employed in roles below RQF (Regulated Qualifications Framework) Level 3, which at the time of writing is the new skill threshold for migrant workers.

The pandemic has further muddied the waters. The sectors hardest hit are the same sectors and many EU workers may have left because they were losing work during that period. But many of these workers also had settled status, meaning they could return to work in their home countries without obligation to return to the UK. It remains to be seen how much these become longer-term changes in migration and therefore also signal another shift in the demographics of the workforce in the UK.

The King's Fund did some extensive research around 2012 on changes and projections for the UK population and demographics.[59] Their primary conclusions were:

- The population is growing. Over the period 2012 to 2032 the population in England is predicted to grow by 8 million to just over 61 million, 4.5 million from natural growth (births – deaths), 3.5 million from net migration.
- The population is becoming more diverse. By 2031, ethnic populations are expected to make up 15 per cent of the population in England and 37 per cent of the population in London.
- More people are living alone. By 2032, 11.3 million people are expected to be living on their own, more than 40 per cent of all households. The number of people over 85 living on their own is expected to grow from 573,000 to 1.4 million.

These were projections based on migration policies at the time. Policy remains quite a political hot potato in this area, not only for the UK but for most of the more developed nations of the world.

With some of the changes we observed in the last chapter, including greater protectionism in more developed nations, set alongside the growing rates of emigration from war zones and countries in the poorer parts of the world struggling to sustain their young and growing populations, it will be a continued challenging debate for the future. And it will require some long-term thinking and solutions.

The rise of the new generations – the 5G workforce

Researching the attitudes and views of the younger generations over the last decade or so has become something of a field of research all by itself. Books and surveys crowd the shelves. This has driven views of several generations all now co-existing in the workplace, all with some defining characteristics.

We are all broadly familiar with the Baby Boomers (born roughly between 1946 and 1964) and the Gen Xers who followed them. Then along came the millennials, and now the so-called Generation Z – the true digital natives.

FOMO, or fear of missing out, has become a somewhat familiar expression of how millennials think. FOBO could be the expression for Gen Z – fear of being offline. And then to round it out, FOBO for us Baby Boomers is probably fear of becoming obsolete. And perhaps for Gen Xs, fear of being overtaken. Before all of them and still active in many organizations are the so-called Silent Generation – the post-war generation usually defined as being born between the late 1920s and 1945.

The workforce today can therefore be described as a 5-generational, or 5G, workforce, each with some generally definable attributes. Understanding and adapting to some of these different needs and expectations is an important part of inclusion, and in attracting and retaining employees across all age groups. Figure 4.5 shows how generations are shifting over time and how the workforce changes.

In the previous chapter, we referenced Strauss and Howe's 1991 work *Generations*, in which the duo spelled out the foundations of their Fourth Turning theory to help explain the nature and power of political and cultural cycles. It was in the same book that Strauss and Howe introduced the term millennial to our vocabulary. The word was initially coined to refer to the specific generational cohort of youngsters born between 1980 and 2000. The oldest millennials, by the authors' definition, would be graduating from high school in the year 2000 – the start of the new millennium.

Today the term serves as a neat yet often simplistic way for the mainstream media to cast demographic generalizations. Millennials and their

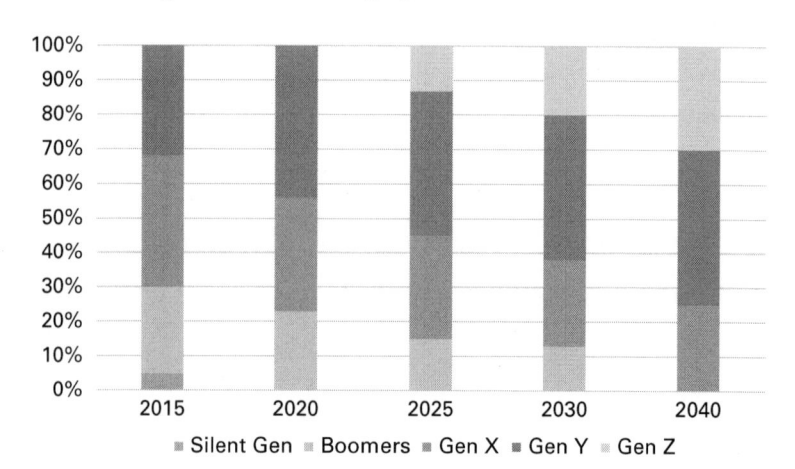

FIGURE 4.5 How generations are changing as a mix of the workforce over time

■ Silent Gen ■ Boomers ■ Gen X ■ Gen Y ■ Gen Z

SOURCE US Census Bureau

younger peers of Generation Z have been too often dismissed as lacking resilience and being entitled. In some cases the phrase has become the catch-all, disparaging descriptor for any young person, which is largely unfair and unfortunate.

Millennials are projected to account for three-quarters of the global workforce by 2025.[60] They have already helped to drive businesses in different ways, to expect more of how businesses behave responsibly – it is no coincidence that the CSR or corporate social responsibility agenda took hold as the millennials joined the workforce and challenged their potential employers on what they stood for and what their purpose was.

They also expect more from their managers and leaders. Research by Accenture[61] published in late 2020 on responsible leadership and expectations of the younger generations highlighted five key attributes that they look for in leaders and responsible businesses:

- stakeholder inclusion – stand in the shoes of all stakeholders when making decisions;
- emotional intuition;
- relentless focus on mission and purpose;
- technology and innovation that benefit people and society as well as business performance;
- heightened insight and commitment to continuous learning.

These are all positive attributes of modern leaders and responsible business, but they are far from universal in their adoption, as we will review further in Chapter 9. Besides these expectations, the younger generations have also learned and been encouraged to speak up more.

It did take a while for many leaders to see and accept this shift. Many leaders I talked to in the early part of the new millennium struggled to deal with a more vocal young workforce when they themselves were taught to 'keep quiet until spoken to' and to 'respect their elders and betters'. Now, the ideas of 'voice' are central in creating inclusive and vibrant workplaces and cultures.

On the heels of millennials, members of Gen Z – generally defined as those born between 1995 and 2010 – are already in the workforce and bringing some different perspectives and expectations even from the millennials just before them. Many of the characteristics ascribed to millennials are thought to be shared by Generation Z, but to an even greater extent.

Research conducted by Zuzana Kirchmayer and Jana Fratričová[62] in Slovakia concludes that more than other demographic cohorts, Generation Zers prioritize enjoying their work, having high-quality relationships with their co-workers and achieving their personal goals, whatever those might be. They are less motivated by money than previous generations and have a significant expectation for a degree of personalization.

Having a voice and the idea of greater personalization and individualism has been a notable trend. This is often observed as the move away from collectivism in the past to individualism today. For example, it is taken as one of the reasons for the decline in interest of young people in being members of unions, but also the greater appetite for starting businesses or working for themselves.

Gen Zers really are true digital natives who don't remember a time before social networks and the ubiquity of mobile phones. They can navigate technology effortlessly and are quick to become used to new digital gadgets. They are often described as self-directed learners as they have grown up in a world with free access to limitless information and knowledge. As a result they are happy to challenge their teachers, parents and work colleagues. In return, older generations challenge them on their ability to think critically, to apply judgement, to seek out alternative perspectives.

A paper by global consultancy McKinsey & Company[63] describes them as the 'hypercognitive generation' – a generation that's comfortable collecting and cross-referencing different sources of information and with integrating virtual and offline experiences. They value expression and avoid labels. They're curious and comfortable standing up for their beliefs, which is perhaps also a byproduct of the fact that they're accustomed to the personal broadcast opportunities afforded to them by the prevalence of social media. They seek connection and communities – either virtual or real life – and aren't afraid to mobilize and take a stand.

Swedish teenager and environmental activist Greta Thunberg, who gained international recognition for publicly accusing world leaders and corporate executives of perpetuating climate change, is often championed as a poster-child for Generation Zers. The passion, fearlessness and energy she channels into her activism, and the many of her generation who stand beside her, can be considered prime examples of stereotypical Gen Z traits.

The relationship between millennials and the older generations does need to be understood and must be balanced. Research by Aviva conducted in 2019 revealed that more than a third (37 per cent) of employees aged 45 and over believe age discrimination to be an issue where they work, with those aged 55 to 59 most acutely affected.[64]

Rising intergenerational tensions?

Intergenerational tensions do exist – in truth they have always existed as upcoming generations have developed their own thinking and challenged those before them. But there are concerns the tensions are growing in the modern era. In 2018, the House of Lords appointed the Select Committee on Intergenerational Fairness and Provision 'to consider the long-term implications of Government policy on intergenerational fairness and provision'. The Committee published its report in 2019.[65] It began with a statement: 'We believe the issue of intergenerational fairness needs to be addressed.'

There are several issues that are the subject of debates of this kind. First, the apparent obstacles that young people face in getting on in life and whether they will have similar opportunities as the generations ahead of them. As the Lord's Committee report cited, there is the prospect of an end to generation-on-generation income progression – for reasons such as education not adequately equipping young people for economic and technological change, the difficulties faced in finding employment that is secure and well paid, or access to affordable housing.

The pandemic and the economic crisis following it have made this more stark – sadly, as with almost every economic crisis, rates of employment among the younger generations always fall.

These may be reasons why there are concerns, not least by their parents, that Gen Zers may be more stressed. A 2019 headline in *The Economist*[66] purported that Generation Z is 'stressed, depressed and exam-obsessed' and numerous pieces of academic research have since provided evidence of this.

The American Psychological Association's annual 'Stress in America' report[67] concluded in 2019 that Gen Z adults indicated the highest average stress level of any demographic cohort, followed by Generation Xers and then millennials. Baby boomers and older adults have significantly lower average stress levels comparatively, the report found. Maybe these are just features of getting older anyway where we tend to become more circumspect.

Furthermore, as we have already explored, the increasingly ageing population raises challenges of adequate support and funding for areas such as long-term care. These demographic shifts will also place greater burdens than in the past on the younger generations.

These issues are of significant political and social importance and will require more discussion of governmental policies, tax and benefit systems in the coming years. They add another dimension to the concerns of equality and fairness in which business must also play its part – for example, in how we support and manage age diversity, understanding the benefits of retaining older workers and adapting work and working patterns to support them.

Generational differences also threaten to be exacerbated by technology. Younger generations are eager to try new technologically enabled ways of working and can sometimes be quick to assume that everyone else feels the same.

In her book *You Can't Google It!: The compelling case for cross-generational conversation at work*,[68] Phyllis Weiss Haserot argues that communication across different demographics is the key to creating workplaces that are inclusive, regardless of age. She says it's important for managers to understand the fears faced by each generation, as these can hamper productivity and motivation. For baby boomers, concerns often centre around the prospect of being displaced by younger managers (FOBO) and new ways of doing things – including but not limited to technology. These individuals are scared of a loss of professional identity, a loss of relevance or a loss of business as a result of them not being able to keep pace with new developments.

Those belonging to Generation X – the demographic that slots in between baby boomers and millennials – face their own unique fears and challenges.

Weiss Haserot argues that these individuals often want to win over the boomers for the purpose of transitioning power and transferring knowledge. At the same time they want to keep millennials on side. They rely on the support of both the older and younger generations to do their jobs, but they also face more external pressures than either of their two peers. They tend to have greater personal responsibilities in terms of children and other dependants to support, so they need their own managers to provide the flexibility and compassion they need to be able to reach their potential.

Finally, millennials have their own set of worries. They're ambitious and impatient to progress professionally. Weiss Haserot says that they are generally eager to understand those of other generations but this is often misconstrued by older generations, many of whom think millennials are trying to wade in and do things their way.

They're scared of failure, being met by disapproval from older generations or being dismissed as unimportant or irrelevant. As a generation raised on social media, and therefore accustomed to being able to broadcast their thoughts and opinions at any time they choose, they also expect to have a voice and be heard. These differences, the author writes, must be understood and appreciated by all in order to create productive workplaces.

So how do we do this? Peter Cappelli, author and Professor of Management at the Wharton School, says that the first way to bridge gaps between generations is to avoid useless labels, like millennial and boomer. For one thing, he says, generalizations about particular demographic groups are often not true.

It's much more important for employers – and for employers to encourage employees – to get to know individuals for who they really are and not for the traits that are lazily attributed to them based on their age group.[69] Not all characteristics and behaviours are derived or developed as a result of the generation to which someone belongs.

Cappelli also argues that a culture of collaboration which doesn't necessarily equate age to seniority when it comes to management hierarchies can help. He points to the US Marine Corps where, he explains, it's relatively common for a lieutenant in their 20s to be in charge of a sergeant in their 40s.

In conclusion

There are many issues of social change reflected through growing issues of inequality and trust. Combined with demographic shifts and expectations and views of the younger generations, they create significant challenges to be addressed by policy makers, political leaders and businesses for the future.

The social and demographic changes we have observed have been growing on us for a long time. But as with the analogy of the frog in the boiling water, we haven't always been sufficiently aware of them.

They are all important in understanding the future of work as every organization operates within these social changes, just as they do for economic and political change.

In particular they relate to our ability to attract and retain the people we need, to understand and support inclusion and diversity, and the changes we have to make in building trust. They speak strongly to the idea of business being part of society, impacting positive change.

We will refer back to the trends and thinking we have covered in this chapter in particular as we discuss people strategies in Chapter 10, leadership in Chapter 9 and the principles of good work in Chapter 11.

Endnotes

1 https://ec.europa.eu/social/main.jsp?catId=738&langId=en&pubId=8219 (archived at https://perma.cc/7ZZN-KVLS)
2 Boin, A, 't Hart, P and van Esch, F (2012) in *Comparative Political Leadership*, ed L Helms, Palgrave Macmillan, London
3 www.edelman.com/trustbarometer (archived https://perma.cc/VBK4-YRUJ)
4 www.cipd.co.uk/Images/where-has-all-the-trust-gone_2012-sop_tcm18-9644.pdf (archived at https://perma.cc/ZR8K-H5H8)

5 www.accenture.com/gb-en/insights/future-workforce/employee-potential-talent-management-strategy (archived at https://perma.cc/UP5U-AGHD)
6 www.theguardian.com/technology/2017/feb/02/travis-kalanick-delete-uber-leaves-trump-council (archived at https://perma.cc/5LCS-BSJF)
7 www.edelman.com/sites/g/files/aatuss191/files/2019-06/2019_edelman_trust_barometer_special_report_in_brands_we_trust_executive_summary.pdf (archived at https://perma.cc/94VZ-ZDXS)
8 www.forbes.com/sites/jeffkauflin/2017/02/06/why-audis-super-bowl-ad-failed/#55c2f85a1786 (archived at https://perma.cc/GFS2-4VKH)
9 www.adweek.com/brand-marketing/audi-defends-its-super-bowl-ad-about-equal-pay-after-it-quickly-becomes-a-flashpoint/ (archived at https://perma.cc/HN34-S33D)
10 www.theguardian.com/us-news/2017/apr/14/fearless-girl-statue-women-new-york-bull (archived at https://perma.cc/F3AK-YWPB)
11 www.theguardian.com/business/2017/oct/06/fearless-girl-company-discriminated-against-women-by-underpaying-them (archived at https://perma.cc/YNF5-9A37)
12 www.nytimes.com/2020/06/06/business/corporate-america-has-failed-black-america.html (archived at https://perma.cc/B5RP-FNL4)
13 www.nytimes.com/2017/09/02/business/munroe-bergdorf-loreal-transgender.html?auth=login-email&login=email (archived at https://perma.cc/FR4V-AZ9K)
14 Carleton, R N (2016) Fear of the unknown: One fear to rule them all? Journal of Anxiety Disorders, 41, pp 5–21
15 www.pwc.com/gx/en/ceo-agenda/ceosurvey/2020.html (archived at https://perma.cc/L222-FBTG)
16 www.mckinsey.com/featured-insights/mckinsey-global-surveys (archived at https://perma.cc/TQ2G-AL3G)
17 www.weforum.org/agenda/2019/03/migration-myths-vs-economic-facts/ (archived at https://perma.cc/65UU-HY6S)
18 Milanovic, B (2011) The Haves and the Have-Nots – A Brief and Idiosyncratic History of Global Inequality, Basic Books, New York
19 https://ec.europa.eu/social/main.jsp?catId=738&langId=en&pubId=8219 (archived at https://perma.cc/7ZZN-KVLS)
20 www.ifs.org.uk/uploads/publications/wps/WP201701%20-%20Exec%20summary.pdf (archived at https://perma.cc/ZA9C-9RHG)
21 Burkhauser, R V, De Neve, J-E and Powdthavee, N (2016) Top incomes and human well-being around the world, January, Paper No CEPDP1400
22 www.payscale.com/data/employee-engagement (archived at https://perma.cc/RG4B-V3DU)
23 Piketty, T (2013) Capital in the Twenty-First Century, Harvard University Press
24 Case, A and Deaton, A (2020) Deaths of Despair and the Future of Capitalism, Princeton University Press, Princeton, NJ
25 www.brookings.edu/blog/up-front/2016/08/15/men-not-at-work-why-so-many-men-ages-of-25-to-54-are-not-working/ (archived at https://perma.cc/6JNF-E258)
26 www.ifs.org.uk/inequality/can-covid-reduce-global-inequality/ (archived at https://perma.cc/24R7-6XDA)

27 https://newrepublic.com/article/118024/piketty-and-marx-where-they-disagree (archived at https://perma.cc/X5WX-8Q2K)
28 www.gov.uk/guidance/equality-act-2010-guidance (archived at https://perma.cc/UE8A-3VRL)
29 www.weforum.org/reports/the-global-gender-gap-report-2018 (archived at https://perma.cc/V2D8-A8Q8)
30 www.pewresearch.org/global/2019/04/22/how-people-around-the-world-view-gender-equality-in-their-countries/ (archived at https://perma.cc/NCA9-5VDH)
31 Allen & Overy UK Pay Gap Report 2020
32 www.ons.gov.uk/employmentandlabourmarket/peopleinwork/earningsandworkinghours/articles/ethnicitypaygapsingreatbritain/2019 (archived at https://perma.cc/BXW4-3LH2)
33 www.ilo.org/global/topics/wages/minimum-wages/definition/WCMS_439073/lang–en/index.htm (archived at https://perma.cc/59Q4-PARZ)
34 https://ceoworld.biz/2019/01/03/countries-with-the-highest-minimum-hourly-wages-in-the-world-2019/ (archived at https://perma.cc/5LC5-G6PP)
35 www.theguardian.com/world/2020/sep/30/geneva-raises-minimum-wage-covid-poverty-switzerland (archived at https://perma.cc/88HU-74MK)
36 www.livingwage.org.uk (archived at https://perma.cc/6HBY-NLQ9)
37 www.bbc.co.uk/news/business-54867444 (archived at https://perma.cc/LG3P-NNNY)
38 www.ifs.org.uk/publications/14154 (archived at https://perma.cc/PW93-LJ7D)
39 https://ec.europa.eu/social/main.jsp?catId=738&langId=en&pubId=8219 (archived at https://perma.cc/7ZZN-KVLS)
40 www.bls.gov/ooh/fastest-growing.htm (archived at https://perma.cc/Y5D5-D6HZ)
41 www.bls.gov/news.release/pdf/wkyeng.pdf (archived at https://perma.cc/UYN3-EHEY)
42 www.brookings.edu/blog/the-avenue/2020/09/09/the-labor-market-doesnt-have-a-skills-gap-it-has-an-opportunity-gap/ (archived at https://perma.cc/38YZ-J5TM)
43 www.americanprogress.org/issues/economy/reports/2019/10/16/475875/design-workforce-equity/ (archived at https://perma.cc/LET9-DX27)
44 https://equitablegrowth.org/fact-sheet-occupational-segregation-in-the-united-states/ (archived at https://perma.cc/TU2W-GWKC)
45 www.ons.gov.uk/employmentandlabourmarket/peopleinwork/earningsandworkinghours/articles/ethnicitypaygapsingreatbritain/2019 (archived at https://perma.cc/BXW4-3LH2)
46 https://www.ilo.org/wcmsp5/groups/public/---dgreports/---dcomm/---publ/documents/publication/wcms_734455.pdf (archived at https://perma.cc/43KE-D63F)
47 www.ilo.org/ilostat-files/Documents/LFEP.pdf (archived at https://perma.cc/2BFL-9WZX)
48 https://www.un.org/en/development/desa/population/publications/database/index.asp (archived at https://perma.cc/7D63-HQZ8)
49 https://data.oecd.org/pop/working-age-population.htm (archived at https://perma.cc/XG7F-G33S)

50 www.cipd.co.uk/Images/megatrends-ageing-gracefully-the-opportunities-of-an-older-workforce-1_tcm18-64897.pdf (archived at https://perma.cc/55N2-MQR4)

51 https://data.worldbank.org/indicator/SP.DYN.TFRT.IN (archived at https://perma.cc/2YT7-HRVM)

52 https://ec.europa.eu/social/main.jsp?catId=738&langId=en&pubId=8219 (archived at https://perma.cc/7ZZN-KVLS)

53 https://edition.cnn.com/2021/01/04/asia/south-korea-2020-births-intl-hnk-scli/index.html (archived at https://perma.cc/9LCC-Y3K9)

54 www.nippon.com/en/japan-data/h00747/ (archived at https://perma.cc/95JA-RHP5)

55 http://www.oecd.org/employment/emp/average-effective-age-of-retirement.htm (archived at https://perma.cc/2X82-QZBZ)

56 https://time.com/5523805/china-aging-population-working-age/ (archived at https://perma.cc/SR7H-JUJM)

57 www.ons.gov.uk/employmentandlabourmarket/peopleinwork/employmentandemployeetypes/articles/ukandnonukpeopleinthelabourmarket/february2020 (archived at https://perma.cc/3AFA-GLTX)

58 www.reuters.com/article/us-britain-eu-immigration/immigration-to-britain-falls-to-five-year-low-ahead-of-brexit-ons-idUSKCN1VC0TW (archived at https://perma.cc/4ERK-EJ5A)

59 www.kingsfund.org.uk/projects/time-think-differently/trends-demography (archived at https://perma.cc/8HQJ-DLSN)

60 EY (2015) Global Generations: A Global Study on Work-Life Challenges Across Generations, p 1

61 Accenture.com/us-en/insights/consulting/responsible-leadership (archived at https://perma.cc/AU47-URMG)

62 www.researchgate.net/publication/324797364_What_Motivates_Generation_Z_at_Work_Insights_into_Motivation_Drivers_of_Business_Students_in_Slovakia (archived at https://perma.cc/3XGP-Z7BU)

63 www.mckinsey.com/industries/consumer-packaged-goods/our-insights/true-gen-generation-z-and-its-implications-for-companies (archived at https://perma.cc/GU8P-9KFS)

64 www.aviva.com/newsroom/news-releases/2019/05/one-third-of-mid-life-workers-believe-age-discrimination-is-an-issue/ (archived at https://perma.cc/QD46-WNDW)

65 https://old.parliament.uk/intergenerational-fairness/ (archived at https://perma.cc/6PLD-BUAK)

66 www.economist.com/graphic-detail/2019/02/27/generation-z-is-stressed-depressed-and-exam-obsessed (archived at https://perma.cc/9UQS-USKW)

67 www.apa.org/news/press/releases/stress/2019/stress-america-2019.pdf (archived at https://perma.cc/W3KQ-F2XA)

68 Haserot, P W (2017) You Can't Google It!: The compelling case for cross-generational conversation at work, Morgan James Publishing

69 https://hbr.org/2014/09/managing-people-from-5-generations (archived at https://perma.cc/U2Y2-5TM7)

05

Technology: Automation, AI and beyond

It's not a faith in technology. It's faith in people.
STEVE JOBS, CO-FOUNDER OF APPLE

Technology in all its forms throughout history has driven great change, reinvention of jobs and work, and societal shifts. Since the first industrial revolution that began in the 18th century with the development of steam power to mechanize production and transportation, thereby dramatically improving productivity, major technological shifts have been the driving forces of subsequent industrial revolutions.

We explored the different eras of industrialization in Chapter 3 and what drove them. Computing technology, automation, the internet and artificial intelligence are now the big drivers shaping the fourth industrial revolution.

From a business perspective, the benefit and outcomes of investing in technology in the past had primarily been focused on productivity – being able to produce more for less. Now we would also see technology as providing greater agility and ability to adapt and respond, enabling new business models, products and services, and new ways of working. What has come to be referred to as digital disruption and digital transformation.

In the third industrial revolution, as computing technology started to be implemented in all businesses, large and small, it took a while to see the productivity impacts. The US economist Robert Solow won the Nobel Prize for Economics for his 'exogenous growth theory', which described the impact of technology on growth and productivity independent of other economic forces. But in 1987 he famously observed that the computer age was everywhere except for the productivity statistics. This phenomenon became known as the Solow Paradox.

It wasn't until the 1990s that productivity increased more rapidly as computing power versus cost changed exponentially. The so-called 'Moore's Law' started to hit its stride. Advances in computing power rose at the exponential rate described by Gordon Moore, co-founder and CEO of Intel, back in 1975 – the number of transistors or components per integrated circuit would double every two years. This not only increased computing power but also reduced size to allow chips to be placed almost everywhere, and at a decreasing proportionate cost.

As economist Richard G. Anderson notes, 'Numerous studies have traced the cause of the productivity acceleration to technological innovations in the production of semiconductors that sharply reduced the prices of such components and of the products that contain them (as well as expanding the capabilities of such products).'[1]

Technology powering the fourth industrial revolution

By the mid to late 1990s, the early versions of the internet and web browsers were appearing. Beginning more as a communications technology, supporting emails and early ecommerce, it wasn't really until the evolution of Web 2.0 in around 2005 that everything started to change. Processing power was now enabling home PCs and increasingly mobile computing that could be put into everyone's hands. The world was becoming interconnected and new social media businesses were creating previously unimagined ways in which people would engage.

The last 10 years have seen an extraordinary acceleration of technology into all fields and aspects of work and people's lives. Social media, artificial intelligence, machine learning, virtual and augmented reality, cloud computing and the Internet of Things connecting the physical and digital worlds. Robots to cobots working alongside humans and enhancing their capabilities, 3D and even 4D printing with intelligent products that adapt to their environments and transform over time. And big data and blockchain promising to transform many business and commercial processes, including the uptake of electronic or crypto currency.

This fourth industrial revolution creates huge opportunities, but also huge challenges. In 2016, Klaus Schwab in describing this new world talked

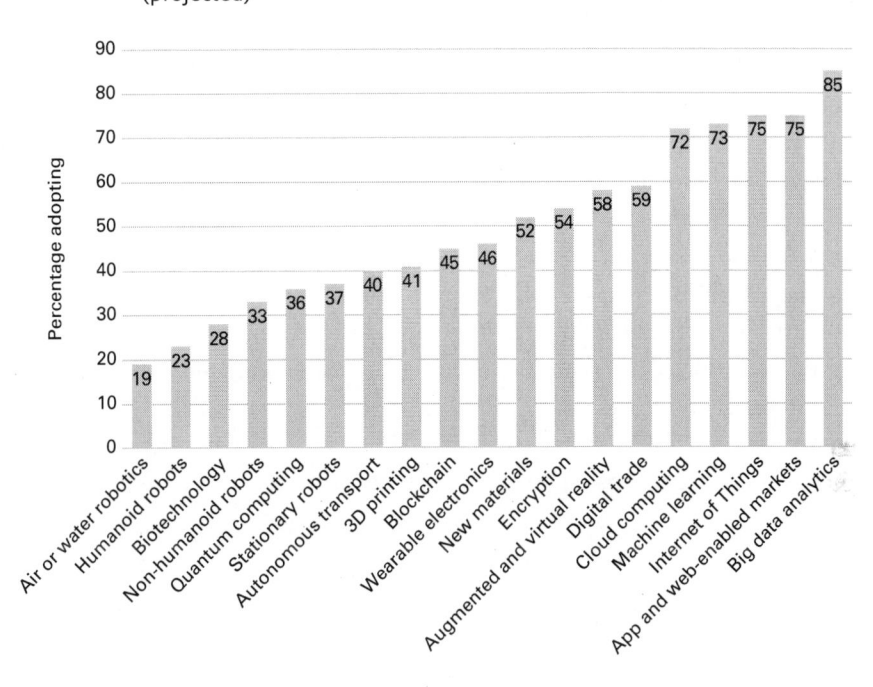

FIGURE 5.1 Technologies by proportion of companies likely to adopt them by 2022 (projected)

```
Percentage adopting
90
80                                                                                      85
70                                                          72  73  75  75
60
50                                              58  59
                                        52  54
40                              45  46
                        40  41
              33  36  37
30      28
   19 23
20
10
0
  Air or water robotics
  Humanoid robots
  Biotechnology
  Non-humanoid robots
  Quantum computing
  Stationary robots
  Autonomous transport
  3D printing
  Blockchain
  Wearable electronics
  New materials
  Encryption
  Augmented and virtual reality
  Digital trade
  Cloud computing
  Machine learning
  Internet of Things
  App and web-enabled markets
  Big data analytics
```

SOURCE WEF, *The Future of Jobs*, http://www3.weforum.org/docs/WEF_Future_of_Jobs_2018.pdf

about how these advances in technology would merge the physical, digital and biological worlds, which he recognized created both 'huge promise and potential peril'.[2] He also highlighted how the nature of the revolution would require us to fundamentally rethink 'how countries develop, how organizations create value and even what it means to be human'. Heady stuff.

Research by the World Economic Forum highlighted in its 2018 report on the future of jobs a broad range of technologies and how organizations saw their potential adoption.[3] Figure 5.1 shows the response rates. These are a bit of a mixture of applications and underlying technologies, but it gives an indication of how businesses are thinking about technology. The big technology drivers that underpin all these are seen as ubiquitous high-speed mobile internet, cloud computing, and artificial intelligence and big data.

Although many things are happening, we are still in the early stages of this revolution, however. We have already seen from the discussion on economic trends and productivity that the next generation of technologies so far seems to be following the Solow Paradox again. There is clearly a lot more to come.

Research by the McKinsey Global Institute in 2018 highlighted how actual practice lags the hype of digital transformation and therefore the impact on business performance and productivity gains.[4] It takes time to transform businesses, to get the technology and data right, to overcome adoption barriers and resistance.

Hype always tends to lead reality. As Bill Gates pithily observed, 'We always overestimate the change that will occur in the next two years and underestimate the change that will occur in the next ten. Don't let yourself be lulled into inaction.'[5]

The fourth industrial revolution, also referred to as Industry 4.0, has the potential to be as era defining as the first industrial revolution. It will impact us all. Technology has therefore been the focus of so much of the debate in recent years about the future of work. But as we have already seen, it is coming together with other significant shifts and changes. Taken together they add up to perhaps a perfect storm, but certainly to a new era.

A new era driven by data and artificial intelligence

Data is the new fuel of Industry 4.0. And artificial intelligence in its many manifestations is the engine that uses that fuel to drive the new era.

Artificial intelligence underpins almost all the new fields of technology. The basic definition of AI is technology that seeks to automate or simulate what we would generally describe as intelligent behaviour. AI in its basic forms has been with us since the 1950s but is now a huge field with many different levels of sophistication and application, enabled by huge advances in data-processing power and capabilities.

To better understand AI and its pervasive range of applications, there are some generally accepted classifications[6] which are based on relating AI to human-type intelligence:

- The most basic AI are 'reactive machines', which automatically respond to limited sets of inputs but have no memory. This level of AI has been with us for decades and widely applied. Just think of heating sensors or speed cameras.
- The next level are 'limited memory machines', which can learn from historical data to make 'decisions' or alter outputs. This level of AI therefore includes machine learning whereby AI systems repeat tasks and refine their predictive outputs, for example in marketing analytics or

chatbots. Within machine learning is so-called deep learning where applications are increasingly able to train themselves to perform tasks without further input – voice- and image-recognition applications would be examples.

These first two levels are broadly where we are today. AI at these levels is limited to specific tasks based on predetermined and predefined ranges. This is also called artificial narrow intelligence (ANI) or narrow AI. However, it is already clear that many higher-order analytical and cognitive tasks can be performed even better than humans can perform them, allowing automation to move beyond basic administrative or routine tasks. Driverless vehicles are a fascinating example – while they may look like they have a wider intelligence, they are operating from huge combinations of very specialized ANI applications.

But AI isn't finished. The dream of technologists over the years is to get much closer to human intelligence and behaviour and even to surpass it. For the rest of us this sounds more like a nightmare. This is where it becomes more speculative and enters the realms of science fiction – at least for now. The next levels of AI classification illustrate this:

- 'Theory of mind' is the third level where AI becomes able to distinguish and understand the entities it is interacting with, their needs and even their emotions, beliefs and thought processes.
- The fourth level is 'self-aware', which is self-explanatory. And scary.

These levels move AI into the realms of artificial general intelligence (AGI), mimicking real human intelligence, and even moving beyond into what has been described as artificial super intelligence (ASI).

Currently, while machines are able to process data faster than we can, we are able to think in the abstract, to rapidly adapt, and to tap into our thoughts and memories to make different decisions or be creative. This also comes from being sentient and self-aware. How this happens is still beyond the reach of neuroscience, but advances in AI are also giving us insights into how our brains work.

Greg Brockman, CTO and chairman of OpenAI, an AI research laboratory founded in 2015, backed by heavyweight entrepreneurs of the likes of Elon Musk, Reid Hoffman and Peter Thiel, announced a $1 billion investment from Microsoft to pursue AGI.[7] Big money is going into this field.

OpenAI describes itself as a 'public benefit Apollo program to build general intelligence'.[8] It's not a bad analogy when some commentators today would say that the most advanced neural networks are roughly equivalent to the capabilities of a bee.

OpenAI estimates that since the tech industry started to properly focus on machine learning around 2012, the amount of processing capacity being applied to training the biggest AI models has been increasing at five times the pace of Moore's Law. That means that in 2020, the most advanced systems would be hundreds of thousands of times more powerful than those used in 2012. This comes from huge levels of investment, but also processing power with parallel computing techniques that can crunch much more data.

If this trend continues it results in an exponential curve which would yield really crazy results. It will require further developments in processing power, perhaps the world of quantum computing (don't ask). But if it turns out this way then a comparison would be battery life having extended from 1 day to 800 years in the last 5 years, but the next 5 years would take it to 100 million years.

In all of this, it is intriguing to think that our most innate human skills, including emotion, self-awareness, and all of our sensory and motor skills, are the hardest to replicate with machines. It's also why many jobs in highly automated environments use these very basic skills, because it is too hard and too expensive to have machines do them. Think of the jobs in many automated warehouses.

Our cognitive and analytical abilities which came later in human evolution, however, are already being shown up by AI in its specialized applications. Look at Google's supercomputing AI machine DeepMind,[9] which uses deep learning to solve extraordinary problems. It hit the headlines when its program AlphaGo defeated the world Go champion in 2016, after which he immediately announced his retirement.[10] The ancient game Go is famously complex, with more possible configurations for pieces than atoms in the known universe, and it was long not thought possible that a machine could master it.

How new technologies are impacting organizations and business models

These advances in technology are already reshaping jobs, roles, organizations, creating entirely new business models and eco-systems, blurring traditional boundaries between industries, as well as impacting how we learn, think and interact. Digital disruption in action.

Ginni Rometty, IBM's former president, chair and CEO, has remarked that she expected AI to change 100 per cent of jobs in the next five to ten years.[11] The cynic might argue that she would say that, wouldn't she, given IBM's obvious interest in the field, but she is far from alone in this view.

Perhaps our greatest challenge is the sheer pace at which this is happening.

The Covid-19 pandemic has acted as a further accelerant as organizations recognized they had started to fall behind and needed to adapt and look ahead. Many organizations and sectors have been greatly disrupted by the pandemic and its economic fallout, and change that might have taken a decade or more happened in months.

Companies like Amazon, Deliveroo, Uber Eats and others in the new economy, which were highly digitally adapted and had distribution models that allowed consumers to be accessed and served from their homes, have thrived. Those with traditional models that had not understood or invested enough in technology to adapt have suffered – companies like Arcadia Group and Debenhams or Bonmarché, and sadly too many others. Of course, some sectors like transportation were caught in a great downturn in demand for which they had no substitute product or service.

It means every business in some way has to see itself as data driven and digital, whether trying to understand customers better – from small restaurants to businesses like Amazon – or performance of people – from sports teams to retailers – or transforming business models from product driven to service driven.

Rolls-Royce has used data and AI to transform its business model from design, manufacture and after-sales support, describing itself as much as a data company as an aero-engine maker. Bernard Marr, recognized by LinkedIn as one of the world's foremost business influencers, wrote a compelling book on these themes, with over 40 examples across all sectors that illustrate the transformations that are taking place.[12]

The challenge that so many face, however, is keeping up. Randy Bean, CEO of consultancy New Vantage Partners, and Professor Tom Davenport from Babson College, Massachusetts, wrote an article in *Harvard Business Review* in 2019 citing a survey across 64 large multinationals which raised concerns about progress.[13] Despite almost all acknowledging an acceleration in investments in AI and big data:

- 72 per cent of survey participants reported that they had yet to forge a data culture;
- 69 per cent reported that they had not created a data-driven organization;

- 53 per cent stated that they were not yet treating data as a business asset;
- 52 per cent admitted they were not competing on data and analytics.

But transformation at scale will happen and those left behind will suffer. The pandemic acted as a stark reminder of that. Not only will these transformations help businesses to be more adaptive and agile and to serve their markets and customers better, but they will see productivity and efficiency gains as well. In the McKinsey report referenced earlier in the chapter, they commented, 'Adding things up for the economy as a whole, our latest research identified potential productivity growth of at least 2 percent per year over the next decade, with about 60 percent coming through digitization.'

Are robots coming after our jobs?

So we know that AI and digital transformation will significantly impact jobs, roles and the skills we need. Are we headed for a world of automation – the joke about the factory of the future being staffed by a person and a dog? The person is there to feed the dog, and the dog is there to ensure the person doesn't touch anything.

The most recent report from the World Economic Forum on the future of jobs is sobering in its predictions based on the extensive surveys it carried out across industries and countries.[14] The report forecast that half of all work tasks would be handled by machines by 2025 in a shift likely to worsen equality.

The WEF described an automation revolution that would create 97 million jobs worldwide but destroy almost as many, leaving some communities at risk in this short time frame. Routine and manual administrative and data-processing jobs were most at risk, while roles relying on human skills, such as advising, decision-making, reasoning, communicating and interacting, would rise in demand. In other words, the new jobs that may be created are far from a like-for-like replacement of old jobs and the skills needed.

We have already observed in Chapter 2 the steady shift in the nature of work and high, mid and low skills. The cocktail glass analogy would create huge challenges in balancing work and opportunity across our economies.

These sorts of predictions have been coming thick and fast over recent years, and have led to much popular debate about the future of work and whether the robots are coming to take our jobs.

Of course, the picture as ever is not as simple as how many jobs go versus how many might be created. Jobs are typically made up of groups of tasks, and for most jobs it will be particular tasks that may be automated, shifting the nature of the job or role but not necessarily eliminating the job entirely. As the CIPD's research from April 2019 reveals,[15] it can be easy to ignore the possibility that removing mundane tasks through automation actually enhances the quality of jobs and therefore the satisfaction we derive from work.

One of the most cited studies that excited the debate a few years ago was by Carl Frey and Michael Osborne of Oxford University. Their 2013 report, 'The future of employment: How susceptible are jobs to computerization?', described the analysis of the activities involved in over 700 different jobs in the US economy and estimated that 47 per cent of jobs were at risk of automation.[16] It seemed to predict a job apocalypse, but that wasn't quite what they were saying. As *The Economist* reported in 2019,[17] it was intended to show just how many jobs or activities could be vulnerable to automation, and there are many other factors that would impact how jobs actually changed.

However, there are many who believe that we will see a dramatic reshaping of work and loss of jobs across economies. And as already noted, it isn't any longer just about lower-skilled, more routine work, but also about higher-skill cognitive and analytical roles.

Richard and Daniel Susskind in their 2017 book *The Future of the Professions: How technology will transform the work of human experts* analysed and described how AI's growing ability to carry out complex analytical and cognitive tasks was going to automate higher-order skills and roles in the traditional professions such as law and accountancy. This 'hollowing out of the middle' could profoundly reshape many professional jobs and roles.[18] Or how careers are developed that have been based on the steady gaining of knowledge and experience through these mid- to higher-level skills.

In Daniel Susskind's latest book, *A World Without Work*, he concludes that ultimately there will be less paid work, which will shake the foundations of our economy and our society.[19] Martin Ford's book *The Rise of the Robots*, a 2016 FT and McKinsey Business Book of the Year, similarly draws on extensive evidence to reach the same conclusion and call for action.[20] As he observes, if a robot could do your job quicker than you and better than you for no pay, would you still be employed?

I have always enjoyed these sorts of debates. In my experience the people who want to reassure us most that technology won't destroy more jobs than it creates are typically the technologists themselves. They don't want to be seen as the bad guys.

This is not the first time in history that there have been predictions of huge losses of jobs and work because of technological advancement. In 1930, in an essay entitled 'Economic possibilities for our grandchildren', the famous economist John Maynard Keynes predicted that by now we would all be working around 15-hour or three-day weeks.[21]

Although he was right that what was being produced in the 1930s in the following decades could be produced with much less labour input, what he hadn't reckoned with was the explosion in consumerism – his view then was that we broadly had enough of what we needed so we had just about reached a finite production output limit, of itself a very interesting philosophical debate – how much really is enough? But today, even if we felt that consumerism in the developed economies had already gone too far and was increasingly unsustainable, there are so many of the world's population who are far behind.

Industry 4.0 and AI without doubt raise the stakes. Automation can and will displace labour in ways we haven't seen since the first industrial revolution. But we need to work together to ensure that automation serves humans positively. It should not end up controlling us or deskilling and disempowering, but instead enable us to improve the nature and quality of the work we do, allow productivity to increase and people to reduce levels of stress and working hours, and provide a better balance to our lives.

It will require forward thinking and great collaboration between all of us – business, education, policy makers and politicians. We have already touched on income and wealth distribution, and we will go on to explore the ideas of the principles of good work and inclusion, and a positive vision for the future. We can learn from the disruption and civil unrest created by the first industrial revolution, and they should not be repeated.

Technology improving people's performance at work

With the beginnings of the second industrial revolution and the development of assembly lines and process thinking, we mentioned F W Taylor and scientific management, and Seebohm Rowntree in his more humanistic approach of welfare and wellbeing. Both in their ways the forefathers of the HR function and profession.

Today we look back on scientific management theory and practice as too formulaic and rather dehumanizing. Scientific management was based on the scientific principles of research, experimentation and the collection and analysis of data, but looked at people in a very deterministic, rational way.

One hundred years later, however, and HR and management practice is again focusing hard on evidence and data. Definitely not all bad as too much of people management practice in the last decades was not sufficiently based on research, insight and evidence, but rather too much on writing rules, defining processes or popular 'best practices'.

With the ability of technology to be everywhere and to monitor and track anything, data science and analytics in understanding people and their performance is a burgeoning field. The CIPD has embedded analytics and evidence-based approaches into the heart of its thinking for the capabilities needed by HR professionals.

With the big shifts to remote working driven by the pandemic, the appetite for more data to understand and predict employees' behaviours will continue to accelerate. People analytics is an important and valuable capability to provide the insights to make organizations more productive and effective. Used in the right ways, people analytics can also help to ensure organizations are more people centric, assessing both quantitative and qualitative inputs to understand how people are experiencing the organization and their work.

But again, we must also take great care in how these technologies and applications are used. The spectre of Big Brother looms over us.

There have been too many examples of organizations, even with positive intent, having over-zealously sought to track employees' productivity.[22] Tracking computer log-in time, or even keystrokes, or presence and use of desks and workstations, or monitoring where and how people interact via emails and even on what subjects. The consultancy firm PwC came under fire for developing a facial recognition tool that logs when employees are away from their computer screens while working from home.[23]

Wearables can now monitor stress and anxiety, and chatbots can ask about your emotional state and provide advice. Through the pandemic, everyone became familiar with and largely accepting of track and trace applications such as those developed by Google and Apple and deployed via the UK's much trusted National Health Service, monitoring our interactions with others and our whereabouts.

These technologies, having gained acceptance for public health applications, are likely to be used or to endure for other applications, not least continuing to monitor or safeguard the health of our workforces. But they must be used with care as they can be hugely intrusive and can greatly undermine trust. If people don't understand how and why they are being monitored, and see the positive outcomes, not surprisingly they will resist. How would I know that data being captured on how well I am is not being used to judge me in other ways that might impact my progression or reward?

Technology may provide insights, but are they the right ones? Undermining trust in organizations causes much more damage than any insights we might otherwise gain. Ethical use of these technologies in the workplace must be a subject of focus for every organization, and will likely attract more regulation.

Other important applications of technology in the workplace relate to learning and developing skills. While the early years of eLearning in the early 2000s yielded mixed results, the field of digital learning has advanced rapidly. Better technology, but also better understanding of how people learn and how to use technology, is leading to significant growth, which again the Covid-19 pandemic has accelerated.

The digital learning market exceeded $200 billion in 2019 and was anticipated to grow at over 8 per cent CAGR between 2020 and 2026, according to Global Market Insights, a global market research and management consulting company.[24] Smart digital learning can understand individual learning behaviours and patterns and adapt learning interventions. Bit-sized and on-demand learning, mobile learning, embedded learning, collaborative learning will all transform how we learn in the workplace, but also in education, something we will come back to in Chapter 12.

Virtual reality vs real life

The fourth industrial revolution calls out the challenges and opportunities of technology in the world of work. But the impact of technology goes way beyond that into almost all aspects of our lives. It's another reason why this time it really is different.

The dominance of technology as a tool for socializing, broadcasting our views and opinions about the world, and communicating is transforming how we learn, behave, form social groups and interact. It is also leading to greater blurring of the lines between personal lives and what we understand to be our professional lives.

Over the last few decades, we've radically changed the way in which we interact with technology. Our mobile devices have become so integral to the way we live our lives that numerous studies[25] – some with more academic rigour than others – suggest we'd sacrifice almost everything for our phones. Gen Z's #FOBO.

Our relationship with technology is being increasingly humanized, in particular by the development of facial and voice recognition devices or home assistants, to the extent that the youngest generations today might struggle to understand that the perceived intelligence of the household's Alexa device is, in fact, artificial. We've all experienced or heard stories of children interacting with these technologies almost as if they are human – real examples like 'I'm bored Alexa, what should I do?' or 'Why are Mummy and Daddy so beastly to me?'!

This personification of AI will go a lot further. AI is getting better and better at mimicking human behaviour and emotion, allowing for much more natural interaction between humans and machines.

No surprise, it has its own classification within the field of AI as emotion AI and is rolling out across many applications, from chatbots in call centres, through advertising to self-help and wellbeing.[26] Studies are showing how humans even feel they are creating a meaningful relationship with these technologies. Let's be honest, even with relatively dumb and unresponsive technologies such as our cars, we have often anthropomorphized them, giving them names and identities and talking to them as if expecting them to respond or behave better.

Japan is at the forefront of smart robotics to help in social care and care for the elderly given the pressing challenges of the country's ageing population, as we touched on in Chapter 4. As reported in *The Japan Times* in 2018[27] and across international media, Shintomi Nursing Home in Tokyo is home to 20 different models of care robots, mimicking cute furry animals, small children, human-shaped 'humanoids' or full-sized lifting and walking robots. Residents 'have taken a shine to their robotic companions'.

The Japan Agency for Medical Research and Development showed that through these robot carers, older people's autonomy, sociability, mood and communication improved along with a better quality of life overall. A wider survey by elder care company Orix Living found that 80 per cent of respondents over the age of 40 welcomed or were open to being helped by a care robot.[28] Tellingly, they were responding to a common fear of becoming a burden on family members and even said they felt more relaxed in the presence of a robot.

A report in *The European Business Review* in November 2020 discussed AI developments in the emotional and 'soft skills' domain in the context of the potential for robot leaders in the future.[29] If the basis of emotional intelligence is to be able to interpret and understand emotions in others, then there are already AI applications that can interpret facial expressions and even respond at some level with emotion-based responses.

The article's authors say that 'if robots can master humour, this suggests that they could be positioned to step into more-human roles that require exemplary soft skills, like leadership roles'.

Indeed, humour was seen to be one of the attributes of the famous Turing test – the point at which we can't tell whether we are interacting with a machine or a human. For specific applications, the Turing test has already been passed – do you really know with certainty when you are interacting with a chatbot and not a person?

Social media – from word of mouth to world of mouth

The incredible rise of social media in the last couple of decades driven by the tech behemoths like Facebook and Google shows no sign of abating. Their wealth and power come from a simple idea that knowingly or unknowingly people will give up data about themselves in exchange for free services and access to the vast networks and resources the social media companies provide.

The saying goes that if you are not paying for the product, then you are the product.

There are huge implications for all of us, and understanding, regulation or control of these channels is way behind actual progress. It is often a rather pitiful experience watching the big tech giants run rings around politicians and regulators who are way behind in their understanding of what these companies and technologies do. An important discussion for other times and places. In few other fields of business endeavour are the issues of trust in business and the purpose and intent of business leaders quite so important. Something we return to in Chapter 7.

But there are some important things for us to think about for social media in the world of work. In 2018, the Washington DC-based Pew Research Center conducted a study of 743 American teenagers aged between 13 and 17 on their attitude towards and habits on social media.[30]

When asked about their primary use of social media platforms, approximately half of respondents said that they posted about their accomplishments while 44 per cent said they posted about their family. Some 34 per cent said they shared things related to their emotions and feelings, while 22 per cent admitted to regularly posting about their dating life. A minority of about 1 in 10 said they shared things relating to personal problems, their religious beliefs or political persuasions.

The survey also found, though, that only about a third of all respondents admitted to often or sometimes deleting or restricting access to things they shared on social media because they were concerned it could negatively impact them later in life.

An individual's online presence and digital footprint have become hugely important constituents of their identity both in a personal capacity and for a potential employer.

A 2015 survey[31] of 2,000 HR employees across a multitude of industries in the US revealed that more than a third said they would be less likely to interview a job candidate for whom no online information could be found. More than half said they used social networking sites to research potential hires, which was up from about 39 per cent just two years earlier. Most strikingly, perhaps, around one-third of respondents to that survey said they had learned something online that had led directly to them making a candidate a job offer.

Anecdotal evidence suggests there is a widespread underappreciation among young people of just how important their online presence might be in determining their future career opportunities. Most of us of the older generations are thankful that we did not live our young lives in the glare of the social media spotlight which may yet haunt this younger generation for years to come.

There are wider social impacts emerging. A 2016 research report[32] authored by Dr Jennifer Lau of King's College London in conjunction with National Citizen Service (NCS) warned of a 'concerning' lack of social integration and level of loneliness among the next generation of young people, and cautioned that this could have a detrimental impact on the UK economy in future.

Dr Lau found that while online interactions, on social media sites for example, are generally positively linked to a young person's social intelligence levels – defined as the ability to apply our understanding of people's emotions to decide the appropriate form of interaction with others – there are downsides too.

'While important as a means of practising social skills, online interaction is not a substitute for real life interaction,' Dr Lau says. 'Not only is online interaction associated with more loneliness in later life – as indicated by our research – this form of communication alone is not adequate in preparing young people for the challenges of the workplace.'

The research indicates one problem to be that people tend to interact with individuals online who are of a similar background to their own and of a similar age. This becomes particularly relevant in light of increasingly multigenerational and diverse workforces in which young people will need to effectively collaborate with colleagues and managers who will be from different generations and backgrounds.

Dr Lau's research also warns that limited social integration may have a significant impact on wellbeing later in life, and particularly may contribute to a sense of loneliness among young people, the type of which we have a tendency to associate with older generations. The rise of remote working, facilitated by increasingly sophisticated technology, risks exacerbating this.

Extensive research[33] shows that loneliness is consistently cited as one of the greatest downsides of remote working.

The global pandemic in 2020 almost overnight dramatically increased remote working as lockdowns restricted movements of people and offices literally switched off the lights. The UK-based mental health charity Mind surveyed more than 16,000 people on how the pandemic had impacted mental health.[34] They found that more than half of adults and over two-thirds of young people said that their mental health had deteriorated during the period of lockdown restrictions. The NHS in the UK also reported that mental health issues accounted for 4 in 10 of all sick notes, which was up 6 per cent since the pandemic started.

Supporting people's mental health and wellbeing is a societal imperative, but it's also critical within the workplace and should be seen as an outcome of responsible business. We will delve deeper into these points in Chapter 13.

Looking further out – utopia or dystopia

There are many people who doubt that technology could ever really emulate true human intelligence or exhibit emotion and empathy, let alone go way beyond to super intelligence. There are countless articles on the human skills that robots can never reproduce, doubtless providing comfort to us all as we consider our own jobs. These may be comforting views to avoid the mind-boggling implications of AGI or even ASI. But let's not forget Bill Gate's observation we referenced earlier.

The great physicist Professor Stephen Hawking expressed his greatest concern that AI could threaten the existence of humanity if unchecked.[35] Even renowned tech entrepreneurs like Elon Musk have warned that AI could be our 'greatest existential threat'. Although he also declared that humanity must merge with AI to continue to evolve and not be surpassed like the primates were in the past.[36]

Could truly ubiquitous, all-seeing and knowing technology create the kind of dystopian future of totalitarianism and human control that science fiction writers of the past have described? Among the best known are Aldous Huxley in his book *Brave New World*. First published in 1931, it describes a world state of total control, where procreation becomes a factory-like activity and genetic engineering defines social hierarchies. And George Orwell, writing in the late 1940s in his famous book *Nineteen Eighty-Four*, imagined a very dystopian view of Big Brother, the Thought Police and total surveillance and control.

Other more recent examples repeat these dystopian ideas – consider the 'Black Mirror' TV series, or the book and now film *The Circle* by Dave Eggers, or *The Handmaid's Tale* written by Margaret Attwood in 1985 and more recently turned into a TV series. The common threads are of control and totalitarianism, of social engineering, and profoundly of inequality and suppression of what we would regard today as basic human rights. All enabled by technology.

Bleak futures driven by technology may be more interesting to write about, and they play to some of our bigger fears and in particular our loss of power of self-determination, our freedoms and perhaps our fears of mortality. It would be short sighted not to think about the possibilities for human-like or super intelligence and how this might impact our future. We cannot sleepwalk into a future where technology or intelligent machines could threaten humanity. But there are signs already of a direction of travel that should be of concern.

1984 has long come and gone. Wind the clock forward to today, however, and the technologies exist to do much of what writers like Orwell describe. We can see surveillance happening in different forms and the spread and reach of today's big tech companies. There is an increasing confusion of commercial interest, political interest, individual rights, and desire through organizations as well as agencies and governments to influence behaviours in various ways.

Perhaps the biggest example is the Chinese social credit system, which is described as a national reputation or trust system that aims to standardize the assessment of citizens' and businesses' economic and social reputations. Data is being collected across many dimensions into a unified system that tracks information such as whether people are paying taxes or bills on time, or anti-social behaviours, while encouraging positive ratings through activities like volunteering. This builds up individual credit scores that can influence where you may be able to send your children to school or your chances of good employment.

This is arguably a huge exercise in manipulating human behaviour and a gross infringement on people's basic rights, and would not be tolerated in liberal democracies elsewhere. But in a country and system long used to higher levels of state control, people may be persuaded by the arguments of building greater trust across society and aligning positive social behaviours.

Looking further ahead, what about super intelligence and the threats of AI that goes not only beyond human capabilities but potentially beyond our control?

It's what the renowned futurologist Ray Kurzweil described as the 'singularity'[37] – the point at which the development of AI is out of human control and hard to predict. Having been prescient on many developments of technology over the last 25 years and received numerous awards, his predictions for the next 25 years are to say the least thought provoking.[38]

Kurzweil believes that we will be able to multiply our intelligence a billionfold by linking wirelessly from our neocortex to a synthetic neocortex in the cloud – a melding of humans and machines. We could then connect with machines via the cloud, but also to another person's neocortex. And all that by 2045. Before then he expects that virtual reality will feel 100 per cent real and that smart nanotechnologies (super small) will help eradicate many diseases and be a lot smarter than biological systems. And of course, we will all be travelling in driverless vehicles.

Some might see these as the more utopian outcomes of technological advance. Not something I would agree with, and it does sound far-fetched and scary in equal measure. But as we work towards greater interconnectivity and virtual collaborative working, to people even 10 years ago it might seem as though we have already advanced significantly down this path.

Spatial is a company that is creating 'shareable augmented workplaces' using augmented reality that look a bit like the movie *The Matrix*. Its vision is of moving from 'personal computing' to 'the world's first collective computer'.[39]

Technology is already being connected into the human body to correct or replace lost capabilities – bringing movements to artificial limbs from brain sensors, or restoring lost senses. Stephen Hawking himself used AI to continue to communicate after motor neurone disease had robbed him of so much.

At a conference in 2019, I met a fascinating person who described himself as the first human cyborg and is even recognized as such by the UK government and Passport Office. In 2004 Neil Harbison, who was born colour blind, had an antenna implanted in his skull that translated colour into vibrations so that he was able to sense colour. He has extended its capabilities to the super-human – being able to sense infrared and ultraviolet light, and now with Wi-Fi enablement allowing it to become a means of direct communication into his head. Through his Cyborg Foundation and Transpecies Society, he has formed a community of people with various technology-implanted enhancements to promote and defend their rights.

In a nice piece of historical symmetry, Julian Huxley, the brother of Aldous Huxley, promoted these ideas as what he called transhumanism.[40] 'The human species can, if it wishes, transcend itself—not just sporadically, an individual here in one way, an individual there in another way, but in its entirety, as humanity.'

The best-selling historian and writer Yuval Harari has extended these ideas and laid out possible futures in his books *Sapiens*[41] and *Homo Deus*.[42] His view is that humanity, at least as we know it, will be radically transformed, whether it be by fundamentally altering the course of human evolution through genetic engineering, or bio-technological replacements of our bodies, or even uploading our consciousness and experiences to a vast artificial neural network along the lines of Kurzweil.

We have organized to meet basic human needs – being happy, healthy and in control of the environment around us. Taking these goals to their logical conclusion, Harari says humans are striving for 'bliss, immortality, and divinity'. This extends further Aristotle's thesis of Eudaimonia as a goal of humanity – the goal of contentment and wellbeing if you will – into a challenging space of superbeings and immortality.

These ideas are no longer just philosophical musings or the imagination of science fiction writers. They are possible extrapolations from where we are now, albeit based on a view that expresses biology and human intelligence as another form of technology that is replicable, interconnectable and ripe for improvement.

I prefer the kind of viewpoint expressed by Klaus Schwab. 'In its most pessimistic, dehumanized form, the Fourth Industrial Revolution may indeed have the potential to "robotize" humanity and thus to deprive us of our heart and soul,' he wrote. 'But as a complement to the best parts of human nature—creativity, empathy, stewardship—it can also lift humanity into a new collective and moral consciousness based on a shared sense of destiny. It is incumbent on us all to make sure the latter prevails.'[43]

Regulation and education

The risks that advancing technology brings are steadily attracting the attention of regulators. As they should. The longer-term projections of how technology can impact us will require deep understanding and challenge on ethical and moral grounds, as well as practical areas of control. But not only does regulation struggle to keep up, it's hard also to find the right balance between control and freedoms that allow innovation and exploration.

One of the first areas has been individual protection. Protection of identity and of individual rights is essential in a world where cybercrime is more sophisticated than ever.

The pandemic itself led to a marked increase in individual and corporate attacks as people worked more from home – reports show at least 30 per cent higher levels. The latest Organised Crime Threat Assessment (IOCTA) report by Europol in October 2020[44] found that 'criminals quickly exploited the pandemic to attack vulnerable people; phishing, online scams and the spread of fake news'. Major threats continue to be malware and ransomware attacks on organizations, payment fraud, and the use of the dark web for organized criminal activities.

Many people are still not aware of the types of defences they need to have in place to safeguard their personal information and security. Measures like General Data Protection Regulation (GDPR),[45] which was implemented into EU law in May 2018, have been a positive step in getting organizations to be responsible for data privacy and security. But at an individual level, more education is needed to help everyone protect themselves as far as possible.

But cybersecurity also spans far beyond keeping your bank details and personal data secure. The anonymity granted to individuals on the internet, and the lack of obvious accountability, also mean that the cyberworld can quickly become a wild west. Cyberbullying and trolling are extremely hard to regulate. Their effects on victims' mental health can be devastating and they set a dangerous precedent for what is acceptable. Employers have a duty to educate their workforces about technology, safety and wellbeing in a comprehensive and inclusive way and to seek external support to do so if they don't have the resources available.

This dependency extends to social media too, something that again became more evident during the pandemic[46] when social distancing was enforced widely. But even before that, platforms like Facebook, Twitter and Instagram were frequently being used by individuals not only as ways to communicate with friends for pleasure but increasingly as a form of intranet to facilitate exchanges relating to work.

This introduces a whole host of risks, both legal and ethical, and raises questions around the responsibility of employers. The rapid rise in the popularity of social media platforms in the last few decades has made it hard for policy-setters to keep up.

Beyond the regulations and obligations to protect data and communications, there is now more attention being paid to the ethical questions being raised by technology.

The idea that machine ethics might take the form of laws or principles was famously explored by the science fiction writer Isaac Asimov back in the early 1940s. He proposed three laws of robotics

---

ASIMOV'S LAWS OF ROBOTICS

- First Law: a robot may not injure a human being or, through inaction, allow a human being to come to harm.
- Second Law: a robot must obey the orders given to it by human beings except where such orders would conflict with the First Law.
- Third Law: a robot must protect its own existence as long as such protection does not conflict with the First or Second Laws.

Not a bad start, but we need to go a lot further now. An exploration of the many different areas was described in *The Stanford Encyclopedia of Philosophy* by Vincent Muller, Professor of Philosophy at Eindhoven University of Technology and a Fellow at Leeds University.[47] These include autonomous self-learning machines, privacy and surveillance, manipulation of behaviour, bias and opacity in decision systems, human–robot interaction, automation and employment, machine ethics, artificial moral agents and on up to super intelligence.

So there is a lot to think about and we are still largely in the early phases of policy thinking or the wider debate that will be needed. We will explore some of this a bit further in Chapter 11 as we look at job design and AI in the workplace more directly.

The essence of ideas we explore in this book, including good work, wellbeing, and greater equality and inclusion, we believe are the cornerstones for building a future increasingly influenced by technology, that is still good for all.

In conclusion

The pace of development in all forms of modern computer-based technologies is accelerating. Alongside all the other shifts we discuss in this book, technology will be the biggest disruptor and driver of change, and of itself is also driving significant social change.

Every business today (and every business leader) has to see itself as a technology company or data business in some way. It is a shift in mindset to understand not only the possible but also the threats to existing business models. We must keep informed, keep being curious, and think systemically about the impact of digital transformation.

Technology will significantly reshape jobs and the skills we need. That is already happening and will accelerate in the coming years. It is critical that the jobs that change and the new jobs and roles that are created are designed from a human-centric perspective. We have to make technology work for us, not us work for technology.

AI will continue to evolve and now is the time to develop clearer principles, guidelines and regulation to understand and manage its application. The dystopian futures are just as possible as the utopian futures. We need to work collectively to ensure AI is good for all, not reinforcing divides in society or even in humanity itself.

Endnotes

1 Anderson, R G (2007) How well do wages follow productivity growth? (PDF) Federal Reserve Bank of St. Louis Economic Synopses
2 Schwab, K (2016) *The Fourth Industrial Revolution*, World Economic Forum
3 http://www3.weforum.org/docs/WEF_Future_of_Jobs_2018.pdf (archived at https://perma.cc/YR5R-Y4DX)

4 www.mckinsey.com/business-functions/mckinsey-digital/our-insights/is-the-solow-paradox-back# (archived at https://perma.cc/UF7H-VZ6N)
5 Gates, B, Rinearson, P and Myhrvold, N (1995) *The Road Ahead*, Viking Press
6 www.forbes.com/sites/cognitiveworld/2019/06/19/7-types-of-artificial-intelligence/?sh=6956bdfe233e (archived at https://perma.cc/FWV3-3267)
7 https://www.ft.com/content/df752cc6-ac98-11e9-8030-530adfa879c2 (archived at https://perma.cc/YX6F-SGHG)
8 https://www.ft.com/content/c96e43be-b4df-11e9-8cb2-799a3a8cf37b (archived at https://perma.cc/C79S-93E3)
9 https://deepmind.com/about/deepmind-for-google (archived at https://perma.cc/JD8N-ZXUS)
10 www.theverge.com/2019/11/27/20985260/ai-go-alphago-lee-se-dol-retired-deepmind-defeat (archived at https://perma.cc/WV2W-ZDB3)
11 www.cnbc.com/2019/04/02/ibm-ceo-ginni-romettys-solution-to-closing-the-skills-gap-in-america.html (archived at https://perma.cc/9JXX-MBRK)
12 Marr, B (2016) *Big Data in Practice: How 45 successful companies used Big Data analytics to deliver extraordinary results*, Wiley, Chichester
13 https://hbr.org/2019/02/companies-are-failing-in-their-efforts-to-become-data-driven (archived at https://perma.cc/KKV5-UY52)
14 www.weforum.org/reports/the-future-of-jobs-report-2020/in-full/executive-summary (archived at https://perma.cc/R2J7-CQZF)
15 www.cipd.co.uk/knowledge/work/technology/emerging-future-work-factsheet (archived at https://perma.cc/56QZ-ADTH)
16 https://www.oxfordmartin.ox.ac.uk/downloads/academic/The_Future_of_Employment.pdf?link=mktw (archived at https://perma.cc/6DRE-AEMG)
17 www.economist.com/business/2019/06/27/will-a-robot-really-take-your-job (archived at https://perma.cc/5THQ-78MT)
18 Susskind, R and Susskind, D (2015) *The Future of the Professions: How technology will transform the work of human experts*, Oxford University Press
19 Susskind, D (2020) *A World Without Work: Technology, automation, and how we should respond*, Penguin Books
20 Ford, M (2016) *The Rise of the Robots: Technology and the threat of mass unemployment*, OneWorld Publications
21 https://www.economicsnetwork.ac.uk/archive/keynes_persuasion/ (archived at https://perma.cc/D62S-2F5H)
22 www.theguardian.com/world/2020/sep/27/shirking-from-home-staff-feel-the-heat-as-bosses-ramp-up-remote-surveillance?CMP=Share_iOSApp_Other (archived at https://perma.cc/7ERB-PKCV)
23 www.personneltoday.com/hr/pwc-facial-recognition-tool-criticised-for-home-working-privacy-invasion/ (archived at https://perma.cc/JD93-WXMB)
24 www.gminsights.com/industry-analysis/elearning-market-size (archived at https://perma.cc/SNH3-YT4N)

25 www.forbes.com/sites/alicegwalton/2017/12/11/phone-addiction-is-real-and-so-are-its-mental-health-risks/#7113a16f13df (archived at https://perma.cc/WG7R-5W5V)
26 https://mitsloan.mit.edu/ideas-made-to-matter/emotion-ai-explained (archived at https://perma.cc/SH9B-6HQY)
27 www.japantimes.co.jp/opinion/2018/06/09/commentary/japan-commentary/japans-robot-revolution-senior-care/ (archived at https://perma.cc/7SWW-DQ32)
28 https://www.japantimes.co.jp/news/2018/11/15/national/80-japanese-positive-robotic-nursing-care/ (archived at https://perma.cc/9KEF-4BLG)
29 www.europeanbusinessreview.com/the-funny-thing-about-robot-leadership/ (archived at https://perma.cc/XJP6-8RB3)
30 www.pewresearch.org/internet/2018/11/28/teens-and-their-experiences-on-social-media/ (archived at https://perma.cc/9QCG-WBLE)
31 www.careerbuilder.com/share/aboutus/pressreleasesdetail.aspx?sd=5%2F14%2F2015&id=pr893&ed=12%2F31%2F2015 (archived at https://perma.cc/RK98-2ZLF)
32 www.kcl.ac.uk/archive/news/ioppn/records/2016/march/report-highlights-loneliness-and-lack-of-social-integration-amongst-young-people (archived at https://perma.cc/TNZ3-XAGT)
33 www.gallup.com/workplace/268076/manage-loneliness-isolation-remote-workers.aspx (archived at https://perma.cc/4UTZ-GBY6)
34 www.mind.org.uk/media-a/5929/the-mental-health-emergency_a4_final.pdf? (archived at https://perma.cc/VQH9-YL7L)
35 www.bbc.co.uk/news/technology-30290540 (archived at https://perma.cc/DSW9-R953)
36 www.axios.com/elon-musk-artificial-intelligence-neuralink-9d351dbb-987b-4b63-9fdc-617182922c33.html (archived at https://perma.cc/5A5D-XMDT)
37 Kurzweil, R (2005) *The Singularity Is Near: When humans transcend biology*, Viking, London
38 https://singularityhub.com/2015/01/26/ray-kurzweils-mind-boggling-predictions-for-the-next-25-years/ (archived at https://perma.cc/D8BY-2GBL)
39 https://www.youtube.com/watch?v=PG3tQYlZ6JQ&ab_channel=Spatial (archived at https://perma.cc/YF7K-UUFP)
40 www.huxley.net/transhumanism/index.html (archived at https://perma.cc/99AY-CA2M)
41 Harari, Y N (2015) *Sapiens: A brief history of humankind*, Vintage
42 Harari, Y N (2017) *Homo Deus: A brief history of tomorrow*, Vintage
43 https://www.weforum.org/agenda/2016/01/the-fourth-industrial-revolution-what-it-means-and-how-to-respond/ (archived at https://perma.cc/WXR5-VU9U)
44 www.europol.europa.eu/newsroom/news/covid-19-sparks-upward-trend-in-cybercrime (archived at https://perma.cc/MS33-KW7P)
45 https://gdpr-info.eu/ (archived at https://perma.cc/S3FH-C2UF)
46 www.nytimes.com/2020/03/24/technology/virus-facebook-usage-traffic.html (archived at https://perma.cc/9G6G-T28U)
47 https://plato.stanford.edu/archives/win2020/entries/ethics-ai/ (archived at https://perma.cc/PJ2L-LPMT)

06

Education and learning

Wisdom... comes not from age, but from education and learning.
ANTON CHEKHOV, RUSSIAN PLAYWRIGHT

As we explore the future of work, one of the most pressing issues we will all keep coming back to is skills, learning and education. The forces for change we have outlined in the preceding chapters place great emphasis and need for societies and organizations to be able to adapt. One of the most critical areas of adaptation is developing the skills needed in our people. As we debate the future of work and the fourth industrial revolution, so must we also debate the future of education and learning.

Education is so fundamental to the functioning of society and our future that it is called out as one of the United Nations' 17 Sustainability Development Goals for the future: Goal Number 4, Quality of Education, 'To ensure inclusive and quality education for all and promote lifelong learning'.

This simple statement raises critical questions. How do we best equip young people for a fast-changing world of work when we don't even know what many of the jobs will be? How do we sustain the variety of education and training that is inclusive and provides opportunity for all? And how do we best upskill and reskill the adult workforce to meet the changing demands and needs of jobs and roles?

Stephane Kasriel, former CEO of Upwork and member of the World Economic Forum council, puts the half-life of a learned skill at about five years. This means that in five years from now, around half of our skills today will no longer be of value – or collectively the current knowledge and skill set of your workforce will be worth about half as much. And this half-life, which would best be attributed to technical and job-specific skills, for many is reducing all the time.

A report by the CBI published in October 2020 based on analysis by McKinsey estimated that 9 in 10 employees will need to reskill by 2030 in the UK at an estimated additional cost of £13 billion a year.[1]

These are big statements that go along with many other huge predictions about how we are educating young people today for jobs in the future that don't yet exist. Jobs will change, and we have always needed to reskill people, so some of these predictions appear a bit melodramatic. But given all the trends we have already discussed, we have to expect that the pace of change will increase. Not only do we need to think about education for the future, but also about what needs to change in our organizations to invest properly in skills development and to reinvent workplace learning to make learning part of work, and work part of learning.

We will need Education and Learning 4.0 to support Work 4.0.

As we will explore in this chapter, we can see real needs for change in education and learning. Many of our systems of education and learning were built in a different time and era, and retain learning philosophies at their heart which become less and less relevant in a world of self-directed learners with limitless access to knowledge and content. We have to ensure we can properly support lifelong learning and rapid and frequent upskilling and reskilling as the skills need for the future of work change.

But to begin, let's look at the issues from a work perspective and where the skill gaps are.

Understanding skills gaps and the imperative for change

Being educated isn't necessarily the same thing as being skilled. Skills are what we need in the world of work, and although we can't expect education to meet all the skills needs in our workforces, we should expect the basic foundations to be there. Education should equip young people for life, but it should also prepare them for the world of work.

Today we see far too many gaps in education and into work. Gaps of opportunity, and gaps in core skills. These gaps may start in education, but they continue into the adult workforce.

From a business perspective, there are rising concerns among businesses everywhere about their ability to find the right skills. Access to skills and talent has been among the top concerns for business leaders in most surveys over recent years, and is seen as a key risk issue in their growth strategies and ability to adapt.

The pandemic for the vast majority of businesses placed an even stronger focus on people. The Fortune/Deloitte survey of a sample of CEOs representing more than 15 industry sectors published in October 2020[2] showed optimism for the most part in how their organizations and their workforces had adapted during the pandemic, and how that was giving them confidence about the future. However, they acknowledged that attraction and retention of people with the right skills was even more critical, and 96 per cent of them agreed that greater diversity and inclusion were a critical strategic priority.

Research by KPMG published in August 2020[3] compared CEO views of risks before the onset of the pandemic in January 2020 and in July/August 2020. There were some striking, and in many ways encouraging, findings. Firstly, the pandemic had accelerated attention on corporate purpose and the drive towards more responsible business, with people more at the centre of the corporate agenda – key themes for us in this book. But the key risk CEOs now identified was about access to skills and talent.

As the report noted, 'While "talent risk" was the threat that CEOs ranked behind eleven other risks at the beginning of the year, it has now risen to be the number one threat to long-term growth. CEOs were also recognising the need to keep their people feeling safe but also connected, engaged and productive.'

Global recruitment company Hays is one of a number of organizations that publishes an annual skills index aiming to examine skill supply and demand across countries on a comparative basis. The research considers a series of metrics, including how flexible the education system is to being able to accommodate changing labour market needs, wage pressures in various types of occupation, and also talent mismatch – an indicator of the gap between the skills businesses are specifically looking for and the skills that are available in the labour market.

Hays' most recent report, 'The global skills dilemma – how can supply keep up with demand?',[4] published in collaboration with Oxford Economics, stated 'Talent mismatch is becoming worse in a number of markets'. The report also highlighted that organizational responses, including the rapid growth in use of technology, the rise of outsourcing, globalization and uncompetitive labour markets, were causes of wage stagnation.

The index looks at data across 34 countries. There is some significant variation in individual countries' skills gaps, but generally across each region of the world, pressures are increasing. For the UK, the report observes that employers are having to work hard to secure the talent they need due to skills shortages, particularly in areas such as technology, construction and some areas of finance.

These findings are reflected further by the Open University's 2019 Business Barometer,[5] which found that 63 per cent of UK organizations are experiencing a skills shortage. Some 55 per cent said their company had struggled because of the skills shortage over the course of the previous 12 months, and three in five senior business leaders admitted that their organization was not as agile as it would ideally need to be on account of a lack of skills.

While the OU survey focused on the private sector, the public sector also suffers from significant skills shortages in many areas, partly because the public sector competes for skills with the private sector but has such different pay and reward structures, and partly because it is very dependent on specific skills. Most notable is the health and social care sector.

In November 2018 a report by the King's Fund, Nuffield Trust and the Health Foundation on the healthcare workforce in England[6] highlighted that the NHS in England was already short of more than 100,000 staff, including 10,000 doctors and 40,000 nurses. 'If the emerging trend of staff leaving the workforce early continues and the pipeline of newly trained staff and international recruits does not rise sufficiently, this number could be more than 350,000 by 2030', according to the report. This amounts to around one in five of all NHS posts being unfilled. The experts blame the situation on 'an incoherent approach to workforce policy at a national level, poor workforce planning, restrictive immigration policies and inadequate funding for training places'.

Then along came the pandemic. The healthcare sector has been particularly hard hit and staff shortages were further exposed with burnout, stress and significant issues of mental health also leading to further exits from the profession.

These issues of skills shortages have been a long-growing concern that has not been adequately addressed, either by businesses in their own investment in skills or through government and education policy. Again, there is a big imperative here for change, driven not only by the accelerating changes in job and skill demands but also by the tightening of migration philosophy and policies in the UK, and in other countries, that will add further constraints to skills access.

However, while it is easy to talk about skills shortages in general terms, to make meaningful headway we have to get a bit more specific.

What skills are really needed for the future

Aligning educational policy and outcomes and government incentive schemes to increase the supply of skills requires understanding of skills demand. Gaining a collective view, however, is very difficult as businesses themselves have not historically done a good job of understanding their future skills needs. Strategic workforce planning is not just an issue for the NHS.

As we have already observed, short-termism and lack of longer-term people and organizational strategy and investment are endemic. Of course there are many examples of organizations with very particular skills needs, such as in engineering, which can describe what they need, but the solutions to any skills shortfalls will need to go far beyond traditional talent supply chains (for instance, recruiting graduates from the same places).

It is also very important to understand the breadth of talent and skills organizations need. The much quoted 'War for Talent', originally coined by McKinsey & Company in 1997, focused the idea of talent as the superstars, the brightest and the best. It felt a bit like *Brave New World*, a view of the 'alphas' and what was seen to be their critical role in the success in any business. A notable model referenced at the time was Enron, and we know how that ended.

By the early 2000s the debate was moving on to recognize that skills shortages were becoming more widespread, influenced as we have seen by demographic shifts and demand for new skills. Businesses needed a wide range of skills and capabilities, and they also needed people with good social skills, communication skills, creativity, teamwork and problem-solving skills in almost any role. Subsequently even the word 'talent' became a more generalized descriptor for people, which for the most part is where it remains today.

As we noted in Chapter 5, the more technology and AI advance, the more talk there is of the essential human skills that cannot be readily replicated or automated. And as skills needs are changing faster, and individuals jobs and careers change, this has also focused more attention on what are the foundational or transferable skills we can all build from. What have also been referred to in the past as employability skills.

An IBM research report published in 2019[7] based on surveys across 50 countries with 5,800 executives showed this shift quite starkly. Figure 6.1 shows in the quite short period between 2016 and 2018 that businesses were now prioritizing behavioural skills over technical skills.

FIGURE 6.1 Shift in demand from technical to behavioural skills

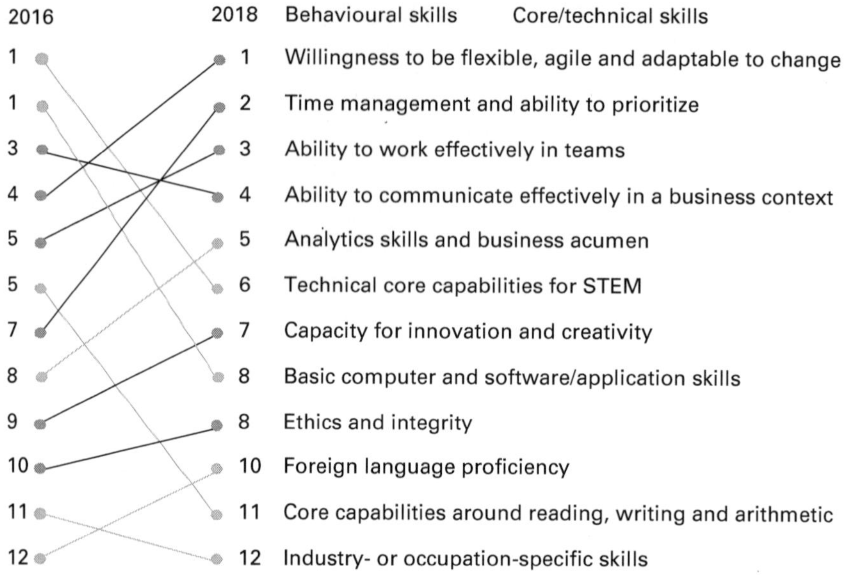

2016	2018	Behavioural skills	Core/technical skills
1	1	Willingness to be flexible, agile and adaptable to change	
1	2	Time management and ability to prioritize	
3	3	Ability to work effectively in teams	
4	4	Ability to communicate effectively in a business context	
5	5		Analytics skills and business acumen
5	6		Technical core capabilities for STEM
7	7	Capacity for innovation and creativity	
8	8		Basic computer and software/application skills
9	8	Ethics and integrity	
10	10		Foreign language proficiency
11	11		Core capabilities around reading, writing and arithmetic
12	12		Industry- or occupation-specific skills

SOURCE 2018 IBM Institute for Business Value Global Skills Survey 2018

But the report goes on to say, 'Half of the chief human resource officers say that people graduating from college possess the necessary technical and digital skills the company is looking to hire employees for. What they're missing are skills in problem-solving, innovation, teamwork, and leadership. The information is crystal clear: "digital and technical skills gaps" are rapidly addressed while behavioral skills are not.'

Other research shows the same patterns. For example, CV-Library, a leading UK job board, reported in June 2019 that the most important skills employers were favouring included the ability to adapt (71 per cent), resilience (57 per cent), willingness to upskill (40 per cent) and ability to change (31 per cent).[8]

These are more attitudinal and behavioural skills than just academic or technical qualifications. Some recruiters and HR teams are even starting to take qualifications off CVs as they are presented to hiring managers so they can focus on these core skills, and to help with the diversity of recruiting.

As Herb Kelleher, co-founder of Southwest Airlines in the United States, neatly summarized in his oft-repeated motto, 'Hire for attitude, train for skill.'

These sorts of behavioural and attitudinal skills are not just skills needed when people set out in their first jobs but are critical throughout people's careers. They are the bedrock for people to be effective and productive at all levels, they are enduring and they are highly transferable between jobs.

FIGURE 6.2 A simple skills framework

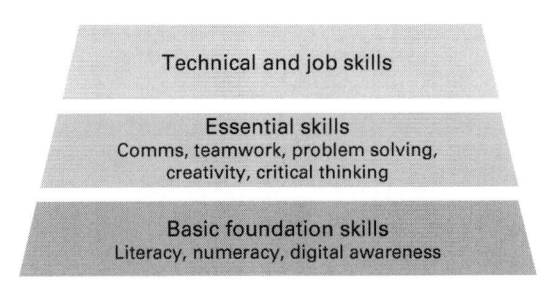

- Technical and job skills
- Essential skills
  Comms, teamwork, problem solving, creativity, critical thinking
- Basic foundation skills
  Literacy, numeracy, digital awareness

Employers therefore should be looking not just to hire for these skills but to recognize, promote and develop for these skills.

While the recognition of these essential skills is being drawn out much more, there is a need for more consistent language. There are many different skills frameworks, and language that is used interchangeably, including how we talk about knowledge, skills and behaviours. This doesn't help the understanding either for employers or for educationalists, and importantly for individuals.

To provide a simple summary, Figure 6.2 shows a basic framework to distinguish three levels and types of skill.

The base skills should be literacy and numeracy, and these are generally regarded as the base educational skills that should be developed in all young people.[9] To these would now be added basic digital skills – the skills required to make use of digital devices and basic online applications, all of which are widely considered a critical component of a new set of literacy skills in the digital era.

At the next level, core or essential skills come into play. These are skills that are in many ways as essential for life and wellbeing as they are for employment. UNICEF, UNESCO and the World Health Organization list the 10 core life skill strategies and techniques as problem solving, critical thinking, effective communication, decision-making, creative thinking, interpersonal relationship skills, self-awareness, empathy, and coping with stress and emotions.

Core or essential skills have been increasingly embedded in many schools, even if not called out directly in core curricula. Employers have also been adopting these ideas as noted and many have been promoting programmes to help young people in these areas. A great example is Barclays and its Life Skills programme, established in 2013 with the aim to inspire young people and equip them with the skills they need to move forward into work. To date, more than 3 million young people across the UK have participated in these programmes with Barclays, alongside many schools, FE colleges and universities.

To help bring together a common language and framework for essential skills, in 2018 the CIPD led the establishment of the Essential Skills Taskforce

FIGURE 6.3 The Skills Builder Universal Framework

in collaboration with the Gatsby Foundation, the EY Foundation, the Careers and Enterprise Company, the CBI, Business in the Community and the Skills Builder Partnership. Having reviewed various core skill frameworks, the Taskforce adopted and worked with the Skills Builder Partnership which had an established framework describing eight core skills used across hundreds of schools and educational establishments.

Consulting with a wide range of employers and testing against other frameworks, the Skills Builder Universal Framework, launched in May 2020,[10] has extended the framework to employers and the workplace. Higher levels of maturity and detail in the eight core skill areas were developed and incorporated further important areas for employers, including coaching, mentoring, strategic thinking and negotiation. The eight skill areas are shown in Figure 6.3. More than 750 organizations across the UK were using the framework by the end of 2020.

Standards like this may act as a Rosetta Stone, helping a much greater coalition and coordination across frameworks and standards through education and into work. In the context we are in for the future of work and the future of skills, it has never been more needed. But its success relies on buy-in not only from employers and education and training providers but also from the government. And the government should also do more to ensure that core and essential skills are embedded in a consistent manner across all training and apprenticeship frameworks.

Finally, both employers and teachers can have a great impact immediately. When hiring, interviewers can focus more on what essential skills a candidate already possesses and whether they have the potential to develop these skills further.

If young people understand the questions, they can be prepared to talk about all the experiences they have had that have helped them develop these skills. Teachers should be able to encourage young people in their understanding of these skills, recognizing that many experiences they have in education are developing skills not just to pass exams but in all these core skill areas. And importantly, other activities such as volunteering and playing team sports also greatly help in the development of these skills and should be further encouraged.

Digital and technology skills

Digital skills have been hotly debated for some time as skills that we all need in an increasingly digital and technology-enabled world. There are now generally accepted views of basic or foundational digital skills in how to use common technologies (smartphones, laptops), how to connect and basic security. Beyond this, it gets a bit more complicated – some people, for example, have advocated views that people should know how to code and how computers actually work. These skills are more related to specific job needs and not skills we all need to use technology effectively and safely.

Against the simple skills framework, beyond the basic digital skills, are the essential digital skills now needed in most jobs and roles, and which are also very transferable. The UK government after much consultation published an 'Essential Digital Skills' framework in 2018.[11] The framework describes five categories of these essential digital skills for work as well as for life more generally.

ESSENTIAL DIGITAL SKILLS

- Communicating – communicate, collaborate, and share online.
- Handling information and content – find, manage and store digital information and content securely.
- Transacting – apply for services, buy and sell, and manage transactions online.
- Problem solving – find solutions to problems using digital tools and online services.
- Being safe and legal online – staying safe, legal and confident online.

At the third level are the job and technical skills that are needed to perform specific roles. These must build on the other two levels and will require many different levels of competence and qualification depending on the nature of the jobs. They also will change more and therefore need ongoing investment and development.

Will our systems of education meet the needs of the changing world of work?

In previous chapters we've explored how generations that have recently entered the workforce, or those who are about to – millennials and Generation Z – are more educated than any before them.[12]

Being educated speaks to principles of wider awareness and understanding of the world, of values and beliefs, appreciation of different things, conceptual understanding, and a curiosity and desire for learning. It is the greatest gift that each generation gives to the one that follows, and which in a modern civilized society should be seen as a basic right for all.

As John Dewey, the influential American educational reformist and philosopher, noted in the 1930s, 'The purpose of education has always been to everyone, in essence, the same—to give the young the things they need in order to develop in an orderly, sequential way into members of society.'[13] His philosophy, which influenced a lot of educational reform at the time, was one of learning through experience and that education needed to reflect real life to achieve its greatest benefits. His philosophy still rings true today.

The World Economic Forum in its report 'Schools of the future – defining new models of education for the fourth industrial revolution', published in January 2020, similarly talked of a wider view of what education is for and the outcomes it should achieve.[14] The report described four critical and universal skill areas needed – global citizenship skills, innovation and creativity skills, technology skills and interpersonal skills. Global citizenship skills speak to the wider awareness of the world we all live in and how it is changing. Awareness of social change, environment, and appreciation for difference and context.

Teaching about the environment and awareness among young people has been a good example, but we have all recently had a stark reminder that education does need to open up its horizons in other ways. The Black Lives Matter movement has highlighted how teaching of history in the West was dominated by a white and predominantly colonial perspective, not giving young people the balance of views they needed. This is now changing and shows that education, like any system, can adapt rapidly when it is pushed.

However, despite the political focus on education for so long, there are still too many gaps, too many young people losing opportunities for the future. The huge shifts we are seeing now as a result of the trends we have already explored are further challenging the traditional pathways from education into work – the essence of social mobility and opportunity for all. As Tony Blair memorably stated at the 1996 UK Labour Party conference when he said that his three top priorities on coming to office were 'education, education, and education'.

In 2006, Sir Ken Robinson, a British author, speaker and international advisor on education in the arts to governments, gave the most watched TED Talk to date on whether schools destroy creativity.[15] He talked of the need for education to take us to a future we can't grasp, and his profound concerns that education was not equipping young people effectively and was designed for a different era.

He described creativity being as important as literacy, but that education was stifling young people's creative instincts. Instead, traditional education was a system based on examination and qualification geared to university entrance, with a hierarchy of maths at the top and arts at the bottom. Traditional education also is based on ideas of intelligence that value academic skills, specialization and ability to focus, and teaches in standard ways. Yet intelligence is diverse, dynamic and distinct.

In today's world we are all bombarded by information and one of the most important skills alongside creativity is the ability to think critically – core skills as we have previously noted. It's becoming less about the knowledge we retain than our ability to ask the right questions and being able to see more than one answer.

Hence the emergence in the younger generations of 'self-directed' learners, able to learn in a digital world where content and learning are everywhere. Memorizing facts to pass the artificial construct of examinations where no collaboration or access to outside sources is allowed now seems totally at odds with real-life experience and real-life learning. And also at odds with what the educational reformers of 100 years ago were describing.

It's no coincidence, then, that those countries with the best-rated education systems also appear the most equipped to meet the challenges of the future world of work. The World Economic Forum's research on 'Education 4.0' mapped out those countries which appeared to have the highest levels of digital skills from its research on global competitiveness, as shown in Figure 6.4.

FIGURE 6.4 Which countries have the digital skills to master the fourth industrial revolution

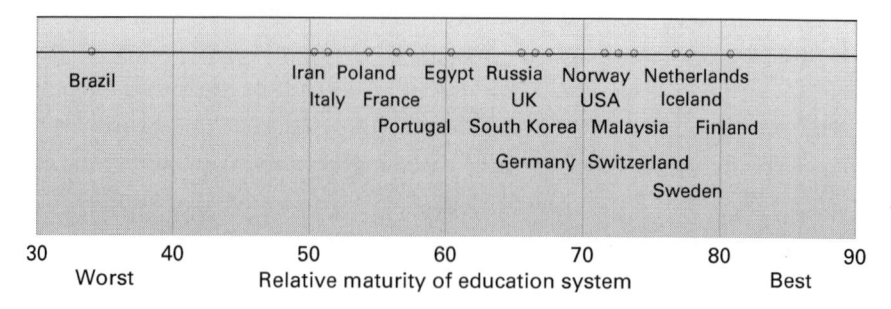

30	40	50	60	70	80	90
Worst		Relative maturity of education system			Best	

- Brazil (~32)
- Iran, Poland, Italy, France (~50)
- Egypt, Portugal (~57)
- Russia, South Korea, Germany (~63)
- Norway, UK, Malaysia, Switzerland (~70)
- Netherlands, USA, Iceland, Finland, Sweden (~77–82)

SOURCE Adapted From WEF 'Schools of the Future' report, January 2020

Good education not only equips workforces and organizations to be competitive and to drive our economies, but also creates national competitive advantage in attracting businesses to locate and invest. Access to good skills and talent is a globally competitive game.

The best educational systems in terms of outcomes are not directly correlated with expenditure. The OECD's most recent 'Education at a glance' report in 2018[16] says that in 2015, the United States spent approximately $12,800 per student on elementary and secondary education. That was over 35 per cent more than the OECD country average of $9,500 but still less than some European countries, including Norway, Austria and Luxembourg. At the post-secondary level, the US spend was 93 per cent higher than the average of OECD countries. But according to data from the OECD's Programme for International Student Assessment (PISA), in 2018 15-year-olds in the US ranked 31st on OECD standardized mathematics tests and their test scores were far below average in reading and science.

The UK also ranks highly in educational investment, but the global report ranks the UK only 14th for reading, 18th in maths and 14th in science – not great, but at least these were improvements from the last survey in 2015. Andreas Schleicher, OECD education and skills director, noted that it will take 'a long time' for the UK to catch up with top-performing countries like China, Estonia and Finland.

Sadly, the study also found just 53 per cent of UK students were satisfied with their lives, compared with 67 per cent across the OECD countries. The level of exposure to bullying at school was also slightly higher than average in the UK – 27 per cent of students reported being bullied at least a few times a month, compared with 23 per cent on average across OECD countries.

This raises questions around what the overall impact of a negative school experience might have on students' ability and motivation to learn, and how that might shape their attitudes towards education at a later stage. It is part of the issue of social divides and growing gaps of student attainment, when also combined with home environments, that are not supportive or encouraging of learning.

However, despite the challenging questions for education for the future, there have been extraordinary advances in access to education globally in recent decades.

Hans Rosling in his wonderful book *Factfulness*[17] questions our typical assumptions about the world and things getting worse by presenting the data and facts (try the Gapminder Test at www.gapminder.org to test your own assumptions). Access to education across the world has increased literacy rates to around 86 per cent globally, from only 10 per cent in 1800. Ninety per cent of girls are now enrolled in primary school education, up from only 65 per cent in 1970.

These are great advances, but progress in education needs to accelerate and in particular on the basic and essential skills. According to the United Nations, more than half of all children and adolescents worldwide are not meeting minimum proficiency standards in reading and mathematics.[18]

In the UK, from research carried out by the Social Mobility Commission and reported in November 2016,[19] over the previous 5 years 1.2 million 16-year-olds who were disproportionately from low-income homes had left school without five good GCSEs. And just 5 per cent of children eligible for free school meals gain five A grades at GCSE.

Of the basic skills, while general levels of literacy have been improving over the last 20 years, numeracy seems to be in a decline. According to the National Numeracy Campaign, an independent UK charity,[20] based on data from the OECD in 2011 only 22 per cent of working-age adults in England had numeracy skills levels equivalent to GCSE C grade or above. This was down from 26 per cent in 2003.

Numeracy skills are essential life skills and link directly to job prospects and overall wellbeing. The charity estimated that around four in five people have low levels of numeracy skills, and 68 per cent of businesses are concerned about employees' ability to sense check numbers.

Underlying causes for poor literacy and numeracy are now better understood to include inherent reading (dyslexia) and numeracy (dyscalculia) difficulties. As reported by the British Dyslexia Association,[21] dyscalculia may affect around 5 per cent of the population, but it also comments that 'mathematical learning difficulties' are prevalent and may affect as much as

25 per cent of the population. This suggests some allowance and more support are needed than was recognized in the past, and that is important, but overall there is still something of a culture of acceptance that 'I'm not very good with numbers'.

In 2020, as the Covid-19 pandemic spread across the world, most countries forced temporary closures of schools to help in containing the spread of the virus. The UN estimated this impacted more than 90 per cent of students worldwide and that by April 2020, over 1.5 billion young people were out of school, of whom almost 370 million were reliant on school meals as their main source of nutrition.

This level of disruption in education has never been seen before, particularly for those who are more vulnerable or marginalized. We don't yet know the longer-term impacts of this, but it is another reason why we have to do more in developing cultures of lifelong learning and educational support.

The rise and rise of higher education

Around the world, higher or degree-level education is seen as the pinnacle and something to be aspired to. Higher education is a global industry and universities around the world compete for students.

The UK punches far above its weight in higher education – not only does it have some of the top-rated universities in the world but it also attracts some of the highest proportions of overseas students.

According to UK government data,[22] the UK is second only to the US in volume of overseas students – the US took 26 per cent of the total and the UK took 12 per cent in 2017. In 2018/2019 there were 485,600 overseas students studying at UK universities, which amounted to 20 per cent of the total student population, with close on a third coming from the EU. Some universities such as University College London and Imperial were at 40–50 per cent.

At postgraduate levels, across the sector the proportions are even higher, with 54 per cent of full-time taught postgraduates and 49 per cent of full-time research degree students. These students pay higher tuition fees and have been a source of huge and growing income for UK universities. Universities UK estimated that in 2014–2015 international students contributed over £25 billion in gross output to the UK economy.[23]

Those countries sending overseas students have changed over the last few years. China sends the most students to the UK and the number has risen by more than 60 per cent over the decade. Other countries have dropped, including Nigeria, which has fallen by 45 per cent, and there has been a steady decline in students from many EU countries. The pandemic also reduced student numbers.

Worldwide, there has been huge growth in graduate numbers over the last 20 years and a 2019 report on an extensive study by the OECD showed some extraordinary progress.[24] The report found across OECD countries that the proportion of 25–34-year-olds with a higher education qualification is now larger than the proportion with upper secondary education only.

This means 44 per cent have a degree, and that number is above 50 per cent in nine countries, including Canada, Japan and the United Kingdom. Nearly a quarter of 25–64-year-olds across the UK have a bachelor's degree, which is 5 percentage points above the OECD average.[25]

When Prime Minister Tony Blair in 1999 set the goal of 50 per cent (which was reached almost exactly 20 years later), it was reflecting a very different preceding couple of decades. In 1980, only 15 per cent stayed in full-time education after the age of 18, which by 1990 had risen to 25 per cent.

So this was a big ambition to give more opportunity to more people to get into good jobs and to progress. One of the biggest successes is that now 57 per cent of graduates in the UK are women.

This trend of women progressing in education is reflected globally and has various causes. Much research has shown girls and boys often have different attitudes towards school education. The Higher Education Policy Institute, an independent educational think tank in the UK, reported that boys are significantly more likely than girls to regard school as a waste of time.[26] Boys seem more focused on whether education is relevant and will help them or not.

Which takes us back to some of the core arguments about philosophies of education and preparing young people for life and work. The great danger is that disengaged young people, particularly boys, grow up to become disillusioned adults who may never fulfil their potential or find their purpose.

These findings on female trends in education are seen globally. The Sheikh Saud bin Saqr Al Qasimi Foundation for Policy Research in the United Arab Emirates[27] has studied gender and education around the world and cites the same effects. Countries as varied as Panama, Sri Lanka, Argentina, Cuba, Jamaica and Brunei have some of the highest female-to-male ratios in higher education.

It is particularly interesting to see in traditionally patriarchal societies such as across the Middle East. At the University of Jordan, women outnumber men two to one. In Saudi Arabia, more than half of the country's science graduates are women.

Having been to these countries myself and met many female graduates and young people, it is wonderful to experience their enthusiasm. All these countries are changing to give more women opportunities to work as women are gaining a stronger voice. Governments are recognizing apart from anything else the huge pool of talent they have been creating but not utilizing effectively.

The OECD expects the global trend of increasing graduate numbers to continue and that 'the global population of university graduates is expected to nearly double over this decade and next to reach 300 million by 2030'.[28] With the population trends and high levels of investment in Asia in education, China and India together will account for nearly half of all degree holders worldwide. This will be a significant driver in increasing the impact of these countries in global talent supply, economic growth and influence in the coming decade.

However, it is also important to note that not all higher education systems or institutions and the graduates they produce are of the same standard. This is steadily changing as educational standards improve, and although in many western countries there has been the assumption of lower standards, say in China, that won't be true in the future.

There is now a growing strategic question for the HE sector in the UK and the West about dependence on overseas students in an increasingly competitive marketplace as university education evolves around the world. The coming years may well see something of a shakeout, and lower-quality courses, faculties and institutions will likely suffer.

The payback for degree-level education – the need for a balanced debate

With the evidence of the growing skills gap coupled with a falling graduate premium in the more mature economies, there are strong arguments to provide a better balance of educational routes into work. Degrees are expensive and the returns both individually and collectively at national economic levels are not always evident.

Joint research published in 2019 by the Higher Education Statistics Agency and the Department of Economics at Warwick University found that graduates born in 1990 earned 11 per cent more than non-graduates at age 26 compared with the 19 per cent graduate premium enjoyed by graduates born in 1970.[29]

OECD research found that those with a degree in the best-paid field of study earned about twice as much as those with a degree in the worst-paid field. People who studied natural sciences, mathematics or statistics, for example, earn over 180 per cent of the earnings of a worker with only an upper secondary education. But those who studied arts, humanities, social sciences, journalism or information earn just 92 per cent of the pay of a worker with an upper secondary education. Clearly the degree subject studied makes a big difference in earning expectations.[30]

Research by the UK Department of Education[31] on a longitudinal view of graduate outcomes over five years similarly showed how subjects which are more vocational (ie related directly to particular professions or jobs) had higher rates of employment.

The same research also showed how minority ethnic graduates tended to earn significantly less, pointing to other issues of routes into employment. 'The lowest earning ethnic group was "Asian or Asian British – Pakistani", which had median earnings of £21,500 (£4,500, or 17 per cent, below the median for all students). "Black or Black British-Caribbean" graduates, and graduates from an "other Black background", also had median earnings at least 10 per cent lower than the median for all students.'

The Institute for Fiscal Studies in the UK have researched the impact of undergraduate degrees on lifetime earnings.[32] They estimated that men will be on average £130,000 better off at discounted present value over a working lifetime, accounting for student debt, taxes and not earning while at university. The figure for women was £100,000.

While not to be ignored, these are not huge amounts over a lifetime of earning – maybe just over £3,000 a year on average. The research also estimated that one in five would be better off not having gone to university.

It's hard to make comparisons over long periods of time, particularly as so many jobs now appear only accessible to graduates when they were not in the past. If just having a degree is not as much a route to higher earnings or sustained employment as it was in the past, then the cost of tertiary education should also be a serious consideration.

Tuition fees in England are higher than in all OECD countries and economies, except the US. When the cap on fees was raised to £9,000 per year effective from September 2012, it sparked widespread student protests, yet by 2020 more than three in four English universities were charging up to the cap. As a result, government-supported student loans have risen dramatically and interest rates are now over 6 per cent for anyone who started studying after 2012.

Not surprisingly, tuition fees remain a highly charged political football. And we all pay for them. According to the UK government's own data,[33] more than £17 billion is loaned for tuition and maintenance fees to around

1.3 million students in England each year. By March 2020, the value of outstanding loans was £140 billion, and this could reach around £560 billion at today's prices by the middle of the century. The average individual debt among the cohort of borrowers who finished their courses in 2019 was £40,000, and based on the repayment criteria and levels of earnings needed, it is expected that only 25 per cent of current full-time undergraduates who take out loans will repay them in full.

However, higher earners also contribute more in income tax, which helps to balance the books. The Institute for Fiscal Studies in the UK in its research on the impact of undergraduate degrees on lifetime earnings estimated an average lifetime financial gain per graduate of around £110,000 for men and £30,000 for women. But the research acknowledged that these figures were driven mainly by the top earners and that there would be a net loss to the economy for around 40–50 per cent of graduates.

Even with an analysis that suggests some overall economic payback for a proportion of graduates, these are astonishing sums of money. It must surely question how we create a better balance in post-secondary education alternatives and how money is spent on education across our populations, particularly with the obvious and growing need for adult and lifelong learning.

The value of a university education is also often described in terms of developing life skills and confidence that help many graduates to progress, which is certainly important. But as we have already discussed, these life skills need to be better recognized and developed throughout education and through other channels as well.

Alternative educational routes – vocational education and training

As more graduates have flooded the entry-level recruitment market, employers and professions have increasingly used a degree as a basic entry-level criterion for all sorts of jobs and occupations that were not always asking for them before – professions such as accountancy, surveying and estate agency, insurance brokers, law, teaching, nursing.

These sorts of professions are vocational and historically they relied on training their own, recruiting straight from school and requiring learning at work followed by professional exams. This is the basis of the apprenticeship system as it has existed for centuries, well recognized for trades as well as professions. In the UK, these traditions were often enshrined through the livery companies of the City of London. The earliest of these, such as the Mercers, Drapers, Fishmongers and Goldsmiths, date back to the Middle Ages. I am proud to have helped to establish the Guild of HR Professionals, one of the modern livery companies.

The alternatives to degree-level education need to be more strongly promoted, not least to improve equality of opportunity for those who cannot or who choose not to go to university. Vocational education and training (VET) must be seen more clearly as an integral part of the system of education and learning to meet the needs of the changing world of work. But there remains much bias and stigma associated with different educational routes, particularly around the perceived value and status of apprenticeships or routes to work that do not include going to university.

In a talk I gave to school careers advisors at a conference in 2018, I asked them what the biggest barrier was to encouraging more school leavers to seek vocational education. With an almost unanimous chorus they said it was the parents.

There remain great social pressures and status associated with a university education, alongside a lack of understanding of the alternatives. Schools pride themselves and are measured by how many of their pupils go to university, but it is rarely about how many students get on to apprenticeship programmes. Yet some of the best apprenticeship programmes are among the most competed-for placements of any kind.

I experienced these pressures directly when one of my daughters decided not to go to university but to go directly to work in the TV and film industry. Her teachers asked her repeatedly why she wasn't going to university and she was given almost no support in preparing for work; she also found herself at odds with her peer group. No wonder so many young people go to university even when it is not the right or the best choice.

There are many issues to be considered in how to get a better balance across our educational systems from academic to vocational. The European Centre for the Development of Vocational Training (Cedefop) research on apprenticeship schemes across Europe[34] found a lack of consistency of standards, definitions and frameworks for apprenticeships and their place in the education and training system. This makes it hard to compare outcomes and value of apprenticeships, but is recognized as needing to change.

There is huge variation in how much apprenticeships are promoted in different countries, as Figure 6.5 shows. Internationally, Germany, Austria and Switzerland are seen as having the strongest apprenticeship systems and a longstanding equality of status, and a level of integration, with academic

FIGURE 6.5 Apprentices in programmes as a share of all students enrolled in upper secondary and shorter post-secondary education (ISCED 3 and ISCED 4C), 16–65-year-olds (2012)

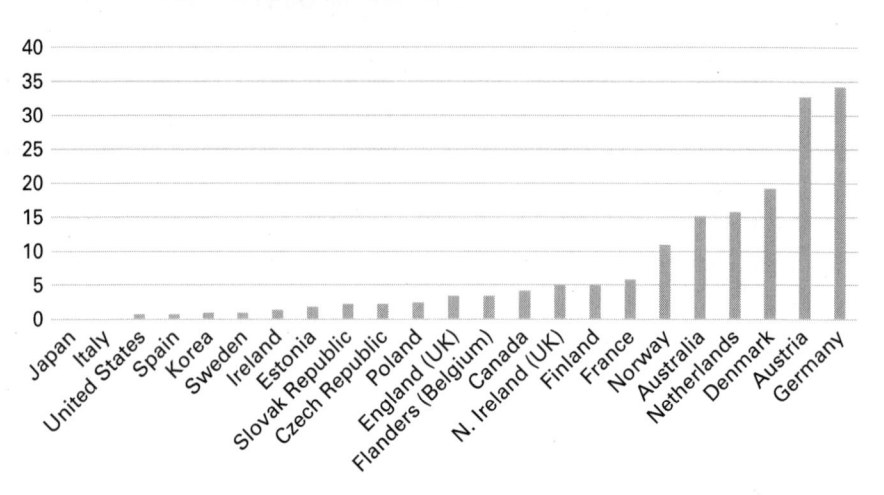

SOURCE OECD, www.oecd.org/skills/piaac/publicdataandanalysis

study. Employers work closely with schools, the chambers of commerce and local government to create effective training schemes that meet the needs of business and individuals. Learning at work and formal learning combined in a 'dual system' are seen as an integral part of education for young people, and employers in these countries are required to take on apprentices. Close to 60 per cent of young people complete an apprenticeship, and the system provides a powerful route into work and is central to how employers recruit. This plays out in the relatively low youth unemployment rates across these countries.

In research on cross-country comparisons of engagement in apprenticeships by Oxford University's Department of Education, significant benefits were found.[35]

For individuals, incentives include the appeal of learning through doing, the opportunities for occupational socialization, the possibility of progression to employment or to additional education, and learning while earning. For employers, there are the obvious benefits of developing job-ready skills and engaged employees, and the opportunity to make a contribution to the wider education and economic systems.

In the UK, apprenticeships have been part of the labour market and training system for centuries. From 1996 when apprenticeship-related data began to be formally collected there were 65,000 individual apprenticeships. With government focus and investment, in England this number grew rapidly, reaching over half a million by 2011/2012,[36] although there is some debate about how changes in definitions of apprenticeships affect the data. However, most recent figures show there has been a sharp drop in apprenticeship starts, 376,000 down from the previous year's 495,000. This falls a long way short of the government's target of 3 million apprentices by 2020, which was set at the time of the introduction of the Apprenticeship Levy in 2017.

The Apprenticeship Levy signalled a big shift in the development of apprenticeships to address issues of quality and provision, and to make employers more accountable. It required all public and private sector organizations with a payroll of over £3 million to pay a 'levy' of 0.5 per cent of their payroll to fund and incentivize uptake. To address quality concerns there were a number of reforms. These included setting minimum standards for duration and off-the-job training, and the launch of a new body, the Institute for Apprenticeships and Technical Education (IFATE), to oversee the quality of the new system.

While the new system has created a much greater awareness of apprenticeships among employers, there are growing concerns about the lack of flexibility in the standards and the time taken for off-the-job training commitments. The significant drop in apprenticeship starts has occurred since the time of the levy introduction, but it is not just about volume, it is also about quality.

However, research on the implementation of the levy, published by the CIPD in July 2019,[37] also showed that its design was actually incentivizing employers to use the funds made available to them in counterproductive ways. Twenty-two per cent of employers questioned said they used their levy money on training which would have happened regardless, while 15 per cent said that they had used the scheme to accredit skills which staff already had. As the apprenticeship data is showing, the system therefore is not creating more opportunities for people to come into work via apprenticeship schemes as was intended.

The review at the time also found that the levy had not significantly enhanced the quality of apprenticeships and it suggested that there may be a level of dead weight, displacement and substitution of training occurring across businesses.

I believe the scheme itself should be much broader. In its current form, it covers only a small number and proportion of UK employers; it should be extended to include small and medium-sized organizations. The levy in the UK is also relatively unique in that it is specifically designed to support apprenticeships and it could be extended to cover other forms of in-work training and VET. Crucially, the amount raised by the apprenticeship levy is considerably lower than the gap in employer contributions resulting from the long-term decline in employer investment.

Do we have too many types of qualification?

The qualification frameworks and systems in the different parts of the UK have thousands of different standards, pathways, programmes, awards, certificates, diplomas, etc.

The OfQual register[38] shows 44,000 different courses for GCSE, A level, AS level and vocational (work-related) qualifications in England and Northern Ireland. For degree-level qualifications there are over 50,000 undergraduate courses at more than 395 providers. As at December 2020, there were just under 600 apprenticeship standards approved for delivery. With the introduction of T levels, another choice opens up at Level 3, alongside A levels or apprenticeships. T levels are two-year courses that combine classroom learning and an extended industry placement of at least 45 days.

This proliferation of schemes and qualifications makes it very hard for young people, parents and employers to understand and navigate. As already noted, most of education isn't generally about specific jobs but about equipping young people for life and wider employment, particularly in a world where these jobs and skills needs are changing so rapidly.

There is a real danger that apprenticeship standards or VET driven by employers can become specific to a job or role need, which may even be seen differently between employers. Vocational education will be more focused on types of jobs and sectors but should not limit the learning narrowly to a particular job type. The German system has a total of around 330 apprenticeship standards and Switzerland around 250.

Overall it seems that the great number of qualifications and standards continues to reflect a view of much of education that is about increasing specialization, assessable standards and outcomes based on these. Equipping people for life and the future of work will of course continue to need some of this, but perhaps more for people in work as they need to develop the deeper job and technical skills through their careers.

For young people, we now need to better address the foundational and essential skills to give them the best platform, whatever their background, for a much more rapidly changing future of work. We should look again at what Ken Robinson said about education, the underlying philosophies of education and what so many have recognized before, to properly shape Education 4.0.

The case for strengthening non-degree post-secondary education and learning through the FE sector

In 2018, the government sponsored a review of post-18 education in England. Led by Philip Augar, the report was published in May 2019.[39] It looked at both university and higher education, and the further education sector. For HE, the review in particular called for reforms to tuition fee schemes and levels of payment, which we discussed earlier. At the time of writing, these recommendations are yet to see the full light of day.

For the further education sector, the review made a number of important observations and significant recommendations for change. FE is a vital part of the educational system, encompassing a wide variety of technical colleges, colleges of further education, adult and community colleges. FE in particular plays a key role in community-based learning, adult and lifelong learning, and vocational and functional qualifications, including apprenticeships.

The Augar review concluded there was a 'powerful' case for change in the FE sector that has been subject to 'inflexible' and administratively costly rules, and which in recent years has had its ability to innovate and plan for the long term 'severely restricted' by the funding regime. The review also recommended the sector needed to be rationalized, with a more consistent focus and purpose supported by proper investment.

This work is much needed and was given additional impetus from the work by the Independent Commission on the College of the Future. I was involved directly in this work as a commissioner, and the remit of the Commission was to look at what we want and need from the college system in the coming 10 years. The conclusions were published in the summer of 2020 and made a powerful case for better investment and support to the FE sector and to raise its profile as a key part of the educational system. There was strong emphasis on the need for adult and lifelong learning and closer connections with employers to provide localized hubs of learning to directly address skills gaps, as well as to increase the quality and diversity of teaching to help raise standards across the sector.[40]

In summary, then, we have a complex and often confusing approach to education. There are many long-held beliefs about what comprises 'a good education', which have often felt more about a closed system structured around paradigms of testing and achieving examinations rather than real-life outcomes.

It seems clear that we must aim for a better balance of different forms of education, but that itself will require a lot more 'education' of young people, parents and employers. Government policy is a key lever for change. But policy needs to look systemically and holistically at all forms of education and routes to work over the longer term to find the right balance and the changes that need to be made

Any significant level of change along the lines of some of what we have discussed will take a lot of collective effort and belief, and a much broader understanding of the shifts in skills demand and educational needs that are becoming more and more visible. We will need to look out further to the future to set a direction, beyond the paradigms and constraints of today, and then come back to a roadmap that might get us there.

However, as with all systems, sometimes the stimulus for change comes from outside.

New models for education – the disruptors

Having discussed the traditional forms of education and where change is happening and is needed, Education 4.0 is also throwing up completely new and different models for education.

These models are the disruptors of the future, meeting educational needs in very different ways. Just as with many industry sectors, education has to embrace, adapt or find itself potentially compromised by these models.

The pandemic has greatly accelerated the development and uptake of digital learning programmes. Across all forms of education and learning, from schools to universities, as well as in the corporate world, teaching has had to adapt and to go more online. The trend for digital and online learning will grow much faster as a result. We have all learned from this experience and it has dissipated some of the resistance from both teachers and learners. However, enforced remote learning has also shown the real importance and value of group and peer learning, and of social interaction.

Just as for places of work and how we work, the pandemic has created the opportunity to shift how we educate – to focus more on face to face as an opportunity for social and peer learning, and to use digital learning to impart direct knowledge and learning in ways that can best suit the individual learner. Digital and online learning is opening up access to learning and education everywhere and providing more choice. It will shape the future of education and learning, and we are still in the early phases of this revolution.

MOOCs are a great indicator of possible futures of education. Massive open online courses officially began in 2007 with the first free online course offered by David Wiley, a professor at Utah State University, enrolling 50 online students from eight countries joining five face-to-face students.

The courses are massive because enrolments are unlimited, open because anyone can enrol and there is no admission process, online as they are delivered via the internet (typically they comprise video lessons and online learning, readings, discussion forums) and are courses because they teach specific subjects.

MOOCs emerged from universities, notably Stanford, Harvard and MIT, and the Open University in the UK. The established platforms of Udacity, Coursera, edX and FutureLearn really took off from around 2011, but others are emerging, such as Swayam, a MOOC sponsored by the Indian government in 2017.

According to Class Central,[41] a search engine, discovery platform and review site for MOOCs, these platforms now support an estimated 180 million learners (not including China), strongly boosted by the pandemic, with over 16,000 courses from a base of almost 1,000 universities worldwide and increasingly from organizations – tech companies like Microsoft and Google, but also professional bodies and other types of learning institutions. The CIPD launched two five-week courses at three hours' learning per week on FutureLearn in 2017 – HR Fundamentals, and People Management Skills – which together have had more than 100,000 enrolments.

Figure 6.6 shows the rapid rate of growth of the number of courses being offered.

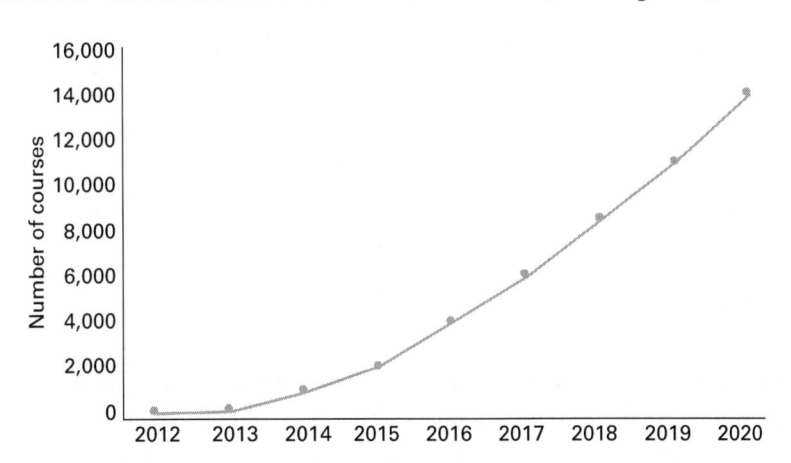

FIGURE 6.6 Growth of online courses offered as MOOCs (excluding China)

SOURCE Class Central

As with any new and innovative business models, it has taken time for MOOCs to develop, to find the best ways to retain students and increase the very low initial course completion rates, and to develop their sources of income. Universities also have found themselves in the interesting position of fuelling the growth of MOOCs but also wondering how they may impact their own business models.

The big shifts for MOOCs and new educational models in general have been emerging from credentialization – from full online degrees to micro credentials. These have given opportunities also to apply charging to students to complete and gain recognized credentials. A big advantage over traditional education systems is great flexibility. Courses can be modularized and delivered in many different ways. So called nano-degrees have emerged which can be completed in less than 12 months.

Digital badging is also rapidly emerging to allow individuals to capture their learning credentials digitally and for employers and others to see and validate them.

Digital badges may capture all forms of learning, formal and informal, from established educators, private training providers or corporations. This will create other challenges of validating the veracity of the training that underpins these credentials, and the need for common approaches and standards. However, as noted, that issue exists in many ways for our existing systems of certification and qualifications.

Corporate universities

The other significant growth in the wider world of education is the way in which corporates have developed and branded their own learning programmes as corporate universities and academies.

There are many good employers which sponsor and encourage their workforce to gain further formal education. Employer-sponsored degrees have a long tradition. According to the Higher Education Policy Institute, 10 per cent of students (235,000 students) across UK universities are on employer-sponsored degrees.[42] The Institute argues, though, that this number can and should be a lot higher.

Many large corporations, private as well as public, have pulled together their training programmes and investments and branded them as corporate academies or universities to give them a stronger focus, and to signal their commitment to training and development. These programmes also help to strengthen the sense of corporate identity and culture, and themselves can be major attractors of talent to an organization.

Initially these corporate institutions tended to focus on executive and leadership development, but most have extended into training at all levels. Some open up their programmes to people outside their organizations, such as suppliers, customers or partners – Disney University is an example – while others, such as Apple University, are very selective even within the organization.

The idea is not new – GE established its well-known Crotonville campus in 1956, and McDonald's set up its Hamburger University in 1962. They have extended this belief in providing education to all their workforce in recent years.

In 2015 McDonald's launched its Archways to Opportunity programme. This gives employees the chance to earn a high school diploma, receive upfront college tuition assistance, access free education advising services and learn English as a second language. It has helped thousands of employees to progress within and beyond the company. One of the success statistics McDonald's is proud of is that over 90 per cent of people in management roles in the company started as crew members serving in the restaurants.

While the US set the trend, partly because the term university was less protected, many others have followed, with some estimates of more than 10,000 globally. They are not accredited or recognized within the traditional educational system, but some do partner with accredited universities and business schools.

A collective association called the Global Council of Corporate Universities was set up in 2007 and now counts thousands of members across all continents. Its certification programme sets out the ambition and purpose for these universities – gaining its certificate requires the institution to show it 'is a true Corporate University, challenges and implements their business strategies, challenges and implements their Corporate Responsibility commitments'.

I personally experienced Accenture's corporate campus in St Charles just outside Chicago many times during my early career. Not only was it a college-like learning experience, but it was the most memorable way in which we could identify with the corporate culture, and was a powerful way of establishing networks and relationships across a highly distributed global firm which never had a single central corporate headquarters. I have subsequently visited many corporate training centres and corporate universities, many with impressive facilities that would rival any traditional business school.

It has been debated for many years whether corporate universities represent a threat to the traditional educational system. What is evident is that corporate universities move and adapt quickly. They have to continue to show a return in the value of applied teaching and learning they bring, and they are therefore focused on the direct, practical learning needs of employees. They have been embracing digital and remote learning alongside face to face, and many now are emerging as virtual centres of learning.

While they may not provide formally recognized qualifications, 'graduating' from these internal programmes is important for career development in most corporates. Carrying the brand of training with large, successful corporations is likely to grow in status with the demand for up-to-date and market-relevant skills. Universities and colleges should learn from these models, but also seek to collaborate.

Looking ahead, we must continue to look for and encourage the blend of the best of both corporate and traditional education. Education and learning of our workforces need to be seen as a shared responsibility between business and the educational system, sharing also in the funding and sponsorship we will need more and more into the future.

Corporate investments in skills development

Having explored corporate universities as generally good examples of how business is investing in the development of people and skills, what is the overall evidence for skills development in employment?

As we have discussed, education itself cannot solve all the skills gaps at work. Employers cannot expect 'oven-ready' employees to roll straight out of education, or indeed other parts of the labour market, and immediately be effective in roles and jobs, where so many specific and contextual skills are needed. These skills are not just technical job skills but also the skills needed to work effectively in the organization, understanding its working practices and policies, cultures and routines.

Yet it seems that too often the narrative within organizations about skills gaps focuses on the lack of skills in the labour market or candidate pool from which they are trying to recruit.

This reasoning at least highlights the need for organizations to search more widely and to be more diverse in their recruitment practices and the candidate pools in which they are searching – important in its own right. But it also appears to place the burden of skills and career development on individual job seekers, and on the educational system at large. The imperative for organizations to invest more in developing the skills they need should be obvious.

As noted by the Brookings Institute in the US,[43] there is not so much a skills gap as an opportunity gap. A change in mindset is needed to encourage organizations to widen their search for more diverse talent and to recognize their role, and their responsibility, in investing properly in skills development.

This view was also observed by PwC in its most recent global CEO survey.[44] 'One reality is clear: increases in automation, changes in demographics and new regulations will make it much harder for organizations to attract and retain the skilled talent they need to keep pace with the speed of technological change. They will have to grow their own future workforce.'

However, the reality is that the level to which organizations are consistently upskilling and reskilling their people is a very mixed bag.

In the past, executives sometimes talked of training their people as being counterproductive, with a distorted philosophy along the lines of 'if I invest in them, then they are more valuable to others and more likely to leave'.

Happily, sense has mostly prevailed and leaders recognize the truth of the counterargument which was often expressed as 'but what if you don't train them and they stay?' If we are not training people then not only will they be less able to do their jobs and be productive, but they are also more likely to leave as people expect their employers to invest in them properly.

This intuitive argument correlates with data and research. For example, the EU in its annual Employment and Social Developments in Europe review[45] highlighted that to continue economic growth, the EU will need to invest in people's skills and innovation. And that the best-performing EU firms are those that invest most in workers' training and high-quality working conditions. 'Indeed, investments in skills, qualifications, and formal adult training support employability of workers, wage growth, and firms' competitiveness.'

However, corporate training and learning is treated as an expense. It always appears in budgets and plans and profit and loss statements as a cost item. As indeed do almost all people-related costs. But these costs are in actuality an investment for any business – an investment in improving productivity and effectiveness of people, in their retention, and in increasing the overall knowledge capital of the enterprise.

Furthermore, these costs are rarely consistently captured, or reported. Training budgets and expenditure often get distributed in many areas of business and across budget holders. Some training is hard to separate and account for – for example, incidental or tacit learning, or embedded learning as part of doing the job. Even where there are centrally managed training programmes such as through corporate universities, there will still be many other localized training initiatives taking place.

Corporate learning often is seen by line managers as bureaucratic, not timely and responsive enough, and not always meeting specific needs they have for their teams or parts of the business.

This points to another widespread issue in business which limits training initiatives and investments: time pressure. Most managers feel themselves under pressure and will be making their own judgements about how and whether to spend their own time and that of their direct reports on training. In times of crisis this becomes even more true.

Towards Maturity, a learning research and benchmarking organization, now part of Emerald Works, highlighted both a lack of real learning culture in organizations and resistance from managers.[46] Almost a third (29 per cent) of L&D professionals say managers are reluctant to make time for learning.

Corporate learning does need to change to be more adaptive and responsive, and we will explore this further in Chapter 12. There is no doubt that organizational agility and ability to respond to changing skills needs will be more and more dependent on corporate training and learning capabilities. Investment in skills development therefore needs to be seen strategically, and not just as an item of expense.

Understanding the value of learning and training

A popular saying about marketing by business leaders is that they know that at least half of their marketing spend is adding value, but that they don't know which half. That would certainly relate to training and learning as well.

Without this clear line of sight, it is too easy for finance teams and executives facing cost pressures to see training spend as a soft target. And that is what happens. Repeatedly through economic downturns or individual corporate crises, spend on skills development in businesses drops. Even if it is in these times when proper training may be most needed. Short-termism and focus on near-term profit as we noted in Chapter 2 clearly exacerbate this issue, since training outcomes are future-oriented and payback may take time.

Even with the caveats of the weaknesses of measurement or accounting for training in organizations, the evidence of declining levels of investment in training in the workplace makes these points clear. And not only declining but also lower average levels of spend in training is particularly apparent in the UK.

The employment rate in the UK, and in many countries, was the highest on record in 2019 at 76.6 per cent, having grown steadily since the 2008 recession. Vacancies were high and the unemployment rate was low at 3.9 per cent.

Yet, employer skills investment fell across virtually all measures during the same period.

Research from the Trades Union Congress indicated that the volume of employer-led training in the UK has declined by a half since the end of the 1990s.[47] The UK government's latest biennial Employer Skills Survey for 2019 showed that an extraordinary 39 per cent of employers admit to training none of their staff over the last year – a rise of 5 per cent from the previous survey.[48] This is much stronger among smaller employers who often lack the resources and funding, and has certainly not been helped by the 45 per cent real-terms fall in the government-funded Adult Education Budget between 2010 and 2018.

Internationally, the UK compares poorly when it comes to workforce training. The amount spent per employee on training in the UK in 2015 was estimated to be just half the average spent across EU countries.[49]

The Continuous Vocational Training Survey (CVTS)[50] shows a marked decline of 23 per cent over the decade in training investment per employee. While there was a slight overall increase in expenditure as a share of labour costs, spend per employee and training cost per hour fell between 2005 and 2015. This was in contrast to growth across the EU of 22 per cent. This is highlighted in Figure 6.7.

As CIPD research has indicated,[51] the relatively lower levels of investment in corporate training across the UK workforce may be related to business strategies that invest less in technology in the workplace, as we have previously noted, and therefore more low-skilled jobs requiring lower

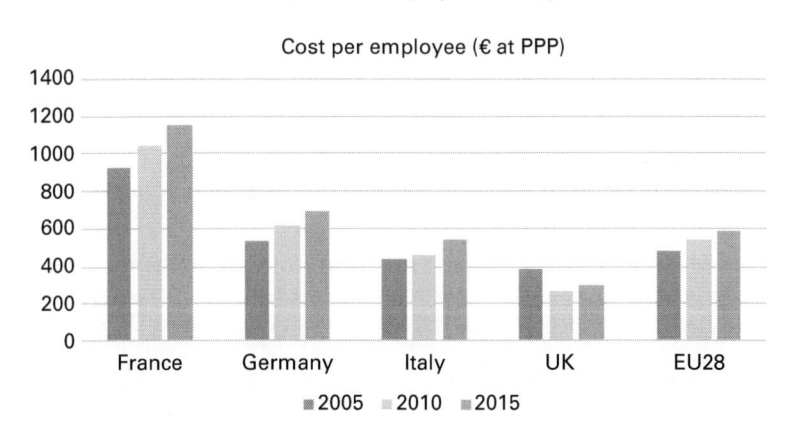

FIGURE 6.7 Relative levels of spend on employee training

SOURCE Eurostat

levels of skills and qualifications. It is also reasonable to assume that the UK's much discussed lower productivity levels are a likely outcome of lower investment in workforce development together with higher levels of low-skilled jobs.

Evidence from the latest UK Skills and Employment Survey assessed by the UCL Institute of Education lends some weight to this view.[52] The SES (1986–2017) points to a worrying fall in the use of high-level literacy and numeracy at work and a stagnation in social skills and self-planning skills, which 'indicate a slowdown in the demand for high level generic skills since 2012'.

However, at the same time, this survey and others have shown the increase in graduate recruitment over the period from the late 1980s. So another important factor in the relative lack of corporate investment in people may even be the expansion of the higher education system itself. Ready access to apparently more qualified people coming out of education has reduced the perceived need for employers to train.

Research by the CIPD in 2018[53] on how employers were viewing different levels of qualifications in hiring showed a strong bias towards graduates. Sixty-seven per cent of employers reported that they had taken on a graduate for their first job. Just a quarter had recruited a 16-year-old school-leaver to their first job, while just under half recruited a 17- or 18-year-old school-leaver, or from FE colleges.

As part of PwC's regular and respected bi-annual CEO survey[54] covering more than 1,500 CEOs globally, they showed an interesting correlation between the maturity of the national education systems and the preparedness of upskilling programmes.

This is shown in Figure 6.8. The graph is based on the questions of how much progress their organization had made in establishing an upskilling programme that develops a mix of soft, technical and digital skills, and what they regarded as most important to close a potential skills gap – showing the aggregated percentage of external sources (eg hiring from outside my industry, establishing a strong pipeline from education).

This data shows this trend of reliance on education to meet the skills needs of organizations, and the related underinvestment or lack of focus on internal workforce development, and the converse where educational systems are less mature

But as we observed earlier in the chapter, attitudes among employers are changing. According to a YouGov poll in 2020, 56 per cent of UK businesses said that a job candidate having a degree was 'not very important' or 'not important at all', with only 39 per cent saying that it was 'very' or 'somewhat' important. An additional 5 per cent said they did not know. However,

FIGURE 6.8 Relative importance of education vs preparedness in organizational upskilling programmes

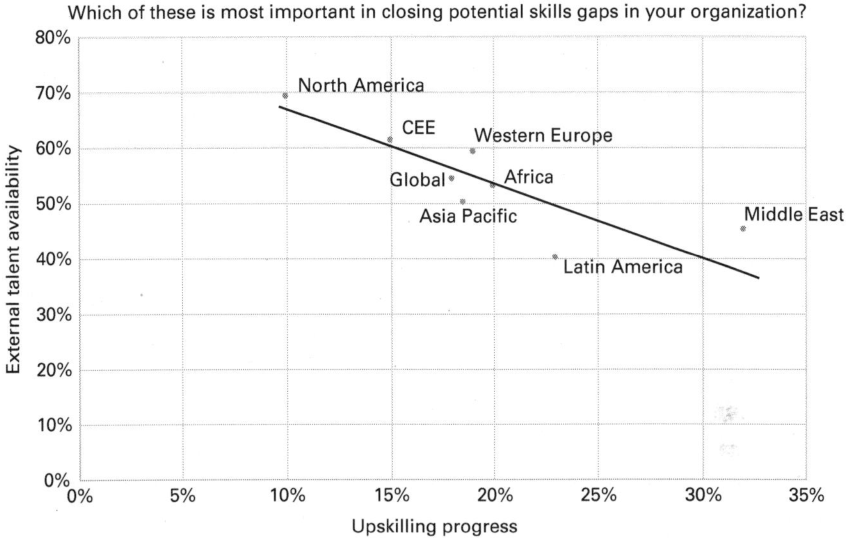

Which of these is most important in closing potential skills gaps in your organization?

[Scatter plot with x-axis "Upskilling progress" (0%–35%) and y-axis "External talent availability" (0%–80%). Data points: North America (~10%, 68%), CEE (~13%, 62%), Western Europe (~18%, 60%), Global (~15%, 55%), Africa (~18%, 55%), Asia Pacific (~17%, 50%), Middle East (~33%, 48%), Latin America (~23%, 43%). A downward trend line is shown.]

SOURCE PwC Global CEO Survey 2020

the larger the business, the more important it seems that a degree is in the hiring process. Fifty-six per cent of businesses with over 250 employees said that a degree was important, compared with only 20 per cent of businesses with less than 10 employees.

In conclusion

The need to support and encourage lifelong learning has never been more apparent. But lifelong learning should be seen as a shared enterprise, across society, educational systems and business. Learning is a gift and something everyone should see and recognize that it never stops. Education is not just something for the young.

Author John Coleman references Doreetha Daniels who in 2015, aged 99, received her associate degree in social sciences from California's College of the Canyons.[55] Daniels indicated that she wanted to get her degree simply to better herself.

Education and learning will also have to adapt, to become more flexible and more related to real-life learning and the different means by which people are learning in a digital world. Different forms of accreditation and means of capturing people's experiences and records of learning will become prevalent. There must be more focus on the core and essential skills that should be critical to educational outcomes. These are the building blocks for everyone to progress in work and in life.

But a lot of policy and investment change will be needed. The huge amounts of investment in education need to become better balanced and spread, and employers need to take more responsibility for investment in training and development – for their own interests as well as for their collective social responsibility. Ideas like providing budgets to individuals to support and encourage their learning and development need to be promoted and revisited, along with individual learning accounts that give people more choice and flexibility in learning throughout their lives, and particularly to support the growing population of the self-employed.

Much closer blending of workplace learning and formal education and qualifications should be part of this. That is why VET and apprenticeships are good models, from basic levels of skills and qualifications up to degree level.

Much needs to be done, but it is encouraging to see more of the strategic longer-term thinking emerging.

In December 2020, the UK parliament Education Committee published its report titled 'Plan for an Adult Skills and Lifelong Learning Revolution'.[56] Its primary recommendations included a shift in funding to spread the investments in education and learning more, a community learning centre in every town, individual learning accounts and boosting part-time higher education and employer-led training. As we have discussed, these are all very good policy areas to work on.

But we should add the need to provide for much better support for careers advice and guidance. Having the skills is one thing, but navigating and understanding the increasingly diverse and complex world of work and work opportunities is another. We will return to this theme in later chapters.

Endnotes

1 www.cbi.org.uk/media-centre/articles/a-radical-new-strategy-for-lifetime-reskilling-must-be-the-bedrock-of-uk-economic-recovery-cbi/ (archived at https://perma.cc/EEU3-RT7G)

2 www2.deloitte.com/us/en/pages/chief-executive-officer/articles/ceo-survey-gauging-priorities.html (archived at https://perma.cc/FB7K-54SF)

3 https://home.kpmg/xx/en/home/insights/2020/08/global-ceo-outlook-2020.html (archived at https://perma.cc/N5DP-ECX7)

4 www.hays-index.com/full-report/ (archived at https://perma.cc/WC2A-6SWH)

5 www.open.ac.uk/business/Business-Barometer-2019 (archived at https://perma.cc/256C-RZQ6)
6 www.nuffieldtrust.org.uk/files/2018-11/health-foundation-king-s-fund-and-nuffield-trust-the-health-care-workforce-in-england.pdf (archived at https://perma.cc/5M57-PDJY)
7 www.ibm.com/downloads/cas/EPYMNBJA (archived at https://perma.cc/M3QN-UAMQ)
8 www.cv-library.co.uk/recruitment-insight/employers-favour-workers/ (archived at https://perma.cc/DM75-5FRE)
9 www.ibe.unesco.org/en/glossary-curriculum-terminology/b/basic-skills (archived at https://perma.cc/49R6-EWLN)
10 www.skillsbuilder.org/blog/announcing-the-skills-builder-universal-framework (archived at https://perma.cc/2RPU-XBP6)
11 https://assets.publishing.service.gov.uk/government/uploads/system/uploads/attachment_data/file/738922/Essential_digital_skills_framework.pdf (archived at https://perma.cc/P9CW-ZLBR)
12 www.pewsocialtrends.org/essay/millennial-life-how-young-adulthood-today-compares-with-prior-generations/ (archived at https://perma.cc/6DBJ-ULQG)
13 Dewey, J (1934) Individual psychology and education, *The Philosopher*, 12
14 http://www3.weforum.org/docs/WEF_Schools_of_the_Future_Report_2019.pdf (archived at https://perma.cc/NJ6B-PMJ7)
15 www.ted.com/talks/sir_ken_robinson_do_schools_kill_creativity?language=en (archived at https://perma.cc/RM44-UGZR)
16 www.cnedu.pt/content/noticias/internacional/Education_at_a_glance_2018.pdf (archived at https://perma.cc/P946-8E5F)
17 Rosling, H, Rosling, O and Rosling Ronnlund, A (2018) Factfulness – ten reasons we are wrong about the world, and why things are better than you think, *Sceptre*, London
18 www.undp.org/content/undp/en/home/sustainable-development-goals/goal-4-quality-education.html (archived at https://perma.cc/5BNS-TH3H)
19 www.gov.uk/government/news/state-of-the-nation-report-on-social-mobility-in-great-britain (archived at https://perma.cc/ZV4Z-YBWV)
20 www.nationalnumeracy.org.uk/what-issue (archived at https://perma.cc/8HG3-SYFR)
21 www.bdadyslexia.org.uk/dyslexia/neurodiversity-and-co-occurring-differences/dyscalculia-and-maths-difficulties (archived at https://perma.cc/EQ5E-BT38)
22 https://commonslibrary.parliament.uk/research-briefings/cbp-7976/ (archived at https://perma.cc/G6C4-57F9)- International and EU students in higher education in the UK FAQs
23 https://www.universitiesuk.ac.uk/policy-and-analysis/reports/Documents/2017/briefing-economic-impact-international-students.pdf (archived at https://perma.cc/AU8F-KQMZ)

24 OECD (2019) Benchmarking Higher Education System Performance, June
25 www.oecd.org/education/education-at-a-glance/EAG2019_CN_GBR.pdf (archived at https://perma.cc/F2BG-WSY9)
26 www.hepi.ac.uk/2020/03/07/mind-the-gap-gender-differences-in-higher-education/ (archived at https://perma.cc/T6C9-AGAU)
27 http://arabfoundationsforum.org/author/AQF/ (archived at https://perma.cc/NGB9-PYGE)
28 https://monitor.icef.com/2019/07/oecd-number-of-degree-holders-worldwide-will-reach-300-million-by-2030/ (archived at https://perma.cc/8LKB-QEPP)
29 www.hesa.ac.uk/news/22-10-2019/return-to-degree-research (archived at https://perma.cc/RWG6-8CPT)
30 http://www.oecd.org/education/thereturntoinvestmentineducation.htm (archived at https://perma.cc/R78Z-MC76)
31 UK Department of Education December (2016) Employment and earnings outcomes of higher education graduates: experimental statistics using the Longitudinal Education Outcomes (LEO) data: further breakdowns
32 www.ifs.org.uk/publications/14729 (archived at https://perma.cc/2VXN-7SRK)
33 https://commonslibrary.parliament.uk/research-briefings/sn01079/ (archived at https://perma.cc/9BZE-LLQE)
34 http://data.europa.eu/doi/10.2801/722857 (archived at https://perma.cc/289W-W5ZQ)
35 Chankseliani, M and Anuar, A M (2019) Cross-country comparison of engagement in apprenticeships, *International Journal for Research in Vocational Education and Training (IJRVET)*, 6 (3), pp 261–83
36 https://commonslibrary.parliament.uk/research-briefings/sn06113/ (archived at https://perma.cc/V75C-NNY6)- Apprenticeship statistics for England
37 www.cipd.co.uk/Images/addressing-employer-underinvestment-in-training_tcm18-61265.pdf (archived at https://perma.cc/2VEW-QJPE)
38 https://register.ofqual.gov.uk/Download (archived at https://perma.cc/T92J-DBS7)
39 www.gov.uk/government/publications/post-18-review-of-education-and-funding-independent-panel-report (archived at https://perma.cc/X7GB-N343)
40 www.collegecommission.co.uk/final-report-uk (archived at https://perma.cc/5ZCS-9D2S)
41 www.classcentral.com/report/mooc-stats-2020 (archived at https://perma.cc/G8PV-UTEA)
42 www.hepi.ac.uk/wp-content/uploads/2016/04/Making-a-success-of-Employer-Sponsored-Education-Report-83.pdf (archived at https://perma.cc/Z68K-CTHL)
43 www.brookings.edu/blog/the-avenue/2020/09/09/the-labor-market-doesnt-have-a-skills-gap-it-has-an-opportunity-gap/ (archived at https://perma.cc/E5C6-TCMK)

44 www.pwc.com/gx/en/ceo-survey/2020/reports/pwc-23rd-global-ceo-survey.pdf (archived at https://perma.cc/B42H-N2YA)
45 https://ec.europa.eu/commission/presscorner/detail/en/IP_19_3412 (archived at https://perma.cc/ZL4S-GCUG)
46 https://emeraldworks.com/research-and-reports/strategy/the-transformation-journey (archived at https://perma.cc/VMM6-NE5Z)
47 Trades Union Congress (ASL0074) Session 2017–19
48 https://assets.publishing.service.gov.uk/government/uploads/system/uploads/attachment_data/file/936488/ESS_2019_Summary_Report_Nov2020.pdf (archived at https://perma.cc/HJ26-JLDF)
49 Social Mobility Commission (2019) The adult skills gap: is falling investment in UK adults stalling social mobility? January, p18
50 http://ec.europa.eu/eurostat/web/education-and-training/data/database (archived at https://perma.cc/M5WS-WGMW)
51 www.cipd.co.uk/Images/addressing-employer-underinvestment-in-training_tcm18-61265.pdf (archived at https://perma.cc/2VEW-QJPE)
52 Henseke, G, Felstead, A, Gallie, D and Green, F (2018) Skills trends at work in Britain: first findings from the Skills and Employment Survey 2017, Centre for Learning and Life Chances in Knowledge Economies and Societies, UCL Institute of Education, London
53 www.cipd.co.uk/Images/reforming-technical-education-report_tcm18-46474.pdf (archived at https://perma.cc/SLB3-9M7E)
54 www.pwc.com/gx/en/ceo-survey/2020/reports/pwc-23rd-global-ceo-survey.pdf (archived at https://perma.cc/B42H-N2YA)
55 https://hbr.org/2017/02/lifelong-learning-is-good-for-your-health-your-wallet-and-your-social-life (archived at https://perma.cc/R7MC-ZZ92)
56 https://committees.parliament.uk/committee/203/education-committee/news/138043/mps-call-for-adult-skills-revolution-to-foster-new-culture-of-lifelong-learning/ (archived at https://perma.cc/AKE4-W3KM)

07

Focusing on the right things

In God we trust – all others must bring data.
                              OFT QUOTED WITH VARIOUS ATTRIBUTIONS

In the previous chapters of this book we explored many of the dimensions of change that are impacting the world of work. The issues are multi-dimensional, fascinating and challenging, in equal measure. They are all being emphasized more through the crises we are experiencing, which themselves are acting as catalysts for change in ways we have not seen in our lifetimes.

It is why this time feels like we are at the beginning of a new era of how we have to think about work and about business – the real shaping of the fourth industrial revolution; about how we move on from many paradigms, standards and norms of work that have been with us for decades, but are being reshaped by technology, by expectations of people and of wider society and by the changing dynamics of our economies. It is a new era of creative destruction.

Work should be good for us, for our wellbeing, for our sense of purpose, development and achievement, and it should be fair and accessible to all. Business is part of society, not apart from society. Business drives our economies, but should do so in responsible ways that benefit all stakeholders, not just financial owners.

In this second half of the book we are not attempting to answer all the questions – that would be impossible as well as delusionary. Rather, the aim is to try to help to progress the thinking, to show what is important and ways we can work together to shape a positive future.

What gets measured gets done

This is a truism that impacts so much of our lives. Things that have no measure remain hard to understand and will lose our focus of attention.

As humans, we're inherently competitive and seek to find ways of measuring our personal success relative to that of others.[1] The types of things we measure on a daily basis – our financial income, of course, but even things like the number on the weighing scales – also create accountability and a means of assessing progress. They're the framework that helps us set appropriate targets and goals.

Businesses, as much as politics and public discourse, are driven by measures and metrics – comparisons to others. It's how we understand progress and what is important, and what our systems of reward and recognition are usually tied to. We've long been exhorted to build so-called SMART objectives – specific, measurable, achievable, relevant and time-limited.

So it seems like a good place to start. To think about what we measure and whether we are measuring the right things – recognizing that measuring the wrong things is equally of concern. How can we be sure we are doing the right things, as well as doing things right?

A maxim that is widely attributed to Albert Einstein, although not originated by him, sums up the challenge in a wonderfully concise way: 'Not everything that counts can be counted, and not everything that can be counted counts.'

This might seem obvious. If something can't easily be quantified – a feeling or an emotion, for example – that doesn't necessarily mean it's devoid of value. However, it is always easier to start with what can be readily counted, even if it may not be the most important thing or the entire picture.

Our measures of business and economic progress for so long have been the hard financial measures of GDP, of revenues and costs, profit and loss and even productivity. But they are not the complete picture or all the things that matter to healthy and functioning businesses and societies. They are the measures of rational economic thinking of people and human behaviour. Our measures of business in particular are very largely backward looking and do not account for all the value or give a clear view of how business is investing for the future.

If we are going to change then we have to measure more of the things that really count. We have to shine a light on the intangibles, the real values of our societies, our impact on the environment, and the wellbeing and happiness of people. We want businesses and business leaders to pay more attention to these things, so we have to find ways of measuring them and incorporating these forward-looking (and thinking) ideas into their reward systems as well. And that is true also for our politicians, policy makers and regulators so we can work collectively to improve our societies as well as our economies.

In Chapter 2 we discussed the issues of intangible value in business, which now accounts for the majority of enterprise value, and we looked at the shortcomings of productivity as a way of assessing the success of a workforce. The measures we predominantly use are tangible and quantifiable, and qualitative or intangible measures take a poor second place.

William Bruce Cameron, a professor of sociology, should be credited with the quote about what counts, Quote Investigator suggests.[2] It cites an article by Cameron in 1963, 'Informal sociology: a casual introduction to sociological thinking', bemoaning the challenges sociologists had in being taken seriously: 'It would be nice if all of the data which sociologists require could be enumerated because then we could run them through IBM machines and draw charts as the economists do.'

I will always remember being told by a CEO of a large company a few years ago that the problem with HR is they brought too much PowerPoint and not enough Excel. I responded by acknowledging the issue of HR getting better with numbers and analytics, but at the same time that business can't be run just from numbers on spreadsheets.

Understanding the corporate culture, how engaged staff are, their wellbeing and levels of innovation, along with recognizing the tacit knowledge capital within an organization, all greatly impact longer-term value and sustainability. These are harder to quantify or count, and instead of value in many of these areas we look at the easier things to measure, reducing people to elements of cost or 'resources'.

Measuring the big things

Let's start by looking at how we measure our economies, our societies and the things that are truly important to life.

In a March 1968 speech at the University of Kansas,[3] Robert F. Kennedy stated that erasing material poverty was important, but that a far greater task was to 'confront the poverty of satisfaction – purpose and dignity – that afflicts us all'. He also drew out arguments about the limits of what we measure, and in particular GDP as the primary measure of a nation's progress.

Kennedy asserted that for far too long, Americans had 'surrendered personal excellence and community values in the mere accumulation of material things', and went on:

> Our Gross National Product, now, is over $800 billion dollars a year, but that Gross National Product – if we judge the United States of America by that – that Gross National Product counts air pollution and cigarette advertising, and ambulances to clear our highways of carnage. It counts special locks for our doors and the jails for the people who break them. It counts the destruction of the redwood and the loss of our natural wonder in chaotic sprawl. It counts napalm and counts nuclear warheads and armored cars for the police to fight the riots in our cities. It counts Whitman's rifle and Speck's knife, and the television programs which glorify violence in order to sell toys to our children.
>
> Yet the Gross National Product does not allow for the health of our children, the quality of their education or the joy of their play. It does not include the beauty of our poetry or the strength of our marriages, the intelligence of our public debate or the integrity of our public officials. It measures neither our wit nor our courage, neither our wisdom nor our learning, neither our compassion nor our devotion to our country, it measures everything in short, except that which makes life worthwhile. And it can tell us everything about America except why we are proud that we are Americans.

More than half a century on, Kennedy's words still sing with relevance. Pollution, the destruction of the redwood and the loss of our natural wonder in chaotic sprawl, are all obvious characteristics of the great climate crisis that we're failing to counteract. By any measure of where we are on climate change, we have gone significantly backwards over the 40–50 years since Kennedy's speech.

The way we measure things still widely assumes our economy is powered by the buying and selling of goods – of physical capital. But technological advances have altered the DNA of our economic system and rendered the metrics we use to measure it inadequate.

Environmentalists have spent years arguing that GDP treats the exploitation of the earth as something that creates economic value when it should be treated as something that incurs a significant cost. Similarly, sociologists and the many different forms of social democratic movements have long argued that our economic measures are not treating people as anything other than units of production or resources. The cost to people of stress at work, inequality and unfairness, or lack of support and recognition, all have a significant individual and collective social cost.

However, there are now much more positive signs. We have greatly increased our understanding and ability to communicate the issues of environment and climate change because we are better at measuring things – global temperatures, the rate of ice cap melting, air pollution, the ozone layer, levels of plastics in our oceans and rates of deforestation.

This is driving change ranging from individual behaviour in how we consume to movements like Extinction Rebellion and a strong voice among the younger generation to challenge those in power to take real action. Politicians everywhere are having to respond, and so are businesses.

We have found a more common language in carbon offset and our carbon footprint, which businesses are signalling and increasingly reporting on. Responsible businesses are looking within their organizations but also into their supply chains, and engaging directly with their customers. Given public sentiment and attention to environmental issues, at least they know it is important for their brand.

There is, however, little consistent – if any – regulation on what businesses should do. Some, like many airlines, have tended to put part of the onus on the customer – add something voluntarily to the price of a ticket to offset the carbon impact of the flight. Or plant-a-tree schemes. Not much data available on the real uptake, and practically as well as morally rather questionable.

But on a positive note and to the point of this discussion, the environment really will be one of the big crises that better measurement is making us more aware of, and showing us where and how to make a difference.

As for all the other issues Kennedy drew out in his speech, and as many others have recognized, we have not made significant progress. As we explored in previous chapters, issues like social inequality and division are as challenging as ever.

It may be that things have to get worse before they can get better, to be at a level where enough people see these things or are directly impacted. Conflicting evidence and beliefs are fuelled by social media, acting as further barriers to change. The pandemic showed this in many ways with conspiracy theories, debates about infringements on personal freedoms, and resistance to vaccination.

Moving on, though, what particularly was inspiring about Kennedy's speech was how he talked about the things that are important to our lives. As he said, GDP measures 'everything in short, except that which makes life worthwhile'.

Life satisfaction, purpose and wellbeing

This idea of what is important in life or even life's purpose has been debated since Aristotle. In perhaps one of Aristotle's most famous works, *Nicomachean*

Ethics, the Greek philosopher argues that all human beings' highest aim in life is *Eudaimonia*, which roughly translates as contentment and wellbeing,[4] or what has been described as the good life. As he said, 'The life of money-making is one undertaken under compulsion, and wealth is evidently not the good we are seeking; for it is merely useful and for the sake of something else.'

Of course, this theme can get deeply philosophical and even religious – is there a purpose of humanity? Not really the purview of this book, but the fact is that humans generally look for and need a purpose. It's a key motivator, as behavioural science has shown us, and it helps align and channel what we do. We will return to this thought in later chapters, particularly in Chapter 8 on responsible business.

These ideas of what is really important have never really gone away, but they are getting something of a renaissance today. How do we as societies, and indeed as organizations, better understand wider purpose and what else beyond economic growth we should be striving for? Arguably the younger generations have brought this more to the fore. They have looked at their parents and often wondered why they work in the ways they do and to what end.

Which is not to say that consumerism doesn't continue to be such a huge force. That of itself is another question that economists and philosophers have been asking – how much is enough?

Robert and Edward Skidelsky in their book *How Much Is Enough? Money and the good life* had a good go at this theme.[5] They began with the prediction by John Maynard Keynes that we referenced earlier in Chapter 5 that we would all be working 15-hour weeks and why that had not happened. Keynes' view was that technology would radically improve productivity and we could therefore produce what we needed with far fewer hours of work. What he hadn't reckoned with was that the more we produced, the more we seemed to consume. The Skidelskys made similar calls for a shift in our focus about what is important and to better understand what really makes for a good life.

These points have all been leading to the broader idea of measures of happiness, wellbeing, social cohesion and other measures of what is important beyond just economic growth and money.

Academics have also joined the chorus calling for a measurement reform. Echoing the words of Bobby Kennedy, Joseph Stiglitz, the influential US economist and Nobel laureate, has argued that GDP fails to capture the impact of climate change, inequality, digital services and other phenomena shaping modern societies.[6]

'Can a modern economy deliver shared prosperity? And can democracies thrive if our economies fail to deliver shared prosperity? These are critical questions, yet the accepted ways by which we measure economic performance give absolutely no hint that we might be facing a problem. Each of these crises has reinforced the fact that we need better tools to assess economic performance and social progress,' Stiglitz wrote.

In 2009, the Stiglitz-Sen-Fitoussi Commission[7] that he led promoted the value of governments shifting emphasis from measuring GDP to measuring citizens' wellbeing or Gross Domestic Wellbeing. The OECD responded to the commission by creating the influential Better Life Index, which measures societal wellbeing across a range of indicators, including housing, civic engagement and life satisfaction.[8]

Writing in the *Guardian* in 2019, the Nobel laureate argued that the world is facing three existential crises: a climate crisis, an inequality crisis and a crisis in democracy, and that it was 'time to retire' metrics like GDP.[9]

The spread of Covid-19 around the world in 2020 only emphasized Stiglitz's argument. Figures like GDP and unemployment obviously go some way to reflecting the damage wrought by the virus, but they won't shine a light on the multifaceted social and wellbeing impacts on individuals, families, communities and businesses.

It is useful to explore where these endeavours have got to, as there are direct parallels with what we want to measure within organizations – we will explore these in subsequent chapters. And if we can focus more on happiness, wellbeing, social support and cohesion, for example as corporate, national and international agendas, it sets a positive context for all of us.

Gross National Happiness – is it for real?

Measuring national happiness as a construct has received a lot more attention since around 2011. Much of the drive for this came from Bhutan, a land-locked Himalayan country with a population of around three quarters of a million. In 1972 the fourth king of the South Asian country, King Jigme Singye Wangchuck, coined the phrase 'gross national happiness' when he declared in an interview that 'Gross National Happiness is more important than Gross Domestic Product'.[10]

The premise of the King's concept was that sustainable development should adopt a holistic approach to notions of progress and treat economic and non-economic aspects equally[11] – areas such as wellbeing, education, time use, cultural and ecological diversity and even good governance. The ideas were rooted in the Buddhist faith and tradition of belief in compassion, calmness and contentment – always in such stark contrast to the predominantly materialistic traditions of the West.

In 2011, the UN unanimously adopted a General Assembly resolution,[12] introduced by Bhutan with support from 68 member states, calling for a 'holistic approach to development' aimed at promoting sustainable happiness and wellbeing. The following year, the UN hosted a High-Level Meeting on *Happiness and Wellbeing: Defining a New Economic Paradigm*. It was designed to bring political and spiritual leaders together, with experts and civil society, to devise an economic paradigm based on the concepts of sustainability and wellbeing pioneered by Bhutan.

From this meeting came the first World Happiness Report with the aim of bringing together the available global data on national happiness and reviewing evidence from the emerging science of happiness. And we can all enjoy March 20 each year as the United Nations' International Day of Happiness.

Although the World Happiness Reports have been based on a wide variety of data, the most important source has always been the Gallup World Poll. This surveys people in now more than 160 countries on issues such as food access, employment, leadership performance and wellbeing.[13]

The eighth and latest version of the World Happiness Report published in March 2020[14] (and therefore based on data before the global pandemic) as it has in recent years places Nordic countries at the top – Finland, Denmark, Iceland, Norway and Sweden make up five of the top seven places.

While these countries have high GDP per capita, there is interesting analysis of factors which make them stand out, specifically the importance of positive trust and social connections. As the report states, 'Together the changes in trust and social connections explain 60 per cent of the happiness gap between the Nordic countries and Europe as a whole.'

The UK lies at 13th in the index, with Germany at 17th, the US at 18th and France at 23rd. China is at 94th and India is at 144th, and most of the African countries lie in the bottom quartile. There is an undeniable link between overall economic prosperity and happiness as measured, but it is clearly not the only driver. Very developed nations like South Korea and Japan lie at 61st and 62nd respectively.

Bhutan itself was last reported in 2019 at 95th, and faces many challenges of poverty, income, inequality, youth unemployment and even the introduction of democracy. Dorji Penjore, an anthropologist who has extensively researched Bhutan's policy of GNH, along with others has warned that the mystical trouble-free Bhutan lives mostly in the imagination of the West.[15]

Another issue identified has been the spread of technological developments which have also created rifts in the country and facilitated a spread of Western-style consumerism, tensions also observable in other countries with less traditionally materialistic and more spiritual cultures.

Some take issue with the methodology of happiness measurement, not least Bhutan itself. The concept of happiness is highly nuanced and has many variations across different languages. The idea we are trying to get at should be a longer-term sense of contentment and feeling positive, and not some transient thing influenced by how good a day I am having. Happiness can be quite ephemeral.

But we all strive for it. In 2018, a course offered to undergraduates at Yale purporting to teach them how to lead a happier, more satisfying life became the most popular ever for the university.[16] In India, meanwhile, the Delhi school system added happiness to its curriculum[17] – explicitly citing Bhutan. In 2016, the UAE became the first country to formally appoint a Minister of State for Happiness and launched the National Programme for Happiness and Positivity.[18]

Gross National Wellbeing

Other countries have unveiled commitments to their own versions of GNH, with a strong focus on wellbeing.

The UK has been at the forefront of trying to understand and measure wellbeing and individual purpose at a national level. The Office for National Statistics in trying to assess personal sense of wellbeing uses four questions (known generally as the ONS4) aimed at capturing three types of wellbeing: evaluative (evaluate how satisfied overall you are with your life), eudemonic (having a sense of meaning and purpose) and affective experience (happiness and anxiety). They are shown in Table 7.1.

TABLE 7.1 Personal wellbeing measures

Measure	Question
Life satisfaction	Overall, how satisfied are you with your life nowadays?
Worthwhile	Overall, to what extent do you feel that the things you do in your life are worthwhile?
Happiness	Overall, how happy did you feel yesterday?
Anxiety	On a scale where 0 is 'not at all anxious' and 10 is 'completely anxious', overall, how anxious did you feel yesterday?

SOURCE Office for National Statistics

The OECD has adopted the UK measures and they are now used across 22 nations. The ONS4 measures are being used across a wide range of intervention types to evaluate effectiveness, including areas like the impact of social care support, volunteering, arts and culture, physical activity and skills training.

The UK's What Works Centre for Wellbeing has carried out the first full analysis of the data.[19] The research shows that sense of purpose and wellbeing varies with age – best for the over-65s and worse for those in mid-life and the over-85s. Factors like self-reported good health, positive use of leisure time including social activity outdoors and involvement in cultural activities were all more important for people's wellbeing and purpose than wealth or material possession. Also those who are self-employed tend to show higher levels of wellbeing.

In May 2019, New Zealand, mired by years of rising wealth inequality, introduced a Wellbeing Budget under which new spending must go to five priority areas: aiding the transition to a sustainable and low-emissions economy, supporting a thriving nation in the digital age, lifting Māori and Pacific incomes, skills and opportunities, reducing child poverty, and supporting mental health for all New Zealanders.

In December of that year, Iceland's prime minister Katrin Jakobsdóttir joined Scottish first minister Nicola Sturgeon and New Zealand's prime minister Jacinda Ardern to promote a 'wellbeing' agenda.[20] Jakobsdóttir explicitly called for new indicators of economic health, beyond GDP. Results will take some time to come through clearly from these initiatives, but New Zealand ranked eighth in the Global Happiness Index; despite their recognized issues, they were not starting from a bad place by this measure.

There seems to be a common thread in that these countries are all led by women. Theresa May, former UK prime minister, also brought some stronger focus to mental health and even introduced a government strategy on loneliness,[21] recognizing it as 'one of the greatest public health challenges of our time'.

Although there has been more attention on wellbeing measures in the UK – the ONS Wellbeing Dashboard was developed in 2011 – there are many gaps and GDP remains the primary measure of the UK's progress at political levels.

In December 2020, the Carnegie UK Trust, a charitable organization committed to understanding and improving work and wellbeing, published its report, 'Gross Domestic Wellbeing (GDWe™): an alternative measure of social progress'.[22] Carnegie takes a holistic approach to thinking about wellbeing, as others have tried to do. Its model, reproduced in Figure 7.1, is a good summary. It identifies measures or 'areas of life' across the SEED

FIGURE 7.1 Carnegie UK Trust's SEED approach to societal wellbeing

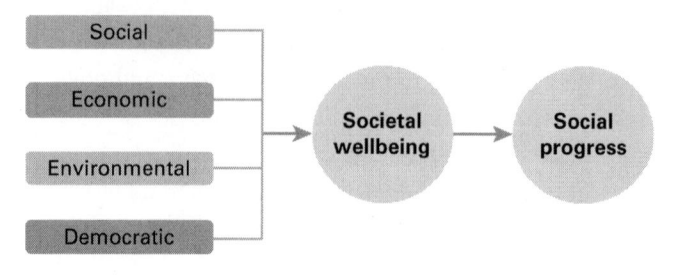

SOURCE Carnegie UK Trust

dimensions, including areas such as health, relationships, what people do, personal finance, and the economy and environment.

Perhaps the most striking finding of the research based on this index looking back over the last six years is that even before the pandemic hit, there was a downward trend in national wellbeing (this based on data for England). And, that when plotted against GDP growth over the same period, there has been a stark disconnect, as shown in Figure 7.2. This is more evidence if needed that we have to move beyond just economic measures to understand the social health of our nations and our people.

FIGURE 7.2 Growth of GDWe™ and GDP as a percentage from baseline in 2013/14

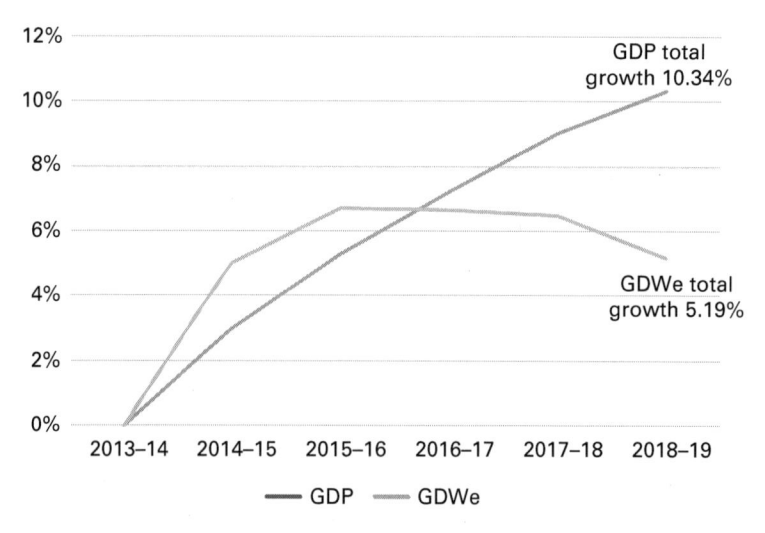

SOURCE Carnegie UK Trust

Acknowledging business responsibilities to all stakeholders

The idea of responsible business has grown in particular from the notions of corporate social responsibility, addressing the issues of trust and meeting the wider expectations of society – in other words, the wider set of accountabilities and responsibilities beyond just the financial owner or shareholder.

A shift, as we discussed in Chapter 2, from the Friedman doctrine of shareholder primacy to a wider notion of stakeholder capitalism.

Following the global financial crisis in 2008, the outcry about business behaviour and what was seen as many businesses' lack of accountability was a pivotal point in time. Of course, business has to aim to make money, but not at any cost or consequence. Understanding a wider sense of accountability to all those impacted by the actions and decisions of businesses gathered pace.

The multi-stakeholder view emphasizes all the stakeholders in a business – all those who are impacted by business actions, and whose viewpoint or needs should be taken into account. The financial stakeholder includes the financial owners and shareholders. But customers, suppliers, employees, communities and society, and the environment are all stakeholders as well.

Focusing on all stakeholders not only creates a wider understanding of the accountabilities of business, it also promotes a longer-term value creation focus. This is sometimes now being referred to as 'enlightened shareholder value', which is enshrined in UK corporate code. Paying attention to all stakeholders can be instrumental in serving long-term shareholder value.

Perhaps most importantly, it helps to drive decision-making that is not just about maximizing profits and enhancing shareholder value at the cost of other stakeholder groups. In other words, it can be part of a more ethical frame of reference for decision-making.

This should be seen as integral to the idea of responsible business. Corporate governance and measures of what businesses do should follow.

Supporters of stakeholder capitalism believe that serving the interests of all stakeholders is essential to the long-term success and health of any business, and that business can create profit for investors and value for society. There is not some inherent contradiction between making money and corporate social responsibility. It is not a zero-sum game.

Alex Edmans, Professor of Finance at London Business School, is a long-term advocate of these views. In his book *Grow the Pie: How great companies deliver both purpose and profit*, published in late 2020, he makes compelling arguments that a wider stakeholder view and purpose grows the pie for all.[23] He calls for a radical rethink and argues that our long existing system of capitalism is in crisis.

But there is not unanimity of views on this. Many still believe that businesses' primary focus must be on profit and are sceptical about genuine shifts in corporate mindset, preferring regulation to oversee responsibility to other stakeholders – back to this idea of whether we need rules, or can trust leaders to do the right things.

Lucian Bebchuk, a professor of economics and finance at Harvard Law School and author of many articles and books on corporate governance,[24] argues that corporate leaders have incentives not to protect stakeholders beyond that which serves shareholder value maximization.

He notes that it would take significant changes in corporate governance to genuinely reflect all stakeholders' interests, and there are questions about practicality. Is it really possible for corporate leaders to understand and balance all stakeholders' interests, and how far could you take that? They are not elected, and stakeholder interests are very broad and not uniform. One person's access to cheap food may literally be a matter of life and death, but the suppliers on whom the pressure is placed to reduce their prices are themselves placed at risk.

It comes back to broader questions of collective roles of business in society. As I have argued, business must see its wider responsibilities, and use these frameworks in helping to make the right decisions to act responsibly. But this can be about mindset and backed up by greater transparency in how leaders show they are acting in these ways. Companies have different purposes and therefore it may be ok to let them have different metrics to demonstrate how they are delivering.

The mainstream now appears to accept that the singular view promoted by Milton Friedman all those years ago is changing. Whether driven by regulation, corporate governance or delivering more on the expectations of us all, fundamentally this is about business acting ethically and responsibly. Trust in business depends on this, given the many examples of poor corporate behaviour over the years.

Even the respected journalist Martin Wolf, since 1996 associate editor and chief economics commentator at the *Financial Times*, has acknowledged that, although a believer in the Friedman doctrine in the past, he was wrong. He called it out very directly in an article in the *FT* in December 2020 titled 'Milton Friedman was wrong on the corporation – the doctrine that has guided economists and businesses for 50 years needs re-evaluation'.[25]

He cites many examples of why change is needed – from companies promoting products that can be harmful or addictive, tax avoidance schemes, over-protection of copyrights and anti-competitive practices, and precarious work practices.

Towards broader corporate reporting and governance

In 1994 John Elkington, the renowned writer and expert on corporate responsibility and sustainability, coined the term Triple Bottom Line – profit, people and planet. It was founded on the view that organizations should commit to focusing as much on social and environmental concerns as they do on profits.

It has become widely recognized and has pushed the development of sustainability reporting with a focus predominantly on non-financial performance of companies. As discussed earlier, with the development of more quantifiable environmental measures and metrics, more of these metrics have become incorporated in corporate reporting.

However, in an article in HBR in December 2018,[26] Elkington 'recalled' the Triple Bottom Line, citing the lack of progress on real change versus rhetoric. 'Fundamentally, we have a hard-wired cultural problem in business, finance and markets. Whereas CEOs, CFOs, and other corporate leaders move heaven and earth to ensure that they hit their profit targets, the same is very rarely true of their people and planet targets. Clearly, the Triple Bottom Line has failed to bury the single bottom line paradigm.'

Tough commentary, but certainly not without foundation. Making real change, particularly cultural and mindset change, is hard.

But progress can be seen in other ways. TPL was also a precursor of ESG reporting (environmental, social and governance) which is becoming increasingly accepted in the investor community. It gives a focus to investors on what companies are doing in driving more holistic value and how they are acting responsibly.

Scores of asset managers and large investors have in recent years focused on socially responsible funds and ESG measures. More investors steer clear of investments in companies that sell alcohol and tobacco, promote gambling or warfare, or contribute to environmental damage. And according to research by Morningstar and Citywire reported in April 2020,[27] there is good evidence the ESG funds outperformed non-ESG funds both in the short term through the pandemic, but also over the longer term.

Chuka Umunna, a former leading UK Labour politician, stated in a December 2020 article in *Forbes* that '2020 was the year that the environmental, social and governance movement in capital markets and financial services came of age'.[28] The article title is interesting in talking about millennials continuing to drive it.

Deloitte forecasts that ESG-mandated assets could make up to half of all managed assets in the US alone by 2025.[29]

Other initiatives to broaden out the measures and reporting that hold businesses to account include the International Integrated Reporting Council (IIRC). It was established 10 years ago in response to the global financial crisis and is made up of a coalition of regulators, investors, companies, standard setters, the accounting profession, academia and NGOs.[30]

The IIRC also challenges corporate reporting as having been too short term, backward looking, too compliance driven and too fragmented. Integrated reporting defines a comprehensive reporting framework based around six 'capitals' – financial, manufactured, intellectual, human, social and relationship, and natural. As the IIRC describes it, by taking these into account when reporting on performance, a company provides a fuller picture of the way in which it creates value.

The IIRC estimates that the concept of integrated reporting is today being used in over 2,500 companies in more than 70 countries. And over 40 stock exchanges refer to it in their guidance. And as we noted in Chapter 1, the Business Roundtable group of top corporate CEOs in the US committed themselves to updating the definitions of purpose to be inclusive of all stakeholders.

Other initiatives have come from groups that campaign for change and encourage businesses to sign up to broader standards of governance and reporting.

B Corp has a certification programme for businesses 'that meet the highest standards of verified social and environmental performance, public transparency, and legal accountability to balance profit and purpose'.[31] The B stands for benefit, and from its beginning in 2006 it has more than 3,700 businesses in its community across 150 industries and 74 countries.

Blueprint for Better Business is a UK-based charity whose purpose is 'to create better society through better business'.[32] It emerged in 2011 from seeing much the same issues but channelled from a perspective of Christian moral and social teachings. Its aim is to work directly with businesses and business leaders 'to be inspired and guided by a purpose that respects people and contributes to a better society'.

It's not hard to be cynical and suggest we have been here before, and it is true that progress overall has been slow. But it certainly feels to me, and through research and work with many organizations, that these ideas' time has come.

Public tolerance (and therefore that of employees, customers, suppliers and communities) is much reduced for poor corporate behaviours, and lack of trust in business is unsustainable for the good functioning of business as well as society. We need more transparency, accountability and higher standards.

However, referring back to the arguments made by Lucian Bebchuk, regulation does have its part to play.

Progress and changes in corporate regulation and standards

Boards should have a primary function and responsibility in holding their executives and businesses to account. If purpose and stakeholder capitalism is to have meaning, it must be anchored within the corporate governance of the organization. We will explore this further in the next chapter.

Boards of quoted companies are greatly influenced by investors, and of course by regulators and compliance. Regulators everywhere focus on corporate behaviours and aim to write rules and regulations to control or at least incent the right behaviours.

Regulation, however, moves slowly, and it does not move consistently or always work consistently internationally. What national regulators require of organizations in terms of reporting and compliance can vary significantly, and this provides a major challenge for businesses with international operations.

It is also hard for regulators to be sure they are driving the right behaviours or measuring the right things – not just from a monitoring and enforcement standpoint, but the fact that rules themselves are not sufficient to drive behaviours, as we briefly discussed earlier.

The Financial Reporting Council in the UK is responsible for regulatory codes and standards, and UK corporate governance has been a leader in the development and application of good standards based on the 'comply or explain' principle. Introduced after the recommendations of the Cadbury Report of 1992, this puts the onus on the company to either comply to the standard or explain why it hasn't. It's then up to the external market and investors to decide whether deviations from the prescribed standards are acceptable. This provides more flexibility than other jurisdictions, but enforcement is harder.

In 2016 I participated in the FRC's Culture Coalition looking at the role of corporate culture and boards. This led into the broader review of the revised UK Corporate Governance Code in 2019. It was a fascinating process to see the challenges of applying standards in a fast-changing and varied business world. The review looked at application of the codes, the need for any changes, but also wrestled with the debate about standards and rule-based systems in dealing with corporate cultures.

Indeed, the outcome of the review by the FRC highlighted that 'Unfortunately, some companies continue to treat the code as a box-ticking exercise. Where this happens, reporting is formulaic and companies do not seize the opportunity to meaningfully explain why they do not comply with its provisions'.[33]

The code does call out the importance of good governance and responsible business behaviour to all stakeholders. It expects companies to establish a purpose which is aligned with its culture and strategy, and to forge strong relationships with key stakeholders.

But it was clear through the review that corporate governance reporting failed to live up to stakeholder expectations. There were too many examples of statements of intent, but far less in explanation of how and what needed to change – for example on board diversity.

The new reporting requirements relate to the directors' duty to promote the success of the company, which is prescribed in section 172 of the Companies Act 2006. It's powerful stuff and highlights so much of what we have talked about. It is listed in the box below.

> **UK COMPANIES ACT: SECTION 172(1)**
>
> A director of a company must act in the way he considers, in good faith, would be most likely to promote the success of the company for the benefit of its members as a whole, and in doing so have regard (amongst other matters) to –
>
> - the likely consequence of any decision in the long term;
> - the interests of the company employees;
> - the need to foster the company's business relationships with suppliers, customers and others;
> - the impact of the company's operations in the community and the environment
> - the desirability of the company maintaining a reputation for high standards of business conduct;
> - the need to act fairly as between members of the company.

Many of these are principles rather than explicit standards. They are worth stating directly by businesses, describing what they believe in and how they can show how they are applying these principles. This would be an approach of 'apply and explain' as a positive driver, alongside the standards-based approach of 'comply or explain'.

This idea was something that the CIPD engaged on with the British Standards Institution as well as working together on development of human capital standards. The suite of British standards on human capital provides a principles-based framework for valuing people, diversity and inclusion, and learning and development.[34] They are not prescriptive standards in the traditional sense but describe principles that lead on valuing people in organizations.

> **PRINCIPLES FOR HUMAN CAPITAL STANDARDS – BSI**
>
> - People working on behalf of the organization have intrinsic value, in addition to their protections under the law or in regulation, which needs to be respected.
> - Stakeholders and their interests are integral to the best interests of the organization.
> - Every organization is part of wider society and has a responsibility to respect its social contract as a corporate citizen and operate in a manner that is sustainable.
> - A commitment to valuing people who work on behalf of the organization and to meeting the requirements of the standard is made and supported at the highest level.
> - Each principle is of equal importance.

Principles-based standards will fall more into the 'apply and explain' approach. But we are all familiar with the wide range of standards promoted by standards bodies and organizations of various kinds, including professional bodies.

Many of these kinds of standards focus on tangible practices, processes and products. Standards as promoted through the standards institutes under the overall umbrella of the International Organization for Standardization are also means of encouraging and benchmarking good practice. Many of these standards are enshrined in policy, alongside those that come from trade bodies and associations. But with a huge range of standards originating from so many sources, most are voluntary.

Standards of these kinds can therefore also play an important role in encouraging good practice and behaviour in organizations everywhere. Many organizations do use them in promoting what they do, to reassure customers or other stakeholders that they pay attention to standards of practice, or suppliers to ensure compliance and complementarity.

Importance and challenge of measuring people

In measuring the right things there has to be a strong focus on corporate cultures and behaviours, already highlighted. And a big part of measurement and understanding value in any organization is about the people.

As Charles Tilley, former CEO of the Chartered Institute of Management Accounting (CIMA) was always fond of reminding me, at the end of the day business has only two things, money and people, and we need to understand both and how they work to drive outcomes and value.

As we have already noted, measures of people are profoundly cost based and give little insight to value. They encourage a view of people as expendable or replicable, yet people are the asset that drives value in all other assets. As Bill Gates, I believe, once quipped, his most important assets come in through the office door in the morning and leave in the evening. He has to make sure they come back the next day.

So it would also be true to think of people as among our greatest risks. We explored in the previous chapter how the high visibility of access to the right skills and talent is one of the greatest corporate risks and concerns for corporate leaders.

Measuring value and the right things about people has challenged us all for a long time. I have always observed that if it were easy, we would have doubtless done it a lot more.

We try to measure productivity, which is always seen as such a key metric. But as we discussed in Chapter 2, it is so often hard to measure at anything other than an aggregated level. It is very context dependent and dependent on many variables, a lot of which are outside the direct control of the individual employee. These include application of technologies, product design, market pricing, and design of the job and the organization it's in.

Some areas of business do, however, lend themselves well to measures of productivity, such as sales, where measures are well established and are often directly linked to reward and commission schemes.

At the CIPD we have done a lot of work on these questions. In 2014 they established a coalition called Valuing your Talent to help develop a framework to understand all the various aspects of quantitative and qualitative people data and how they could relate to outputs and outcomes.[35] The work was in collaboration with the then UK Commission for Employment and Skills (sadly disbanded in March 2017 after UK government funding was withdrawn), and

FIGURE 7.3 Valuing your talent framework

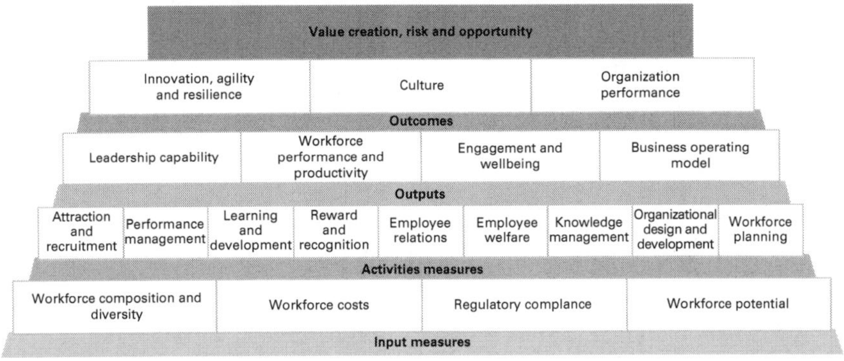

Value creation, risk and opportunity

Outcomes:
- Innovation, agility and resilience
- Culture
- Organization performance

Outputs:
- Leadership capability
- Workforce performance and productivity
- Engagement and wellbeing
- Business operating model

Activities measures:
- Attraction and recruitment
- Performance management
- Learning and development
- Reward and recognition
- Employee relations
- Employee welfare
- Knowledge management
- Organizational design and development
- Workforce planning

Input measures:
- Workforce composition and diversity
- Workforce costs
- Regulatory compliance
- Workforce potential

CIMA, which as a profession has just as much interest in understanding people value as the HR profession as well as with the Chartered Management Institute (CMI) and Investors in People (IiP).

The original report of the work 'Value of your talent: a new methodology for human capital measurement' was written with Dr Anthony Hesketh of Lancaster University Management School. It was further updated in the summer of 2016 and work done by Ulster University Business School to look at human capital reporting across the FTSE100. The model was based on the simple construct of inputs, activities, outputs and outcomes that is most readily thought of in a manufacturing process but is broadly applicable to almost any part of business. The framework is shown in Figure 7.3.

The VyT framework provides a good structure for understanding people and people analytics within organizations, and it has had good take-up in that regard.

People analytics is a critical capability which is at last receiving a lot of attention within organizations everywhere. Most importantly, it should be a collaboration with finance, and with other functions such as marketing, to help make the connections and linkages which are so important to fully understanding value. We explore this further in Chapter 10 on people strategy.

What has always proved hard, though, is to get consistent external reporting standards or frameworks for people metrics. The Ulster University research showed that at that time in 2016 large businesses were reporting more on people metrics, but it was inconsistent and hard to make comparisons. That remains for the most part true today. Hence the more regulated approach being taken on reporting specific people metrics that we will explore next.

The challenge ranges from historic lack of investment in good people systems and analytics capabilities, to the data collection challenge. There is no doubt that it is not easy, not least because people-related data is often hard to capture consistently. How many times have you heard arguments between your HR and finance leaders about what the headcount is?

People data in organizations suffers from the classic four Vs of big data – volume, velocity, variety and veracity. There is a lot of it, it changes frequently, there are many sources and views of it and it is hard to tell what is accurate, particularly when it comes to the significant amounts of qualitative data that we rely on.

Even capturing workforce demographic data, important as it is, is not straightforward. First, on headcount – do we count contractors and contingent workers or not, or open positions, or people on various leave arrangements and backfills, and how do we make the right calculations for part-time workers?

People's willingness to declare, for example, their ethnicity or race, or sexuality, or disabilities or socio-economic status are all subject to their trust in how this data might get used, and cannot be forced. Much of the data we need to understand cultures, and important areas like engagement and wellbeing, is largely subjective and can be greatly influenced or biased by the nature of the question and people's trust.

Furthermore, laws on data collection, standards and regulatory reporting requirements vary across countries, making it tough to consolidate. As noted, however, there is more work on standards in these areas which we will need to implement and build from.

Regulatory approaches to reporting on people

Despite or maybe because of these challenges in people measures, policy makers have been showing much more interest in requiring organizations to report on aspects of people and culture. Generally this is to be applauded. It is showing an appreciation for the importance of understanding the people aspects of business and for greater corporate transparency.

As we noted in Chapter 4, policy and regulated reporting has been focusing particularly on fairness and inclusion – reporting of pay gaps and disparities, and on diversity demographics, particularly at top levels.

On 1 January 2019, regulation came into effect in the UK compelling publicly listed companies with over 250 employees to annually disclose executive pay, justify the level of compensation for top bosses and account for how those salaries relate to wider employee pay.[36]

The first reports were due at the start of 2020. It's too early to draw any conclusions around the impact of greater pay-ratio transparency on levels of compensation or links to performance metrics, but it's a step in the direction of more considered governance and responsibility given the gaps in top levels of pay we discussed in Chapter 4. We explore later in this chapter the issues related to the measures used to determine particularly top-level pay.

In 2018, the UK government introduced compulsory reporting of mean and median gender pay gaps for any business or charity employing at least 250 people. Gender equality is the most obvious area of inclusion that needed to be improved. The reporting needs were specific and required breakdowns across quartiles for means and medians, and the inclusion of all forms of payment.

The UK law followed measures implemented by other countries to improve equality in the workplace and equality of opportunity. The Nordic nations have perhaps unsurprisingly been trailblazers. In Norway, for example, tax returns and therefore salary information have been publicly available for years. In 2018, Iceland became the first country in the world to establish processes to legally enforce equal pay.[37]

However, one of the dangers of required reporting of numbers is that they are seen primarily as exercises in compliance and rules. The numbers also have to be real, and must have accompanying narrative that shows insight and understanding.

Some signs are not encouraging. For pay-gap reporting, all data must be based on a snapshot of earnings from April 5 of the previous year. The great majority of entities at the last time of reporting in 2019 had left the task of reporting their numbers to the very last minute.

Employers that don't report on time or post inaccurate figures risk facing legal action from the Equality and Human Rights Commission (EHRC), and could be subject to court orders and fines, but policy makers and advocacy groups have criticized enforcement for not being punishing enough. This, however, can further reinforce that this is just about compliance. Positive drivers are more effective than negative drivers.

Regarding accuracy, we have already reviewed some of the not insignificant challenges in collecting and understanding people-related data.

In 2018, an investigation by the *Financial Times*[38] showed that 1 in 20 gender pay-gap reports filed were statistically improbable and therefore most likely wrong. Well over a dozen companies, for instance, initially claimed to have a gender pay gap of zero. In true *FT* style they reminded people how means and medians should be calculated and that it was therefore 'highly improbable' they could be the same.

We have to be careful that just getting numbers will ensure that things get done, or at least the right things get done. The laws of unintended consequences are everywhere. This issue is exemplified in other ways in many examples of what we report within organizations to drive focus and performance.

Globally, there's still much to be done to show progress on diversity within organizations at all levels to get better balance and equality, but it is encouraging to see that issues of diversity have become mainstream and no business can ignore the clarion calls for change. We will look at these issues in other ways internal to organizations in Chapter 10.

Improving diversity and opportunity – does regulatory reporting work?

Looking at pay gaps internationally, the latest OECD data from 2019[39] showed that Japan and Korea have the highest gender pay gaps of 23.5 per cent and 32.5 per cent for people in employment. Finland, a little surprisingly, is up at 18.9 per cent, but all other Nordic countries were around 10 per cent or lower. The combined figure across reported OECD countries was 12.9 per cent. The US and the UK are significantly above this at 18.5 per cent and 16 per cent.

The data also separate out the self-employed. It is less complete but shows that gaps are a lot higher and there is far greater variability across countries. The US gap shows as the highest at 56 per cent.

There are unsurprisingly some cultural influences at play, such as in the more patriarchal societies of countries like Japan and Korea. Also, those countries with relatively higher average levels of pay, such as the UK and the US, have bigger gaps reflecting the imbalance of women at senior levels. For countries like Poland and Italy, which traditionally have high proportions of self-employed (even when they are working within corporations), it is noticeable their data show small gaps for those employed but large gaps for the self-employed.

The pay-gap data in the UK are captured by the Office for National Statistics differently from the OECD. At the time of writing the latest UK report from the ONS[40] was for data up to April 2020. It therefore also included people on furlough at the time, although this was not seen as having much impact on pay gaps.

The key headlines were that the gender pay gap among all employees (ie part-time and full-time) was 15.5 per cent in 2020, down from 17.4 per cent in 2019. For full-time employees the gender pay gap was 7.4 per cent, down from 9.0 per cent in April 2019. The gender pay gap remained close to zero for full-time employees aged under 40 but was over 10 per cent for older age groups.

Possible evidence of pay-gap reporting influencing corporate actions on gender is that, up until 2019, there had been less than 1 per cent change since 2012. Figure 7.4 shows the ONS data on gender pay since 1998.

The focus on gender pay gaps has highlighted many issues which were historically much harder to see, and it has challenged us in getting to the real insights and issues. The numbers include the difference of pay for women and men in the same jobs. Equal pay legislation in most countries ensures this is small and getting smaller. But more recently there has been some exposure of gaps in pay between jobs that can be defined as equivalent but have different rates of pay between men and women.

The BBC came under intense scrutiny in 2019 for a history of paying male presenters and broadcasters more than women, something they have had to make efforts to correct. Large general retailers have also been under particular scrutiny for what are seen to be largely equivalent jobs in the stores which are more female dominated vs jobs in the warehouses which have a lot more men.

FIGURE 7.4 Gender pay gap for median gross hourly earnings (excluding overtime)

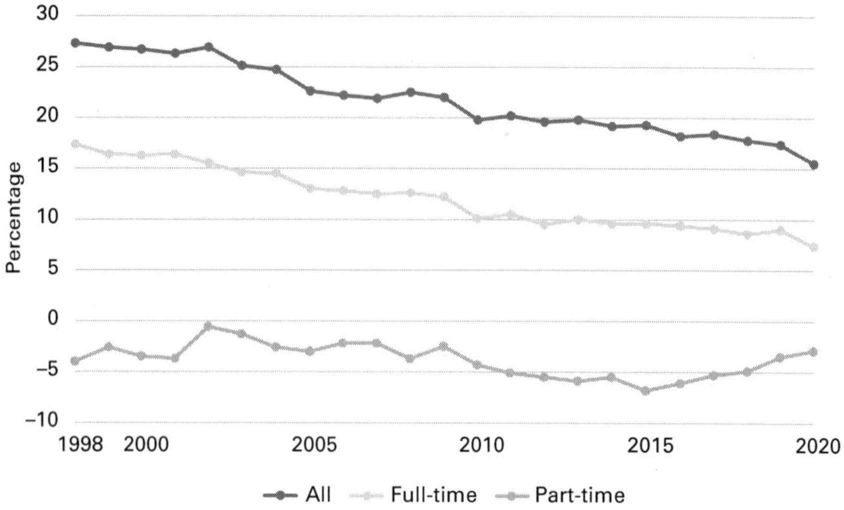

SOURCE ONS

Representation of men and ethnic minorities at senior levels

The biggest driver of gender pay gaps is the disparity of progression, and the reality of the chronic imbalance at more senior levels. This is true also for ethnic minorities, with the often referred to 'glass ceiling' and the 'glass elevator' that has favoured the progression of white men.

Research from 2019 showed there were more FTSE100 CEOs called Steve than there were women.[41] Similarly, in the US, according to research by *The New York Times* in 2018,[42] there were almost as many Fortune500 CEOs called John as there were women, although 3.3 per cent of the male population was called John, while women represent 50.8 per cent of the total population.

In recent years there has been much more scrutiny on proportions of women, and now ethnic minorities, at the highest levels of business. In 2010, Dame Helena Morrissey, then CEO of Newton Investment Management, established the 30% Club to promote gender diversity on boards. The organization is now international and promotes gender and ethnic diversity at board and senior executive levels.

Some major investors have backed this up directly. In February 2019, Hermes Investment Management, a prominent UK investment company, said it would be taking a tougher stance on gender diversity by voting against FTSE100 chairs who fail to address executive committees or boards that lack gender diversity. Such concrete action, however, is still rare.

Governments have also got behind these agendas, and in the UK there have been a number of government-led reviews to highlight the issues. In 2011, the Davies Review, led by Lord Davies, the former chairman of Standard Chartered PLC, focused on gender diversity on boards across the FTSE350. The percentage of women serving on FTSE100 boards increased from 12 per cent in 2011 to 25 per cent in 2015 and the figure for FTSE250 boards increased from 9 per cent in 2011 to 22 per cent in 2015. The Hampton-Alexander Review took this work forwards and set targets of 33 per cent representation of women on FTSE350 boards, but also for executive committees and direct reports, by the end of 2020. This is vital in increasing the pipeline of women into the highest roles.

As reported by the Hampton-Alexander Review,[43] by February 2020 the proportion of women had reached over 33 per cent for FTSE100 boards, and just under 30 per cent for FTSE250 companies. For executive levels and direct reports there has also been progress, and numbers range from just below 20 per cent to just below 30 per cent.

Similarly, there is now a lot more focus on ethnic diversity.

In 2017, Sir John Parker, a senior businessman and at the time on the Cabinet Office board, led the Parker Review looking at ethnic and cultural diversity on UK boards.[44] The review proposed that each FTSE100 board should have at least one director from an ethnic minority background by 2021, and each FTSE250 board the same by 2024.

By February 2020, 11 per cent of FTSE100 board directors were black, Asian or minority ethnic. There were only six ethnic minority directors in the position of chair or CEO in the FTSE100, and nine in the FTSE250. Over a third of FTSE100 companies did not have any ethnic minority board members. For FTSE250 it was even lower. Of the 173 FTSE250 companies analysed, 119 (69 per cent) had no ethnic diversity on their boards.

These figures were a slight improvement on 2017, when half of boards had no ethnic minority representation. But the 'one by 2021' target at the time of writing is looking tough.

The 2017 McGregor-Smith Review[45] led by Ruby McGregor-Smith, then CEO of Mitie and the first Asian woman to run a FTSE250 company, highlighted the wide range of challenges in improving ethnic diversity across organizations.

At the time, the employment rate for ethnic minority workers was only 62.8 per cent compared with 75.6 per cent for white workers. And while 14 per cent of the working age population were from an ethnic minority background, they made up only 10 per cent of the workforce and only 6 per cent of top management positions. Ethnic minorities were also more likely to work in lower-paid and lower-skilled jobs despite being more likely to have a degree, the report found.

Race and ethnicity as issues in all our workplaces have been strongly emphasized as a result of the Black Lives Matter movement and events in 2020. It is critical we make progress and we will explore more of the ways in which we can create more inclusive workplaces and cultures in Chapter 10 in particular.

Among the recommendations from the McGregor-Smith review was the requirement for a lot more transparency and reporting of workforce demographics and pay differentials by race.

There has been some progress with some companies and organizations leading on this such as Zurich Insurance, the Bank of England, a number of professional services firms and media companies like ITN.

Analysis reported by PwC in September 2020[46] found that two in three companies surveyed are now collecting ethnicity data, but so far only one in ten have reported their ethnicity pay gap, although this is up from only 3 per cent a couple of years ago. However, almost 50 per cent of companies say they are planning to disclose in the next three years.

I would also advocate that ethnic pay-gap reporting becomes a requirement, similarly to gender pay-gap reporting, which at the time of writing was still in government consultation.

The combination of required pay-gap reporting and the scrutiny of board and executive diversity is making a significant and important difference. Executive and board-level recruiters I talk to all comment on how much the focus has turned to getting real diversity into candidate lists for executive and board appointments.

But it will take time, and the issues as noted are complex. For example, with gender pay we have to be mindful of the knee-jerk reaction to the data. Having, say, 70 per cent women at the lower levels but only 50 per cent women at the higher levels creates a large pay gap – not uncommon in some sectors like retail or health and social care. These levels are also close to what we see in our own profession of HR, and similarly are seen in the marketing profession.

We could adjust for those numbers in a variety of ways, such as hiring a lot more men into the lower levels. But would that really work at fashion retailers like Asos or Cath Kidston, which report pay gaps into the 30 per cents?

It is something the CIPD is looking at for the HR profession at large in encouraging more men in, but we have to also be looking at maintaining or growing female progression into the higher levels. Likewise, for health and social care, more can be done to attract men into nursing, for example, but there must be attention also on progression of women into the senior roles.

Construction and financial services, long seen to be dominantly male, have the highest gender pay gap. Shifts in these sectors will take time and will require significant cultural changes both within organizations but also more broadly societally.

For smaller businesses, losing or gaining even one senior female or ethnic minority person can make a big difference to the pay-gap data.

Explaining and understanding these contexts must be an important part of any corporate narrative. Many organizations are not providing coherent narrative and we believe this should be a requirement alongside the numbers. You wouldn't expect to report profit or loss numbers and not have deep insight, analysis and narrative to explain them and where you are expected to be heading in the future.

What about quotas?

Growing numbers of jurisdictions have implemented quotas in order to force companies to make changes to increase diversity. Norway led the push in this direction when from 2008 it required listed companies to have women occupying 40 per cent of board director positions.

Other European countries have followed, including Belgium, France, Germany, Spain, the Netherlands and Iceland, all of which have quota legislation for numbers or ratios of women on boards, ranging from 30 to 40 per cent. India and Pakistan also use quotas, and California in 2018 started mandating publicly traded companies to include women on their boards.

In some of these countries, companies that fail to comply can be fined, dissolved or banned from paying existing directors. Germany, Spain and the Netherlands don't back up their quotas with sanctions. As noted, the UK uses guidelines and takes the more liberal comply-and-explain approach.

Quotas can be a bit of a blunt instrument and I have engaged in many discussions about them, including with the head of the Confederation of Norwegian Enterprise. Many advocates argue that quotas force the changes that otherwise happen slowly or don't happen at all. There is of course good evidence that backs it up – for example, Norway doubled the number of women on boards from 2003 to just over the target of 40 per cent as the legislation came in. Other countries showed a similar dramatic shift.

But as we have discussed throughout this chapter, hard rules and metrics can also throw up other issues. As quotas were introduced, some companies delisted to avoid complying, or played the game by reducing board sizes to increase the ratio of women.

There is also the question of squaring what may be positive discrimination with equality laws. A common concern too is that people might get promoted because they fit particular diversity criteria and appointments are seen as tokenism – not good for the individuals concerned or the organization. Also, the pool of talent might be too small and quality therefore declines, and those who have experience can get thinly spread across many positions. While there doesn't appear to be much evidence that would substantiate these concerns, they are easy perceptions.

Quotas will tend to target very specific outcomes – board constitution, for example. However, the issues of diversity and inclusion spread much deeper, and there is evidence that quotas have not helped diversity beyond their specific target.

As a February 2018 article in *The Economist* reported, quotas 'have had no discernible beneficial effect on women at lower levels of the corporate hierarchy'.[47] Various analyses have shown that women still make up a small proportion of the top executive or senior management roles. Korn Ferry data has shown that in France, Germany and the Netherlands only 10–20 per cent of senior management jobs are held by women, and this has barely changed since quota legislation was introduced.

This is in many ways surprising. Having more role models in senior levels, whether for women or ethnic minorities, is important in encouraging others to follow. For example, research by the World Economic Forum on the 'role model effect'[48] has found that improving political empowerment for women corresponds with increased numbers of women in senior roles across the broader labour market.

For the UK at least, we see little appetite from policy makers, or from business in general, to go down a quota route. Progress as noted is being made, albeit slowly, but we believe that continued pressure from all quarters and stakeholders and a greater sense of importance and accountability for diversity will make the changes happen.

Top executive pay and reward – is this part of the problem?

The final area to explore in this review of what we measure and what drives behaviour is our reward systems.

As we observed in Chapter 4, CEO and top executive pay in many organizations and countries has grown disproportionately to that of the rest of their workforces. Yet over recent years as reward has risen, corporate performance has not only not always followed, but corporate behaviours and trust have declined.

The debate about rewarding for performance, and what performance we are measuring, is longstanding. We have already discussed in this chapter a lot about what companies should really be held to account for, yet executive reward systems are still some way away.

We have seen and reported[49] that responsible business has been steadily climbing up the corporate agenda, driven by growing investor and regulatory interest in responsibility and sustainability, and an organizational focus on values and purpose.

In CIPD research in conjunction with the High Pay Centre on 'CEO pay and the workforce' published in December 2020,[50] the extent to which FTSE100 CEOs are incentivized to invest in and protect the interests of their workforces was explored. It was found that while investors have become increasingly interested in the ESG agenda, this is not reflected in the way these companies incentivize and reward their senior executives.

Pay plans are still overwhelmingly weighted towards financial measures of success, with little incentive for CEOs to protect the interests of other stakeholders. Only a third of the largest PLCs use employee measures in their CEO performance-related pay plans, and then less than 6 per cent of their variable pay on average relates to this. Not surprisingly, all FTSE100 firms do use financial metrics in performance-related pay, and over 82 per cent of total variable pay is related to hitting these targets.

At present therefore there is a disconnect. While many investors are advocating for ESG and broader corporate accountabilities, the connections to executive pay are not being more directly made. Legal & General Investment Management's most recent executive compensation guidelines[51] are telling in this respect, as they do not mention ESG metrics as a factor to consider when deciding whether to vote on a remuneration policy.

In January 2020 the FRC's new 2020 Stewardship Code came into effect. Based on 'apply and explain', it encourages asset managers, institutional investors and related service providers to adhere to a stronger set of principles which include specific reference to ESG. They want to see improved ESG disclosures in order to make it easier for investors to understand the material ESG issues relevant to companies. Early days, but again another strong signal of intent.

Beyond the issue of linking performance-related pay more directly to reinforce the ideas of stakeholder accountability, we need to challenge much of the culture that has built up around performance-related pay in general.

Behavioural science research has long shown that there are many facets of how people respond to pay and reward. These have been important areas for research in helping to provide guidance to professionals who work in the reward arena. In 2015 the CIPD published a report, 'Show me the money – the behavioural science of reward', with a call for a 'renewed look at how we design and apply reward strategies'.[52]

Reward systems should do all they can to incent the right behaviours and associated performance. But there are many subjective and emotional elements to reward. They range from perceived fairness and comparability – which has been a big part of the pay-gap debate – to cognitive biases such as how we discount deferred pay to immediate pay, particularly where that longer-term reward is at risk (which it usually is). Hence deferred bonus or the popular long-term incentive plans (LTIPs) for executives tend to have much less impact than immediate pay. Another reason for the bias of short-termism.

As we have also seen, what to measure in looking at performance challenging. And not only is the impact of the individual vs the team hard to separate, but people tend to overrate their performance and contribution anyway.

LTIPs and performance-related or variable pay structures have in many cases become unwieldy and hard to understand. They have also become the largest proportion of pay for CEOs and many top executives. If they are hard to understand or influence, then their motivational impact is greatly diminished, if not negated.

PwC in its comprehensive report in 2015 'Making executive pay work – the psychology of incentives'[53] also highlighted so many of these issues, but little has changed. One of my favourite quotes the report cited from an executive who was clearly showing some disarming honesty was, 'I don't assign any value to my share allocations. I consider them in the same way as a company lottery ticket.'

All of this begs significant questions about what we are rewarding for and how we could reset reward strategies at the highest level.

It is important that remuneration committees and those looking at reward at the top take a broader view of top executive reward as part of total reward strategy for the organization.

The arguments about having to pay top dollar to get top talent get increasingly self-serving and should be challenged. Executive search consultants often have been remunerated as a proportion of the pay package, which doesn't help. Investors are showing more interest but it's still rare that executive compensation gets seriously challenged or changed. Even regulators should take some different views – seeing clawback of long-term share options or bonuses as a mechanism to keep CEOs in line should not be the constraint for change.

In conclusion

Whatever we might like to think about human behaviour, it rings true that what gets measured gets done. We now need to push harder to make sure that we really are measuring the right things. Shifting from short-term thinking requires measures that incent long-term direction and investment.

Responsible business is about understanding and considering all the stakeholders any enterprise has responsibility for. If we take care of them, they will take care of the numbers.

Responsible society likewise needs measures that encompass what is important to all of us in creating a better future, so we can shape the policies, the investments and the collaboration we all need for healthy society to flourish.

We need to keep pressing on the issues of inclusion, and that is hard to do without good information, transparency and insight. Fair opportunity for all.

And within our organizations, we need to measure appropriately what is happening with our people. What supports them to give of their best, to be engaged and motivated in what they do, and to look after their wellbeing. We will look further at this in the upcoming chapters.

Endnotes

1 www.theatlantic.com/magazine/archive/2015/10/why-we-compete/403201/ (archived at https://perma.cc/K3J5-RWS4)
2 https://quoteinvestigator.com/2010/05/26/everything-counts-einstein/ (archived at https://perma.cc/2V2V-RBCV)
3 www.jfklibrary.org/learn/about-jfk/the-kennedy-family/robert-f-kennedy/robert-f-kennedy-speeches/remarks-at-the-university-of-kansas-march-18-1968 (archived at https://perma.cc/PU3J-EWLG)
4 https://plato.stanford.edu/entries/aristotle-ethics/ (archived at https://perma.cc/7UYX-S3UE)
5 Skidelsky, R and Skidelsky, E (2013) *How Much is Enough? Money and the good life*, Penguin Books
6 www.theguardian.com/commentisfree/2019/nov/24/metrics-gdp-economic-performance-social-progress (archived at https://perma.cc/7UWY-KMAN)
7 https://spire.sciencespo.fr/hdl:/2441/5l6uh8ogmqildh09h4687h53k/resources/wp2009-33.pdf (archived at https://perma.cc/3HZ6-LXKQ)
8 www.oecdbetterlifeindex.org/ (archived at https://perma.cc/24Q9-5HCA)
9 https://www.theguardian.com/commentisfree/2019/nov/24/metrics-gdp-economic-performance-social-progress (archived at https://perma.cc/DYC7-8LAB)
10 https://ophi.org.uk/policy/gross-national-happiness-index/#:~:text=The%20phrase%20'gross%20national%20happiness,approach%20towards%20notions%20of%20progress (archived at https://perma.cc/3DJV-2F6R)
11 www.grossnationalhappiness.com/ (archived at https://perma.cc/MSX3-HQH9)
12 www.un.org/esa/socdev/ageing/documents/NOTEONHAPPINESSFINALCLEAN.pdf (archived at https://perma.cc/NK68-SAD6)
13 www.gallup.com/178667/gallup-world-poll-work.aspx (archived at https://perma.cc/BCK5-D2WG)
14 https://happiness-report.s3.amazonaws.com/2020/WHR20.pdf (archived at https://perma.cc/7EDM-G6BT)

15 www.npr.org/sections/parallels/2018/02/12/584481047/the-birthplace-of-gross-national-happiness-is-growing-a-bit-cynical (archived at https://perma.cc/N97Y-LQQV)
16 www.nytimes.com/2018/01/26/nyregion/at-yale-class-on-happiness-draws-huge-crowd-laurie-santos.html (archived at https://perma.cc/948D-2LX3)
17 www.indiatoday.in/education-today/news/story/here-s-how-happiness-curriculum-in-delhi-govt-schools-can-build-a-healthy-mind-1311804-2018-08-11 (archived at https://perma.cc/6K94-6ZCA)
18 https://u.ae/en/about-the-uae/the-uae-government/government-of-future/happiness (archived at https://perma.cc/BQB8-DHFB)
19 https://whatworkswellbeing.org/blog/ons4-evaluations-what-works-to-improve-personal-wellbeing/ (archived at https://perma.cc/M7NF-NXZJ)
20 www.bbc.com/news/world-europe-50650155 (archived at https://perma.cc/EB4F-42G7)
21 www.gov.uk/government/news/pm-launches-governments-first-loneliness-strategy (archived at https://perma.cc/U5KB-9HFM)
22 https://d1ssu070pg2v9i.cloudfront.net/pex/carnegie_uk_trust/2020/12/03170016/LOW-RES-4708-CUKT-GDWe-Social-Progress-Summary.pdf (archived at https://perma.cc/WHR7-HFPX)
23 Edmans, A (2020) *Grow the Pie: How great companies deliver both purpose and profit*, Cambridge University Press
24 www.hks.harvard.edu/centers/mrcbg/programs/growthpolicy/illusory-promise-stakeholder-governance-lucian-bebchuk (archived at https://perma.cc/M4SX-N3YH)
25 Wolf, M (2020) Milton Friedman was wrong on the corporation, *Financial Times*, 8 December
26 https://hbr.org/2018/06/25-years-ago-i-coined-the-phrase-triple-bottom-line-heres-why-im-giving-up-on-it (archived at https://perma.cc/8J4W-HD8X)
27 https://citywire.co.uk/wealth-manager/news/have-esg-funds-outperformed-non-esg-funds-during-the-crisis/a1343642?section=global (archived at https://perma.cc/7UQH-WXFV)
28 www.forbes.com/sites/chukaumunna/2020/12/18/esg-investing-came-of-age-in-2020millennials-will-continue-to-drive-it-in-2021/?sh=3fc3794e409a (archived at https://perma.cc/8NH7-HNAW)
29 www2.deloitte.com/us/en/insights/industry/financial-services/esg-investing-performance.html (archived at https://perma.cc/P7XG-G2C2)
30 https://integratedreporting.org/the-iirc-2/ (archived at https://perma.cc/P8JV-WBL2)
31 https://bcorporation.net/about-b-corps (archived at https://perma.cc/9VH8-AT9C)
32 www.blueprintforbusiness.org (archived at https://perma.cc/A6PX-2R2G)
33 www.frc.org.uk/news/november-2020/reporting-on-the-new-corporate-governance-code-is-a-mixed-picture (archived at https://perma.cc/8RA3-EVKY)

34 www.cipd.co.uk/knowledge/strategy/hr/standards-factsheet (archived at https://perma.cc/G3FQ-JC68)
35 www.cipd.co.uk/knowledge/strategy/analytics/valuing-talent (archived at https://perma.cc/3STU-JPA9)
36 www.gov.uk/government/news/new-executive-pay-transparency-measures-come-into-force (archived at https://perma.cc/3EYB-L726)
37 www.bbc.com/worklife/article/20180209-what-iceland-can-teach-the-world-about-gender-pay-gaps (archived at https://perma.cc/Z2TK-6ZL9)
38 www.ft.com/content/ad74ba76-d9cb-11e7-a039-c64b1c09b482 (archived at https://perma.cc/GE5M-BU4A)
39 OECD (2021) Gender wage gap (indicator), DOI: 10.1787/7cee77aa-en
40 www.ons.gov.uk/employmentandlabourmarket/peopleinwork/earningsandworkinghours/bulletins/genderpaygapintheuk/2020 (archived at https://perma.cc/72BC-6TSK)
41 www.independent.co.uk/life-style/ceo-women-business-sexism-ftse-100-a9073391.html (archived at https://perma.cc/BG9K-KTZ6)
42 www.nytimes.com/interactive/2018/04/24/upshot/women-and-men-named-john.html?auth=login-email (archived at https://perma.cc/EL22-C8JZ)
43 https://ftsewomenleaders.com/targets-progress/ (archived at https://perma.cc/33Y4-R8RC)
44 www.gov.uk/government/publications/ethnic-diversity-of-uk-boards-the-parker-review (archived at https://perma.cc/WQ64-LP4U)
45 www.gov.uk/government/publications/race-in-the-workplace-the-mcgregor-smith-review (archived at https://perma.cc/26EK-MDP5)
46 www.pwc.co.uk/human-resource-services/assets/pdfs/ethnicity-pay-report.pdf (archived at https://perma.cc/5PDX-PK92)
47 www.economist.com/business/2018/02/17/ten-years-on-from-norways-quota-for-women-on-corporate-boards (archived at https://perma.cc/76WQ-TP4B)
48 www.weforum.org/reports/gender-gap-2020-report-100-years-pay-equality (archived at https://perma.cc/Z9X5-QPAT)
49 Hope, H V (2020) Responsible business through crisis: senior leaders on trust and resilience during COVID-19, CIPD, London
50 www.cipd.co.uk/knowledge/strategy/reward/ceo-pay-workforce (archived at https://perma.cc/VSQ6-BKBH)
51 LGIM (2019) LGIM's principles on executive remuneration, Legal & General Investment Management, London
52 www.cipd.co.uk/Images/show-me-the-money_2015-behavioural-science-of-reward_tcm18-9560.pdf (archived at https://perma.cc/KYG3-QQ56)
53 www.pwc.com/gx/en/hr-management-services/publications/assets/making-executive-pay-work.pdf (archived at https://perma.cc/3JN3-WH84)

08

Building responsible business

It takes 20 years to build a reputation and five minutes to ruin it. If you think about that, you'll do things differently.
WARREN BUFFETT, INVESTOR AND CEO OF BERKSHIRE HATHAWAY

As we think about organizations for the future, we have already discussed many aspects of what makes a responsible and sustainable business and how important that is. We talked in Chapter 4 about trust and its importance, yet how much it has been damaged over many years of corporate and political scandals.

Every business leader knows how important reputation is, and Warren Buffett's point is exactly the same as that we made about trust.

In this chapter we'll expand on these themes, looking at the rise of corporate social responsibility, reappraising the points made in Chapter 7 about measuring the right things and greater transparency, together with multi-stakeholder accountability.

We've already referenced how the views of Milton Friedman influenced, or perhaps just reflected, the belief system of much of the last 50 years. The profit motive, the primacy of the shareholder and too much of a 'greed is good' culture, particularly during the last decades of the 20th century.

The issues of trust, and responsible and ethical business behaviour, are central – Edelman described their findings on trust being 'a wake-up call for our institutions to embrace a new way of effectively building trust: balancing competence with ethical behaviour'.[1] A crisis, particularly one of these proportions, is a time for businesses to make good on commitments to do good.

Research shows that individuals believe that a company has clear values only when they see management making a decision that sacrifices short-term profitability for the sake of adhering to those values.[2]

In December 2020, the Institute of Business Ethics published its 18th annual survey on the attitudes of the British public to business ethics.[3] It questioned people on how much they felt UK businesses and the decisions they made followed good principles. While the survey noted there has been some improvement in recent years, 59 per cent of respondents thought that business generally behaved ethically, but 33 per cent thought they did not.

Interestingly, the top issues that people felt needed addressing were corporate tax avoidance, environmental responsibility and executive pay. But high on the list were issues of discrimination, bullying and harassment, and openness of cultures in which people could speak up – all issues notably where women scored higher than men.

The ideas of purpose, of principles and values therefore are a very good starting point for a new era of responsible business. If we now disagree with Friedman's view, then we have to be clear on what we do believe the purpose of business is, both in general and in particular.

In Chapter 7 we laid out many points about responsible business in general, so let's start by looking more at purpose as a way for all businesses to describe what they stand for beyond making money.

Framing corporate responsibility and intent through purpose

In a global study of nearly 500 executives published in April 2018,[4] EY found that well over 80 per cent believe a strong sense of purpose drives employee satisfaction and affects an organization's ability to transform. They describe business purpose as 'an aspirational reason for being which inspires and provides a call for action for an organization and its partners and stakeholders and provides benefit to local and global society'.

With all the trends in work we have explored and what we have learned from crises of the past, the idea of purpose and what a business stands for has become very resonant. And much research suggests that businesses with a strong sense of meaningful purpose perform better.

The EY report showed that executives who treat purpose as a core driver of strategy and decision-making reported greater ability to drive successful innovation and transformational change, as well as deliver consistent revenue growth; 53 per cent of executives who said their company has a strong sense of purpose also said their organization is successful with innovation and transformation efforts.

According to Gallup's most current 'State of the global workplace' report that we referenced in the discussion about happiness, '[Employees] are now driven more than ever by company mission and purpose, and require a workplace culture that delivers it'. And they are right. Research also shows that more than 9 out of 10 employees are willing to take a pay cut for more meaningful work.

Simon Sinek's bestselling 2009 book *Start with Why* and his TED talk, the third most watched, have been a reference point for many. 'People don't buy WHAT you do; they buy WHY you do it.' And as he also observes, 'We want to be around people and organizations who are like us and share our beliefs.'

Purpose links closely to engagement but is also an important attractor to new talent. Going back to our evidence-based thinking, some might argue that direct causal links are hard to establish as they often are in broader constructs of this nature, but there are good correlations. Strong purpose, if embedded as part of a corporate culture, really will drive other positive behaviours – a focus on wider outcomes than just profit making, on ethical behaviours and ultimately also a stronger employee and customer brand.

As Sinek suggests, most businesses have focused on the WHAT – what products we make, what markets we sell to etc, and then the HOW – how to market and promote, deliver to our customers, etc. All very rational, but missing the clear thinking of WHY.

Related to purpose are the constructs of vision and mission, and some delight in arguing the difference between them all. A purpose should really be the why – what do you exist for? The vision then can express more of the what – what you do in aiming to fulfil your purpose – and a mission statement can be the how – how do you do it.

But in all honesty these differences can be a bit pedantic. Many organizations coalesce them into a single statement which they hope best reflects their overall brand positioning. Most customers, employees and stakeholders just want to hear a clear, relevant, meaningful and legitimate statement about what your business believes and what it is trying to achieve – something that is inspiring, but also realistic to the nature of your business. Generally making people happy, making the world a better place or doing no harm are a bit hard to tie down.

> **GOOD PURPOSE STATEMENT EXAMPLES**
>
> - Uber – 'Uber is evolving the way the world moves. By seamlessly connecting riders to drivers through our apps, we make cities more accessible, opening up more possibilities for riders and more business for drivers.'
> - Google – 'To organize the world's information and make it universally accessible and useful.'
> - Ikea – 'At IKEA our vision is to create a better everyday life for the many people. Our business idea supports this vision by offering a wide range of well-designed, functional home furnishing products at prices so low that as many people as possible will be able to afford them.'
> - Coca-Cola – 'To refresh the world... to inspire moments of optimism and happiness... to create value and make a difference.'
> - Walmart – 'We save people money so they can live better.'
> - LinkedIn – 'To connect the world's professionals to make them more productive and successful.'

For the CIPD, one of my first actions on becoming CEO was to create a purpose as there wasn't a clear one other than statements about improving the science of human resource management. We came up with 'Championing Better Work and Working Lives'. It has proved to be a strong inspirational statement but linked closely to what the CIPD does and the difference it wants to make, both as the organisation itself and as a purpose for the profession at large.

One of the most powerful and enduring purpose/mission/values statements that I have seen is the Johnson & Johnson credo. It was originally crafted by one of the founding family members just before the company went public in the 1940s. It is the first thing you see on entering any J&J office or factory, and is so embedded that employees talk about actions, behaviours or language being 'on' or 'off' credo. It starts with a focus on customers, but then responsibility to employees, communities of which they are part, and then finally a 'fair return' to stockholders.

It is a remarkable statement that captures all of what we have been discussing about understanding responsibility to all stakeholders. Notable that the financial stakeholder is mentioned last, and customers then employees are mentioned first. Perhaps also another reminder that sometimes we forget more than we know. The ideas we have been exploring are not new. It's just that we allowed many other priorities and demands to overtake them and lost sight of much of what is really important.

The crisis of the pandemic led to a surge in corporate commitments to being 'purpose-driven' and acting for the greater good, perhaps largely in response to a crisis that impacted everyone and where we all had to play our part – a sense of collective responsibility where businesses found themselves having to put people at the front and centre of their thinking.

However, purpose statements that either are so general they are meaningless, or have no obvious backing in terms of how an organization behaves, can certainly backfire. This was humorously demonstrated by Scott Galloway, an author and professor of marketing at the New York University Stern School of Business, in a blog post in 2019.[5]

Galloway argued that the brand era had created a notion that inanimate objects could take on animate characteristics. In a rush to scale and win over deep-pocketed investors, companies resort to marketing concepts, feelings and images, rather than just the services and products they can actually claim to be selling.

A kind of anthropomorphism; but the professor came up with a catchier term of 'yogababble' to describe the frequently vacuous verbiage that companies – particularly new ones – sometimes use to dazzle prospective investors and customers.

He created the tongue-in-cheek Yogababble Index, which measures the use of what he suggests to be such nonsensical purpose or mission statements against that particular company's equity performance after listing on the stock market. And whether it's coincidence or not, there seems to be at least some correlation.

Galloway took video-conferencing company Zoom's mission statement – 'to make video communications frictionless' – and asserted that it was accurate, with no obvious pompousness or overpromising.

Zoom's stock appreciated more than 100 per cent over a six-month period after the company listed on the stock exchange in March 2019. And it has gone a lot further than that. As the company and technology that did so well during the pandemic, its name became synonymous with how so many of us were spending our days. When a company name becomes a verb you know you've made it – 'I'm all zoomed out' became a common refrain for the symptoms of Zoom fatigue. And some are now referring to Gen Z as the Zoomer generation – probably becomes it neatly rhymes with the boomer generation of their parents.

Next, Galloway looked at Peloton's mission statement, which at the time read: 'On the most basic level, Peloton sells happiness.' Peloton is a company that makes and sells indoor exercise bikes and the software that supports them. Completing a Peloton workout may indeed make someone happy, but Galloway was far from convinced and neither were investors. Six months after the company went public, its shares were roughly unchanged in value.

A high-profile example of a company that's fallen victim to overpromising without truly articulating its real mission is WeWork. Though the infamous unicorn faced a whole host of structural and financial problems that ultimately led to the downfall of its co-founder and CEO Adam Neumann, the rhetoric around its vision and culture certainly didn't help.

In terms of brashness and confidence, Neumann was on another level even within the domain of hubris-fuelled startups. He arranged festival-style summer camps for employees and flaunted his sudden wealth – private jets and weekend homes – publicly announcing that he wanted to become the world's first trillionaire and 'president of the world'.[6]

This apparent obsession with power and money jarred with the values and mission he espoused for WeWork. He repeatedly stated that WeWork's mission was 'to elevate the world's consciousness'.

This is an extreme example of a blinding disconnect between values stipulated and those demonstrated, and a misalignment with what anyway was a meaningless yogababble purpose statement. But countless other examples exist – they just don't necessarily make the headlines. Another cause of trust being undermined.

Purpose and mission statements are there to be acted upon. As we noted in the first half of the book, the workforce of today and the demographic cohort about to enter the labour market are possibly more driven by purpose than any generation that came before them. So it's critical that companies get this right if they want to be able to attract and retain the best talent, and retain the trust of their customers and stakeholders.

Why are values important?

As organizations responded to the Covid-19 pandemic and focused more on their people, they also thought more about their corporate cultures. Were they caring enough, how did people behave when they were more separated, less visible, and in turn had to be trusted more? In other words, what were their values and what did they care about and how were these being reflected in how the corporate culture worked.

Values, when well expressed, should be statements that define cultural norms and behaviours, describe an organization on its best day, and how it would like to be seen by all its stakeholders. That may sound a bit grandiose, and indeed too many value statements are just that – fluffy rhetoric with little substance to back them up. All hat and no cattle, as our Texan friends might describe it.

Just as with purpose and vision or any statements which organizations make about themselves, they have to be meaningful, relevant and actionable, and backed up by reality. Values are typically expressed even in one word or a few short words to help them to be memorable, whereas purpose and vision will usually be more wordy. Value statements should also be enduring.

We see value statements everywhere – up on office walls or in corporate foyers, or on websites and in so many 'about us' statements. It is good that we are expressing these more visibly than ever before, but they have to be embedded and reinforced constantly.

Values can refer to what we focus on as well as how we behave. Customer or people, or environment, alongside respect, or accountability, or passion or as is quite popular, fun. Integrity is probably the most common value statement – certainly it appears at the top of most lists. Others can be a lot more quirky but in that way also say something of the culture. Zappos, an online shoe retailer, have a value of 'Create fun and a little weirdness'. Won't work for everyone, but it works for them.

Many common value statements have often struck me as blindingly obvious and should be givens – if you are not acting with integrity, then what are you doing? But nonetheless, they are important reminders of what any organization should regard as important and expressions of what they believe in.

Accenture has long had the same six values – Stewardship, The Best People, Client Value Creation, One Global Network, Respect for the Individual, and Integrity. Their mission and purpose is 'helping our clients create their future'.

Having worked there for many years, these value statements resonated with me and it was clear they did express what the organization did and its key cultural attributes. Perhaps the value that most resonated for me was stewardship. A powerful and simple idea that speaks to responsibility to others, to leave things better than we found them. And it applies to all stakeholders.

At the CIPD the values are expressed as Customer First, Collaborative, Expert, Impactful and Innovative. Is the organisation always those things? Not always, but they also set a direction to aspire to and to keep working on.

Embedding values and aligning culture to them is a long process. That is why they should be enduring, but also realistic. They have to go beyond the posters on the wall. They should be measurable, at least in the sense we know when people are behaving according to the values and when they are not. They should be built into the recruitment processes, performance management and reward processes, emphasized through management development programmes, and reinforced through everyday behaviours and actions. Leaders must role-model them – disconnects of the kind we saw at WeWork undermine belief in them for everyone else.

CSR – doing well by doing good

It was Benjamin Franklin, one of the great figures of US history and one who helped in drafting the Declaration of Independence, who coined the phrase of doing well by doing good.

In many ways it captures the idea of what a responsible individual should be as well as a responsible business – the balance, and the synergy, of doing good with regard to others (all stakeholders) which in turn helps an individual or organization to do well.

However, doing good to do well has a chequered past in relation to business, as we have observed.

If our only responsibility was to the financial stakeholder, then why would we care about doing good in other ways, unless it bolstered our brand and made customers buy more from us? Since even that connection wasn't clear, in a world where consumers themselves were less driven by these ideas, then for the most part we saw the business world doing philanthropic-type activities alongside the business – donating to good causes, pro-bono, volunteering. But not connected much to the heart of strategy.

Corporate social responsibility or CSR started to take hold from the 1970s. In 1971, the concept of the 'social contract' between businesses and society was introduced by the Committee for Economic Development in the US. In a paper they published on *Social Responsibilities of Business Corporations*,[7] they promoted the idea that since companies function and exist because of public consent, there is an obligation to contribute to the needs of society. This defined the term. But it wasn't really until the late 1980s and 1990s that CSR became mainstream and part of the language of business.

In my experience, this was very connected to the arrival of millennials into our workplaces – as we reviewed in Chapter 4, a generation with stronger views and expectations on purpose and a broader awareness of environment, society and the interconnection of things. We educated them well.

However, a lot of the early stages of CSR were more virtue signalling. More of a quick response to changing demands from new cohorts arriving in our workplaces and some good PR spin. We'll have a few people focused on it, write something into our annual reports and try to show we care.

A bit of a cynical view perhaps, but the fact that there were separate CSR teams looking for good things to do rather made the point that it wasn't really integral to the whole ethos and thinking of the corporation. Enron won several CSR awards from the US Environmental Protection Agency among others shortly before it ignominiously collapsed in 2001.

But over the last couple of decades there has been more sustainable progress. As we discussed in Chapter 7, the interests of all stakeholders have grown in wanting to see businesses behave responsibly and play their part in the betterment of society, the environment and humanity at large. And that has to be a lot more ingrained and integral to what a business does than some PR-friendly philanthropic activities on the side.

There are now many good examples of companies that have integrated these philosophies into the core of how they operate as a business. A good and often quoted example of one that exemplifies these ideals is Patagonia.

In 1965, rock climbing enthusiast Yvon Chouinard partnered with Tom Frost to create Chouinard Equipment, a business dedicated to developing climbing equipment. Motivated by a desire to protect the environment they derived so much pleasure from, they developed aluminium chocks to replace the more traditional pitons, which eliminated damage to rock surfaces.

In 1973 Chouinard Equipment became Patagonia, which today is a privately held corporation that employs approximately 1,000 people internationally. Its environmentally sustainable ethos has always driven it. Its purpose and mission statement is to 'Build the best product, cause no unnecessary harm, use business to inspire and implement solutions to the environmental crisis.' It has consistently demonstrated that making a profit is not its top priority, and the people who work for the company, as well as the communities in which it operates, have benefited from this ethos in many ways.

Although ahead of its time, the environmental commitment that Patagonia demonstrated has consistently heightened its appeal with consumers, employees and investors.

Though rankings of good places to work should always be treated with caution, it's noteworthy that Patagonia regularly appears at the top of a whole host of them. One found that in 2020, 91 per cent of Patagonia employees considered their company a great place to work compared with 59 per cent of employees at a typical US-based company.[8] Some 95 per cent of respondents said they felt good about the ways Patagonia contributes to the community and 94 per cent said they were proud to tell others where they work.

When Covid-19 started to spread in March 2020, forcing retailers of non-essential goods to shutter their physical stores and shift their focus online, Patagonia was one of the first, not only to announce that it was closing its shops, but also that it was temporarily ceasing internet sales out of concern for the health and wellbeing of its employees.[9]

Like other retailers, Patagonia suffered a hit from lockdowns and social distancing. But its strategy based so strongly on the idea of a triple bottom line has created a company widely reported to have been valued at around $1 billion over the last few years before the Covid-19 crisis.[10] Doing well by doing good.

We mentioned B Corp in Chapter 7 as an organization that since 2006 has been certifying companies that operate for the wider good of society while still making money.[11] Certified companies are known as B Corps and are required to have verified social and environmental performances, while also paying close attention to factors like sustainability, income inequality and the impact on local communities.

Patagonia was certified in 2011, but today it's one of over 3,000 B Corps across more than 70 countries and 150 industries. Well-known brands like The Body Shop and the *Guardian* newspaper are certified, as are Ben & Jerry's, Innocent Drinks, funding platform Kickstarter and some divisions of the publicly listed French consumer goods giant Danone.

A study from 2016[12] found that many B Corps choose to become certified because they want to distinguish themselves 'in the midst of a greenwash revolution', and they want 'to help consumers sort through the marketing hype to find businesses and products that are truly socially and environmentally responsible'. It's a way, the research concluded, of validating the authenticity of an enterprise's core business principles.

But less obviously, there might also be a benefit just from assuming an identity that's different from the industry norm. A 2011 research paper[13] by Northwestern University Kellogg Business School professor Ned Smith concluded that a clear 'non-conforming' identity among hedge funds had an advantageous impact on investors' capital allocation decisions.

Smith found that investors tended to reward non-conforming funds, which he defined as hedge funds that used atypical trading strategies relative to the norm. Investors showed a greater propensity to invest in those funds after short-term success and to penalize them less after poor performance.

From the wider investor community perspective, these ideas of responsible business and looking for measures beyond just profit are coming together in the ESG movement, as we saw in Chapter 7.

Challenges remain in having consistency of measures and metrics for ESG, and how to balance all these measures and weigh them for materiality, together with the difficult questions that arise about balancing tradeoffs between stakeholders. This is known as the 'net benefit test' which seeks to answer the big question of whether a company delivers a net benefit to society.[14]

Blueprint for Better Business, working with leading investors from a range of asset management companies with combined assets under management of over $8 trillion, came up with a set of eight questions to help assess whether and how a company really is purpose led and understanding its obligations to all stakeholders:[15]

QUESTIONS TO ASSESS PURPOSE AND MULTI-STAKEHOLDER FOCUS – BLUEPRINT FOR BETTER BUSINESS

1. In simple terms, what is the company in business to deliver and for whom? How does that differentiate you?
2. What does success look like and how do you measure and review it?
3. How does your pay policy link to long-term success?
4. How are your board discussions and agenda anchored to your purpose? Can you give some examples of how your purpose has changed your decisions?
5. What positive and negative impacts does your company have on society? How are you maintaining your 'licence to operate'?
6. How are your people? Can you give examples of how you have responded to specific concerns?
7. Which external relationships are most important to achieving your purpose (eg customer, supplier, regulatory)? What key measures do you use to assess the strength of these?
8. [For Chairs] How do you as a board know you are doing a good job?

These are undoubtedly good questions, and executives and boards should be asking themselves the same questions in seeking to become responsible businesses. But the answers are rarely simple, and quantifying net benefits to society in economic terms is complex and often ambiguous, as Professor Alex Edmans, whom we referenced in Chapter 7, acknowledges.

That is also why we would continue to emphasize the many intangible benefits – ability to attract talent, build trust and reputation over the long term, and the inherent belief in doing well by doing good. To go back to the Einstein quote of not everything that counts can be counted, we have to also build responsible business from belief, principles and values, as we have reiterated throughout.

In an interview in 2019,[16] Andrew Kassoy, co-founder and CEO of B Lab (the organization that oversees all B Corps certifications), said that the broader impact of initiatives like the one championed by his organization is gradually becoming obvious. Some jurisdictions have started to implement laws to ensure that businesses operate in a way that prioritizes people and the planet as much as profit. As noted in Chapter 7, as an example, this is a direction in which the UK Financial Reporting Council are moving.

Chris Turner, executive director of B Lab UK, tells us that while there is still a lot of work to do, they are already seeing a shift in business culture and awareness around the wider responsibilities that companies should have towards all their stakeholders. As he said, 'We're essentially building a community and a network and thereby helping companies to inspire each other.'

In the end, the reality is that we have to be careful not to confuse altruism with business. I am not making a plea here for businesses to be all altruistic and put lots of other interests above their own. More, it is about understanding how these ideas of wider purpose, recognizing the interests of all stakeholders, and trying to do good, actually link to business strategy. We need a clear line of sight as to how this will also help our business to do well. Unless we link CSR, or multi-stakeholderism or wider purpose to positive business outcomes, they are hard to sustain, particularly when times get hard.

These connections won't all be directly causal and quantifiable. But ultimately it is about building brand and reputation as a responsible business, making all our stakeholders want to do business with us. In today's world, as we have discussed, the expectation that business will do these things has never been higher, so we need to work harder to weave these ideas into our business strategies.

People-centric cultures

Having explored the wider dimensions of responsible business and the links to the ideas we discussed in Chapter 7, it is worth some more time on what a responsible business looks like from the inside. How it treats and manages its people.

A responsible business can't be responsible or sustainable unless it is first responsible to its people.

As stated several times, and as should be obvious, businesses all depend on people for their success. The language of high-performing teams and organizations has been popular for years. We're all looking for some secret sauce, but in reality there is no great magic. Having the right people with the right skills in the right places, working together to common goals and objectives, is what's needed – feeling inspired and motivated to give of their best, with supportive cultures that reinforce openness, trust, collaboration and innovation.

Clear and inspiring purpose, embedded values that define the key elements of cultures, measuring and incenting the right things – all are critical foundations.

But truly people-centric cultures also understand that all workers and employees are whole people, they are individuals, they have needs and expectations, they want to be listened to and see that others care about them.

In so much of the history of work, though, people seem to have been treated as assets and resources. Our language of human resources, of human capital, all speak to this. They are measured as a cost and while in the past we might have preferred simplistic models of control through rules or algorithms, people are not robots.

Happily, over recent decades management thinking and practice has steadily embraced the notions of humanity and of understanding human behaviour and motivations. The Covid-19 pandemic, which was above all things a human crisis, has greatly accelerated a more humanistic and holistic view of people at work.

As so many people were forced to work from home and we started to interact via video calls, staring at each other's living and home environments in the background, it made us all appreciate our colleagues in different ways. Obvious symbols of hierarchy and power dropped away, and leaders and managers at all levels communicated more and worried about each other's wellbeing. Even though so many were working remotely and were not physically connected, work became more human.

Inclusion and diversity as drivers of good business

One of the consistent themes throughout this book is the value and importance of inclusion and diversity – from inequality to the needs to access all skills and talent, breaking the mould of group think, and as a source of innovation.

Inclusion and diversity are part of people-centric cultures. We have noted the increasing pressure on businesses everywhere to show they are creating more diverse organizations, and addressing issues of opportunity and progression, as can be shown for example through pay gaps.

Building more inclusive organizations has received a lot more attention in the last year or two. The Black Lives Matter movement highlighted many things, not least the slow progress and action across the business world in creating more ethnically diverse organizations and cultures of respect with zero tolerance for racism or discrimination in any form.

For businesses therefore this is not just some social trend or about being 'woke'. Inclusion should be seen at the heart of thinking about sustainable and responsible business, and should link to connection with and understanding of all stakeholders.

For the workforce, an inclusive culture creates the ability to attract more diverse talent and breadth of experience. These are vital ingredients for addressing skills gaps and building the workforce of the future that reflects the demographics of our populations. We also know that innovation comes from diversity. We have to think differently, take on board different perspectives and experiences. And diversity is the crucible.

Our customers expect to see organizations that reflect them. We have to communicate with our customers, representing them inclusively, not as some subset. And we have to understand all our customer segments and diversity to be successful. Having a workforce that has those insights, because they also reflect the diversity of the customer base, becomes obvious.

Channel 4, a UK-based broadcaster, recognized this many years ago. They are very visible in their commitment to diversity for these reasons, expressed through their 360° Diversity Charter[17] first launched in 2015. As they call out, Channel 4 is an industry leader in diversity, both within broadcasting and more widely. Diversity has always been essential to Channel 4's mission, and since launching the 360° Diversity Charter their aim has been to be 'truly reflective – both in what we do and who we are – of the diversity of Britain today'.

For the communities and societies of which any organization is part, diversity reflects all these points.

The power of empowerment

Swedish music streaming company Spotify is known for its culture of experimentation and its test-and-learn approach, but it also always ensures that risk is contained through a 'limited blast radius'. It champions open dialogue and data-led thinking in favour of anything that's opinion-oriented, and its organizational structure is designed around small teams – or squads – that work mostly autonomously under self-determined leadership to give employees a sense of ownership.

The same sort of culture and philosophy has been highlighted in organizations like Zappos and Buurtzorg, a Dutch social care organization which we will return to in Chapter 10. Organizations that empower their people effectively result in more engagement, more innovation and adaptability, and a better focus on the real outcomes and customers of the business.

One of my favourite examples, though, is that of the military. No one would deny that the military is hierarchical. From top to bottom, even in the smaller national military forces, there would typically be more than a dozen ranks from private to general that have existed by tradition for centuries. And you are never in doubt about who is where in this hierarchy, with badges of rank and regalia to remind you, reinforced by a culture of discipline.

This is the antithesis perhaps of prevalent management thinking about flat structures and minimizing management layers. However, this is not how the military works in practice.

The changing geopolitical world, described succinctly by the VUCA acronym, made it clear that military operations in highly uncertain and changeable environments could not be undertaken with long chains of command to decide every action that needed to be taken on the ground. Decision-making had to be devolved as far as possible to those directly on the front line. And the teams on the ground would require all their functions and disciplines to work together to execute their mission.

The mission must therefore be clearly communicated from the senior ranks, and the boundaries within which the teams can operate must be unequivocal. Within those boundaries, the teams led by junior officers must be able to make the calls.

This is the concept of Mission Command, adopted in the modern era by the US and the UK and now largely across NATO forces. It embodies so much of what we have been talking about – clear mission and purpose, strong communications, trust and empowerment.

An article in *The Army Leader* by a former British officer summarized it well with five key points.[18] Have a clear vision and mission; over-communicate clearly (at least two levels down); delegate until you feel uncomfortable then delegate some more; encourage all to speak up starting with the most junior; and trust other teams as if they were part of your own.

But for every example where people are properly empowered and given autonomy, there are many more where the opposite is true. Some of this has come about from trying to create models of efficiency, enabled by smart technology, which in some cases has taken organizations back to the days of scientific management. Classic examples are in workforce scheduling and how best to manage and deploy resources to multiple tasks or locations, such as field service engineers, social care workers or logistics operations.

I have witnessed many examples of workforce scheduling technologies that use clever algorithms to optimize travel times between jobs and how much time a job should take, or to control how people do tasks and in what sequence to best fulfil orders. The great danger is that while there may be some optimization of activity, the people have no agency or autonomy and become disengaged.

In one organization involving field service engineers I worked with a few years ago the problem was so extreme that I was surprised they continued to work there. They described how they would arrive at their depots in the morning, and download the optimized schedule of house visits they had been given, with the calculated standard time each job should take. The GPS trackers in their vans or trucks told central control where they were, and if it appeared they were not near enough to where they were supposed to be, they would get a call. If they ran over their allotted time for the job, they would get a call. If they finished early, they had no incentive to do anything other than go and sit in their van and wait for the next job to come up – not even to go and help out a colleague who might be nearby and need assistance.

This was not how they operated in the past when they would collaborate to organize the best ways of working. Now they felt completely disempowered to the extent that there was a somewhat odd camaraderie which excluded even former colleagues who had now moved up to line management roles. They said the only reason they stayed was because of the relatively good pay and pension rights.

We can still use optimizing technologies, but let's use the principles of empowerment and delegate as much as possible to the workers and teams to find what works best in optimizing all outcomes.

The importance of listening and speak-up cultures

The wisdom of the crowd is a good paradigm for another important element of sustaining ethical and responsible organizations.

We talked earlier about the mission command principles within the military, and gaining input and feedback from all levels, even starting with the lowest in the pecking order. In the most demanding of circumstances where actions have huge and immediate consequences, the importance of listening to all is recognized. It helps to get to the best decision, to see all the angles, and make sure all consequences and outcomes are considered. Essential to any responsible organization as we have seen.

Feeling able to speak up, particularly where people see something that is not right, is an important part of the checks and balances in ensuring ethical and responsible behaviours. But it goes further than that, in helping to create the feedback loops where organizations learn from past mistakes and continue to grow.

Carol Dweck, a professor of psychology at Stanford University, described the idea of growth mindset based on her research on how individuals respond to failure and how they learn.[19] She contrasted a fixed mindset where failure was something to be avoided or punished, with growth mindset where we recognize the opportunity for continuous learning and growth.

Matthew Syed, the widely acclaimed author and speaker on what creates high performance, built on these ideas as mindsets for organizations. In his book *Black Box Thinking*,[20] he describes how organizational mindsets of growth facilitate cultures of open and honest feedback and continuous learning. He cites as an example the airline industry which has developed incredible levels of safety most of us now take for granted – any person at any level can challenge a decision, call things out when they think something is wrong, and failures are opportunities to learn.

For any individual, being able to speak up requires a sense of trust and a feeling of safety, that they won't be unfairly judged or discriminated against for having challenged others or particularly their superiors in the organization. Sadly, not a sufficiently common attribute of organizations today.

Good indicators of open cultures are how organizations listen and respond to issues of conflict, of misconduct, harassment and bullying, and discrimination – all issues that relate to ethical practice and responsible business. As noted earlier, the Institute of Business Ethics' survey highlighted how important these issues were to people's belief in ethical business – roughly a quarter of women surveyed highlighted discrimination issues (which had grown significantly from the year before), bullying and harassment, and ability to speak up.

Most organizations have reporting systems or confidential helplines in place to enable people to report misconduct in the workplace in all its various forms. But even where these confidential channels are used or available, there is typically a sense from employees that nothing will happen.

CIPD research on managing conflict in the workplace published in January 2020[21] confirms this. Nearly half (47 per cent) of workers didn't think that their complaint would be treated seriously, 42 per cent didn't think that any action would be taken against the perpetrator, and many were concerned that raising issues would rebound on them personally. The most common word that people used to describe a good workplace culture was 'listen', followed by 'respect' and 'trust'.

Not all conflict is necessarily negative, and disagreement and debate is part of healthy dialogue and decision-making. But conflict that impacts people's trust, wellbeing and ultimately their performance is a common occurrence at work, according to a significant proportion of both employees (26 per cent) and employers (20 per cent).

The research found that just over a third of respondents had experienced some form of interpersonal conflict, either an isolated dispute or ongoing difficult relationship, over the past year.

Other recent surveys have suggested that during the pandemic there were some increases in bullying and discrimination. Remote working creates an even stronger need for people to feel trusted and able to share their concerns openly.

So it's clear that feedback channels or confidential helplines won't address the issues if people don't trust that they can speak up or that any real action will happen as a result.

Whistleblowing is another mechanism by which people will challenge organizations where they see broader issues of fraud, or unsafe activity or illegal actions. It can also apply to the other issues we have discussed, so it is not distinct, but it is the heading under which legal rights and protection are given. It has received more public attention in recent years – with high-profile cases such as that against WikiLeaks founder Julian Assange, or the whistleblowing by Michael Woodford, the CEO at Olympus, on corporate fraud that was widely reported.

Many countries have been reviewing and tightening legislation. The EU introduced new directives from 2021 to provide more consistency across member states on whistleblowing as it relates to areas including public procurement, financial services, money laundering, public health and product and transport safety. They will apply to all companies with 50 or more employees.

Channels of support and advice to whistleblowers play an important role where whistleblowers want to raise issues they feel are not being listened to internally. Protect (formerly Public Concern at Work) is a UK charity[22] with more than 30 years' experience in helping people and organizations. They have a useful benchmark that helps organizations understand how well their own internal channels and speak-up cultures are working.

Prevention is always better than cure. Open and speak-up cultures start at the team and manager level. But more needs to be done to train managers to listen, to understand concerns, recognize and address bullying or discrimination, and help to manage conflict. These are all critical parts of good people management.

Good corporate governance

The final area to consider in driving towards more responsible and sustainable organizations for the future is corporate governance. It is a big and involved field in its own right and I have touched on it in various ways, but it is important to emphasize certain areas that build on our views of guiding responsible business behaviours.

Corporate governance relates to the oversight and responsibilities of boards in the strategic direction of the organization, protecting the interests of all stakeholders and holding the organization and its executive to account.

Regulators in every country prescribe codes and regulations for how boards should operate. As we noted in the last chapter, regulators like the FRC in the UK are taking a much broader view of what good corporate governance is. The new Corporate Governance Code, in effect from 1 January 2019, asks boards to create a culture which aligns company strategy with purpose and values, and to assess how they preserve value over the long term.

The OECD, partnering with the G20, developed a series of six key principles of good corporate governance in 1999, most recently updated in 2015,[23] which could be seen as an international benchmark. They focus mostly on publicly traded companies, but the principles can be seen as more broadly applicable:

> **THE SIX OECD PRINCIPLES OF GOOD CORPORATE GOVERNANCE**
>
> - Ensuring the basis of an effective corporate governance framework
> - The rights of shareholders and key ownership functions
> - The equitable treatment of shareholders
> - The role of stakeholders in corporate governance
> - Disclosure and transparency
> - The responsibilities of the board

Of particular interest are the role of stakeholders in corporate governance and disclosure and transparency.

As the OECD emphasizes on the principle on the role of stakeholders, 'Corporate governance is also concerned with finding ways to encourage the various stakeholders in the firm to undertake economically optimal levels of investment in firm-specific human and physical capital. The competitiveness and ultimate success of a corporation is the result of teamwork that embodies contributions from a range of different resource providers including investors, employees, creditors, customers and suppliers, and other stakeholders.

'Therefore, in the long-term interest of corporations to foster wealth-creating co-operation among stakeholders, the governance framework should recognize the interests of stakeholders and their contribution to the long-term success of the corporation.'

On transparency, the report makes the important point that 'A strong disclosure regime can help to attract capital and maintain confidence in the capital markets. By contrast, weak disclosure and non-transparent practices can contribute to unethical behaviour and to a loss of market integrity at great cost, not just to the company and its shareholders but also to the economy as a whole.'

As with all principles regarding transparency, there is an emphasis on materiality. The idea of materiality as defined through international accounting standards is any facts or data which have a material bearing on the 'decision making of a reasonable user'.

I would contend that information about an organization's culture, purpose, values and how these are understood and enacted, their people and the investment in them, the demographics and other data about the organization, are all material in this definition. They are certainly of material interest to most external stakeholders and the ideas of responsible business.

Again the OECD stresses that companies, in addition to their commercial objectives, should be encouraged to disclose policies and performance relating to business ethics, the environment and, where material to the company, social issues, human rights and other public policy commitments.

In particular, there is encouragement through the G20/OECD principles as well as national regulators to get more employee participation in corporate governance.

There are various ways in which the voice of the employee can be heard in the structures of corporate governance. For starters, understanding how the employees feel, where the issues are, and areas like cultural alignment should be part of the insights shared at board level consistently and regularly.

Actual employee representation within the board or board committees is more challenging. Even countries such as Germany with its much-vaunted supervisory board structures and the regulated requirements for employee representation have issues which organizations everywhere might be familiar with. The VW 'Dieselgate' scandal was a bit of a dose of reality.

It is very difficult for an individual as an employee to be able to represent a whole workforce, or necessarily be able to act effectively in board environments. There is no one approach, but each organization should consider how it gets the voice of the workforce clearly heard.

One important way of improving corporate governance, particularly as it relates to the organization and people, is to extend the role of remuneration committees.

Historically, the remit of most remcos was to focus on executive pay. Arguably, this has been part of the problem of the growth and imbalance of executive pay as we have observed, particularly as it has become out of kilter with pay within organizations and CEO pay ratios have become increasingly excessive.[24] For the financial year ending 2019, FTSE100 CEOs took home a median pay package worth £3.61m, which was 119 times greater than the median earnings of a UK full-time worker (£30,353). In the US, the numbers are far higher.

Remuneration committees should have oversight of pay across the wider workforce, and the overall remuneration strategy for an organization. It should then look at executive pay in this context, and not just against external benchmarks.

Even good companies like Starbucks with a pay ratio of 1,049-to-1 and McDonald's with a ratio of 3,101-to-1 show how far the pay differentials have gone. Each company is different, and the emphasis should be on determining what's reasonable for each individual company, but it is hard to argue in any circumstance that a CEO can really be making that much difference to deserve these levels of pay. And as noted earlier, CEO pay is a key issue on the minds of many people about ethical behaviour and trust in organizations.

Beyond overall pay strategy, remcos could become the focal point for all culture- and people-related issues within an organization. Alongside the finance or audit committees looking after the money, a remco could look after the people.

Board constitution and diversity

Finally, good board governance is also about board constitution and balance of experience. It is more important than ever before given the range of challenges facing organizations today that boards have the right mix of experience and backgrounds – diversity applies distinctly at board level as well.

A fascinating article and research from Harvard Law School Forum on corporate governance, titled 'Director skills: diversity of thought and experience in the boardroom',[25] in 2018 showed where significant skills and experience gaps in boardrooms remain.

Figure 8.1 taken from the report highlights some of the issues, both at board and at executive levels, at the largest US companies. Similar breakdowns of skills and experience are common for boards in organizations everywhere.

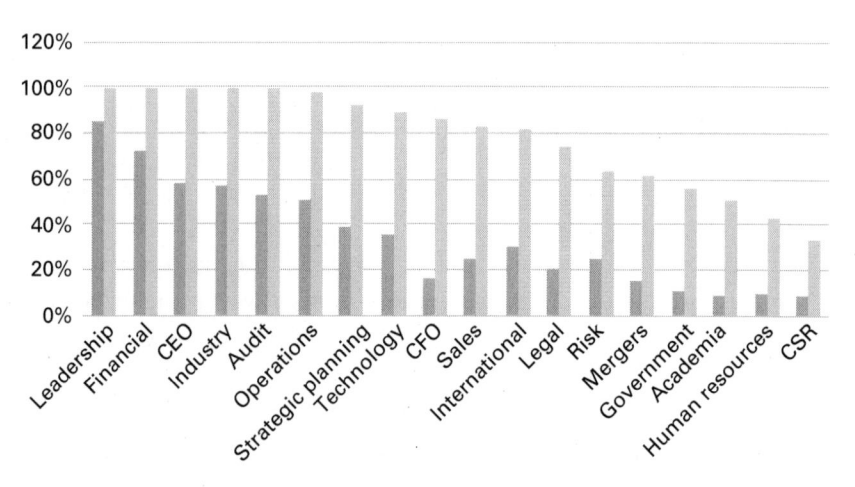

FIGURE 8.1 Percentage of directors and companies with each skill in the 1,000 largest companies in the US by market capitalization

SOURCE ISS Analytics

FIGURE 8.2 Assessed levels of risk relating to ESG policies mapped against diversity of skills on the board

[Bar chart showing percentages for Governance policies, Social policies, and Environmental policies across three categories: Fewer than 13 unique skills, 13–16 unique skills, and 17 or more unique skills]

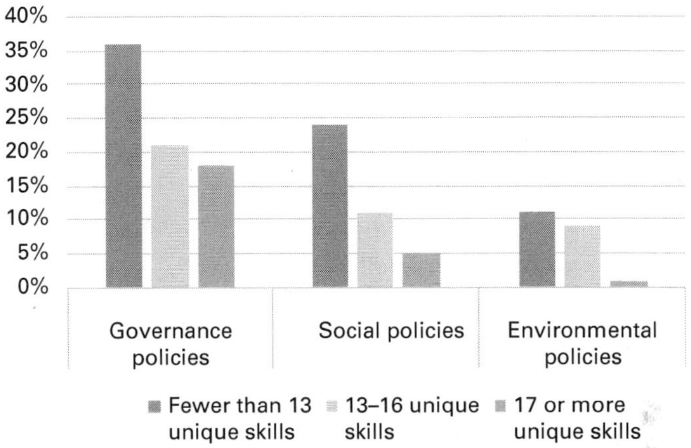

SOURCE ISS Analytics

Both experience in HR and corporate social responsibility fall way off to the right. As the researchers noted, 'Skills such as human resources and corporate social responsibility, which likely have the strongest correlation to the current focus on E&S (ESG) issues, remain some of the least prevalent skills both at the director- and board-level.'

The research also highlighted how a stronger female gender balance often compensated for some of these gaps. It found that those organizations with the widest mix of skills and experience on the board did a much better job of reporting on ESG issues and were more likely to adhere to best practice. They found that 'companies with less diversity of skills on the board have higher rates of risk across all three pillars' of ESG, as shown in Figure 8.2.

So, greater diversity of skills and experience on boards should be the hallmarks of good governance and responsible business for the future.

In conclusion

There are many attributes of what makes a good and responsible business. Typically, it starts with a clear sense of purpose and values that are embedded and lived – purpose that reflects more than commercial outcomes, but also is real and measurable.

Doing well by doing good is such a powerful construct. But it is doing good in line with what a business stands for, and being embedded in the organization, not at the fringes.

Open and positive corporate cultures and how people are treated, with the importance of inclusion and diversity throughout the organization, are all critical attributes of responsible businesses. Also, corporate governance which holds the executive and the organization to account, measuring and recognizing the right behaviours and strategies.

This sets the framework within which leadership should operate, and the framework for good work and quality jobs – themes we will explore next.

Endnotes

1 https://www.edelman.com/trust/2020-trust-barometer (archived at https://perma.cc/B94G-Y98E)
2 https://hbr.org/2020/04/coronavirus-is-putting-corporate-social-responsibility-to-the-test (archived at https://perma.cc/AET3-ZDE8)
3 www.ibe.org.uk/resource/ibe-survey--attitudes-of-the-british-public-to-business-ethics-2020.html (archived at https://perma.cc/Y4NH-PEYU)
4 www.ey.com/en_uk/purpose/why-business-must-harness-the-power-of-purpose (archived at https://perma.cc/L6BY-WYSB)
5 www.profgalloway.com/yogababble (archived at https://perma.cc/F4GW-B2ZK)
6 www.nytimes.com/2019/11/02/business/adam-neumann-wework-exit-package.html (archived at https://perma.cc/8KZF-M3XP)
7 www.ced.org/pdf/Social_Responsibilities_of_Business_Corporations.pdf (archived at https://perma.cc/K9CH-P36U)
8 www.greatplacetowork.com/certified-company/1000745 (archived at https://perma.cc/4G9K-KY3F)
9 www.forbes.com/sites/angelauyeung/2020/04/23/outdoor-clothing-chain-patagonia-yvon-chouinard-starts-selling-online-again-after-unusual-decision-to-pause-its-e-commerce-due-to-coronavirus-pandemic/#718dc8e31c48 (archived at https://perma.cc/27T4-BUH7)
10 www.ft.com/content/1564e99a-5766-11e8-806a-808d194ffb75 (archived at https://perma.cc/56A8-4CWJ)
11 https://bcorporation.net/ (archived at https://perma.cc/FNA6-GCPR)
12 https://papers.ssrn.com/sol3/papers.cfm?abstract_id=2794335 (archived at https://perma.cc/WDC3-RD3G)
13 https://journals.sagepub.com/doi/abs/10.2189/asqu.2011.56.1.061 (archived at https://perma.cc/U5JC-BL7E)

14 Edmans, A (2020) *Grow the Pie*, Cambridge University Press, Cambridge
15 www.blueprintforbusiness.org/wp-content/uploads/2018/05/Blueprint-how-can-investors-identify-a-purpose-led-company-May-2018.pdf (archived at https://perma.cc/LV7F-2XN8)
16 www.nytimes.com/2019/10/17/business/certified-b-corps.html (archived at https://perma.cc/ZW99-KCMF)
17 www.channel4.com/media/documents/corporate/diversitycharter/Channel4360DiversityCharterFINAL.pdf (archived at https://perma.cc/XX55-AS5C)
18 https://thearmyleader.co.uk/five-rules-of-thumb-to-build-a-mission-command-culture-part-1/ (archived at https://perma.cc/RT6F-96LB)
19 Dweck, C S (2006) *Mindset: Changing the way you think to fulfil your potential*, Random House, London
20 Syed, M (2015) *Black Box Thinking: Marginal gains and the secrets of high performance*, John Murray (Publishing), London
21 www.cipd.co.uk/Images/managing-conflict-in-the-workplace-1_tcm18-70655.pdf (archived at https://perma.cc/M9AQ-JEFH)
22 https://protect-advice.org.uk (archived at https://perma.cc/9VZH-885E)
23 www.oecd.org/daf/ca/Corporate-Governance-Principles-ENG.pdf (archived at https://perma.cc/XPK5-XEHX)
24 www.cipd.co.uk/Images/ftse-100-executive-pay-report_tcm18-82375.pdf (archived at https://perma.cc/2LN3-VJ7Y)
25 https://corpgov.law.harvard.edu/2018/10/10/director-skills-diversity-of-thought-and-experience-in-the-boardroom/ (archived at https://perma.cc/JAE6-U6B4)

09

Leadership for the future

A good leader inspires people to have confidence in the leader.
A great leader inspires people to have confidence in themselves.
ELEANOR ROOSEVELT, US DIPLOMAT, ACTIVIST AND POLITICAL FIGURE

Much of what has been thought about in the world of work, about performance and productivity, about strategy and cultures, or about role models and visionaries, has centred on leadership.

For centuries the concept of good leadership has fascinated and mystified us. Numerous historical myths have withstood the test of time by telling tales of the damage wrought by bad leaders and the prestige achieved by the good.

The popularity of fictional leaders through the ages has shaped many of today's ideals and standards of what makes a great boss. We all will have our views of what makes a good or bad leader or boss. We have all experienced it. Many of us have tried to practise leadership, and we usually find ourselves learning as we go no matter how much 'development' we may have had. We develop good habits and not so good habits, and every now and again we get a reminder or a refresher of what we should be doing.

More books have been written on the theme of leadership almost certainly than any other subject in business. Typing 'books on leadership' into Amazon comes up with over 40,000 results, and just for 2020 it shows more than 5,000 titles. The pandemic is creating another flurry.

When I talk about leadership, one of the slides I use shows covers of various books on leadership which are usually about lists, laws or guides; from the *Leadership Secrets of Santa Claus*, *The 21 Irrefutable Laws of Leadership* – or if you prefer the shortened version, *The Eight Universal Laws of Leadership* – or perhaps my favourite, *The Complete Idiot's Guide to Leadership*.

Doubtless all worthy – indeed, if you are interested, *The 21 Irrefutable Laws* appeared among *Soundview Magazine*'s 25 best ever books on leadership that it compiled in December 2020.[1]

But we cannot possibly consume all this, and there will be many contradictory views of what makes the best leaders, fads and trends that come and go, and quite clearly just how many 'laws' there really are. Having read a lot, I am happy to report that I was aware of more than two-thirds of the best 25, and have read (at least the bite-sized summary of) seven or eight of them, some of which are referenced in this book.

What this tells us is that leadership remains a paradox – what it actually is, what is important about it and how it is best developed. Leadership in actuality is both a noun and a verb.

Leadership really is more art than science. Leadership development is a combination of knowing, doing and being – our base of knowledge, how we learn through experience and how we act, how we behave and our values and beliefs.

Good behavioural science such as adult developmental ideas can help inform the art. We can learn from leadership in different contexts, such as sport, the military or the corporate world, but we have to adapt, to contextualize. And we have to recognize we are always learning.

Described as 'the Dean of Leadership Gurus' by *Forbes* magazine, Warren Bennis in his classic book *On Becoming a Leader* (book number one on the Soundview list) persuasively argues that leaders are not born, they are made.

Many would argue that people do have inherent strengths, and weaknesses, which help them as leaders, but we learn as we go. Experience is the best teacher, and it shapes us more than formal learning. As the great Galileo observed, 'You cannot teach a man anything, you can only help him find it within himself.'

But formal learning can at least teach us to make best use of our learning experiences, to give us frames of reference and to better understand ourselves. Good coaching helps to reinforce our learnings, to understand ourselves better and to develop our own developmental plans.

So any book about work or business has to include something on leadership. That is not to say the aim is to add to the pantheon, but in any scenario we envisage for the future of work we will continue to require leaders – leaders who are people, albeit perhaps with more assistance from technology and AI.

What is leadership – is it different from management?

Without getting lost in a subject which generates reams of commentary and research, if we simplistically define leadership as doing the right things, and management as doing things right, then we can see things changing.

We have come from a long history of regarding managers as those who do stuff, organize work and make sure things get delivered. We have, however, generally failed to develop them effectively as leaders of people and to empower them to make decisions and to be more accountable. This historic lack of training for managers from the first time they step up to lead is extraordinary. We have revered and recognized the technical competence and then not trained the breadth of skills needed to manage effectively.

In the 1960s, Canadian educator Laurence Peter set out to conduct an intense study of why so many poor or incompetent managers exist. In his subsequent book,[2] Peter and co-author Raymond Hull concluded that organizations tend to reward a high-performing employee by promoting that person to a management position regardless of whether he or she possesses the skills needed for that responsibility or not.

This Peter Principle, as it has become known, might seem like a nonsensical pattern of management, and it would be reasonable to assume that we've learned from our past mistakes. But more recent research indicates that we likely haven't, and the principle remains alive and well.

A 2019 paper published in the *Quarterly Journal of Economics* examined the career progressions of more than 50,000 salespeople across 214 companies in America between 2005 and 2011.[3]

It concluded that individuals who closed twice as many deals as the average salesperson were promoted to management positions about 14 per cent more often than their peers. But it also found that the better a salesperson was, the worse manager they were likely to be. Sales fell by an average of 7.5 per cent in teams led by a manager who used to be a salesperson. Managers who had previously been poor salespeople, on the other hand, were more likely to perform better in their current roles as managers. They were more likely to recognize their limitations and work through others.

The same can be said of football managers – the best and most enduring almost always were not the top-flight players when they were younger.

Similar findings have been found in many other areas of business such as in programming teams – the tendency to promote the most productive programmer, which is easily measurable as it is for sales, and then find team performance drops. The productive programmer can no longer solely focus on churning out code, and their management approach to others discourages rather than encourages.

However, with all the changes that are happening, it is becoming more apparent that we need leaders at all levels. If leaders were to be defined as those who can engage and get the best out of their people, have a sense of purpose and can communicate, who can be change agents as much as they can manage the status quo, who can innovate where they need to, and who can coach as much as they direct – then we need them everywhere.

As is sometimes attributed to John Quincy Adams, the sixth US president, 'If your actions inspire others to dream more, learn more, do more, and become more, you are a leader.'

All these skills are essential in being able to adapt and respond to fast-changing needs and context, as much as they are essential in creating open and engaging cultures that help get the best out of everybody. Thinking like this also helps to get leadership closer to all our people, and to the real action and the front line.

Leadership therefore should not be seen as just about a single person or senior group. It is as much about a mindset and pervasive culture of empowerment. And in reality it is more about actions and behaviours than it is about role or position in a hierarchy. More the verb than the noun.

As we discussed in Chapter 7, models of workplace democracy, 'humanocracies' or holacracies are powerful ideas built around these perspectives. They move us on from old command and control cultures to something that puts people at the heart of business thinking. People will follow those they trust and respect, not necessarily just because of their position – particularly as we have seen with the younger generations and the wider issues of trust across society.

Another driver for this change will be technology and AI. As we touched on in Chapter 4, we can see that AI is increasingly helping with the performance of traditional management-type tasks – scheduling and managing resources (robots as well as people) to be as efficient as possible, or performing many tracking and analytical tasks that would have been part of management activity in the past.

The fourth industrial revolution is more and more emphasizing the real value of the human skills that lie at the heart of good leadership.

A brief history of leadership models – are they helpful?

With all the research and books on leadership, what are some of the things we have learned?

Good leaders come in all shapes, sizes and forms, as do bad leaders. Leaders are rarely good at all times or bad at all times. Appreciation of context and need, and the ability to adapt without losing sight of core values, beliefs, vision and purpose, means also that there is rarely one leadership model that will work at all times.

Given the intense and longstanding interest in leadership as a field of research, it is not surprising that over time various models for leadership get developed and promoted. They can be seen as the next big thing or trend, the answer to all the failings of leadership that have gone before them.

Looking back over the history of leadership research and the models that have evolved, we can see aspects of all of them not only still very much alive, but with relevance in different circumstances.

Scientific management and the work of F W Taylor in the early 1900s that we have referenced before is often taken as the start point.

It was a very task and process-oriented approach to management, but there are still many tasks and operations that need to be approached in a systematic and disciplined way. Furthermore, his belief in using science and not just intuition or rule of thumb has echoes today in the ideas of evidence-based management.

The trait theories of leadership that followed sought to define specific character traits of good leaders from the belief that these were inherent. As Taylor also believed, the view at the time was that good leaders were born and not made. All these ideas changed by the early 1970s.

Ralph Stogdill, a professor in management science and psychology at Ohio State University, compiled much research and evidence that showed people don't become effective leaders because of pre-destined traits. He argued that a leader's behaviours must be relevant to the demands of the situation, and the needs and concerns of the followers.

Many other models and ideas have followed, from transformational leadership, to authentic, charismatic, values based, and servant leadership. All have aspects of truth about them, but even as Stogdill noted, they are not singular universal truths.

We each need to understand what our strengths and weaknesses are and what our natural style of leadership is. Our styles will differ depending on our personalities, our experiences and other leaders we have learned from. Any leadership programme I have been part of or seen almost always starts with building self-awareness.

Being self-aware helps us to be authentic and show consistency in our behaviours and actions, things others look for in leaders. But being authentic does not mean being inflexible – empathy is about understanding others and being able to adapt to them as well. Authenticity isn't about a licence to just be yourself regardless.

As human beings, we are also subject to biases and what the entrepreneur and influential speaker and writer Margaret Heffernan has described as wilful blindness.[4]

In her book of that title she examines the cognitive and emotional mechanisms by which we make choices and decisions, often not consciously, and remain unseen in so many situations. 'Whether individual or collective, wilful blindness doesn't have a single driver, but many. It is a human phenomenon to which we all succumb in matters little and large. We can't notice and know everything: the cognitive limits of our brain simply won't let us. That means we have to filter or edit what we take in. So what we choose to let through and to leave out is crucial. We mostly admit the information that makes us feel great about ourselves, while conveniently filtering whatever unsettles our fragile egos and most vital beliefs.'

Many failures of leadership can be attributed to this, and she gives many examples in her book – from Enron to Harvey Weinstein – where actions of leaders and organizations do not benefit the greater good, or work against any sense of ethical or moral value.

Quite a good way to think of this is what someone once described to me as Newton's First Law of Motion reflected in a First Law of Leadership Development – every leader continues in his or her state of rest, or in the habitual direction they were heading, unless compelled to change that state by external forces acting upon them.

But as we have explored, we can learn and change. Our habits and our thinking can evolve. We need the frameworks and the evidence to cement these learnings, and to overcome our natural confirmation biases that tend to take us back to what we have always done.

It is why I argued in Chapter 7 the case for more transparency, more focus on understanding the impact on and needs of all stakeholders, and more focus on principles and not just rules – to make us all more conscious of these realities of how we think, and to influence better outcomes.

What and how we learn from crises

Crises accelerate our learning as leaders. We have to respond, often with imperfect information, and help to lead our teams or our organizations or even whole countries through what may be uncharted waters. Cometh the hour, cometh the person.

The topic of leadership and leaders themselves enters the spotlight during crises. As Joshua Rothman, editor of *The New Yorker*, wrote in a 2016 article for the magazine: 'Without an answering crisis, a would-be leader remains just a promising custodian of potential. (Imagine Lincoln without the Civil War or FDR without the Depression.) Before a leader can pull us out of despair, we have to fall into it. For this reason, a melancholy ambivalence can cling to even the most inspiring stories of leadership.'[5]

A bit gloomy perhaps, but the pandemic gave us many examples of this. It speaks to the need for clear and open communication. What is the situation and the reality, and what will we need to do next? Everyone wants facts as far as possible, not unfounded optimism. They want to be treated like adults and will want to know how they should respond and how they can help.

Crises large and small happen all the time and shape our individual learning. Whether it's a huge existential crisis, or a smaller internal crisis, the same principles will apply, and in each case they will teach us something – often, unfortunately, as much through our mistakes as our successes. Crises are the ultimate crucibles of experiential learning, tough as they can be.

As a former colleague of mine, Bob Thomas, described in his book *Crucibles of Leadership*,[6] 'practice and performance are part of the same process'. We learn as we perform, but we also recognize what we need to learn or practise more. Perhaps most importantly, significant events teach us much about ourselves and shape what we each stand for.

Large system-wide crises happen rarely, and when they do they can shape our collective learning.

The economic and public health crises we have faced, the ongoing environmental crisis and the many uncertainties ahead of us will require a new breed of leaders. But these new contexts have also provided extraordinary learning experiences, creating leaders who see the wider context, can think systemically, can deal with paradox and uncertainty and understand their responsibilities to all stakeholders – those who can communicate clearly, build or reinforce trust, and show resilience and clear thinking.

Early on in the Covid-19 crisis, New Zealand's prime minister Jacinda Ardern was praised by *The New York Times*' editorial board as having taught the 'master class' in crisis leadership,[7] a sentiment that was widely shared by commentators around the globe.[8] She explained the restrictions she was imposing rationally and confidently, but with deep empathy too. 'Please be strong, be kind and united against Covid-19.'[9] She empathized with people and showed she was human too with the same anxieties and concerns for her young family.

Leaders of other countries garnered acclaim for their quick and decisive policy reactions which helped to contain the spread of the disease and save lives. South Korea and Taiwan stood out in Asia. Elsewhere, Greece and Iceland as well as Germany were applauded for their responses in the early phases of the pandemic.

Several media outlets noted that many of the leaders earning plaudits during the crisis were female. Louise Champoux-Paillé and Anne-Marie Croteau from the University of Concordia, in an article in *Management Today* in May 2020, argued that 'resilience, pragmatism, benevolence, trust in collective common sense, mutual aid and humility' are all features that are common to the women leaders who were deemed to have excelled.[10]

In terms of individual businesses recognized for demonstrating effective leadership during the coronavirus crisis, all share many of the characteristics displayed by country leaders who have been praised. They communicate often, clearly and directly, they demonstrate compassion and authenticity, and they take swift and decisive action.

Kevin Johnson, the CEO of Starbucks responsible for employees and customers in more than 80 markets globally, was praised for his empathy. In an early April memo to all staff he admitted that he was 'reflecting on the fragility of the human experience' and on the challenges associated with dealing with 'the loss of life, feelings of isolation and loneliness, concerns about health and fears of economic uncertainty'.[11]

Even two decades ago, such rhetoric would have jarred awkwardly with the desirable image of assertive leadership in a capitalist system. It might even have been ridiculed, but Johnson's message is sensitive and compassionate.

In terms of transparency, Marriott CEO Arne Sorenson was commended for his candour and for abstaining from sugar-coating the horrendous impact of the crisis on the industry when he delivered an emotional video message to staff and other stakeholders.[12] 'Covid-19 is like nothing we've ever seen before. For a company that's 90 years old – that's borne witness to the Great Depression, World War II, and many other economic and global crises – that's saying something,' he said. He added that the crisis was having a more severe and sudden financial impact on the business than 9/11 and the 2008 financial crisis combined.

By outlining the appalling severity of the fallout, he's certainly not comforting stakeholders, he might even be instilling anxiety in employees and investors, but he's showing trust and openness and demonstrating that he believes the people who work for the company are resilient and pragmatic enough to deal with the true facts. He's treating them like adults and with respect, which is usually the best way to ensure reciprocation.

Research the CIPD carried out with Professor Veronica Hope-Hailey from the University of Bath Business School during the crisis in 2020[13] set out to see how leaders had responded and what they had most learned.

Through interviews with more than 60 senior leaders, including HR directors, across larger public and private sector organizations, a number of important and consistent themes were found. As the report concluded, trust matters in a crisis because vulnerability drives both a need and a propensity to trust. The more vulnerable we feel, the more we seek leadership. Trust therefore helps organizations generate resilience to deal with volatility and uncertainty.

But trust cannot be created overnight. A critical element of how organizations were able to respond was the pre-existing 'trust fund' that an organization or its leaders had. Findings from research that Professor Hope-Hailey had done back in 2012, 'Where has all the trust gone?',[14] suggest that even among organizations that would describe themselves as responsible businesses, employees were not sure that senior leaders were concerned or cared about their needs. They also did not believe that leaders were open or always 'walked the talk'. All the same sorts of issues we noted through the Edelman Trust Barometer findings in Chapter 4.

The research highlighted the shifts in leadership thinking and behaviours that the pandemic brought about – embracing home working and breaking down previous long-held prejudices, putting health and wellbeing to the fore, and implementing a stronger focus on culture, core values and purpose. There was also more devolved decision-making, connecting and communicating across organizations, with more transparency and walking the talk.

Many management decisions were taken on the front line and not in head office. This was summed up in the research report rather pithily by Sara Bennison, chief product and marketing officer at Nationwide, the UK-wide building society, during our research – 'What the branch manager says on hand sanitizer is more important than what Boris Johnson says on hand sanitizer.'

At the same time, however, CEOs were having to step up to lead their companies from the front, and be more visible than they may ever have been before.

Amazon founder Jeff Bezos in the years before the pandemic had devoted himself to long-range strategic thinking at the group. According to *The New York Times* in an April 2020 article headlined 'Bezos takes back the wheel at Amazon',[15] he started 'holding daily calls to help make decisions about inventory and [Covid-19] testing, as well as how and when – down to the minute – Amazon responds to public criticism'.

While that was true for most leaders, that didn't mean they were there to take all the decisions. They had to be there to understand what was happening, to reassure and to guide. As initial stability was found, then leaders had to pick up their heads and look outwards and forwards. What was the pandemic going to mean for medium- and longer-term strategy? What structural changes might be needed, was there a need for real transformation or was it an opportunity to accelerate on strategic change that had been in the works for a while?

Ironically, despite its constraints, virtual working enabled time to be used effectively in these ways – moving from meeting to meeting or group to group without the need for travel or the usual logistics of meeting rooms and other parts of corporate life we had all become so familiar with. To understand how to respond and what to do next, we all had to listen to our people at all levels, to try to appreciate what was happening and be able to adapt and prioritize differently as needed.

It is clear that some extraordinary things happened through the crisis, with many positives that must be taken forwards.

It was indeed a huge crucible of learning for leaders everywhere. Leaders had to learn more than they may have experienced in their careers to date about listening, trusting and empowering, and communicating. People look to their leaders in uncertain times.

What we must take forwards from here – the mindsets and capabilities leaders will really need

The crises and the many different drivers of change we have discussed throughout are all putting new demands on leaders. The context in which every leader is acting at any level of an organization is more complex, more varied and uncertain than at any time any of us can recall.

The consulting firm BCG came up with a good list of priorities for CEOs at the start of 2020.[16] This was before the pandemic hit but they illustrate quite well the different ways of thinking that CEOs needed given all the changes and demands we have been discussing.

- 2020 is not time to be average.
- Look for opportunities to change the game.
- You're a tech company – regardless of industry or sector.

- Every business will still be a people business.
- Be more flexible in organizing and managing work.
- Go 'multilocal' and develop purpose that is good for society.

These are very different times for leaders than many of them experienced as they built their careers over the last couple of decades. The old paradigms of leadership – command-and-control cultures and authoritarian leadership – have little place in a world where no one has all the answers, where people expect compassion and to be treated fairly, where greater transparency and recognition of wider accountabilities is demanded, and where context is shifting all the time.

So what will be the anchors on which we need to base leadership for the future, and what do we really take forward from the pandemic and the other crises that are reshaping our thinking and our beliefs?

The key capabilities and attributes for leaders that are important now and for the future would seem to be the following. They are broad principles and mindsets – a combination of knowing, being and doing:

- Leaders must be **adaptive, agile and resilient**. Dealing with paradox and uncertainty, multiple truths and knowing when to adjust course. Ability to listen, to appreciate different perspectives and learn from others. Able to think confidently on their feet, unafraid to acknowledge what they don't know, even changing their mind when necessary, while making decisions and still navigating to a clear sense of purpose and vision.
- Leaders must be **systemic and multidisciplinary**. Competence in not just an area of specialization, but in other broader areas particularly as they relate to people management, communication, understanding of culture and of context. Able to think systemically, curious and with a willingness to learn constantly. Humble enough to be both teacher and leader, or student and follower at any given time.
- Leaders must be **empathetic and human**. Listening to and being aware of individuals' needs and expectations, showing care and understanding. Recognizing people, coaching and supporting. Self-awareness, unafraid to show weaknesses and frailty, opening up whole self. Open and honest communicator, visible and approachable.
- Leaders must be **ethical and principled**. Clear values, beliefs and a strong sense of purpose, individually but also aligned to those of the organization. Must recognize all stakeholders in actions and decisions. Exercising judgement, holding true to principles and being transparent. Acting and behaving as a role model.

- Leaders must **embrace diversity**. Diversity in all its forms, to bring the wide range of experiences needed, and able to coalesce diversity into inclusive ways of working and thinking. Prepared to break the comfortable mould of conformity and homogeneity and able to attract and retain all the talent needed.

We'll touch on each of these in different ways through the rest of this chapter as guiding principles of leadership we need for the future.

Importance of evidence and measuring the right things

As we discussed in Chapter 7, measuring the right things is critical to driving any business in the right direction. We should not always be counting the things that count, lacking data and insight into so many areas which are critical to making the right decisions.

One of the more recent movements within the world of leadership and management is evidence-based management (also known as EBM or EBMgt). It is a management approach that involves using multiple sources of scientific evidence and empirical results as a means of attaining knowledge.[17] In essence, making decisions informed by the best available evidence.

Evidence-based thinking has become increasingly pervasive in many disciplines and fields, from medicine to teaching to policing, and beyond. As already mentioned, it's important to keep pushing for more evidence-based HR and people management.[18]

What has always seemed so odd is the obvious question about what we were doing before. If we were not basing decisions in any field on best available evidence, then what were we basing them on? Certainly in my experience in the field of management and business, too often the answer in the past was a combination of intuition or gut instinct (hope for the best), what everyone else was doing (best practice), or what we had done before (experiential bias).

I like the work of the Center for Evidence-Based Management (CEBMa) based in the Netherlands. Led by Eric Barends and Professor Rob Briner, it is a not-for-profit leading authority on evidence-based practice in the field of management and leadership, connecting some of the leading lights in management thinking internationally. Sources of evidence they describe are shown in Figure 9.1.

FIGURE 9.1 Sources of evidence

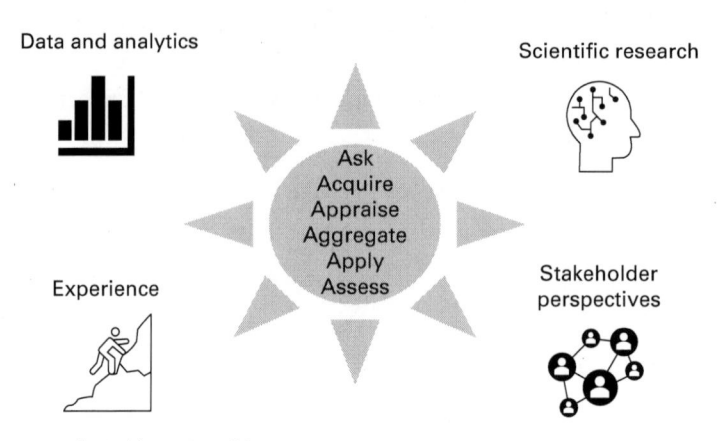

Data and analytics

Scientific research

Ask
Acquire
Appraise
Aggregate
Apply
Assess

Experience

Stakeholder perspectives

SOURCE Center for Evidence-Based Management

One of the first and most important sources of evidence is proper research, or scientific literature. Obvious, right? Yet the worlds of academe and business have long been too separated.

I have observed over many years that academics are recognized for what they write in academic journals. But not only will you never find the journal of anything on any business leader's desk, with the possible exception of *Harvard Business Review* (often there for effect rather than actually to read), but the academic style and method of writing required makes it very difficult for time-poor business leaders to digest. There is a genuine lost-in-translation issue.

The research method and the requirements for rigour in academia take time. Often to find the provable outcome, many variables have to be controlled and this can often also lead to narrow conclusions.

That is not to say it is all their fault. Far from it. Business practitioners as already stated have not paid enough attention to real evidence.

I remember at a conference a few years ago being introduced along with an applied psychologist. The person introducing us was an experienced HR leader and commented in introducing the psychologist that he was just an HR guy so didn't really know anything about psychology. Ouch. Shouldn't the basis of human resource management be an understanding of human behaviour?

Other plausible sources of evidence include organizational data. As we have discussed, we need to do more to build good data and evidence within our organizations to understand people and culture in particular. The views of all our stakeholders are also important as we have emphasized. And professional expertise also must be a legitimate source of evidence, but we will need to do more to invest in our professions and professionals to keep their knowledge current.

CEBMa also outlines a straightforward methodology to help us all understand evidence:

- Asking – begin with taking a problem and asking the right questions.
- Acquiring – systematically search for and retrieve the evidence.
- Appraising – critically judge the relevance and trustworthiness of the evidence.
- Aggregating – weighing and pulling together the evidence.
- Applying – incorporating the evidence into the decision-making process.
- Assessing – evaluating the outcome of the decision-taking.

Developing a stronger evidence base for management and HR practice is an important part of the role of professional bodies – helping practitioners to understand research evidence, but also helping practice shape research priorities. Continued professional development is central to what it means to be a professional in any field, and building the understanding of gathering, reviewing and developing evidence must be a core skill set.

Key metrics and the balanced scorecard

Part of our challenge, however, is that we can be overwhelmed with data and struggle to analyse effectively. Analysis paralysis can set in. And it is hard to manage any business with too many metrics. Any leader needs to be able to see the forest for the trees.

The idea of the balanced scorecard was introduced in 1992 by Robert Kaplan, a professor at Harvard, and David Norton, a strategy consultant, in their *Harvard Business Review* article, 'The balanced scorecard—measures that drive performance'.[19] The four categories of a balanced scorecard they described are financial perspective, internal business perspective, customer perspective, and learning and growth perspective.

The balanced scorecard construct remains very relevant and again calls out the need to understand business from any lens and viewpoint, not just financial measures.

Kaplan and Norton also recommended that a good balanced scorecard had no more than 20–30 metrics, although there would be an underlying depth of analyses to facilitate the deeper dives. The key measures need to filter down through the organization. What we want to drive from the top needs to reflect in how we measure, recognize and reward at all levels.

Traditional metrics will always include costs and budgets, sales pipelines, revenues, etc – the quantitative and fundamental measures of business operations and performance. But to these we must add the more qualitative measures, particularly about our people. If we believe as we should that areas like engagement, wellbeing, diversity of our teams, and how our people are living our values, are important, then we must signal that by making sure these measures roll down too.

These measures should then be linked to leaders' and managers' performance at all levels. We can't only measure and incent performance by looking at what has been done. We must understand how it has been done – did the manager hit the sales targets but leave wreckage behind them in terms of team morale, trust and engagement? If they did, and we let that happen, it will do more damage to the cultures of trust that we need than the sales themselves may deliver in short-term profit.

But of course, as noted, we live in an imperfect world. We don't have all the information we need, not just because we still are not measuring all the right things but also because we live in an uncertain and fast-changing world. There are many unknowns.

With more uncertainty, a key ability for organizations and leaders is to be able to make decisions and act with imperfect information. Taking appropriate risks and making decisions have been identified as key leadership strengths that have emerged more strongly in recent years.

Julian Birkinshaw, Professor of Strategy and Entrepreneurship at London Business School, together with Jonas Ridderstrale, consultant and author, in their book *Fast/Forward*[20] called out these capabilities by arguing that leaders had to be able to act on instinct as much as on data.

They argued that in a fast-changing world, an endless flow of data and vast pools of analytics can get us only so far. They contend that a default assumption that more and better information is always better for an organization is false and can significantly impinge on a company's ability to move fast. 'To navigate the future, the ability to act with decision and purpose will trump big data,' they write. 'Priorities need to be reversed.' They advanced the idea of what they called 'adhocracy' as a contrast to bureaucracy, to open up decision-making and agility.[21]

Decisions that need to be taken with incomplete and imperfect information should, however, also encourage leaders to listen more, to work collectively and collaboratively, and to bring diverse opinions and views to the table. This gives you the best chance of making the right decisions.

These principles need to apply not only at the top level of leadership, but through the organization.

Leading from principles – a 21st-century model of compassion and safety

The work of British paediatrician and psychoanalyst Donald Winnicott, born in Devon in 1896, is considered some of the most pioneering in the field of developmental psychology. One of his most influential concepts was that of the 'holding environment'.

He observed that for infants and children, being held by their mother was critical to healthy development, but he also extrapolated that idea more broadly to the idea of psychological holding and safety as adults. Being held, he argued, didn't mean being sheltered from trauma and discomfort. Instead, it meant being able to develop the resources and processes to manage whatever comes your way. The essence of resilience.

Gianpiero Petriglieri, an associate professor of organizational behaviour at INSEAD, and a medical doctor and psychiatrist by training, builds on Winnicott's work in his own research.[22] He draws a distinction between interpersonal holding and a broader concept of institutional holding. Effective corporate leaders, he says, should be able to provide both.[23]

Institutional holding is perhaps the more obvious one in this context. It speaks to open and supportive cultures where people feel safe – safe to be themselves, express views, to share and participate fully, and even to make mistakes without fear of unfair or undue judgement.

These constructs are central to creating inclusive and diverse organizations and are receiving a lot more attention in this regard. But psychological safety is also at the heart of adaptability and agility as we have discussed. The Spotify example from the previous chapter to encourage experimentation and risk taking to become more innovative illustrates this well.

As Petriglieri also highlights, an effective leader must be open to understanding people's immediate experiences and worries, to give them the permission to experience emotions without the risk of being shamed or overwhelmed. Listening and being empathetic, as noted, are critical skill sets.

People don't care how much you know, until they know how much you care. Or, as a senior leader once reflected to me, if you care about the things your people care about, they will care about the things that you care about.

These ideas have evolved into what many call compassionate management. Being compassionate does not, however, mean not being direct in feedback where needed, and not having clear objectives and expectations – no surprises. It also therefore does not mean people can't challenge or be challenged, so that leaders also have to be able to take the tough messages from those they lead.

One of the areas where the idea of compassionate management is being promoted is within the NHS. Michael West, Professor of Work and Organizational Psychology at Lancaster University, and the work of the Kings Fund have long led for a change in culture from command and control to greater empowerment, trust and compassion.

An article they wrote in May 2019[24] laid out very clearly why this was important and what the myths that get in the way really are. It was driven by the high levels of stress in the NHS (at the time noted to be 50 per cent higher than the general population), and as they said, the need for 'radical innovation – transformational change. That can only come through releasing staff from the rigidities of bureaucracies, command and control hierarchies, and relentless top-down scrutiny and control. And the evidence from research is clear that compassionate leadership is the vital cultural element for innovation in organizations'.

In another bestselling book, *Leaders Eat Last*, published in 2014,[25] Simon Sinek talks passionately about the ideas of leaders taking care of the people, of the cultures of safety, and helping people find meaning in their work. As he says, 'leadership is not just about managing numbers, it's about helping people to thrive and find meaning in their work. When leaders and organizations take care of their people, the numbers will take care of themselves'. But he recognizes and calls out that many leaders have lost sight of this fundamental truth.

Compassion, cultures of safety and care are also clearly linked to themes of wellbeing and seeing wellbeing as a goal of any organization, as we will discuss further in Chapter 13.

Developmental models of leadership – navigating the uncertain and thinking systemically

One of the biggest challenges facing leaders and leadership is that of uncertainty. Another quality of 21st-century leadership that contrasts sharply with the ideals we've modelled ourselves on in the past is an ability to show vulnerability when navigating uncertainty. That's proved tough because it's forced us to confront some of our more deep-seated fears.

Illustrating this point, a 2016 study which looked at the way people responded when playing a video game in which they had to overturn rocks that might have snakes hidden under them, and would receive an electric shock whenever they found a snake, concluded that uncertainty is even more stressful than knowing something bad is definitely going to happen.[26]

Overcoming flight or flight instincts, and being able to deal with contradictory information, paucity of data and the paradox of multiple truths, all of which are characteristics of uncertainty, requires different mental models.

A useful model that describes this well, and how we can evolve our thinking, is called Spiral Dynamics. Developed by Don Beck and Christopher Cowan,[27] and based on the work of developmental psychologist Clare Graves, Spiral Dynamics is a model that aims to chart the development of people, organizations and society. It's centred around the value systems of individuals and organizations as they move through different stages of development, which are sometimes referred to as stages of consciousness.

The first levels of the model take us from the thinking and behaviour that is driven by basic survival, to following the crowd or the tribe, and up to more independent thinking. Initially this independent thinking is more short-termist, self-serving and power-oriented. It is not thinking of others. This is known as the red stage or power phase, and many people get stuck at this level and barely move on. Over-sized egos – but so often hiding deep-rooted insecurities.

As most people develop, though, they move on to the next phases which start with understanding of order and obedience. Thinking is shaped by hierarchy and systems of right or wrong – a rules-based world.

But then we begin to escape the rule-bound thinking and go beyond herd mentality, seeking more purpose and meaning. At this fifth level, it is typically a mindset that views science, and rational, practical thinking as the dominant forces.

The highest levels, however, move into the space of pluralism, caring for others, and decisions require many perspectives and inputs. There is not necessarily one single truth. We start to think much more systemically, seeing the world as a collection of interlocking systems and forms. It drives greater flexibility and spontaneity in how we think, and our ability to deal with paradoxes, competing priorities and evidence, taking holistic views of the world.

Figure 9.2 attempts to summarize these ideas.

FIGURE 9.2 Leadership development and mindsets

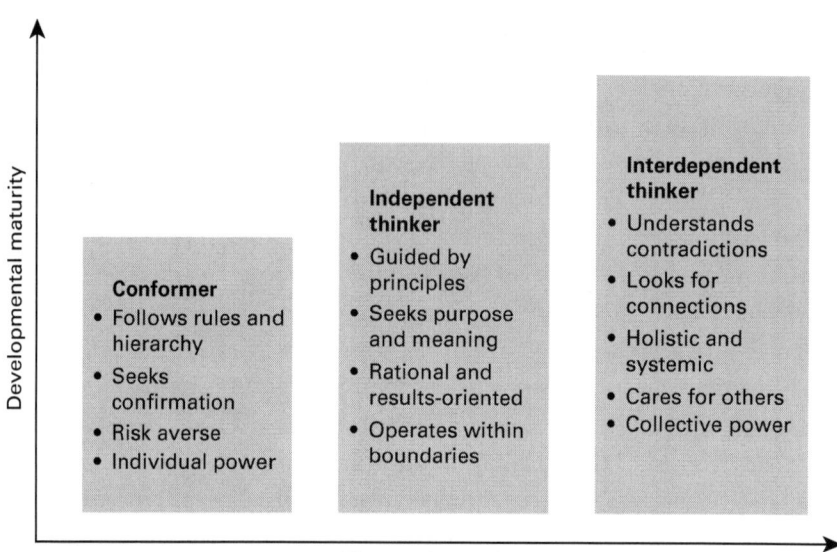

```
Developmental maturity ↑
                                                          ┌─────────────────┐
                                                          │ Interdependent  │
                                                          │ thinker         │
                                        ┌───────────────┐ │ • Understands   │
                                        │ Independent   │ │   contradictions│
                                        │ thinker       │ │ • Looks for     │
                    ┌─────────────────┐ │ • Guided by   │ │   connections   │
                    │ Conformer       │ │   principles  │ │ • Holistic and  │
                    │ • Follows rules │ │ • Seeks purpose│ │   systemic      │
                    │   and hierarchy │ │   and meaning │ │ • Cares for     │
                    │ • Seeks         │ │ • Rational and│ │   others        │
                    │   confirmation  │ │   results-    │ │ • Collective    │
                    │ • Risk averse   │ │   oriented    │ │   power         │
                    │ • Individual    │ │ • Operates    │ │                 │
                    │   power         │ │   within      │ │                 │
                    │                 │ │   boundaries  │ │                 │
                    └─────────────────┘ └───────────────┘ └─────────────────┘
                                    Time and experience →
```

In our lives and in our careers, we tend naturally to move up these levels. As children we lack the maturity and experience to make judgements or understand paradoxes, so we operate and are taught in more rule-bound ways.

The levels are not absolutes, and we may move between modes of thinking and behaviour as circumstances change. That's why the model is presented as an emergent sequence and not as a fixed ladder-like structure.

The model at its higher levels relates closely to the increasingly popular constructs of systems thinking. Systems thinking is based on the theory of systems which are broadly defined as aggregations of interrelated and interdependent parts that work together in achieving particular outcomes. The disciplines of systems thinking include being able to see connections and patterns, not just parts but wholes, not just silos but relationships, and moving from analysis to synthesis. All vital elements of a broader mindset and ability to deal with complexity and uncertainty.

But organizational thinking, reward for deep specialist knowledge, rule-bound cultures and norms often constrain movement of people up to the higher levels, where they can think and operate more for themselves, work within broader boundaries and deal with uncertainty and paradox.

Most research using models like Spiral Dynamics shows that there are significant gaps in many of our leaders. They may be held back by their own insecurities to push more into the unknown, to have their perspectives or views challenged (the anxiety issues we noted earlier), and to be able to accept that if all they have is a hammer, then everything isn't a nail. Even the sense of imposter syndrome. Or conversely, they may be simply driven by overconfidence.

There is a fine line between the positive aspects of confidence and knowing where you are getting in too deep. It requires high levels of self-awareness and the ability to think more broadly to see that you may be wrong and that there are other perspectives you must take into account.

We do need to see confidence in our leaders, alongside humility in being open to what they don't know or what is troubling them. Nothing creates fear and doubt more than seeing a vacillating leader, but overconfident leaders are usually seen through and will create just as much fear and doubt.

In an interview with the *Guardian* in 2015,[28] Daniel Kahneman said there are various flaws that bedevil decision-making that can't be corrected, the most damaging of which is overconfidence. Kahneman said that overconfidence 'is built so deeply into the structure of the mind that you couldn't change it without changing many other things'.

There has been plenty of research that demonstrates that confident CEOs can be more innovative and therefore more successful.[29] They are more likely to take risks. Apple co-founder Steve Jobs reportedly sidled up to AT&T about partnering on a new kind of mobile device at a time when he had absolutely zero expertise in the mobile market.[30] Surely a case of extreme overconfidence, but there's a good chance the result is sitting in the palm of your hand or pocket right now.

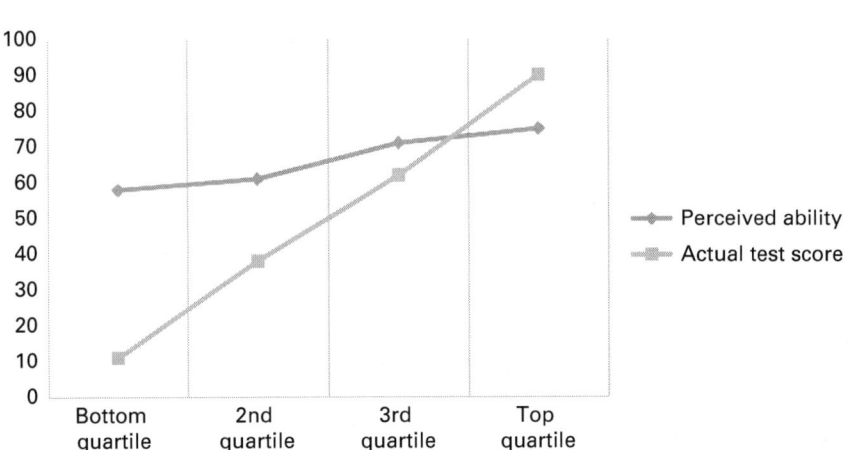

FIGURE 9.3 The Dunning-Kruger effect

SOURCE Journal of Personality and Social Psychology

But we've all witnessed the Peter Principle – we've felt it in ourselves and certainly seen it in others. Echoing Kahneman's sentiment, overestimating our abilities is what's widely become known as the Dunning-Kruger effect. Based on the research of these psychologists published in 1999,[31] it is the cognitive bias many have that makes them believe they are more competent than they actually are. Figure 9.3 shows graphically their key findings.

It can be problematic and irritating if someone is a poor manager, but it can become almost intolerable for colleagues, clients and others if that person believes themselves to be an excellent manager. The comedic value of that idea has been brilliantly exploited in the hit TV series *The Office*.

This is not an uncommon cognitive bias, and in my experience something that men are a lot more prone to than women. Indeed, women often need more encouragement to put themselves forward for the next job or promotion. Whereas men will often view a list of competencies or experiences they might need as 'I can do most of them or blag the rest', women often need to feel they can tick all the boxes properly. This requires different approaches in coaching and developing leaders.

The coronavirus pandemic altered a whole array of things, from the way we think about operational resilience, to the way we consider employee wellbeing. Perhaps this health pandemic will also bring about the demise of the overconfident leader and force a bit more self-awareness as to the limits of our knowledge and capabilities.

Building leadership capabilities

According to data from *Chief Learning Officer* magazine and its Business Intelligence Board,[32] in 2018 nearly 95 per cent of organizations planned to increase or keep their current investment in leadership development. They also suggested that estimates put the spend on leadership development worldwide at as much as $50 billion. Over many years, leadership and management development have been seen as the biggest priority in overall skills development within organizations.

The top priorities for leadership development include strategic planning and business acumen, but increasingly the priorities have been shifting to the 'soft' skills of coaching, employee engagement and improving communication skills.

Chief Learning Officer magazine cited its own research across a wide range of business leaders, finding that leadership development is typically positioned as high-touch and in-person with a strong focus on soft skills. Almost three-quarters of organizations used instructor-led leadership training and almost two-thirds used executive coaching.

But are these programmes effective? Looking at the fact that leadership and management development still remain such priorities and are cited as we have seen as among the biggest corporate risks, the question remains very much open.

According to McKinsey research published in 2014,[33] most of these leadership programmes were failing to create desired results. Key observations were that there was too much one size fits all and too much content in these formal learning programmes – like drinking from a fire hose is an expression I have often heard in this context. Can we possibly remember 21 laws or even 8 laws anyway?

There is often too much emphasis on reflection rather than application. Habits are best developed, or reset, by focusing on a few things at a time then applying what has been learned and repeating often. Similar to how we best learn to play a sport like tennis or golf.

The research also observed another real truism – underestimating the culture and cultural barriers. As they neatly put it, 'No leadership training program can truly succeed unless the organization is willing to look beyond these seven words: that's the way we've always done things.'

Developing leaders at all levels is an imperative. Some of it can be taught, beginning with developing self-awareness to understand mindsets and frames of reference against models like Spiral Dynamics. But much will come from experiential learning.

Working from principles as much as from rules. Giving people more autonomy and empowering them. Exposing them to new challenges, pushing them beyond their comfort zone and then rewarding what they have learned, not punishing what they might have got wrong.

These are also very strong arguments for greater diversity in our leadership. Diversity of background, experience, ethnicity, gender and ways of thinking in leadership teams are an obvious way to bring breadth of insight and perspective we need.

As we discussed in Chapter 7, we need to make more progress in the diversity of leadership teams for many reasons, but there is much evidence now that diverse teams perform better precisely because they bring different disciplines, skill sets and perspectives to address problems and challenges in business.

As Albert Einstein observed, we cannot solve our problems with the same thinking we used when we created them.

But we have to be more courageous in working to these sorts of principles. Even how we recruit into senior levels exhibits the biases and the concerns of risk by pushing people beyond their core knowledge and experience or recruiting people who are different – for example, the strong bias in so many organizations to hire leaders from within their sectors.

A study done by Monika Hamori, a professor at IE Business School in Madrid, and Burak Koyuncu, assistant professor of management at Rouen Business School in France, concluded that hiring a CEO with specific industry experience might even be detrimental to performance of both the CEO and the company.[34]

Examining the professional background and performance of S&P500 CEOs, the researchers found that people tend to draw heavily on experience from past jobs and events, which encourages the formation of 'knowledge corridors'. These can inhibit a person's ability both to act differently in a new role within the same specialist field, and to modify their decision-making templates to fit their new role.

As the academics explain, 'professionals who are well versed in the norms, culture, and routine of one organization may fail at another, due to the fixed assumptions they develop about how tasks should be done'. And they also found that CEOs learn to adapt to a new organization and position more quickly when the experience immediately prior does not conflict with the knowledge, skills and abilities that the new position requires.

When asked what advice he would offer to other CEOs and companies looking for new leadership, Archie Norman, the former chief executive and chairman of Asda, said that 'a lot of chief executives look very successful and are very successful in a company at a point in time'. In fact, he said, 'They look like geniuses.'[35]

'But the real test is if you take that genius and put him in a totally different situation to succeed again. And to do that, they have to be able to listen, able to understand, able to hear why the culture is totally different … the behaviour that worked where you worked before ain't gonna work here,' said Norman.

Talking it through – open leadership

A study conducted in 2017 revealed that a large proportion of employees don't know what their CEO looks like. Some couldn't even name them.[36] That will surely have changed over the last year or so.

Regardless of the nature of the crisis, or indeed the nature of the organization, experts widely agree that communication is the uncompromisable foundation for successful leadership, and particularly in a crisis and times of uncertainty.

Amy C. Edmondson, Professor of Leadership and Management at Harvard Business School, writes that 'if sunshine is the best disinfectant, the opposite is also true: Dark, hidden corners are great places to grow something truly horrible'.[37] Transparency, she says, is 'job one' for leaders in a crisis.

Edmondson cautions, however, that it's important to make clear distinctions between what you know, what you don't know and what you're doing to learn more. People need to see honesty not hubris. Only when employees have accurate information, she argues, can they turn their attention, skills and energy to helping to develop ways to combat these newly visible problems.

In 2002, Paul Argenti, a professor of corporate communication at the Tuck School of Business at Dartmouth College, conducted research into the power of internal crisis-communications strategies practised by large corporations in the aftermath of the 9/11 attacks on the World Trade Centre.[38] Argenti examined the experience of employees and managers at Morgan Stanley, Oppenheimer Funds, American Airlines, Verizon, The New York Times, Dell and Starbucks – all firms severely impacted by the attacks in one way or another – and found that in a time of crisis, internal communications should take precedence over everything else. 'Before any other constructive action can take place – whether it's serving customers or reassuring investors – the morale of employees must be rebuilt,' Argenti writes.

Ray O'Rourke, managing director for global corporate affairs at Morgan Stanley in New York, is quoted by Argenti as reflecting like this on the immediate aftermath of the 9/11 attacks: 'We knew within the first day that, even though we are a financial services company, we didn't have a financial crisis on our hands; we had a human crisis. After that point, everything was focused on our people.' Many leaders have reflected exactly the same idea through the pandemic.

There have been many other good examples.

In autumn 1982, Tylenol capsules manufactured and sold by Johnson & Johnson were laced with cyanide and sold in the Chicago area. Seven people died and Johnson & Johnson was catapulted into the headlines, casting its whole future in doubt.[39] The company adopted an approach of speaking early, often and directly with employees and consumers. That involved issuing a national alert, establishing a toll-free number for consumers to call with questions or concerns, and holding regular press conferences from company headquarters from the very beginning. The company recalled over 30 million bottles of Tylenol, and created new tamper-proof packaging in the immediate aftermath at a great cost.

Chairman James Burke was widely praised for being unconditionally transparent and keeping a cool demeanour throughout the crisis. Today Tylenol is again a trusted over-the-counter drug which few people would associate with seven tragic deaths that occurred in 1982.

It's not only an example of the power of stakeholder capitalism, as we've discussed in the previous chapter, but also of compassionate, confident leadership under which the safety and wellbeing of customers, employees and the broader environment is never compromised. In 2021 and beyond, as the full impact of Covid-19 continues to become evident, this is more relevant than perhaps ever before.

Judgements and ethical decision-making

Making the right judgements, and considering all the impacts and possibilities, is what leaders have to do all the time. And it is very challenging in circumstances with imperfect or conflicting information, or when our beliefs and values are in conflict – what is known as cognitive dissonance.

The term cognitive dissonance was first used by American social psychologist Leon Festinger to explain the discomfort or anxiety that we feel when we hold two or more beliefs about something or someone that are inconsistent with one another. You might use disposable coffee cups despite knowing they're bad for the environment, or smoke even though you know it increases your chance of developing lung cancer.

Research published in the *Journal of Management Control* in 2018 examined the role of cognitive dissonance in performance measurement.[40] The research found that too often the metrics we use to judge performance can be in conflict – conflicting objectives or outcomes. If unresolved, it leads to significant stress, or a reversion to the easiest to measure parts of a job or task as a means of resolving the dissonance. Then it's not only organizational performance that suffers as a result, but also culture, and what the authors of the paper describe as the important practice of 'collegiality'.

What is even more troubling is the moral and ethical conflicts we create at work where rules and metrics dominate our behaviours, but those behaviours really don't align to our normal sense of moral or ethical values.

This aspect of cognitive dissonance was brutally demonstrated in the now infamous experiments by social psychologist Stanley Milgram in the 1960s. In what are sometimes known as the electrocution studies, he sought to understand just how far people would go in causing what they understood was harm to others in a strongly rule-bound and authoritative context.

Roger Steare, a consultant and 'corporate philosopher', in his powerful book *Ethicability: How to decide what's right and find the courage to do it*,[41] described these issues clearly. Based on moral philosophy and research into human psychology and behaviour, he describes three moral consciences or levels.

The Ethic of Obedience is defined by rights, rules and legal duties. As we have observed, that underpins the idea of compliance, but of itself can be contradictory and can never be complete. The next level is Ethic of Care. This extends our frame of reference to thinking about others, about the consequences of our decisions and actions. It embraces the idea of empathy and the concept of social contract. The highest level is Ethic of Reason. This is based more on values, principles and virtues. Not just about empathy, but about rational thinking in a wider context.

This is a powerful frame of reference for this debate about doing what is right, and clearly amplifies the issues of rules versus principles and higher ideals and responsibilities.

Steare developed an approach to understand how these different levels work in actuality. Called MoralDNA,[42] which has now been used by thousands of people, it has called out some fascinating contradictions. Our ethic of care appears largely constant throughout our lives, while our ethic of reason grows dramatically and inversely to our ethic of obedience which declines. Also, women demonstrate a much higher level of ethic of care than men. Won't be a surprise, certainly to most women.

But in the context of our work lives, there is a huge and worrying variance between what drives us at work versus what drives us in life.

The ethic of obedience is very much higher at work, but our ethic of care goes the other way – a profound reflection of rules-based cultures and command and control. Leaders and others are doing things at work because those are the rules or expected norms or what they think they are most measured and rewarded by, and not feeling that sense of personal accountability to others.

This conflict has led to many examples with bad outcomes. In February 2020, US bank Wells Fargo and one of its subsidiaries agreed to pay $3 billion to resolve a legal case relating to a practice between 2002 and 2016 of pressuring employees to meet unrealistic sales goals.[43] Thousands of employees had provided millions of accounts or products to customers under false pretences or without consent, often by creating false records or misusing customers' identities, according to the Department of Justice.

As summarized by the leading prosecuting attorneys, this was seen as an egregious example of a business that 'traded its hard-earned reputation for short-term profits', and that 'when companies cheat to compete, they harm customers and other competitors'. All true, and while it was also clearly seen as a failure of leadership at multiple levels within the bank, it pointed to a culture of obedience and metrics that only considered the profit motive.

It wasn't because the bank subsidiary hired bad people. It was because they put them in a context where their behaviour became determined by rules and metrics of success that removed any wider sense of accountability to those they were selling to. An outcome those Milgram experiments graphically demonstrated.

Sadly, it happens everywhere. Even where there is not any obvious profit motive and the clearest objective is one of care for others. The scandal of the Mid-Staffordshire District General Hospital in the UK is a notable example where it came to light that hundreds of patients had died through poor patient care between 2005 and 2009.

In the subsequent inquiry and report, concluded in 2013,[44] it was stated, 'The inquiry chairman, Robert Francis QC, concluded that patients were routinely neglected by a trust that was preoccupied with cost cutting, targets and processes and which lost sight of its fundamental responsibility to provide safe care.'

Again, the issue wasn't that the front-line medical staff were bad people, but that they were driven by a culture that was paying more attention to process and cost-related metrics than the real purpose and outcome of patient care.

Concerningly, Francis reported in an article in January 2020[45] that NHS staff are still scared to speak up where they see failings in the system of this kind.

In conclusion

Leadership is a set of behaviours and capabilities that are needed not just at the top of organizations but throughout.

Leaders should be driven not just by rules and the old cultures of command and control but by a strong emphasis on guiding principles, ethics, values and alignment to purpose.

Good people management is at the heart of good leadership, and is a resonant theme throughout this book, but we need to do much more to build good people management understanding and skills at all levels.

Leadership is a learned experience, and we learn as much by practice and application as we do from theory or reflection. Understanding and dealing with uncertainty is the normal for the future. We all learn through crises which act as crucibles of learning and they teach us all that we can't know everything.

Dealing with uncertainty and paradox, and being able to think systemically, are critical capabilities of more evolved leadership capabilities, and essential in an increasingly uncertain and changeable world. We have to move beyond rules, beyond command and control, to act and think ethically and encourage others to do the same.

Endnotes

1 www.summary.com/magazine/the-25-best-leadership-books-of-all-time/ (archived at https://perma.cc/YV39-PQLF)

2 Peter, L J and Hull, R (1969) *The Peter Principle*, William Morrow & Co, New York

3 Benson, A, Li, D and Shue, K (2019) Promotions and the Peter Principle, *The Quarterly Journal of Economics*, 134 (4), November, pp 2085–34, https://doi.org/10.1093/qje/qjz022 (archived at https://perma.cc/3VAY-X3G6)

4 Heffernan, M (2011) *Willful Blindness: Why we ignore the obvious at our peril*, Simon & Schuster, New York

5 www.newyorker.com/magazine/2016/02/29/our-dangerous-leadership-obsession (archived at https://perma.cc/D5B5-3MBS)

6 Thomas, R J (2008) *Crucibles of Leadership: How to learn from experience to become a great leader*, Harvard Business Press, Boston, MA

7 https://theconversation.com/three-reasons-why-jacinda-arderns-coronavirus-response-has-been-a-masterclass-in-crisis-leadership-135541 (archived at https://perma.cc/6TRH-5Q27) www.nytimes.com/2020/04/30/opinion/coronavirus-leadership.html (archived at https://perma.cc/2CP5-9WZ8)

8 https://theconversation.com/three-reasons-why-jacinda-arderns-coronavirus-response-has-been-a-masterclass-in-crisis-leadership-135541 (archived at https://perma.cc/6TRH-5Q27)

9 www.nytimes.com/2020/04/30/opinion/coronavirus-leadership.html (archived at https://perma.cc/2CP5-9WZ8).
10 https://www.managementtoday.co.uk/why-women-leaders-excelling-during-coronavirus-pandemic/leadership-lessons/article/1683889 (archived at https://perma.cc/T5R9-YZZ6)
11 https://stories.starbucks.com/stories/2020/a-message-from-starbucks-ceo-kevin-johnson-preparing-for-the-next-phase-in-the-us/ (archived at https://perma.cc/JY23-KL62)
12 www.forbes.com/sites/carminegallo/2020/03/21/marriotts-ceo-demonstrates-truly-authentic-leadership-in-a-remarkably-emotional-video/#65f898d01654 (archived at https://perma.cc/GBY4-Z76T)
13 https://www.cipd.co.uk/news-views/changing-work-views/future-work/thought-pieces/responsible-business#gref (archived at https://perma.cc/L5ZN-KXE5)
14 www.cipd.co.uk/knowledge/culture/ethics/has-trust-gone-report (archived at https://perma.cc/C5YR-C6JQ)
15 https://www.nytimes.com/2020/04/22/technology/bezos-amazon-coronavirus.html (archived at https://perma.cc/Q7G3-Q5M6)
16 https://ceoworld.biz/2020/02/26/ceos-priorities-for-the-2020/ (archived at https://perma.cc/59EF-5U4H)
17 Barends, E, Rousseau, D M and Briener, R B (2014) *Evidence-Based Management: The basic principles*, Center for Evidence-Based Management, Amsterdam
18 www.cipd.co.uk/knowledge/strategy/analytics/evidence-based-practice-factsheet (archived at https://perma.cc/L6YC-J3WE)
19 https://hbr.org/1992/01/the-balanced-scorecard-measures-that-drive-performance-2 (archived at https://perma.cc/88N4-TRBG)
20 Ridderstrale, J and Birkinshaw, J (2017) *Fast/Forward: Make your company fit for the future*, Stanford Business Books, Stanford, CA
21 www.london.edu/think/adhocracy-a-new-management-approach (archived at https://perma.cc/2S45-R26P).
22 https://journals.aom.org/doi/epub/10.5465/annals.2017.0007 (archived at https://perma.cc/VJ53-7MNW)
23 https://hbr.org/2020/04/the-psychology-behind-effective-crisis-leadership (archived at https://perma.cc/3XNH-NBZA)
24 www.kingsfund.org.uk/blog/2019/05/five-myths-compassionate-leadership (archived at https://perma.cc/BN3K-E8B2)
25 Sinek, S (2017) *Leaders Eat Last: Why some teams pull together and others don't*, Penguin Books
26 www.theguardian.com/commentisfree/2016/apr/04/uncertainty-stressful-research-neuroscience (archived at https://perma.cc/7JJU-QA4J)

27 Beck, D and Cowan, C (2005) *Spiral Dynamics: Mastering values, leadership and change*, Wiley-Blackwell, Chichester
28 www.theguardian.com/books/2015/jul/18/daniel-kahneman-books-interview (archived at https://perma.cc/FZX5-5F8R)
29 https://onlinelibrary.wiley.com/doi/abs/10.1111/j.1540-6261.2012.01753.x (archived at https://perma.cc/A597-LU9T)
30 www.forbes.com/sites/petercohan/2013/08/16/how-steve-jobs-got-att-to-share-revenue/ (archived at https://perma.cc/NJ46-M2R2)
31 Kruger, J and Dunning, D (1999) Unskilled and unaware of it: how difficulties in recognizing one's own incompetence lead to inflated self-assessments, *Journal of Personality and Social Psychology*, 77 (6), pp 1121–34
32 www.chieflearningofficer.com/2018/03/21/follow-the-leadership-spending/ (archived at https://perma.cc/6YJE-BGWX)
33 www.mckinsey.com/featured-insights/leadership/why-leadership-development-programs-fail (archived at https://perma.cc/2X6L-GB9A)
34 www.ie.edu/insights/articles/new-ceo-better-without-prior-experience-2/ (archived at https://perma.cc/G5FN-ENUT)
35 https://sloanreview.mit.edu/article/the-ceo-experience-trap/ (archived at https://perma.cc/J9CZ-S2B8)
36 www.entrepreneur.com/article/293827 (archived at https://perma.cc/KC98-WWG8)
37 https://hbr.org/2020/03/dont-hide-bad-news-in-times-of-crisis (archived at https://perma.cc/U77S-3HDP)
38 https://hbr.org/2002/12/crisis-communication-lessons-from-911 (archived at https://perma.cc/4LDG-77AA)
39 https://www.crimemuseum.org/crime-library/cold-cases/chicago-tylenol-murders/ (archived at https://perma.cc/S5HL-NCSV)
40 van der Kolk, B and Kaufmann, W (2018) Performance measurement, cognitive dissonance and coping strategies: exploring individual responses to NPM-inspired output control, *Journal of Management Control*, 29, pp 93–113
41 Steare, R (2013) *Ethicability®: How to decide what's right and find the courage to do it*, 5th edn, Roger Steare Consulting Limited, London
42 https://moraldna.org (archived at https://perma.cc/LZ9R-C5ZW)
43 www.justice.gov/opa/pr/wells-fargo-agrees-pay-3-billion-resolve-criminal-and-civil-investigations-sales-practices (archived at https://perma.cc/83GB-YMZR)
44 www.gov.uk/government/publications/report-of-the-mid-staffordshire-nhs-foundation-trust-public-inquiry (archived at https://perma.cc/W6GX-H9PW)
45 www.independent.co.uk/news/health/nhs-mid-staffs-inquiry-robert-francis-patient-safety-a9283671.html (archived at https://perma.cc/V4X7-DH5Y)

10

People strategy at the heart of business strategy

The war for talent is over, and talent won.

ANON

A common refrain about the future of work is about the jobs that will change and the skills that will be needed. As we saw in Chapter 6, skills gaps are already a significant concern in most businesses. The mismatch between our systems of education and training and the world of work is apparent and growing. Education 4.0 will need to work closer with Work 4.0.

But we also know that businesses everywhere will have to step up in their abilities and investments in people and skills development. This will be essential to their ability to adapt and compete in the future, and we develop this theme more in Chapter 12.

It is essential therefore for any business to be able to understand its people, skills and capability needs in support of business strategy for the future. And the many options that exist in how to source the skills needed, to shape the organizational operating models and cultures and the jobs that get the best out of the people, and the core competencies that make each business unique.

These questions are as fundamental to strategy as any debate about markets, products and financial models. Without it, there is a missing leg from the stool.

Yet most businesses historically have not done a good job in thinking these through. Workforce planning has often been along the lines of 5 per cent more here and 5 per cent less there, or how we can reduce levels of operating costs and people costs. Operating models have often evolved rather than really being planned, and corporate cultures have not been well understood. Organizations are regularly changed with the view that a restructuring will drive a different dynamic and focus. As Peter Drucker famously observed, culture can eat strategy for breakfast.

These are the elements of people and organizational strategy. And in the future they are going to become ever more important in determining any organization's success and sustainability.

People and organizational strategy, and HR

These areas of business are the primary focus of the strategic end of HR. It requires a range of strategic skills and capabilities, but it also requires close engagement and understanding with the business and business leaders.

Too often in the past I have heard business leaders complain of HR not being strategic enough. But at the same time I have also questioned business leaders' understanding of what strategic HR really is.

It is not just about bringing accurate numbers on headcount, or figuring out how to manage down workforce costs, or laying off people, or recruiting faster, or compliance and risk management. These are some of the operational essentials for HR, but as for any part of business, they have to be done in a strategic context with clear linkage to business vision, values and direction.

HR, however, has long been challenged to step up more into the strategic space, to be better at the numbers and analytics and able to think and challenge across the business on strategy and strategic need.

The need has long been there, but as with so many things we have observed, the pandemic has greatly accelerated that need. HR itself came to the forefront of business in the response to the pandemic everywhere, and HR people everywhere never worked harder or innovated faster.

The demand, and the opportunity, were neatly summarized in an article in *The Economist* in March 2020 entitled 'The coronavirus crisis thrusts corporate HR chiefs into the spotlight'.[1] As the article said, 'When the financial crisis rocked the business world in 2007–09, boardrooms turned to corporate finance chiefs. A good CFO could save a company; a bad one might bury it. The covid-19 pandemic presents a different challenge—and highlights the role of another corporate function, often unfairly dismissed as soft. Never have more firms needed a hard-headed HR boss.'

This also means a function that is more analytical and has a greater breadth of business skills and capabilities, alongside the traditional areas of HR competence.

This is a big area of focus for the HR profession. As also reported in *The Economist* article, Russell Reynolds Associates, a US-based executive search firm, found that HR heads appointed to Fortune 100 companies in 2016–19 were around 50 per cent more likely than earlier hires to have worked abroad, in general management or finance.

Referring back to the earlier observation in Chapter 7, that business is really about people and money, some businesses see a triumvirate at the top of business – the CEO, the CFO or COO, and the CHRO. Certainly in all my conversations with HR leaders over the last year they have been drawn right into the heart of decision-making and many have reflected how the pandemic has put people at the heart of the business agenda.

The trend of HR leaders getting more of the seat at the top table they have so often talked about had been growing even before the pandemic.

Many already have offices or desks close to the CEO, and we've also witnessed a trend of shareholders increasingly inviting external HR chiefs to be on corporate boards. From 2005 to 2017, the number of HR executives on US public company boards increased from 84 to a record high of 243, according to data from Equilar, the compensation and corporate governance data analysis firm. That analysis includes board seats held by HR executives at companies belonging to the Russell 3000 index, which accounts for about 98 per cent of all US public companies.[2]

Acknowledging the importance of an HR function that is properly integrated into executive strategy has also translated into greater investment. Equilar data cited by *The Economist* shows that in America HR heads' salaries remain lower than those of CFOs but have nonetheless risen 20 per cent faster since 2010.[3]

In the HR domain, a lot of the capabilities that are being seen as more strategic are within the area of OD or organization design and development. Of itself there is still plenty of debate around how to define this space, but it generally captures those areas of HR beyond the traditional hire to fire, or better put, core talent management. The boundaries are fuzzy and many see areas like employee relations and engagement also as part of OD, but it is carried out by many in HR who wouldn't necessarily recognize or call it that.

In general, OD will be critical to how much of HR is shaped for the future. As technology and AI will allow many of the more traditional and administrative parts of HR to be done much more efficiently, it should allow the function to focus attention more on the really value-adding parts of what it does. We will need therefore to develop more capabilities in this area. We already have many gaps and good OD skill sets are in relatively short supply but in growing demand.

So much of what I have covered in this book is really the strategic agenda for HR and OD in the future. What it is all called and exactly how it is structured as a set of capabilities within any organization should be about what works best in their context.

As a side note, it is curious that a lot of the work historically done in this area, on understanding human behaviours, corporate cultures, and job and organizational design, wasn't generally part of HR in the past. It was occupied more by sociologists, or systems engineers, or broad-based strategists.

I believe it must be part of HR and that we must bring together the various siloes of HR practices from talent management, OD and learning and development into an integral whole. We need all these areas to work together, and with the business, to truly understand our people and organization strategies and all the many levers and specialisms that must be applied.

Even addressing specific challenges like inclusion and diversity requires everything from strategic workforce planning to recruitment and resourcing, learning and development, culture and behavioural understanding to come together.

People and organization strategy versus HR strategy

In the past and even today I still find too much confusion behind a very important distinction of the difference between HR strategy and people and organization strategy. Figure 10.1 is something I have used for a long time to explain it.

HR strategy is what HR needs to figure out how best to run the function. That will include the capabilities it needs, how best to structure and organize, and how to interact best with the business. Just like any other enabling function.

Much attention in the past has been paid to HR operating models and strategies. The pursuit of standardization and best practice, shared service models, and other solutions to make HR more efficient. Some have worked well, but much of this work was very inward looking. It wasn't always about

FIGURE 10.1 The different strategy domains

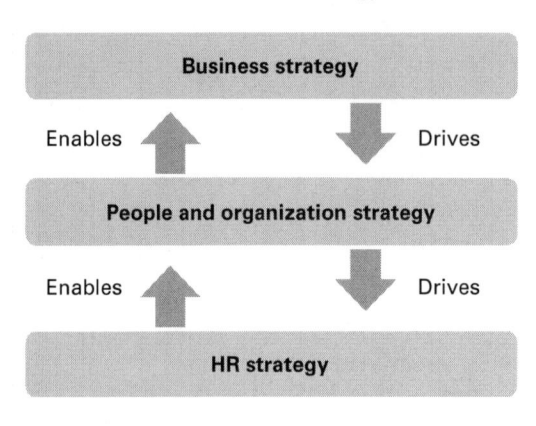

```
        Business strategy              • Business priorities
                                       • Business needs
  Enables  ↑        ↓  Drives

  People and organization strategy     • Skills and capabilities
                                       • Leadership
                                       • Organization and operating
                                         model
  Enables  ↑        ↓  Drives          • Culture

        HR strategy                    • HR capabilities
                                       • HR structure and operating
                                         model
                                       • Practices, policies and processes
```

how best to work with the business, or to understand the specific and unique characteristics that required the best-fit solutions. Too often it was about standardizing and reducing cost of HR delivery as the key goal.

Shared services models were a goal of many, energized by the work of Dave Ulrich, a well-respected and longstanding academic and consultant in the field of HR. So much so that the model became known as the 'Ulrich model'. In reality it was never unique to HR, as Ulrich would be the first to say – the idea of combining common transactional services into a central resource to serve across the business, the role of centres of excellence for specific specialisms, and for business partners to work closely with the business and understand their needs.

Much of this standardized thinking was hardly unique to HR in the past. The obsession with best practice and standard models or heuristics was pervasive in the 1980s, 1990s and 2000s. It was the drive to efficiency and business process reengineering.

The operating model for HR should be whatever best fits the business. Pushing a centralized shared service model with lots of standard processes onto a devolved, loose organization and culture will be hard to achieve.

It is also important that HR looks outwards to the business. Delivering effective HR – good people management, engagement and employee experience, and supportive open cultures – is much about training line managers and leaders at every level to be effective people managers.

As we discussed in the previous chapter, this has been a missing component in the past. HR don't manage the people (apart from within the function), but they are there to understand the needs of the people and the business, to provide the insight and the changes and interventions that need to happen, and to enable, to guide, to support and to ensure compliance where it is needed.

Across all areas of HR or the people profession, we all now need to have the confidence to innovate more, to adapt our thinking. We must focus on the evidence base, the principles that should be driving us and the outcomes that are important.

Forget best practice and think more about best fit – what this problem or context needs, and the evidence that supports what we do to fix or improve it.

Core competencies and strategic workforce planning

One of the most important areas of people and organizational strategy is strategic workforce planning – the need to understand future demands for skills and resources, recognize the gaps between supply and demand and work through the many ways in which those gaps might be filled. This has become recognized much more as a critical need in business thinking. As noted earlier, much workforce planning of the past wasn't really strategic. It was more operational.

With all the changes happening in our economies, the geopolitical shifts causing talent supply lines to change, the changes in skills needs as work and job roles change with the impacts of automation, and the demands of new generations of workers, there is a lot to think about.

To set the context, it is an important part of business strategy to be able to understand what the organization's critical and core competencies are and need to be. It is impossible for any organization to be good at everything, even though in the past perhaps many have tried.

The idea of core competencies was first put forward in a 1990 article in *Harvard Business Review*, 'The core competence of the corporation' by CK Prahalad and Gary Hamel.[4] They described three conditions a business activity must meet in order to be a core competency:

- The activity must provide superior value or benefits to the consumer.
- It should be difficult for a competitor to replicate or imitate.
- It should be rare.

The article pointed out the contrast of how businesses operated in the 1980s versus how they should operate in the 1990s. It asserted that in the 1980s, business managers were 'judged on their ability to restructure, declutter, and delayer their corporations. In the 1990s, they'll be judged on their ability to identify, cultivate, and exploit the core competencies that make growth possible.'

This thinking definitely still applies today, and if anything, needs to be sharpened. Not only must organizations be able to understand and focus on their core competencies, they must also be acutely aware of where those competencies might start to hold them back, can be reproduced in another way or be digitally disrupted, or need to be upgraded. Too many businesses got lost in the past because they did not understand that what had made them distinctive and unique in the past was no longer what was going to make them successful in the future.

Schumpeter's creative destruction again. Think of Kodak, Polaroid, Palm, Wang, Blockbuster, or the more recent spate of traditional retailers like Woolworths, Debenhams and Top Shop losing out to more nimble digital rivals. Michael Porter's famous five forces model is alive and kicking.

Incidentally, the same can be said of people and leaders. An attribute of a good leader is also knowing when they become more part of the problem than part of the solution.

But there are many great examples of highly durable core competencies such as the globally standardized operations of McDonald's, Walmart's huge buying power and supply chain management, or Apple's style and product innovation.

So with our business strategists having figured all this out and established what the company really needs to be built from, of course, there will still be many competencies and functions that may be less distinctive but are nonetheless essential. Finance, marketing, HR, procurement, IT, legal, for example. But all these functions also can come under scrutiny as to how to best deliver what the organization needs – indeed, they have all been popular areas in recent years for outsourcing.

Strategic sourcing and partnering capabilities therefore don't just apply to the traditional areas of procurement, they also apply to how we think about organizational capabilities and skills.

The most agile businesses are able to work with their partners in adapting and responding, and that becomes an essential part of their operating model. It should also be regarded as an essential competence in almost every business today.

As we then focus on all the skills and capabilities we still need, there are many options to think through. A simple but comprehensive mnemonic is whether to 'Build, Buy, Borrow or Bot':

- **Build** – develop the skills and capabilities within the workforce.
- **Buy** – access all the pools of talent and skills to hire in the skills needed.

- **Borrow** – bring in freelancers, consultants, agencies or other service providers.
- **Bot** – automate tasks or roles.

Build is an essential part of any people strategy and a strategic capability even the smallest of businesses need: how to develop people and skills efficiently and effectively. This is the subject of Chapter 12 on agile learning.

The bot option is what is covered in the next chapter on good work. Automation and AI are great enablers of agility, productivity and efficiency. But as has been a core theme throughout, we need to use technology responsibly and with a strong people-centric focus. As we innovate and reimagine jobs, roles and tasks working with technology, we must actively design the work around people so that we are creating good work and quality jobs. And this needs to come together as part of the overall organization and operating models for the future.

The buy option is all about talent sourcing and acquisition, finding the diversity of the talent and skills we need and attracting it into our organizations.

Talent sourcing and recruitment – diversity

I have emphasized throughout the importance of inclusion and of diversity, of having diversity in our leadership teams, the importance of diversity of experience, and organizations that reflect the customers they serve and the communities they are part of.

Another big strategic driver for businesses to act on diversity is in being able to open up new talent pools and supply chains. Businesses that have most complained of talent and skills shortages in the past have often not done enough to open up their thinking to different sources of talent.

In the McGregor-Smith review referenced in Chapter 7, a strong economic case was described for more diverse workforces, estimating that the UK's GDP would be 1.3 per cent higher if black, Asian and ethnic minorities were fully represented across the workforce.

Sources of talent are everywhere, but many segments of the workforce or working-age population have not been sought out or given the opportunity. Organizations have stuck to the tried and tested, and HR and recruitment teams have been pressured to get people in quickly, to minimize risk – often code for bringing in people like the ones we already have.

People diversity covers many dimensions, some of which are readily visible and some of which are not. Age, gender, socio-economic background, race and ethnicity, nationality and culture, personality, ability and disability, neuro-diversity, life experience.

This mixture in our workforces brings richness of thinking, ideas and approaches, supports adaptability and relevance, and breaks down traditional barriers of conformity.

In talent sourcing and recruiting, there has been much more recognition in recent years of the importance of diversity and overcoming the biases in our systems, processes and behaviours. But we still have much work to do. It's easy to get stuck in a mindset of recruiting the familiar. René Carayol, the broadcaster, author and consultant, once challenged me and a group of colleagues by asking when we had last hired someone truly scary. By which he meant someone very different.

Behavioural science has long taught us about our inherent bias towards those that look and behave like us. As I've heard Tara Swart, a leading neuroscientist now at MIT Sloan, describe it succinctly: as humans we are deeply narcissistic.

In her 2016 book *Pedigree: How elite students get elite jobs*, Northwestern University professor Lauren Rivera examined bias in recruitment, particularly in the elite professional services firms.[5] She found that when asking maths questions to potential new hires, teams of white, male managers paid little attention when white men got answers wrong, but close attention when women or ethnic minorities did. The testing, Rivera argues, amplifies bias rather than squashes it because we tend to treat people favourably if they resemble us.

There have been so many examples of this in the past. Recruitment adverts that don't show diversity, or language that can be exclusionary, and assessment processes that favour particular groups. Even language like 'cultural fit' can appear quite innocent and appeal to the idea of cultural alignment, but it is sending a strong signal about conformity and preference for 'people like us'.

It's equally important that recruiters and hiring managers are taught better in understanding bias, to make them more aware as they recruit of the dangers of inherent bias, assumptions and generalizations.

There has been growing popularity in trying to address these issues also by 'sanitizing' CVs and applications – removing details such as names, indications of age, even qualifications. These have always felt more like addressing symptoms than causes. More evidence is needed as to whether these practices really work in the longer term, particularly on how people from more diverse backgrounds then stay and progress within the organization.

I touched on AI in recruitment earlier and the particular challenges being addressed in eliminating the building in of bias, but also how AI can help us better understand human bias. This must be an important focus, but AI will continue to roll out in the area of recruitment and can genuinely help in sourcing, acquisition and selection of talent.

Other stereotypes are being broken down, and some notable organizations are showing they are prepared to take more risks, to be more imaginative in how they recruit.

For example, companies like Timpson and National Grid working actively to recruit people with criminal records. Business in the Community has for some time run a campaign to 'ban the box' – to remove the need for people to have to declare a former criminal record for minor offences. This has now been extended into UK law with some relaxation around DBS (Disclosure and Barring Service) checks for minor offences.

Timpson, a family-owned specialist retailer, has recruited several hundred members of its staff from jail, many working in the day and returning to their cell at night.[6] Great for their rehabilitation and positive for Timpson in terms of accessing good skills. Ex-offenders now make up 10 per cent of the company's staff (what it terms foundation colleagues). This has also proved to be positive for Timpson's reputation in demonstrating social responsibility and support to the communities it is part of.

What the pandemic has changed in talent sourcing and recruitment

The economic downturn and impact on many businesses not only reduced recruitment but also tended to see organizations reverting to the tried and tested – not taking too many risks and getting people in where needed as quickly as possible.

In addition, as organizations had to restructure and people were let go, often it was the younger or older workers – those either with less experience or who were perceived to be less adaptive or able to cope with change. Similar patterns have been seen in downturns in the past.

Furthermore, since there are higher proportions of ethnic minorities working in lower-paid jobs and in sectors like hospitality that were badly impacted, there were disproportionate job losses in those communities as well. Many have expressed concern that the pandemic therefore will have set us back in terms of workforce diversity.

That is disappointing but not altogether surprising. Downturns do not impact everyone the same way, and we will need to work hard to recover and ensure people do not unfairly or disproportionately get left behind.

On the more positive side, the pandemic has shown how many jobs and roles can be performed remotely. This has opened up thinking for many about being able to attract and recruit people from more dispersed locations and not necessarily be so dependent on office locations.

More hybrid forms of working, where people have more choice in where and when they work, and how often they might come into the office, are powerful ways of attracting talent from different places. Making this more the norm for organizations will give them much more opportunity to attract and retain more diverse workforces in the future.

But another impact of the pandemic will be in significant shifts of people across sectors, from those sectors that have been contracting in to those sectors that are growing. Combined with changes in people migration in and out of the UK as a result of Brexit, and even directly as a result of the pandemic, these could be some of the biggest shifts we have seen in a generation.

Organizations should therefore be open to recruiting beyond their sectors, focusing on the core and transferable skills we described in Chapter 6.

Governments will need to help, too. Many people will need advice and guidance in seeking work beyond their sectors or jobs they have experienced, to be given the confidence to look elsewhere, particularly older workers. These shifts will be another strong stimulus to address lifelong learning and how to provide more financial security and support for people moving between jobs.

Starting recruitment with the young – working with education

Many businesses and sectors are recognizing they have to dig deeper and further in their long-term recruitment strategies, going into schools and working with teachers and careers advisors to open up young people to the opportunities of their organizations or careers.

As we explored in Chapter 6, giving young people more exposure to the world of work and better careers advice and guidance is an essential societal and educational agenda, as well as being good for business.

Sectors like technology, science and engineering have for a number of years now been focusing on attracting young girls into the STEM subjects and building the pipelines of women into businesses in these fields. There is an International Women in Engineering day and it is now common to see advertisements more openly seeking to engage women.

But what we have learned is we have to start young. Young people's preconceptions about jobs, about what they may be able or destined to do, and particularly around gender stereotypes, are established at primary school.

The Education and Employers charity based in the UK and its Inspiring the Future and Redraw the Balance campaigns[7] have done great work in focusing attention at this early age, running internationally, engaging many schools and employers to challenge the gender stereotypes of young people in relation to many jobs – such as firefighters, construction workers, nurses, doctors, engineers and pilots.

In the original project 66 primary school children were asked to draw a picture of a firefighter, a surgeon and a fighter pilot – 61 drew men, 5 drew women. They were then asked if they would like to meet real-life versions of their drawings, all of whom were women. Their reactions were worth watching.

The Gatsby Charitable Foundation in the UK, established by Lord David Sainsbury, has done great work in pushing for better career guidance in schools and engaging businesses to support. The Foundation is committed to strengthening science and engineering skills across the UK, and in 2016 under the leadership of Sir John Holman, a former headteacher and founder of the National STEM Learning Centre, carried out a review of career guidance across schools.

From this review came a framework of eight benchmarks,[8] which include having encounters with employers and employees as well as experiences of workplaces. These are now internationally recognized and are promoted widely across schools, supported by the Careers and Enterprise Company (CEC), which was established by the UK government in 2015 to focus and strengthen careers support to young people.

Every business can help by engaging with schools through these kinds of channels. Having employees volunteer to work with schools or talk to young people is good for the future development of young people and the supply of skills business needs. But it's also proven to be good for the employees themselves in developing their awareness, confidence and areas like presentation skills,[9] and their positive engagement.

Borrowing talent and skills

Almost every organization has some dependency on temporary, interim, agency, contingent or contract workers to fill specific or short-term skills gaps. Some sectors like construction are greatly dependent on these sources of skills. They work through myriad contractors and small businesses providing all the different specialist skills needed on a project-by-project basis.

However, in my experience, most organizations have not done a very good job of looking at this area of talent sourcing in a strategic context.

Much of this 'borrow' sourcing is done as a short-term contingency – specific short-term skills shortages or backfills. However, as skills shortages have grown in so many organizations and sectors, contractors or agency staff are increasingly deployed to address systemic staffing issues rather than just to fill short-term gaps.

Government regulations are changing on this, with IR35 regulation in the UK to address who really are the self-employed and who are contractors but working in conditions that to all intents and purposes are employment.

The public sector has historically been a big user of agency and temporary staff, and this has been growing particularly in areas like the health service and education as demand for skills is outstripping the formal routes of supply.

A review of use of agency staff across the public sector in the UK by the National Institute of Economic and Social Research commissioned by the Office of Manpower Economics was published in February 2017.[10] It has been recognized that spending on agency staff, including doctors as well as nurses and ancillary staff, has accelerated over recent years in the NHS, and there has been a substantial shift towards private agencies for the recruitment of supply teachers within schools.

In the NHS, hospitals in England spent £6.2 billion on agency and NHS bank staff (an entity managed by a trust or third party who contracts staff to take on temporary shifts) in 2019–20, up from £5.4 billion two years previously.[11] This is not of itself the full picture as it doesn't take out the cost of employing people to do these jobs if they were available. However, the higher costs of agency staff are significant. The research found some other important aspects of how contract or agency workers are used, including:

- There has been a trend towards longer-term placements, as agency staff are increasingly deployed to address systemic staffing issues, not as a deliberate strategy but rather as an ad hoc response to recruitment and retention difficulties caused by local and national skill shortages.
- Agency workers often describe feeling frustrated and undervalued, and report low levels of support from host employers. Furthermore, agency staff often describe tense and hostile relationships with permanent members of staff over perceptions of inequality and differences in pay and/or responsibilities.
- The research concluded that many public education and health sector employees are 'pushed' rather than 'pulled' into agency working. As the research stated, 'Many decisions to enter agency working would seem to be associated with experiences of deteriorating job quality and subsequent desire to escape permanent employment.' This is amid concerns about increased bureaucracy, target setting, insufficient resources, unmanageable workload and a lack of work–life balance.
- Agency workers also can be attracted by higher hourly pay rates, even though they may lose other aspects of the security of regular employment.

While these are big challenges across the public sector and require more strategic and long-term thinking to address, the same issues are prevalent in many other organizations, public and private.

Use of borrowed resources should be part of overall strategic workforce planning. There should be well-defined principles in how and when they are used. When these resources are used, they should be considered as part of the overall workforce. They should be treated as for any other part of the workforce as far as possible – not excluded or left outside when team meetings happen, or ignored in discussions about performance, or even when some training happens, especially when it is compliance related.

HR should take an overall responsibility for these parts of our workforces as well. Yet frequently they are not even counted. Too often organizations realize how many contractors they have when there is a bit of an audit or check on costs and use of contractors – usually initiated by the finance team.

A lot of the acquisition of contract resources happens through the procurement function and is directly initiated by managers. Yet we are working hard to ensure we have fair recruitment processes for employees managed through HR, that we understand and manage any risks. Just bringing in a contractor because they have a specific fit to a skills gap without much of the due diligence that happens in recruiting is exposing the business to risk.

Crowdsourcing talent and skills

As the internet opened up and allowed access to knowledge and people everywhere, the opportunities for crowdsourcing emerged – quite literally putting work out and seeing who wants to bid for it, or accessing people who are prepared to do something for the sheer pleasure of doing it and want to innovate and share ideas.

Wikipedia is a great example. Launched by Jimmy Wales and Larry Sanger in January 2001, it now has more than 50 million articles on it and attracts more than 1.7 billion visitors a month. Microsoft's Encarta, launched in 1993 with a large paid staff and a traditional model, had disappeared by 2009. At the time Encarta had about 62,000 articles, most behind a paywall, while Wikipedia had over 2.8 million English-language articles in open access.[12]

These kinds of sourcing models may well continue to grow. Other more traditional companies have used these ideas in helping to innovate and develop new products. Ask your consumers what they think and they will come back with new ideas – the emergence of the 'prosumer', both a consumer and a producer.

Examples include the LEGO and the LEGO Ideas platform, where users can submit their ideas for new LEGO sets. Consumers can vote and offer feedback for ideas submitted, and those ideas which get more than 10,000 votes are reviewed by LEGO. If taken forward, the submitters can work with the LEGO team to make their idea a reality and will get royalties on sales.

Or Unilever through the Unilever Foundry, which enables innovators and start-ups to act on particular briefs. Third-party reviewers look over submissions and the shortlisted ones are forwarded to the Unilever team. After an in-person pitch to a panel, winners are selected and co-create pilots with the company.

Or Amazon Studios, which has many points in its production pipeline that seeks input from the crowd, including letting anybody submit concept videos and scripts.[13]

There are now platforms that help create these kinds of connections, such as InnoCentive and Planbox. They work well for the company by providing virtually free access to skills and ideas, but they are also good for the many people who have ideas and want to contribute.

Acquiring capabilities through M&A

Besides market growth, business synergies, or even take-out of competitors, mergers and acquisitions are also about acquiring additional or specific capabilities. However, much of what is being acquired in terms of value is intangible – the brand, the market knowledge, and of course the skills and capabilities of the people.

However, the history of M&A is hardly covered in glory, as touched on in Chapter 2. Failures to deliver the promised synergies and value are legion. The common view is that at least two in three fail to achieve the stated goals and do not boost shareholder returns, and some suggest up to eight or nine out of ten,[14] with many deals ending up destroying value between the combining entities.

A decade of data from an annual McKinsey survey of M&A executives shows that issues such as cultural differences contribute substantially to almost 50 per cent of the failure of mergers to meet expectations.[15] Another compelling reason for greater understanding of corporate cultures and the role of HR in strategic business decisions and execution.

In 2017, when Amazon acquired Whole Foods, the deal was celebrated as strategically brilliant, giving Amazon a foot in the door of the high-end bricks-and-mortar grocery market while Whole Foods would be able to trim prices, potentially luring in a whole segment of new customers. Whole Foods' CEO John Mackey reportedly gushed that it was 'love at first sight'.[16] But things didn't quite turn out as planned. It was clear to almost any outsider that there were hugely different corporate cultures, values and philosophies.

So it wasn't surprising that a year after the combination, Whole Foods workers weren't exactly brimming with enthusiasm for their new owner.[17] A group of them reportedly tried to unionize, accusing Amazon of 'exploiting' their 'dedication' to their jobs.[18]

The loss of staff, and the knowledge that goes with them, when companies combine and the corporate cultures clash is a significant part of the value that is lost. Amazon and Whole Foods continue to work together and much has changed, but it has been a rocky journey.

Michele Gelfand, cultural psychologist and author of *Rule Makers, Rule Breakers: How tight and loose cultures wire our world*,[19] argues that corporates either have a tight culture or a loose culture, and that a merging of the two often leads to problems. Tight company cultures value consistency and routine, she explains. They don't tolerate rebellion or people straying from strict rules and processes. Loose cultures, in contrast, are far more fluid, encourage creativity, experimentation and new ideas, and value discretion. In the above example, as you might have guessed, Amazon is a prime example of a tight culture while Whole Foods falls into the loose category.

Gelfand together with academics from the University of Western Ontario, the University of Maryland and the Jagiellonian University in Poland collected and examined data relating to over 4,500 international corporate mergers that took place in 32 countries between 1989 and 2013.[20]

They looked at factors including deal size, monetary stakes, industry and cultural compatibility, and found that mergers between companies with a more pronounced tight–loose divide resulted in the combined entity performing worse in the years after the transaction than in cases where the divide was less pronounced.

On average, the acquiring companies in mergers with tight–loose differences saw their return on assets decrease by 0.6 percentage points three years after the merger, or $200 million in net income per year, Gelfand and her colleagues found. Those with particularly large cultural mismatches saw their yearly net income drop by over $600 million.

Productivity and performance

Having acquired the talent the organization needs, attention turns to optimizing performance. This is also a theme touched on in many ways through the book, and in particular linking to encouraging the right cultures, supporting engagement and wellbeing, and developing leadership at all levels.

We've also reviewed the issues with understanding and measuring productivity. But as technology and AI advance, the opportunity to collect more data and insight on people within organizations will prove increasingly irresistible to business leaders and to HR professionals.

There are of course many issues with data privacy, transparency and the rules of managing ethical practice around AI in the workplace, which are picked up in a bit more detail in the next chapter.

AI that uses algorithms and big data is now regularly employed to spot risks and opportunities when it comes to staffing, labour market trends and potential skills gaps, as well as the work rate and performance of individuals, or even their health.

An aspect of wellbeing that became popular was in the use of wearable devices that could track aspects such as numbers of steps walked and levels of exercise, or sleep patterns. Generally no bad thing for individuals, but when it strays into the organizational context, it can get a lot murkier.

Capturing and using data of this kind can easily stray across the boundary of privacy laws, but also what is ethically acceptable. If my exercise or physiological data is captured, how can I trust or do I know how that information might be used – will I not get promoted because my BMI has gone up?

There are growing concerns over the use of technology for employee surveillance – usually done in the interests of understanding how people are working and perhaps with an overall eye on how to improve productivity. The huge shift to home working as the Covid-19 pandemic took off also raised many worries in bosses' minds about whether people really were working – the presenteeism bias and mindset I have talked about.

A story reported in *The Times* in January 2021 was of cushions given to staff at a Chinese technology company, supposedly for their wellbeing, but which were in fact surveillance devices that alerted management when they were not at their posts. One employee at Hebo Logistic Technology in Hangzhou said that she and others had initially welcomed the 'smart cushion' that could monitor their vital signs, including heart rate and breathing as well as fatigue and posture. It reminded anyone who stayed still for too long to move around. But when workers were being contacted by the HR team to find out why they had been away from their desks, it became apparent the company had full access to all the data from the cushion.[21]

Examples of technology products that often come under the heading of 'productivity intelligence' include Prodoscore, which monitors things like keystrokes, but also email flows, calendar appointments and possibly even phone calls. Apparently, the company posted a sixfold increase in sales from the start of the pandemic.[22]

By some estimates, the market for HR analytics will have grown by a double-digit percentage figure in the five years to 2024. A 2015 report by Deloitte concluded that 35 per cent of companies were already actively developing data-analysis capabilities for HR.[23] Since then, and particularly fuelled by challenges like the coronavirus crisis, that figure is likely to have risen sharply.

Predictive analytics are also increasingly being used to understand hiring needs going forward, to model likely turnover trends and to construct an appropriate pipeline of talent. Data can prove extremely valuable for garnering insights, particularly in large organizations, but people decisions should never be purely data driven.

Google famously adopted an intensely data-centric approach to hiring and even developed a formula to help streamline the process it uses to decide who gets promoted.[24]

When that formula was back-tested, it proved to be highly aligned with the decisions made by actual humans, but the company ultimately decided never to use the formula. Quantitative evidence is great for informing decisions and evaluating all options, but people decisions, it concluded, needed to be made by actual people. This balance will play out increasingly in organizations as we use technology more and more to understand people and performance.

Optimizing the organization

As noted earlier, an important part of strategy alongside understanding people, competencies and capabilities is how best to operationalize and organize work.

For decades, traditional management and organizational theory worked on the principle of organizing work and tasks in blocks, functions and operations that were then managed through a hierarchical structure. This ensured lines of command and control to ensure accountability and lines of sight. But even with these hierarchies, that is not really how organizations work – they need to work horizontally, to network and connect the different functions and operations to deliver to the markets and customers the organization serves.

In recent years, many different organizational forms have emerged, and new entrepreneurial organizations have often started from quite different principles. Hierarchies, backed up by lots of rules, feedback mechanisms and metrics, don't get the best out of people and often create layers of bureaucracy that can slow down decision-making or stifle innovation.

In the last chapter empowerment as part of modern leadership principles was discussed. In Chapter 8 I also talked about the principles of empowering and trusting people more, moving away from rules and command and control to multifunctional teams empowered to make the decisions needed and to act, within wider guidelines and mission parameters. Looser cultures bound by shared principles and values, understanding of objectives, but built on greater trust.

Tim Kastelle, who teaches at the University of Queensland Business School, argues that needing any kind of hierarchy for a business to succeed is a fallacy. He also says that there is a common misconception that people who do the work are of lower status than those who decide what work to do.[25] Flat structures, he argues, can be enormously effective for companies, while small autonomous teams can be more nimble in an uncertain business environment and can help employees to feel more empowered and therefore engaged.

Particularly in the 1990s, customer-centric organization charts were touted as the key to success, but more recent thinking suggests that these might also not be appropriate for every business.

Other organizations have opted for an even more radical revamp of the traditional organization chart, aiming to give people much more accountability, letting them act as business owners, with truly decentralized management, flat structures, self-organizing teams, and a true voice in what gets done. What has broadly become known as holacracy.

Gary Hamel, founder of the strategy consulting firm Strategos, Professor at London Business School and recognized as one of the most influential business thinkers, has long advocated the view that organizations have become overly bureaucratic and sclerotic. He seeks to 'hack' the corporation and rails against corporate bureaucracy that stifles progress and innovation, and that he sees as fundamentally not human. The CIPD ran a hackathon with him in 2013 to hack HR, which challenged many of the traditional views of what HR, was really there to do.[26]

In a 2017 *HBR* article, Gary Hamel and Michele Zanini argued that many companies attempt to radically overhaul their management structure because of an awareness of just how costly being unnecessarily bureaucratic can be.[27]

The authors estimated that excess bureaucracy costs the US economy more than $3 trillion in lost economic output per year. Across the 32 countries of the OECD, the cost of excess bureaucracy amounts to almost $9 trillion. Based on this, they admit that the incentives for dismantling bureaucratic processes may seem substantial, but they also warn that it can be easy to underestimate the risks with radically scrapping the way things are done.

Hamel and Zanini developed these ideas into what Hamel calls humanocracy and their book *Humanocracy* cites many fascinating examples.[28] Organizations like Buurtzorg mentioned earlier, a Dutch social care provider whose motto is 'humanity above bureaucracy', and whose 15,000 workforce is divided into 1,200 self-managed and fully-empowered teams. Or

Zappos, the US-based online shoe retailer which had a philosophy of no rules. Or Haier, a Chinese manufacturer of household appliances with its culture of everyone is an entrepreneur. Or Nucor, which inverted the organizational pyramid to empower the frontline workers to do what is right for the customer.

These companies and examples have been much studied and argued over. Very free-flowing, unstructured organizations don't work for everyone or in every circumstance. As Tony Hsieh, the CEO at Zappos, observed, 'It can be a challenge for those people to learn and grow in the new environment,' explaining that in response, Zappos had implemented measures to help those people adapt, such as offering 'mentorship through the process of professional development and life-training'.[29]

Overall, the company has shifted from the entirely holacractic arrangement that Hsieh might have envisioned back in 2014. Today it is arranged more like a collection of small businesses. It's still very much decentralized, but the individual circles operate a bit like a marketplace in that they're in charge of their own performance and interact with each other in the way competing companies in the broader economy might.

Other companies, like blog platform Medium, or the software development platform GitHub and social media company Buffer, have experimented with a holacracy model and reportedly then decided to change tack.[30]

The reality, as with so many things, is there is not one size fits all or some perfect new solution.

Most people do need some kind of structure to be effective, and we need to know who is in charge at least for the big decisions – navigating pure holacracies can be confusing for employees as well as for customers, as Zappos recognized. Many cultures such as the civil service would struggle mightily if it was suggested they should go to an unbounded self-organizing way of working.

Voice and empowerment as organizing principles

Giving people voice and empowering them is important, and it can be done in more structured environments as well.

I have enjoyed the views of Vineet Nyar, the former CEO of HCL, a huge Indian IT services company that espoused the view of employees first and customers second, which Nyar described in his book of that name.[31] He recommended we invert the traditional top-down pyramid of organizations and organizational thinking to recognize that all the other structures we put in place must really be there to support the front line and those who engage directly with the customer.

These views have also been captured in the ideas of what has been called servant leadership. A servant leader shares power, putting employees first, inverting the hierarchy and the customer and front line at the top. Ultimately, instead of the people working to serve the leader, leaders should exist to serve the people.

So there are some good principles here, which have been espoused in other chapters in the book. But there is no magic bullet or perfect organizational model because each context is different.

If you run a nuclear power plant, or a railway network, you have to have rules to maintain safe operations and the parameters for experimentation will be limited.

But that does not stop us listening to our people, engaging them in change, seeking their input for how we improve things. If some layers of management can be removed to simplify decision-making, or cross-functional teams can be established to serve customers in more agile ways, then go ahead and try it. Look for ways to strengthen the networks that really make the organization tick. Experiment and innovate. Not everything has to be done to the organization all at once or in the same way.

For sure we should look at our rules and policies, so many of which have grown up like sedimentary layers over time, and add little value or get in the way. Some organizations have literally gone through a zero-basing approach, particularly in the area of HR. Take them all out, then then go ahead and put back what really makes sense.

As a side note, AI itself has given us plenty of examples of how hard it is to develop rules that guide all behaviours in the right ways. AI generally works off algorithms which are logic systems based on rules which it interprets literally and with no other judgement.

There are legions of examples where early AI attempts have gone off the rails because the rules led to odd outcomes. Think of Microsoft's Tay chatbot, which was supposed to have casual conversations in the language of a typical millennial. It was taken down 24 hours after its launch with profuse corporate apologies because it started making sexist and racist comments.

These are important changes in the traditional mindsets of our working cultures. And they need to be thought through as part of the overall people and organizational strategy and culture. We shouldn't just keep on doing things the way we have always done them, easy as that might seem. As Albert Camus, the great French philosopher and writer observed, 'Integrity has no need of rules.'

In conclusion

Any business strategy requires real understanding of skills and capabilities that will be needed, the best ways of working and organizing, and cultures that help get the best out of people.

This requires clear understanding of what makes the organization unique, what its core competencies are, but also its culture and style of operating. These are not immutable and should be considered as part of the overall strategy for the business and how it needs to adapt for the future.

HR has a big role to play and should lead on all these areas of strategic thinking, working closely with business leaders and aligning to the overall strategy, purpose and mission of the organization.

In fulfilling skills and capability needs, there are many different sourcing options which must be part of an overall strategic framework for the organization.

Opening up channels of recruitment and acquiring talent to embrace diversity in all its forms is a strategic capability that helps to fill the skill gaps, to create more diverse cultures and breadth of experience and ideas, and to meet other stakeholder goals.

Operating models and organizational structures and principles should be challenged. Look for the opportunities to simplify, to ease decision-making, and in particular to empower, engage and give voice to people at all levels.

Endnotes

1 https://www.economist.com/business/2020/03/24/the-coronavirus-crisis-thrusts-corporate-hr-chiefs-into-the-spotlight (archived at https://perma.cc/93VQ-DUYH)
2 www.workforce.com/uk/news/teslas-chro-director-pick-points-new-era (archived at https://perma.cc/LQ4F-HURU)
3 www.economist.com/business/2020/03/24/the-coronavirus-crisis-thrusts-corporate-hr-chiefs-into-the-spotlight (archived at https://perma.cc/Q9EH-CZWT)
4 Prahalad, C K and Hamel, G (1990) *The Core Competence of the Corporation*, Harvard Business Review, Boston, MA, May-June
5 Rivera, L (2015) *Pedigree: How elite students get elite jobs*, Princeton University Press
6 www.supportsolutions.co.uk/blog/client_groups/offenders_and_ex-offenders/timpsons_give_former_prisoners_a_second_chance.html (archived at https://perma.cc/5KNS-8NHG)
7 www.educationandemployers.org (archived at https://perma.cc/2LZD-5KAH)
8 www.goodcareerguidance.org.uk (archived at https://perma.cc/M8CC-446X)
9 www.educationandemployers.org/research/the-value-of-volunteering/ (archived at https://perma.cc/JD9V-92W3)

10 https://www.niesr.ac.uk/publications/use-agency-workers-public-sector (archived at https://perma.cc/8HYW-CV48)
11 https://liaisongroup.com/blog/hospitals-spent-6-2billion-on-agency-and-bank-staff-in-2019-20/ (archived at https://perma.cc/S9S4-UHMW)
12 https://en.wikipedia.org/wiki/Encarta (archived at https://perma.cc/ZB8C-X9X5)
13 www.planbox.com/4-companies-that-are-killing-it-with-crowdsourcing/ (archived at https://perma.cc/8GR6-YMTF)
14 www.forbes.com/sites/georgebradt/2019/08/01/what-ceos-must-do-to-avoid-the-83-of-mergers-and-acquisitions-that-fail/?sh=127e8b376152 (archived at https://perma.cc/UT4E-58LK)
15 www.mckinsey.com/business-functions/organization/our-insights/managing-and-supporting-employees-through-cultural-change-in-mergers (archived at https://perma.cc/QHG2-6CHG)
16 www.bloomberg.com/news/articles/2017-06-19/whole-foods-ceo-says-amazon-connection-was-love-at-first-sight (archived at https://perma.cc/N3BA-PSYQ)
17 www.theguardian.com/business/2018/oct/01/whole-foods-amazon-union-organization-grocery-chain (archived at https://perma.cc/D534-JVN6)
18 https://techcrunch.com/2018/09/06/whole-foods-workers-seek-to-unionize-says-amazon-is-exploiting-our-dedication/ (archived at https://perma.cc/T6UK-BR8H)
19 Gelfand, M (2018) *Rule Makers, Rule Breakers: How tight and loose cultures wire our world*, Scribner, New York
20 https://hbr.org/2018/10/one-reason-mergers-fail-the-two-cultures-arent-compatible (archived at https://perma.cc/N47V-GQ3D)
21 www.thetimes.co.uk/article/chinese-workers-get-to-the-bottom-of-smart-cushion-spies-rwh60pw5z (archived at https://perma.cc/Q44G-ZCA7)
22 www.thetimes.co.uk/article/is-your-employer-spying-on-you-as-you-work-from-home-5pdglfpp0 (archived at https://perma.cc/4L6B-E5LJ)
23 www2.deloitte.com/us/en/pages/human-capital/articles/introduction-human-capital-trends.html (archived at https://perma.cc/2PVW-J5HL)
24 http://qz.com/299112/google-came-up-with-a-formula-for-deciding-who-gets-promoted-heres-what-happened/ (archived at https://perma.cc/72AY-27B4)
25 https://hbr.org/2013/11/hierarchy-is-overrated (archived at https://perma.cc/N49T-ZKEG)
26 www.managementexchange.com/hackathon/contribution/presenting-hacking-hr-hackathon-report (archived at https://perma.cc/J86Y-9PYX)
27 https://hbr.org/2017/05/assessment-do-you-know-how-bureaucratic-your-organization-is (archived at https://perma.cc/B9YT-Q3L9)
28 Hamel, G and Zanini, M (2020) *Humanocracy: Creating organizations as amazing as the people inside them*, Harvard Business Review Press, Boston, MA
29 www.workforce.com/news/qa-with-john-bunch-holacracy-helps-zappos-swing-from-job-ladder-to-job-jungle-gym (archived at https://perma.cc/N8QL-NSVL)
30 https://fortune.com/2016/03/04/management-changes-at-medium/ (archived at https://perma.cc/2VJ5-ERJ4)
31 Nyar, V (2010) *Employees First, Customers Second: Turning conventional management upside down*, Harvard Business Press

11

Good work as a goal

Work frees us from boredom, vice and need.
VOLTAIRE, PHILOSOPHER AND WRITER
OF THE FRENCH ENLIGHTENMENT

The word 'work' has many connotations. It's another of those words that is both a verb and a noun – I worked hard or I got the work done. It can be paid or unpaid. It can be physical and/or mental. Indeed, most work that is performed is not recognized formally as work at all. The work we do around the house, for example.

In the context we are writing about, work is about the jobs we do and the roles we perform. Our occupations and our careers.

Jobs and work are so much more than just means to earn money. Voltaire was right, and work should be good for us. It should help to give purpose and meaning, and be good for our wellbeing, which as we have seen are vital goals for our societies.

I have discussed the many issues of fairness and equality, of opportunity, and the importance of responsible business in helping to address these issues. These must be goals for the future of work. If we are to effectively harness AI and automation for the good of people, then we must build to principles of what is good work. The future of work above all must be human.

The pandemic crisis is acting as a catalyst for change and helping to transform thinking about work. We need also to break many of the old paradigms of work, of standard jobs and roles, working routines, and through this to create more inclusion and more opportunity for more people to be engaged productively.

This chapter will pull together many of these ideas and help to provide some of the frameworks and principles for how we shape and design work and the jobs and roles for the future.

Our working lives and what is important as good work

Full-time work at around 40 hours a week consumes more than a third of our waking hours over a working career. A working career may be 50 years or more, and over that time we would spend more than 90,000 hours at work. That is a lot of time, so we should endeavour to do all we can to make work as good as possible for all of us.

But as we review the world of work today, there are many trends that have not been headed in a positive direction. We have already reviewed the issues of inequalities and fairness – in opportunity, in reward, in progression, in having a voice. Work also seems to be getting harder for many people, and issues of stress and the detrimental impacts on people's wellbeing have to be of real concern.

Work is of course fundamentally a means of generating income. But it should also be a source of satisfaction, of accomplishment, of finding and developing one's talents, and of having purpose and meaning. These would be attributes of a good job or good work at whatever level, but they are clearly far from present everywhere.

There is arguably a spectrum between those who work to live and those who live to work. There is no single answer for everyone. Realistically for many people, there are other aspects of their lives which more define them and which they will see as more important. Indeed, those who live to work can become unhealthily obsessed with work.

In 2019, according to the ONS, 16.2 per cent of all UK employees were in low-paid jobs.[1] Low-paid, in this context, is defined by the OECD as earning less than two-thirds of national median earnings. In the US, the Brookings Institute in November 2019 published research showing that 44 per cent of all workers aged between 18 and 64 qualify as 'low-wage', which equates to 53 million Americans.

Low-paid jobs are not necessarily bad jobs, but too often along with low pay come job insecurity, lack of progression, lack of control over work schedules or ways of working, or respect at work or having a voice.

Addressing these sorts of issues can make even relatively low-paid jobs, good jobs. So the idea of what is good work has to cover a wide range of issues, and help to provide the right balance in making work good for people in all circumstances.

The principle of good and decent work is enshrined as one of the United Nations' 17 Sustainable Development Goals (SDGs) – Goal 8 'Decent Work and Economic Growth'.

The SDGs were adopted by all United Nations Member States in 2015 as a shared call to action to end poverty, protect the planet and ensure that all people enjoy peace and prosperity by 2030.

Several other SDGs link to the principles of good work, including Goal 3 on good health and wellbeing, and Goal 10 on reduced inequalities.

> **UNITED NATIONS SUSTAINABLE DEVELOPMENT GOAL 8 – DECENT WORK AND ECONOMIC GROWTH**
>
> To promote sustained economic growth, higher levels of productivity and technological innovation. Encouraging entrepreneurship and job creation are key to this, as are effective measures to eradicate forced labour, slavery and human trafficking. With these targets in mind, the goal is to achieve full and productive employment, and decent work, for all women and men by 2030.

The International Labour Organization (ILO) has described decent work as where 'all women and men should work in conditions of freedom, equity, security and human dignity.'[2]

Are we working harder?

Many aspects of how work is changing have been reviewed in the first half of this book. While work is changing, it isn't necessarily getting better from the perspective of how people feel about their jobs, how they are supported at work, their interpersonal relationships, and what motivates and commits them to work.

In the years leading up to the pandemic in 2020, many countries were seeing the highest rates of employment and participation in employment in decades. More people were participating in work, particularly women, but also older workers. In the UK, according to ONS data from the Labour

Force Survey, the number of people over the age of 50 in work doubled from 5.4 million in 1993 to 10.7 million in 2020 – a significant increase even taking into account the ageing workforce demographics.[3]

Participation rates in employment as a ratio of the employed to the working-age population across OECD countries had steadily risen from 65 per cent in 2006, with a dip following the GFC to around 64 per cent, to almost 69 per cent up to 2020.[4]

Japan had the highest workforce participation rates at almost 78 per cent – a sign of how effectively they were engaging their older workforce. The ILO, however, is projecting participation rates will decline in the latter part of this decade due to ageing populations, by as much as 2–3 per cent outside Africa and Latin America.[5]

Work intensity or how hard people feel they have to work, has also been steadily increasing over the last couple of decades.[6]

For example, the UK Skills and Employment Survey found that the proportion of employees who strongly agreed with the statement 'My job requires that I work very hard' had increased from 32 per cent in 1992 to 45 per cent by 2012.

This appears to be due to increased workloads and tighter deadlines in most cases, rather than an increased pace of work. Forty-one per cent of employees felt under excessive pressure at work at least once or twice a week, and 13 per cent said they were under excessive pressure every single working day.

These trends were not necessarily because people are working longer hours. Across most countries, average hours worked per year have been falling for decades and the average working week for a full-time employee has fallen since 1998.

Technological change has been an important driver of increased work intensity. It can enable both greater efficiency in work processes but also easier monitoring of employees' effort levels.

The result of these trends has been a steadily rising sense of stress in the workforce, which are discussed further in Chapter 13. These are concerning trends and the antithesis of what some in the past, like Keynes, had predicted for the future of work.

Engagement as a way of understanding good work

One of the areas of understanding people at work has been the interest in the theme of engagement.

Workplace attitudes and employee satisfaction have long been measured, but the term engagement and its extension into a much wider-ranging debate was seen to have started in 1990 with the work of William Kahn, a professor of organizational behaviour at Boston University.[7] His paper 'Psychological conditions of personal engagement and disengagement at work' focused on how people can employ and express themselves physically, cognitively and emotionally at work – what was described as being able to 'bring oneself' into work makes people more engaged with the work process.

Since then, the field of engagement and employment relations has grabbed the attention of academic researchers, survey companies and consultants, and HR practitioners and has exploded into an industry almost of itself. The definition of engagement has expanded and now encompasses a range of ideas and variables from how people share a company's values, feel a sense of pride and are committed to working for their company, to having favourable perceptions of their work environment. Commitment to go above and beyond is also popular.

The intention has been to find ways of improving productivity and organizational effectiveness. Outcomes of positive engagement cited include improvements in customer satisfaction, reduced burnout or staff turnover, improvements in safety, overall job performance improvements, and many more.

However, because engagement has suffered from lack of consistency in how it is defined, measured and understood, it makes it hard to pin down. One of the challenges has been the frequent disconnect between academic research and practitioner approaches. Academics tend to take a narrower view to allow the variables to be controlled and measured, whereas practitioners have tended to take a much more holistic view and are more interested in what might be applied.

Engagement research and practice is therefore a classic example of where the evidence base in practice can be lacking rigour, but academic research can lack in relevance. This has long been a challenge for all areas of management science and practice, which we have referenced before, but it is true in areas like education as well. It is neatly illustrated in Figure 11.1.

Academics tend to be more aligned to the rigour axis, and practitioners and consultants much more to the relevance axis, and hence the challenge. The scientists shown in the quadrants are typically given as exemplars.

The ideal alignment is to be in the top right quadrant and it speaks to a closer collaboration between academics and practitioners, both of whom could greatly benefit. As discussed in Chapter 9, taking more evidence-based approaches to the world of work must be a critical element of how we build for the future.

FIGURE 11.1 Rigour versus relevance in research and in practice

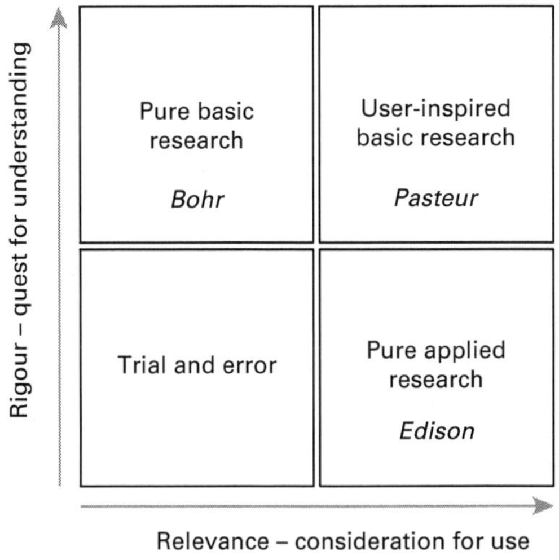

Rigour – quest for understanding ↑	Pure basic research *Bohr*	User-inspired basic research *Pasteur*
	Trial and error	Pure applied research *Edison*
		Relevance – consideration for use →

Understanding the drivers of engagement

Most would agree that if someone is feeling positive about their work and their working relationships, they would be more committed, likely to work harder and to support their colleagues. Whether this links directly to performance outcomes depends on many other things such as wider organizational alignment, operating models and priorities, and even overall strategy.

What makes people feel positive also comes from many different directions, not least the quality of the job, access to good learning, peer networks and feedback – in other words, many of the variables that are part of what makes a good job.

The CIPD published an evidence review of employee engagement in January 2021,[8] with research support from the Center for Evidence-Based Management. It was aimed at exploring the meaning of employee engagement, how it should be measured, what drives it, and the link between engagement and performance. The research distinguished the different areas that tend to get conflated when talking about engagement. These include:

- work engagement – how much people engage with their work and feel energized by it;
- organizational commitment – the extent to which people feel emotionally attached and committed to the organization;

- organizational identification – how employees associate and identify themselves with the organization's values, goals and purpose;
- work motivation – factors that lead people to be interested in and committed to their job.

In summary, employee engagement can be used as an umbrella term describing a broad area of people strategy, but specific constructs can be drawn out and measured to prioritize areas of concern. Work engagement, however, is the most robustly researched and would be the best way to focus engagement from the broader umbrella term.

Regarding measurement, there are many questionnaire-based measures but most are not tried and tested to scientific standards – that old rigour challenge. Nevertheless, they have been used for many years and show some interesting trends, which we will return to shortly.

For work engagement, the Utrecht Work Engagement Scale (UWES) is the most commonly used measure in academic literature. It has predictive validity and is quite easy to use, coming in various forms from the full 17-item measures down to an ultra-short three-item form.[9] These three items are:

- 'At my work, I feel bursting with energy' (vigour)
- 'I am enthusiastic about my job' (dedication)
- 'I am immersed in my work' (absorption)

For the other areas of engagement that relate to organizational alignment and commitment, the constructs of purpose, autonomy and mastery that Daniel Pink described in his popular book *Drive: The surprising truth about what motivates us*[10] have always resonated with me. Pink drew on many years of research from many sources and made it understandable and practical. Perhaps he intended the title to be ironic. The truth was that the insights he summarized about human motivation had been known for years; it was just that we hadn't understood or applied them in any consistent ways in the world of work.

We've already spent some time discussing purpose and why it is important. This is also linked to prosocial behaviour – doing good for others. The old adage of helping to teach someone to fish being more rewarding and enduring for the recipient as well as the giver than just giving someone a fish.

The second intrinsic motivator is what Pink calls mastery and is the basic human instinct of wanting to improve and learn how to do things better. People expect their employers to give them the tools and resources to be effective and productive, and to provide the learning and support they need.

Part of the psychological contract, and it is very based on this idea of mastery. This is explored further in Chapter 12 on learning.

In the context of our traditional models and cultures of work, autonomy is in many ways the most interesting. Autonomy is about agency – having more control over what you do and how you do it. This idea is so fundamental to a positive culture of trust, of empowerment, and encouraging innovation and people taking responsibility and accountability. Yet it has not been the common practice and jars directly with the more traditional command-and-control thinking that has been so common.

Academics in researching engagement usually use the various public national surveys carried out on random selected individuals surveyed at home, such as the OECD Life Satisfaction surveys, or the European Social Survey and European Working Conditions Surveys. These are good sources of data but tend to be reported a year or two after the surveys are conducted.

Duncan Gallie, Professor of Sociology at Oxford University, has been a long-time pioneer in the research on the quality of work and social inequalities. He has researched many different factors of work quality and engagement. His recent research on factors which motivate people at work has findings that echo themes such as autonomy, and the ideas of mastery and sense of accomplishment.[11,12]

A key research question has been, do people work just for the money or do they have a wider commitment to work? Figure 11.2 from Gallie's research shows a high level of commitment to work based on sense of accomplishment – linking to the ideas of mastery.

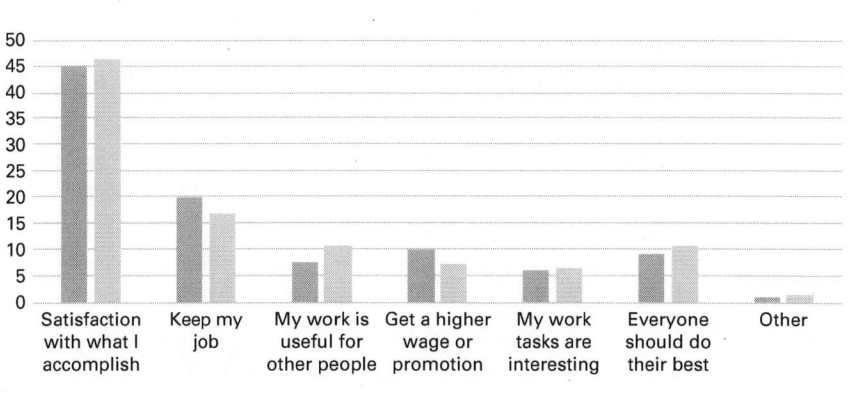

FIGURE 11.2 Motivating values – UK employees: accomplishment vs the work ethic

SOURCE Gallie 2021

FIGURE 11.3 Trends in sense of autonomy and voice

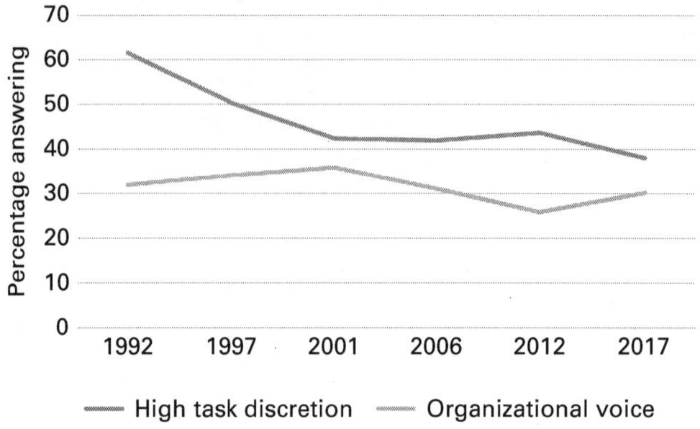

```
70
60
50
40
30
20
10
 0
    1992   1997   2001   2006   2012   2017
Percentage answering

——— High task discretion      ····· Organizational voice
```

SOURCE Gallie 2020

In European comparisons, it appears that Nordic countries have the highest levels of commitment to work. The southern and eastern European countries are at the other end of the scale, where their commitment to work is more related to a sense of duty. The UK, along with countries like France and Germany, falls roughly in the middle.

The majority of British employees are committed to their work for more than financial gain, and commitment has risen since the early 1990s – most noticeably because of the positive trends among women.

Other important variables relating to engagement that research calls out include the importance of being able to use initiative and having task discretion (autonomy), and having a voice at work – being listened to and asked to contribute, what Gallie describes as sense of involvement in their work.

However, as Figure 11.3 indicates, people's feelings of empowerment and having discretion over the tasks they perform, as well as having a voice, have been trending downwards since the 1990s. This is a trend that needs to be reversed.

Having discretion over how tasks are performed becomes ever more important with the implementation of technology and AI. We will come back to that in exploring job design with technology.

Giving people voice in the workplace

There are so many ways in which employees can be given a voice, and it is surprising to see that this remains an issue for so many. I have touched on voice and open cultures, feeling of psychological safety elsewhere. Voice is about being listened to, feeling safe to speak up, being able to contribute but also to challenge.

There is a great proverb, apparently Cherokee in origin, that says, 'Pay attention to the whispers so we won't have to listen to the screams.'

The channels for voice range from engagement surveys to employee forums, to team leaders speaking and listening to their people. Internal social media-type channels also provide that opportunity, and then there are the more confidential channels which are needed when other channels fail – whistle-blowing.

Research on whistleblowing trends is generally showing that it is on the rise. Perhaps it's younger generations wanting to be more vocal and being less tolerant of behaviours they see around them.[13] In most countries, legislation has been increasing to protect whistleblowers, who too often in the past found their confidentiality compromised and action then taken against them. For example, the EU Whistleblowing Directive passed in November 2019 requires member states to protect whistleblowers with anonymous reporting channels and safeguards against retaliation.

Unions have always had an important role to play in reflecting the voice of the workers. It is their primary purpose and they have long influenced the world of work, including employment rights, pay and bargaining, but also in supporting the training and development of people.

However, union membership has been on a steady decline for years. The share of employees that were members of a trade union in the UK in 1995 was over 32 per cent, but by 2019 it was 23 per cent, although the decline has flattened off in recent years and shown a small increase. The public sector has a far higher membership, at over 55 per cent, than the private sector which is under 15 per cent.

Across Europe, union membership figures vary greatly. On average it is 23 per cent but in the Nordic countries it is more than two-thirds, although this is influenced by the fact some of those countries have unemployment benefits paid through unions. The EU average is held down by relatively low levels of membership in some of the larger EU states: Germany with 18 per cent, France with 8 per cent, Spain with 19 per cent and Poland with 12 per cent.

The UK has some of the tightest union laws. France is notable in having low union membership, but liberal union laws allow people to make a lot of noise and mobilize mass strikes. Interesting also to note is that the Nordic countries have a stronger sense of voice in the workplace alongside the higher union membership.

The decline of union membership in general has been ascribed to the tightening of union laws, the growth of individualism in the young, and even the nature of jobs where there is less routine and similarity in jobs as the nature of work changes. The many other channels by which voice can be heard and also perhaps the shift towards better employee relations in general are part of this trend.

If union membership is to increase, unions have to be seen to be relevant in the modern workplace. In a positive way they can help in challenging the growing inequalities we have talked about, and in supporting the growing number of independent workers and helping to protect their interests. As Acas' chief executive Susan Clews observed in a September 2019 article in *HR Magazine*,[14] 'It shouldn't be a power struggle. On an individual workplace level HR wants to engage with employees, and if there is a union there then that's a good channel as it's a ready-made voice arrangement.'

Seeing engagement in a wider context

Given the growing interest in engagement as an indicator of corporate culture and therefore the link to greater corporate transparency and governance we discussed in Chapter 8, it does feel that it is time now to bring together more of the academic and the practitioner – more consistent language and approaches.

This, however, is not an insignificant challenge given the many commercial and other interests in this field. But it would help to raise engagement understanding and a wider acceptance of a construct which, despite its imperfections, continues to resonate strongly as an important part of our understanding of work and working cultures. Engagement has become one of the three most used employee metrics being linked to CEO bonuses and long-term incentive plans,[15] so we need to know that it is built on reasonably solid foundations.

Another sign of the wider acceptance of the importance of understanding engagement was the promotion of the theme by the UK government. In 2008/9, the then Secretary of State for Business, Lord Peter Mandelson, commissioned David McLeod and Nita Clarke to do a review of the research and practice around engagement.

The subsequent report, 'Engaging for success: enhancing performance through employee engagement',[16] was widely received, and encouraged the government in 2011, then under David Cameron, to set up the Engage for

Success movement. Led by McLeod and Clarke, it was established as a not-for-profit, voluntary movement with sponsorship from senior chief executives across the private and public sectors, specifically to raise awareness and understanding of engagement in the workplace.

The movement continues, with thousands of practitioners, researchers and others collaborating voluntarily to share experiences and thinking.

A very practical outcome of the report and the movement was a simple framework to help organizations practically focus on the things that they saw together had the biggest influence on overall engagement – the four enablers.[17] These are having a clear strategic narrative, engaging managers so that they engage with and support their people, giving employees a voice, and organizational integrity and alignment to values. These all link well to other areas we have already covered.

What have been the trends in engagement?

The various commercial engagement survey companies that have evolved over the last 20 years are very widely used in companies around the world.

The approach today to engagement measurement has largely moved on from the extensive and comprehensive annual surveys of the past (engagement as an umbrella) to shorter, more targeted and more frequent 'pulse' surveys. These can help business leaders understand how their organizations are reacting to current circumstances or change initiatives, which is often more relevant in the fast-changing world we are in.

Looking at overall trends, most engagement surveys have tended to paint a similar picture over recent years. Leading firms in the field, such as Gallup, Peakon and Kincentric (a division of Spencer Stuart, which was acquired from Aon Hewitt in mid-2019), now have huge bases of data spreading over many years. These surveys generally classify people into categories of engaged, disengaged or actively disengaged where they may even work against the interests of the organization.

Peakon's annual report of engagement in January 2020 covered 80 million survey responses across 160 countries.[18] It reported 41 per cent of employees globally were engaged, 38 per cent were disengaged and 21 per cent were actively disengaged.

This appears to correlate roughly with UK national measures of job satisfaction. Figure 11.4 shows the trends since the early 2000s for the proportions of people who say they are mostly or completely satisfied with their job, based on the UK Household Longitudinal Study from the University of Essex.[19]

The Peakon engagement surveys also show breakdowns across various dimensions. For example, they found that energy as a sector had the least engaged employees at 33 per cent, while technology had the highest at 44 per cent. Also, as others have found, engagement drops from a high at the start of employment over the first five years and then tends to stabilize. Sad to think that we employ engaged people and make them more disengaged over time. Managers and above tend to be more engaged at 49 per cent whereas below only 41 per cent were engaged.

Kincentric, based on over 5 million employee responses across more than 4,100 organizations in 86 countries between 2018 and 2019,[20] reported that two in three employees were engaged. This was a high point, up from below 60 per cent in 2011. It also reported regional differences but not quite at the same level as Gallup.

Gallup's engagement surveys paint an even bleaker picture. Its State of the Global Workplace reports[21] over recent years have shown only around

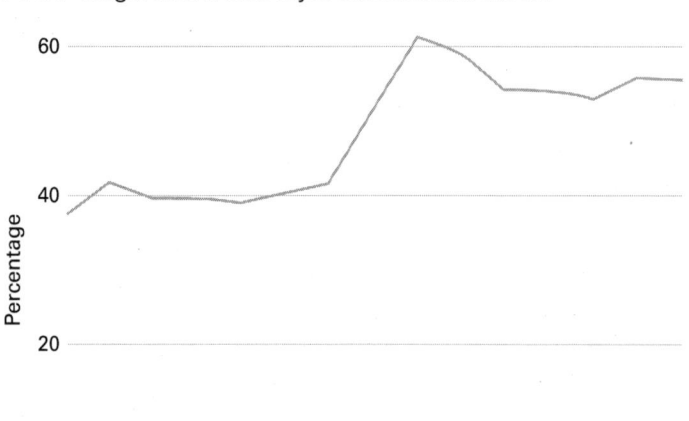

FIGURE 11.4 Longer-term trends in job satisfaction in the UK

SOURCE University of Essex

15 per cent of employees are engaged in the workplace. They point to a large variance across countries, from the US where they indicate around one in three of employees are engaged at work, to Western Europe where only one in ten are engaged, and even worse, the UK, which was at around 8 per cent engaged.

These huge reported differences across different surveys again illustrate the issue of consistency of measurement and definition. But we also have to be careful with comparisons across cultures. UK culture tends to be more cynical than US cultures and people won't necessarily answer the same question the same way. In Japan, I have often been reminded that three out of five would be regarded as a good score.

But these concerns aside, one can't help thinking these are pretty poor numbers. While most indicate they have seen improvement over the last 10 years or so, perhaps as organizations have focused more on the general drivers of engagement, the overall trend indicates large numbers of employees and workers are not particularly happy at work.

Most of the firms involved in conducting engagement surveys claim these levels of engagement are costing organizations hundreds of billions of dollars worldwide.

As Gallup put it, 'This means that the majority of workforce around the world are either viewing their workplace negatively or only doing the bare minimum to make it through the day, with little to no emotional attachment.'

However, it is very interesting to see how all survey firms agree that the pandemic led to a significant rise in engagement. As we have already noted, the pandemic drove a much stronger focus on people at the heart of our organizations. Leaders had to communicate much more and to connect with their people as they worked remotely, there was a great increase in attention to people's wellbeing and people responded positively to more flexible ways of working.

Peakon, in its report 'The impact of Covid-19 on employee engagement',[22] published in October 2020, stated that employee engagement increased by 2 per cent between January and July of 2020 globally, and that the finance and energy sectors had the biggest rise at 4 per cent. Peakon found that employees 'were particularly impressed by the opportunity to work remotely, their working environment, and their organization's support for their mental wellbeing. Scores to these questions increased by 10 per cent, 6 per cent and 5 per cent respectively between January and July 2020.'

The principles of job quality and movement towards good work

From all this work on understanding factors in engagement and the studies of work quality, we have needed a stronger set of guiding principles to embed those drivers that impact how people respond to work and to shape the future of work in positive ways.

In the first half of this book, the advances in technology and impact on jobs, the changing shape of organizations, the different expectations of our workforces and the pressure on improving organizational outcomes were discussed. Also explored were the issues of fairness and growing inequalities which are becoming increasingly unsustainable and also have to be addressed.

In designing the future of work, we need good principles to guide us in meeting all these challenges. We need to shape a future of work that is good for people, as well as good for business.

One of my favourite concepts or models that perhaps captures the ideal of good work is built from the Japanese word 'Ikigai', meaning a reason for being, or more prosaically, getting out of bed in the morning. It combines the ideas of passion, mission, vocation and profession and is illustrated in Figure 11.5. It sums up an ideal for work and what good work ultimately means.

A critical piece of work that has propelled the idea of good work in the UK was former Prime Minister Theresa May's sponsored review by Matthew Taylor of modern working practices. His report, 'Good work: the Taylor

FIGURE 11.5 The concept of 'ikigai' and connection to the idea of good work

review of modern working practices', was published in July 2017. The review was 'based on a single overriding ambition: All work in the UK economy should be fair and decent with realistic scope for development and fulfilment'. The review recognized all the many challenges we have described and drew together much of the research in recent years.

Many organizations contributed to the review, and it referenced groups like the Good Work Commission which was established by the Work Foundation in 2016.[23] They had described good work as being 'shaped by working practices that benefit employees through good reward schemes and terms and conditions, having a secure position, better training and development, good communication and ways of working that support task discretion and involve employees in securing'.

Of the various models of quality of work, the review proposed the 'QuInnE' model of job quality, developed by the Institute of Employment Research at Warwick University, and others as part of a pan-European research programme.

Building on the work from the Taylor review, and with the RSA and team that supported the research, the CIPD worked with Professor Chris Warhurst and his team at the Institute of Employment Research to take the constructs of job quality and good work forwards.

In the report of this work published by the CIPD in January 2018, titled 'Understanding and measuring job quality', Professor Warhurst presented an extensive review of the state of research in this field. The diagram shown in the report shows the variety of concepts that link to the idea of job quality – see Figure 11.6.

The outcome of this work was to define a comprehensive yet manageable set of dimensions to understand good work, drawing from the best existing indicators found in other surveys internationally, but adding some new measures to plug gaps. The focus was on objective indicators of job quality which can be acted on and designed into work for the future, most of which are then observable through the subjective indicators such as we discussed earlier around the theme of engagement.

The seven factors of good work and job quality are shown in Figure 11.7. Each of these factors is fairly self-explanatory and many we have already discussed in the context of prior research.

- Pay and benefits is not just about amount but about perceived fairness and clarity.

- Terms of employment are based on legislation (in the UK, the Employment Rights Act 1996) and as defined in the individual's employment contract and terms and conditions. Not only is it important that everyone has an employment contract, they need to understand it; yet from our own research and others', it's clear many don't.
- Job design and nature of work relates to many aspects we have explored about the job itself – is it using the individual's skills effectively, are objectives and requirements clear and is it manageable?
- Social support and cohesion relates to the nature of support an individual has in their job or role and the interpersonal relationships to help them do the job effectively.
- Health and wellbeing are fundamental to how people feel about their work. Is the work detrimental or additive to a person's wellbeing?
- Work–life balance is about how we support people to be able to manage their work alongside their other commitments and an appropriate balance.
- Employee voice is, as we have observed, a fundamental aspect of an individual's sense of inclusion and empowerment.

FIGURE 11.6 Hierarchical mosaic of job quality-related concepts

SOURCE Warwick University Institute of Employment Research

FIGURE 11.7 Objective factors in job quality and good work

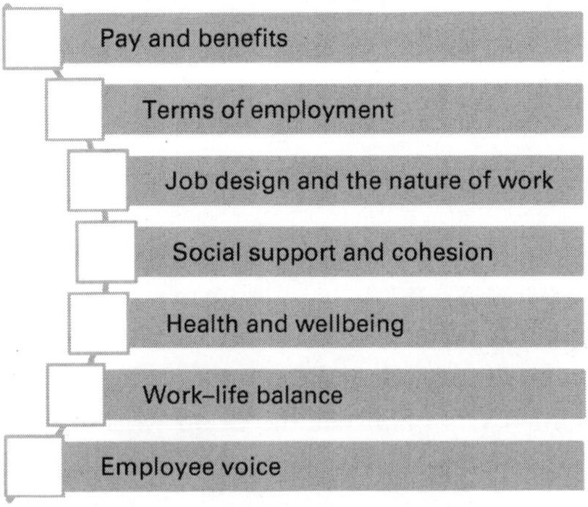

- Pay and benefits
- Terms of employment
- Job design and the nature of work
- Social support and cohesion
- Health and wellbeing
- Work–life balance
- Employee voice

SOURCE CIPD and Institute for Employment Research

All of these factors are objective and should be understood and focused on in any organization, and in particular as we look ahead to create progressive and effective jobs and workplaces for the future.

It is encouraging to see how these principles are being taken forward and supported at national and regional levels across the UK.

- The Industrial Strategy Council, set up in 2018 as a non-statutory advisory group to monitor and assess the progress of the UK government's industrial strategy, has committed to the principles of good work as cornerstones of economic development.
- The Fair Work Convention in Scotland was established in 2015 to act as an independent advisory body to Scottish ministers with the vision that by 2025 people in Scotland will have a world-leading working life where fair work drives success, wellbeing and prosperity for individuals, businesses, organizations and society.
- The Fair Work Commission in Wales sets similar goals where workers are fairly rewarded, heard and represented, secure and able to progress in a healthy, inclusive environment where rights are respected.
- The Good Employment Charter in Manchester, the Good Work Standard in London and the Fair Employment Charter in Liverpool are all good examples of city regions and their respective mayors committing to support the principles of good work.

The CIPD is directly supporting these initiatives and has created a Working Lives Index which surveys people to be able to track overall job quality and good work across the economy.

Surveying job quality and working lives in the UK

Since 2018, the CIPD has been measuring job quality through its UK Working Lives Survey of more than 5,000 workers across different sectors and occupations. Each year, survey respondents have been asked about key aspects of their work and employment.

In June 2020, the CIPD published the Good Work Index 2020, based on the UK Working Lives Survey.[24] Over the three years since the survey started, one of the key findings has been a worrying decline in health and wellbeing.

Workload and pressures at work, concerns of work–life balance, and increasing financial pressures with relatively flat wages growth have all combined. Consistently the research has found that the most important determinant in these factors of good work to people's overall motivation and view of their job is usually how it impacts their wellbeing – mental, emotional and physical.

The survey highlights that some jobs are undeniably better than others – not just in terms of essentials like pay and contracts but also in terms of our day-to-day experiences of work and its impact on our lives. While some differences in job quality are inherent to the nature of work and the structure of the labour market, the report finds that changes in people management and employment practices could significantly improve job quality in many cases. In particular, it finds job design and relationships at work could make a big difference to working lives and to performance at work.

I will come on to job design next, but this is particularly important as we see the growing impacts of technology in the workplace and in the jobs that people do.

The report also shows occupations which lead to particularly poor experiences for workers and those where there are trade-offs to be made between different aspects of job quality, such as pay and wellbeing. For example, while managerial and professional occupations tend to score well across most aspects of job quality, those working in highly paid jobs in legal services, healthcare and conservation report the poorest work–life balance and overall health and wellbeing scores. Meanwhile, those working in low-paid jobs in animal care, housekeeping, cleaning and sports and fitness report better wellbeing, work–life balance and relationships at work.

Use of skills at work

A key theme covered throughout this book is the subject of skills. I have highlighted the issues of skills shortages, of skills mismatches, of changes in job skills and demand, and of the challenges in education and learning.

An important part of good work is the alignment of skills to the job. This is important in job satisfaction – making good use of the individual's skills, but also supporting their ongoing development. But it's clearly also important in getting the best use out of people and the workforce at large, and an important factor in our productivity.

As the OECD has observed, the focus of skills policy is often on the supply side, but making optimal use of existing skills, preventing waste and attrition of skills due to mismatch or lack of use, and encouraging employers to demand higher levels of skill in stagnating regions or sectors are equally important elements of skills policies.

According to OECD data, in 2015 the UK ranked fourth from the top of developed nations in terms of the proportion of workers who are either over- or under-qualified for their jobs.

Alongside this challenge, the UK also stands out in international comparisons, on the high proportion of jobs that require no qualifications, reflecting a higher proportion of jobs in the UK with a low demand for skills.[25] That issue was highlighted earlier in this book and is also connected to the relatively low level of investment in workplace technologies and in investment in skills development relative to many other countries.

Mismatches of skills, either through people being over-qualified for their roles or under-qualified, critically impact both productivity in getting the best out of the people and the individual's sense of their job quality and general levels of stress and engagement. It can also of course directly impact their pay and reward – a factor in the erosion of the graduate pay premium discussed in Chapter 6.

In the research on job quality and good work, there has been growing evidence of the mismatch of skills into jobs. The CIPD carried out research in this area in 2018 and summarized it in a report, 'Over-skilled and underused: Investigating the untapped potential of UK skills'.[26] The research was referenced elsewhere as it also looked at the provision of training and development opportunities, and the extent to which employees feel they have opportunity to develop skills and progress in their career.

In summary, the research found that more than one-third of workers have the skills to cope with more demanding duties than they currently have. Moving or being promoted to another job can help address that, but over a quarter (26 per cent) of those surveyed reported that a lack of opportunities was the biggest barrier to career progression, followed by a lack of confidence in their ability to do more (14 per cent).

Positively, relatively few (12 per cent) of the respondents cited personal discrimination as a barrier to their career. However, the proportion was more than twice as high for non-white workers (26 per cent versus 11 per cent), suggesting there is still a lot more work to be done to address issues of ethnic minority career progression.

The findings also supported previous research that suggests that those in low-paid work experience less mobility in the labour market. Just 12 per cent of those earning less than £20,000 per year reported that they had been promoted in the current organization, compared with 45 per cent of those earning £40,000 and above.

Educational attainment and social class also play important roles, with those with degree-level qualifications much more likely to have been promoted than those without (32 per cent and 15 per cent respectively). Also those from higher social grades were found to be more likely to have experienced progression (32 per cent in ABC1 compared with just 15 per cent in C2DE).

At the opposite end of the scale, 1 in 10 said they lacked all the skills needed to do their job effectively, in many ways even more stressful, but also pointing to the lack of support in these circumstances, including access to appropriate learning and development.

The research also found interesting differences across industry sectors, as shown in Figure 11.8

The issues of addressing skills mismatches is therefore also a vital agenda going forwards. There are many aspects to it – from providing better training and development, as will be addressed further in Chapter 12, to careers advice and guidance and support for fair and open progression.

But there are also real issues of job design. Of developing and shaping jobs that are good for people but also use their skills effectively. Particularly as we look ahead with growing sophistication in technology, AI and automation, we have to work a lot harder in designing the jobs around people and not just around either our long-existing job definitions and categories or that which is most expedient.

FIGURE 11.8 Skills mismatch by industrial sector: proportion of workforce over/under skilled and matched (%)

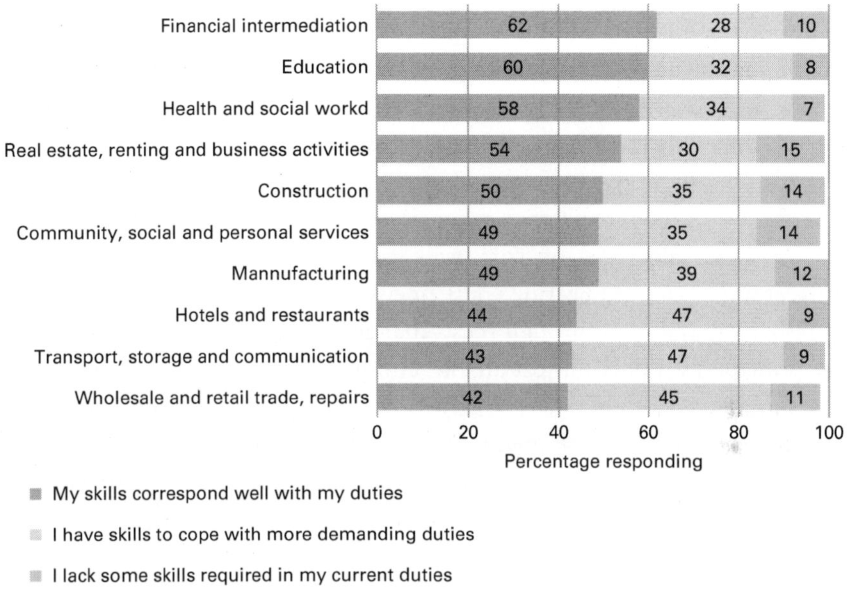

Sector	My skills correspond well with my duties	I have skills to cope with more demanding duties	I lack some skills required in my current duties
Financial intermediation	62	28	10
Education	60	32	8
Health and social workd	58	34	7
Real estate, renting and business activities	54	30	15
Construction	50	35	14
Community, social and personal services	49	35	14
Mannufacturing	49	39	12
Hotels and restaurants	44	47	9
Transport, storage and communication	43	47	9
Wholesale and retail trade, repairs	42	45	11

Percentage responding

■ My skills correspond well with my duties

■ I have skills to cope with more demanding duties

■ I lack some skills required in my current duties

SOURCE CIPD

Design of jobs and work

As we know, the impact of technology on jobs and work is hard to project with certainty, given the rapid pace of developments and the early stages of application. We will see job destruction, job creation, job changes and job shifts.

How we design jobs in the future to make the best of people and technology will become a big part of organizational capability and thinking. Writing in *Harvard Business Review* in May 2020, labour market expert Becky Frankiewicz and Tomas Chamorro-Premuzic, Professor of Business Psychology at University College London and at Columbia University, noted that the coronavirus pandemic was likely to mean that digital transformation becomes an even bigger imperative for organizations in the short-term future.[27]

They say that humans are generally prewired for familiarity, routine and simplicity. Most of us have a tendency to learn less on the job the more time we spend in it, eventually enabling us to almost work on autopilot. It means we're less challenged, which might feel comfortable in the short run but also prevents us from developing new skills and talents, and therefore from reaching our full potential, in the long run.

This crisis, they postulate, could change this, but the onus is on employers to provide opportunities for upskilling and reskilling as a matter of urgency. Technological innovation, however brilliant, is completely useless without having humans who are skilled enough to put it to use in the most appropriate way. Innovation intrinsically involves creativity but the creative aspect of innovation is entirely dependent on people, they say.

They also recommend that when it comes to training and recruiting, employers should focus on soft skills rather than technical abilities, like programming and engineering – a theme we explored in Chapter 6.

However, as we go through these changes, we must continue to hold to the principles outlined in job quality and good work, which are enduring and should apply to all jobs. How people feel empowered and have voice, how they are supported by their managers and given the resources they need to be effective, how they are paid fairly and recognized for what they do, how their skills are used and developed, and how these also support their wellbeing.

The specifics of the jobs and the tasks to be performed by people will change, however, and in particular we have to think about the interaction of people and technology.

The evolution of work, particularly from the second industrial revolution and the development of process and assembly line thinking, has followed a pattern. Generally we have sought to standardize and optimize, to reengineer existing processes with applications of technology to make them more efficient. Automation has followed this same largely sequential and linear flow, sometimes taking out humans where robots can do the job better. Automotive assembly is a good example, partly because this is where a lot of the thinking began, and now as a sector has gone further than most others in adopting automation and robotics.

As a result, we have not always created good jobs. We have put humans in where a multi-sensory operation is needed in the midst of robotic operations. We have even had to protect humans physically in environments with lots of machines. We have broken down tasks of knowledge workers into smaller chunks and bounded them more with rules. We have disempowered with clever work scheduling systems. And we are adding more and more means of measuring what people are doing, allowing even more control over them.

Digital Taylorism is all around us. We have often designed too much from the perspective of what the technology can do, and not enough from the perspective of what is best for the human. As some have rather colourfully described it, we have added 'meatware' to our hardware and software.

The fourth industrial revolution can and must take us in a different direction. We will have to think differently and innovate how we reinvent jobs and organizations to make them human centric.

Humans working together with automation

In their book *Human + Machine*,[28] Paul Daugherty and James Wilson from Accenture emphasize how they see AI as fundamentally changing how we design for jobs.[29] Moving from the thinking of the last era of industrialization to much more fluid, organic and adaptive ways of working. From assembly lines to 'organic teams that partner humans with advanced AI systems'.

It becomes a transformation of business processes and even organizational models and boundaries. They argue strongly for the idea that technology and AI are not just about job displacement but 'technology's greater power is in complementing and augmenting human capabilities'. They describe how in some of the most automated environments we are seeing a 'renaissance of human labour' – AI freeing up time and people's creativity, helping them add more value but also better using their skills, and to 'work more like humans and less like robots'.

I have heard Gary Kasparov, the former world chess champion, make this point very strongly in the context of chess. Winning at chess is no longer about the smartest machine against the smartest human but rather the combination of the human and AI chess player together that beats all.

Daugherty and Wilson propose a model to think about job design and characteristics of what tasks are best done by people, by AI or by the combination of the two. Their contention is that we have not focused enough on the combination of the two in the middle – what they call the 'missing middle'. Figure 11.9 shows their framework and the kinds of capabilities that help determine where a human, machine or combination can work best.

In the framework they also describe new roles and skill sets that people will need as we work with AI. For example, from the explainers who understand the technologies but also their application, to the trainers who work

FIGURE 11.9 Framework for evaluating job design between human and machine

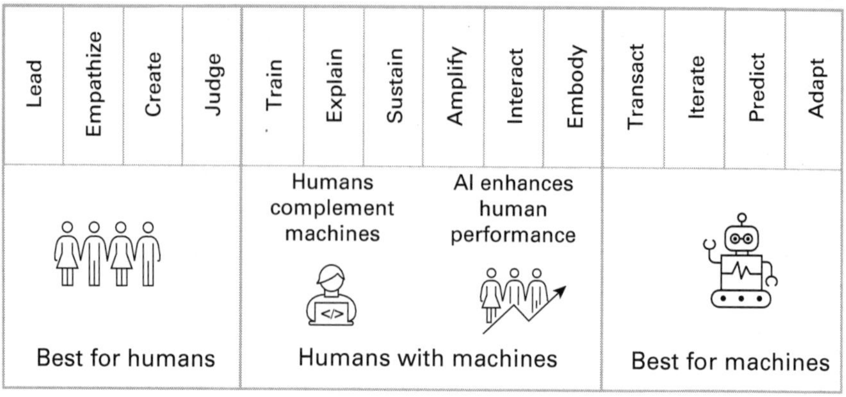

Lead	Empathize	Create	Judge	Train	Explain	Sustain	Amplify	Interact	Embody	Transact	Iterate	Predict	Adapt
Best for humans				Humans with machines (Humans complement machines / AI enhances human performance)						Best for machines			

SOURCE Daugherty and Wilson, Accenture

to train the AI systems to best effect. This kind of research and thinking demonstrates the shift that the fourth industrial revolution is bringing. But it also highlights the challenges in the shifts in mindsets, leadership and innovation to rethink existing processes, structures and ways of working.

Job and process design of the future cannot be about concreting over the cow paths of historical practice but about finding whole new ways to reimagine work.

The issues of bias – keeping our values and ethics front and centre

In research conducted by Accenture in 2016 and referenced in Daugherty and Wilson's book, it was noted that less than one-third of companies had a high degree of confidence in the fairness and auditability of their AI systems, and just as concerning, that less than half had confidence in the safety of those systems.

WEF research has also found that around one in three people are fearful of AI, which is broadly what other research surveys have indicated. Of course, in part it's fear of the unknown and the stories of robots taking people's jobs, or AI controlling us all, or the big debate about bias – all reinforced as we discussed before by popular science fiction over many decades.

But the need to manage AI, to ensure it does not get out of hand, and that we apply it fairly in our workplaces, is vital. Daugherty and Wilson propose that organizations should have AI safety engineers and ethics compliance managers. Certainly there needs to be a strong focus in every organization on these issues.

Bias is a particular challenge when it comes to AI making judgements about people. The popular areas often cited are in recruitment and in tracking people's performance. We are seeing AI being increasingly used in recruitment, with the intent of removing or reducing the time-intensive activities around sourcing, initial screening, applicant tracking and responding. This starts to allow recruiters to focus on the more value-adding shortlisting and finalizing of recruitment.

AI applications such as Textio are also being used to help write job descriptions that resonate best with candidates and remove bias in language such as more masculine-dominant wording. AI is also being used directly in the assessment and interview processes, from tools like Pymetric which focus on assessing behavioural attributes through various forms of testing, even to technologies which listen in on interviews observing aspects such as facial expression to give another view to the recruiter of a candidate.

The EU is moving to implement legislation limiting the use of facial-recognition technology, so this is a controversial space.

Many other AI applications in the workplace are beginning to be used to assess different data points on individuals' performance, or tracking their movements and actions. In all these areas there is the concern of bias and how to address it and ensure it is minimized if not eliminated.

Furthermore, there is widespread concern over data privacy. If information is being collected on individuals in the interests, for example, of understanding wider behavioural trends or attitudes, then there has to be reassurance over the protection of personally identifiable information (PII).

People need to be reassured also about how any data is being used. These are now legal rights in most countries, for example under General Data Protection Regulation (GDPR), which applies across the EU and the UK.

Understanding bias in AI though has really emphasized the reality of human bias. While the approach to ethical AI usually talks about transparency of the rules and algorithms used, the human brain is in many ways the ultimate 'black box'.

In a 2019 *HBR* paper titled 'What do we do about the biases in AI?', the three authors from McKinsey[30] described the paradox that AI can help identify and reduce the impact of human biases, but it can also greatly exacerbate them by 'baking in and deploying biases at scale'. Bias usually comes in as AI applications are trained, either through biased human decisions or historical norms and inequities, or sampling that doesn't reflect a full population.

The McKinsey authors recommend a couple of imperatives for action – first that we must use AI to improve human decision-making and bias, and second that we must accelerate the progress being made in addressing bias in AI.

On this second point, an area of focus has been 'fairness', which ultimately should be the benchmark. However, it is not always easy to assess. At least we should all take the time needed to properly assess outcomes from AI-based decisions to look for potential unfairness and correct. We must keep humans somewhere in the loop and we will need multiple perspectives.

There are various frameworks being used to help us all understand and manage the development and application of AI.

The Asilomar framework has some big names behind it and has 23 principles which incorporate AI research, ethics and values, and longer-term issues. It was developed at the Asilomar Conference on Beneficial AI organized by the Future of Life Institute in 2017 in California. Firms like Oracle are using it to guide their work in the development and application of AI. The ethics and values principles include points like safety, transparency, responsibilities, alignment to human values, shared benefit, and human control.

As we continue the development and roll-out of AI and automation, it will be important for every organization to state its values and principles in the use of these technologies. To be open and transparent, and to align to their own corporate values, so that trust is maintained. People are becoming more concerned, and particularly in these times of greater uncertainty and where trust is not high. Open dialogue is important.

Some companies have been particularly upfront. *The Times* reported in February 2017 that the insurance company Aviva was asking staff to let them know if a robot could do their job better.[31] Insurance is a sector where automation and AI are expected to have a significant impact on jobs up to mid- and higher-skill areas. Aviva was aiming to get out in front and show also that it would try to help reskill or find other roles where jobs were being displaced.

The opportunity of flexible working

Among many of the paradigms of work that the pandemic must really impact is that of flexible working. Giving people more choice about how and when they work, being able to balance work and life more, and better supporting wellbeing are key aspects of the principles of good work for the future. They are also expected and demanded more by the younger generations now in work, who are the future of our workforces everywhere.

As noted earlier, research on engagement has shown that one of the biggest improvements in work that people saw during the pandemic was having more flexibility in their working times, and for many, being able to work from home. It was the biggest 'experiment' we have ever had in working from home. As with most countries, almost half the workforce in the UK rapidly switched to home working in late March 2020 when the first lockdown started.

As a result, we have learned that people can be trusted to work remotely and that working from home is not 'shirking from home'. Also, people want choice and flexibility. Having worked from home, it is not good all the time and most people want the social connection and to check in with colleagues, or even the change of scenery and getting away from other distractions. But equally, the relentless routine of always going into the office, the commute times and other pressures can be greatly relieved with days or even parts of days working at home. So-called hybrid working.

We have stuck for so long to the traditional parameters of work – working hours and workplaces. I explored earlier in the book the origins of the standard five-day working week which is deeply embedded in our cultures and defines our rhythm of life – think of songs like Dolly Parton's 1980 hit '9 to 5', or Sheena Easton's 'Morning train (nine to five)', or The Bangles' 'Manic Monday'.

The OECD reports that only around 17 per cent of the workforce works other than what is usually described as a 'standard' full-time job.[32] These statistics have moved little in the last decade or more, although people working part-time involuntarily, not surprisingly, does increase during crises and times of higher unemployment. According to ONS data in the UK, involuntary part-time working is usually around 10 per cent but rose to 18 per cent of all part-time workers post the GFC.[33]

But having more choice and the ability to work flexibly has significant benefits for stress and wellbeing, as well as for inclusion and access to the wider and more diverse pools of talent every business needs.

Chapter 4 reviewed changing social attitudes. Younger people look for more flexibility at work and are more focused on work–life balance or integration. They don't all want to be slaves to their jobs in ways many of them saw their parents were. According to a 2013 survey by Deloitte, over 90 per cent of the millennial generation say that flexibility is a top priority.[34]

Other surveys around the world have shown that more people would trade longer time off work for pay. A survey by Samsung in 2014[35] reported that 27 per cent of its interviewees would trade flexible working over a pay rise.

With increasing female participation in the workforce, women are combining childcare and work more, but they need flexibility, as do others with caring responsibilities. The country in Europe with the highest level of women working part-time is the Netherlands where more than three-fifths of employed women work part-time hours. Not coincidentally, the Netherlands also has one of the highest female participation rates in the workforce.

In the UK, just over 40 per cent of women work part-time, and just over 12 per cent of men – an indicator of other issues about how many men, too often with good reason, think that working part-time will hold them back. There is also a presenteeism bias in how managers evaluate people and their 'commitment' to work.

In October 2019, Laura Jones of the Global Institute for Women's Leadership at King's College London published a research report on women's progression in the workplace with a particular focus on flexible working.[36] She identified what she calls an 'implementation gap': many organizations appear committed to flexible working but aren't providing it in practice, and even when they do offer it, there are problems.

The research found evidence that part-time and flexible workers were being marginalized. There appeared to be a mismatch between these ways of working and organizational cultural norms which equated commitment with the ability to work long hours and how focused people are on developing their careers. The research also cites a separate study from 2018[37] showing that 32 per cent of UK employees believe that working flexibly decreases the chances of a promotion, underscoring the existence of a palpable stigma.

Flexible working is not just about part-time working though. It includes hours worked, location of work and patterns of work. However, the uptake of different forms even of flexible hours working has been limited, as shown in Figure 11.10. It also includes forms of employment that we discussed earlier in Chapter 2.

Contract workers and the self-employed may choose to work in those ways because it gives them more flexibility. Zero-hours contracts, which have been the source of some political debate, when executed fairly between employer and worker can also provide great flexibility and choice in hours and schedules worked.

FIGURE 11.10 Use of different forms of flexible hours working

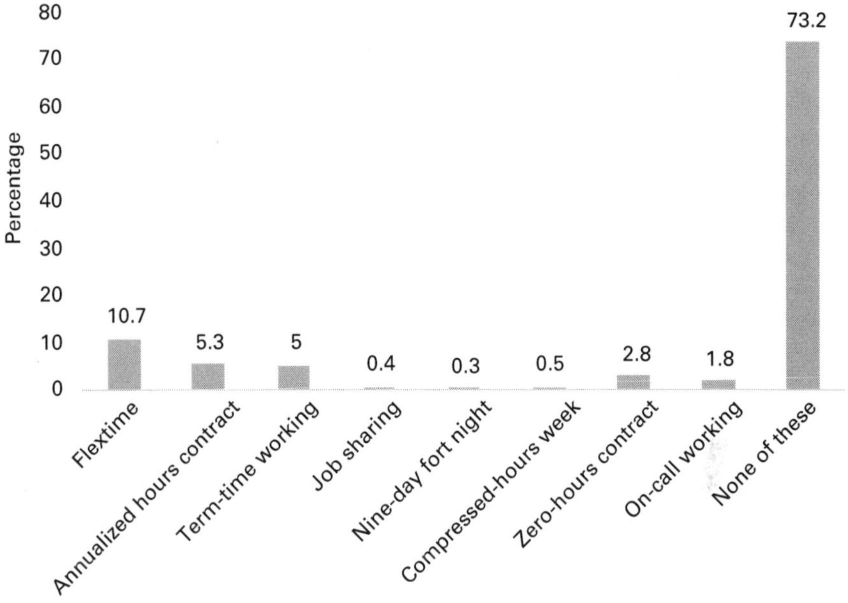

Category	Percentage
Flextime	10.7
Annualized hours contract	5.3
Term-time working	5
Job sharing	0.4
Nine-day fort night	0.3
Compressed-hours week	0.5
Zero-hours contract	2.8
On-call working	1.8
None of these	73.2

SOURCE ONS data, CIPD analysis

Alan Lockey and Fabian Wallace-Stephens wrote in a June 2020 report for the Royal Society for the Encouragement of Arts, Manufactures and Commerce (RSA) that flexible working arrangements which have emerged as a result of zero-hour contracts and the gig economy can also be 'one-sided'.[38] Employers, they argue, often seek to 'transfer risk onto the shoulders of workers in ways that make their lives much more insecure'.

The pair notes that flexible arrangements have added intense insecurity to a labour market that is already grappling with rising in-work poverty, low wages and stagnant productivity. 'Most worrying of all, this "age of insecurity" has coincided with a labour market which has excelled at job creation.'

Strong views. It is clear, however, that different forms of working properly balance the rights of the worker with the needs of the individual and of the employer. Good employers will have clear contracts of employment in all circumstances that make the rights of the employee or worker clear – in particular what the obligations of the employer actually are.

Agile working has also become a phrase to extend further beyond the more traditional flexible working ideas. The British Computer Society describes agile working as 'a way of working in which an organization empowers its people to work where, when and how they choose – with maximum flexibility and minimum constraints – to optimize their performance and to do their best work'.[39]

Laudable goals for the future of work. Agile working helps us think more broadly about how we work and how we use our time more effectively.

As the pandemic recedes into the past, we must take forward the learnings of remote working. At the peak of the pandemic, almost half the UK workforce were working from home.

We all learned a lot about the benefits of flexibility and choice about where and how people work, and the approach to what became known as hybrid working. Positive impacts on an individual's ability to balance their work and life commitments, reducing time spent commuting to offices and even in reducing stress. In particular, how flexible working in these ways can provide more opportunity for everyone to participate in productive work even where they have constraints such as mobility or caring responsibilities.

Giving people more choice – unlimited holidays

Building on the work on employment dosage, organizations have been recognizing more that giving people more time off and more control of when they take time off can have positive benefits.

Offering unlimited holidays or simply getting rid of holiday policies and letting people decide what vacation time they need has become popular among companies in some sectors. This idea started to appear in the technology industry some years ago as an incentive for attracting the best talent, but it has since spread to other sectors.

According to the international online job site Indeed, the number of postings advertising unlimited holiday days as a benefit rose from about 450 per million in May 2015 to almost 1,300 per million in May 2019 – a huge increase of almost 180 per cent.

But evidence has emerged that the policy's side effects can be hugely detrimental, particularly in competitive and results-oriented environments, or for individuals who are passion-driven. Some of the research about passion-driven workers, people who live to work, has already been reviewed. Some employees even say that it encourages a 'race to the bottom' – taking even less time off to prove your commitment and worth.

Software company Buffer in 2012 announced that it was offering unlimited paid holidays but a few years later management decided to reverse the policy because it was promoting a dangerous culture of presenteeism.[40] It subsequently introduced a period of recommended minimum leave and decided to offer all employees a $1,000 bonus to be used on travel expenses around a holiday of their choice.

Analysis conducted by management showed that under the unlimited leave policy the highest percentage of vacation days taken by staff had been in the range of 5–10 days over a whole year. Under the new policy, the average rose to 18.2 days. Critically, the executive team took the most number of days off, setting an important example and reference point for others by actively endorsing the practice by visibly tending to their mental health.

As a principle of empowering people more and reducing workplace rules and policies, unlimited holiday practices feel like a significant step. The policy can encourage better collaboration where colleagues work together to balance their needs for time away. But it has to go along with understanding cultures, particularly in high-pressure environments, and encouraging people to look after their wellbeing, to take breaks away from work. It clearly won't work in every circumstance, but it may be something to experiment with in a more enlightened working world of the future.

It's also important to recognize those who are self-employed. They usually don't have line managers or others to provide support or look out for their wellbeing. Particularly in the early stages of a business, the distinction between a founder's personal and professional life often doesn't exist. In her 2019 book *The Entrepreneurial Myth*,[41] author Louise Nicolson argues that – shaped predominantly by the media – we've developed a habit of portraying entrepreneurs as all-powerful, never-fail gurus who shoulder our collective necessity for enterprise. With reference to dozens of case studies and extensive academic research spanning more than three decades, Nicolson contests that this misrepresentation is damaging entrepreneurs' mental health and exacerbating business failure rates considerably.

How we use our time

I talked earlier about the productivity paradox and Solow's paradox of seeing technology everywhere but in the productivity statistics. As work appears to have become more intense with growing issues of stress and workload, we are not apparently working smarter.

Michael Mankins and Eric Garton from Bain & Company in their book *Time, Talent, Energy*[42] reported research that showed managers tend to have fewer than seven hours each week of uninterrupted time to do what the authors call deep versus shallow work. The rest of their week is taken up with meetings, emails and other tasks, leaving only short increments of 20 minutes for them to work on any given project. This fractious schedule might at best mean that real productivity slumps and inspiration fails to materialize. At worst it could lead to burnout.

Then for many, when we are not in meetings, we are staring at screens emailing people, copying in everyone who might need to know, or those we might want to impress. Technology also means that the boundaries between work and the rest of our lives are becoming blurred – working into the evenings or weekends on emails. The phenomenon of 'leavism' has been described as when employees use leave to catch up on their work backlog, perhaps because that is also when they are not being constantly interrupted.

This is hardly good work, and not a goal anyone in the past would have wanted to describe for the future of work.

These working cultures have just evolved. No one had a guidebook when emails and other office technologies first appeared. In 2003 one rather frustrated CEO announced that he was banning all internal emails as he thought his staff were spending too much time sending and receiving emails and not enough time dealing face to face with customers.[43] I don't think that lasted long.

In France in 2017 a law was introduced that gives French workers the right to ignore business emails that arrive after hours. This will at least be a reminder to think about these workplaces, but hard to see how this can be enforced, and not a direction many other countries seem to be following.

Google famously allows employees to spend 20 per cent of their time working on their own ideas, and they are encouraged not to fear failure because it is precisely this – a fear of wasting time – that might actually be keeping us from using our time in the most efficient way.

The future of work, we strongly believe, should be about greater flexibility in how and where we work. We need to break the cycle or the paradigms of work that are leading to issues of health and wellbeing, loss of productivity and innovation, and also can be excluding to many.

As of 2014, all employees with over six months' service in the UK have legally had the right to request flexible working hours from their organization, regardless of caring responsibilities.[44] The policy was long overdue, particularly for women, who still bear the brunt of caring duties but often can't afford to spend several years out of the workforce if they choose to have children.

Flexible careers

Flexible working also extends into the potential for more mobility between jobs. If the future of work is more about a life of jobs rather than a job for life, then providing support for people as they move between jobs, roles and organizations becomes an important policy need.

In Chapter 6 the issues and needs for change to support more lifelong learning were discussed. This has to be part of the wider system of change, but there are also other social security implications – providing financial support as well as training support where people are changing jobs and employment.

In the 1990s Denmark led the way by establishing a system of what it described as a 'golden triangle' between flexibility in the labour market, combined with social security support, and labour market policy with rights as well as obligations for the unemployed – bringing together a model of the welfare state with a pro-active labour market policy. This became known as 'flexicurity', a term coined by the Social Democrat Prime Minister at the time, Poul Nyrup Rasmussen.

The European Commission now views flexicurity as an integrated strategy to both enhance flexibility and build security in the labour market.[45] It is about finding the right balance between flexible job arrangements and secure transitions between jobs, hopefully also giving employers more space in helping to create better jobs and make their own more rapid adaptations.

Flexicurity is designed and implemented across four policy components:

1. Flexible and reliable contractual arrangements for employees and workers.
2. Comprehensive lifelong learning strategies.
3. Effective active labour market policies, encouraging workers to retrain and find new jobs.
4. Modern social security systems providing adequate income support during employment transitions.

This looks like much more integrated thinking of the kind we will need for the future. But the flexicurity concept was developed in countries with higher wages and taxation systems. Nordic countries follow this model of higher taxation to support strong social welfare systems which are extending in these ways to support a more flexible labour market.

These will become debates in many other countries in the future as we see more movement of people between jobs and organizations as the nature of jobs and work changes more rapidly.

Flexibility in labour markets also relates to employment legislation and getting the best balance between protection of workers and the needs of employers.

The UK is widely recognized as having one of the most flexible labour markets in the world and was rated as having the fifth most efficient labour market in the World Economic Forum's Global Competitiveness Report 2016–17, behind only Switzerland, Singapore, Hong Kong and the United States.[46] Many would argue that some of those countries do not protect workers enough.

As the CBI noted in its input to the Taylor Review, flexible labour markets tend to have higher employment rates and lower unemployment than those with more rigid approaches and – as CBI research from 2014 shows – over many decades they have better protected the labour share and delivered more real-terms wage growth than more rigid systems.[47] This is why flexibility matters.

In conclusion

In this chapter many of the trends and themes that are driving the future of work have been brought together and 'consilidated' into the principles of job quality and good work.

We need to design jobs, working environments and cultures, organization, and ways of working that are human-centred. That are built on good understanding of how best to enable people to be effective, to be engaged in what they do, and to support their wellbeing.

Many of these aspects of work are qualitative – how people feel about their work, how engaged and motivated they are, and what helps them to give of their best. We need to continue to build a stronger evidence base, connecting research and academia better with business, and to find more consistent language, but they are as important as the more quantitative aspects of work we are familiar with.

We have the opportunity to change work for the better, now more than ever. The pandemic has taught us a lot, not least about more flexible ways of working. But it has also further exacerbated issues of inequalities which will take a long time to improve upon. These are economic, political and societal agendas for all of us, and responsible businesses must see their role in ensuring their own organizations are fair and give opportunity to all.

The principles of good work are now being taken more seriously and act as a strong guide. They should lead us to the goal of good and fair work for all as outlined in the UN SDGs, as a fundamental driver for the future.

Endnotes

1. www.ons.gov.uk/employmentandlabourmarket/peopleinwork/earningsandworkinghours/bulletins/lowandhighpayuk/2019 (archived at https://perma.cc/YC8L-ZAU9)
2. https://www.ilo.org/global/topics/decent-work/lang--en/index.htm (archived at https://perma.cc/44V4-8TLF)
3. https://www.gov.uk/government/statistics/economic-labour-market-status-of-individuals-aged-50-and-over-trends-over-time-september-2020 (archived at https://perma.cc/CXK8-DUK5)
4. OECD (2021) Employment rate (indicator), DOI: 10.1787/1de68a9b-en (archived at https://perma.cc/Q2MS-AC57)
5. www.ilo.org/global/topics/future-of-work/trends/WCMS_545626/lang-en/index.htm (archived at https://perma.cc/BE93-QUE7)
6. www.cipd.co.uk/Images/megatrends_2013-working-harder-than-ever_tcm18-11406.pdf (archived at https://perma.cc/BX25-AC6Q)
7. https://theirf.org/research/irf-history-of-employee-engagement/1555/ (archived at https://perma.cc/BN2E-H2AY)
8. www.cipd.co.uk/knowledge/fundamentals/relations/engagement/evidence-engagement (archived at https://perma.cc/NMZ2-UBE7)
9. Schaufeli, W, Shimazu, A, Hakanen, J, Salanova, M and De Witte, H (2017) An ultra-short measure for work engagement: the UWES-3 validation across five countries, *European Journal of Psychological Assessment*, pp 1–15
10. www.amazon.co.uk/Drive-Daniel-H-Pink/dp/184767769X (archived at https://perma.cc/756E-5UA9)
11. www.eurofound.europa.eu/sites/default/files/wpef19061.pdf (archived at https://perma.cc/M8YX-67WJ)
12. www.eurofound.europa.eu/publications/policy-brief/2020/how-does-employee-involvement-in-decision-making-benefit-organisations (archived at https://perma.cc/RJV6-XZF7)
13. https://blog.whistleblowersecurity.com/blog/whistleblowing-trends-what-does-2020-look-like (archived at https://perma.cc/77CS-WHHM)
14. www.hrmagazine.co.uk/article-details/a-new-dawn-for-trade-unions (archived at https://perma.cc/CW9E-L6RB)

15 CIPD/High Pay Centre (2020) CEO pay and the workforce: how employee matters impact performance-related pay in the FTSE 100, Chartered Institute of Personnel and Development, London
16 MacLeod, D and Clarke, N (2009) Engaging for success: enhancing performance through employee engagement, Department for Business, Innovation and Skills, London
17 https://engageforsuccess.org/the-four-enablers (archived at https://perma.cc/2VJV-Q288)
18 https://peakon.com/heartbeat/data/employee-engagement/#section-5 (archived at https://perma.cc/59G4-22HR)
19 University of Essex (nd) Understanding Society: The UK household longitudinal study, Institute for Social and Economic Research, University of Essex, https://www.understandingsociety.ac.uk (archived at https://perma.cc/SAH6-DS7L)
20 www.kincentric.com/-/media/kincentric/pdfs/kincentric_2019_trends_global_employee_engagement.pdf (archived at https://perma.cc/MX7Z-BQ8M)
21 State of the Global Workforce, Gallup Press 2017
22 https://peakon.com/heartbeat/reports/the-impact-of-covid-19-on-employee-engagement/ (archived at https://perma.cc/4H72-9JAL)
23 https://www.lancaster.ac.uk/news/articles/2016/the-work-foundation-launches-commission-on-good-work/ (archived at https://perma.cc/9A3M-5PQ4)
24 www.cipd.co.uk/Images/good-work-index-summary-report-2020-1_tcm18-79211.pdf (archived at https://perma.cc/CHK2-A9AE)
25 www.oecd.org/eco/growth/Skill-mismatch-and-public-policyin-OECD-countries.pdf (archived at https://perma.cc/9539-Z9B6)
26 www.cipd.co.uk/Images/over-skilled-and-underused-investigating-the-untapped-potential-of-uk-skills_tcm18-48001.pdf (archived at https://perma.cc/JBY4-8EKA)
27 https://hbr.org/2020/05/digital-transformation-is-about-talent-not-technology (archived at https://perma.cc/3WTX-UEP6)
28 www.amazon.co.uk/Human-Machine-Reimagining-Work-Age/dp/1633693864 (archived at https://perma.cc/V3CU-K7QV)
29 Daugherty, P R and Wilson, H J (2018) *Human + Machine: Reimagining work in the age of AI*, Harvard Business Review Press
30 https://hbr.org/2019/10/what-do-we-do-about-the-biases-in-ai? (archived at https://perma.cc/ZA8G-6SJA)
31 www.thetimes.co.uk/article/insurer-asks-its-16-000-staff-could-a-robot-do-your-job-2jj5nskxl (archived at https://perma.cc/B8SK-7DRX)
32 www.oecd-ilibrary.org/sites/9ee00155-en/index.html?itemId=/content/publication/9ee00155-en (archived at https://perma.cc/5NSV-6YH9)
33 https://www.ons.gov.uk/employmentandlabourmarket/peopleinwork/employmentandemployeetypes/articles/labourmarketeconomiccommentary/january2019 (archived at https://perma.cc/4LZA-W7L9)

34   https://www2.deloitte.com/content/dam/Deloitte/global/Documents/HumanCapital/dttl-humancapital-trends5-workplaces-no-exp.pdf (archived at https://perma.cc/J5VS-7BFL)
35   www.samsung.com/uk/news/local/research-from-samsung-reveals-that-a-quarter-of-employees-would-give-up-a-pay-rise-for-flexible-working. (archived at https://perma.cc/8BVB-G37N
36   Jones, L (2019) Women's progression in the workplace, Global Institute for Women's Leadership, King's College London
37   https://doi.org/10.1007/s11205-018-2036-7 (archived at https://perma.cc/H8LY-NTMU)
38   Lockey, A and Wallace-Stephens, F (2020) A blueprint for good work: eight ideas for a new social contract, Royal Society for the Encouragement of Arts, Manufactures and Commerce, June
39   https://www.advanced-workplace.com/difference-agile-working-flexible-working/ (archived at https://perma.cc/UAQ5-BRSB)
40   https://open.buffer.com/unlimited-vacation-tips/ (archived at https://perma.cc/5HXM-SUFJ)
41   Nicholson, L (2019) *The Entrepreneurial Myth: A manifesto for real business*, LID Publishing
42   www.amazon.co.uk/Time-Talent-Energy-Organizational-Productive/dp/1633691764/ref=sr_1_1?dchild=1&keywords=Time%2C+Talent%2C+Energy&qid=1615914739&s=books&sr=1-1 (archived at https://perma.cc/ZM34-S5F8)
43   www.theguardian.com/technology/2003/sep/19/business.mobilephones (archived at https://perma.cc/WM34-HYPC)
44   www.gov.uk/flexible-working (archived at https://perma.cc/P4AG-ZLZK)
45   https://ec.europa.eu/social/main.jsp?langId=en&catId=102 (archived at https://perma.cc/8AQ9-25RU)
46   Schwab, K (2016) The Global Competitiveness Report 2016–17, World Economic Forum
47   www.cbi.org.uk/media/2704/work-that-works-for-all-cbi-submission-to-matthew-taylor.pdf (archived at https://perma.cc/BJ9M-LV5V)

12

The agile learning organization

Tell me and I forget, teach me and I may remember, involve me and I learn.

BENJAMIN FRANKLIN, SCIENTIST, PHILOSOPHER
AND A US FOUNDING FATHER

In Chapter 6 we explored many of the dimensions of the skills gaps and learning needs for the future. There was an emphasis on the role of education as much as the role of organizations, and the need for change. And the importance of the distinction between base and core skills, attitudinal and behavioural skills and job- and role-specific skills.

In a world where jobs are changing and new skills are needed, learning and development must be seen as a strategic organizational capability. This capability will lie at the heart of any organization's ability to adapt – to be able to develop its own workforce, as well as to retain and to attract the right people. But as has been discussed, too often business is some way away from this thinking and even the apparent investments in corporate training have been reducing.

Towards Maturity is a UK-based learning research and benchmarking organization. Their work on understanding high-performing learning cultures and organizations over the last 15 years has developed a maturity roadmap, and it shows that progress has been too slow.

Their report 'The transformation journey' published in February 2019, which I briefly referenced in Chapter 6, summarized the shifts in expectations for learning and development from learning processes and efficiency, to driving business change, agility and performance. But the reality is that across the hundreds of organizations surveyed, they described progress against these broader business goals over the last 15 years as at best static, and only one in five organizations surveyed are achieving goals linked to agility and culture change.

The report also cited the key barriers to more impactful change in the value and delivery of learning – in particular, digital disruption (adapting and effectively using new digital learning approaches and technologies), organizational cultural resistance, and the capability and skills within the learning and development function itself.

These findings were reinforced in research the CIPD did with Accenture on the current state of organizational learning. The report, 'Learning and skills at work 2020', published in June 2020,[1] captured a UK-wide picture of learning and development professionals challenged by limited resources, a lack of robust evaluation and measurement, and a sluggish adoption of the emergent technologies that make learning both more efficient and more engaging. However, organizations were quick to assert how vital learning is for performance, productivity and agility.

These critical gaps between belief and reality have to be addressed. The capacity and capabilities for organizations to support and embed effective learning and development should be a strategic pillar for businesses everywhere to be future fit. However, this is not some standalone discipline or function, but one that must be integral to the context of the organization, its strategy and operational needs. It is also more and more important that learning capabilities are agile – able to flex with changing needs, and agile and effective in delivery.

It is these principles which describe an agile learning organization.

Becoming an agile learning organization

The idea of a learning organization was first proposed by Peter Senge in his influential book *The Fifth Discipline*, first published in 1992.[2] Senge is the founding chair of the Society of Organizational Learning which is now a global network of organizations, researchers and consultants dedicated to the 'interdependent development of people and their institutions', and a Senior Lecturer at the Sloan School of Management MIT.

As a systems engineer by training, he views organizations as dynamic systems in states of continuous adaptation and improvement. Hard to disagree with that. He described five characteristics or disciplines that underpin a learning organization. These can be considered as good general principles for effective organizations, and various of these ideas are expanded upon elsewhere in this book.

The core disciplines Senge laid out were having a shared vision for the organization, consistent mental models of how the organization and culture work, ability to work and learn effectively in teams, and affinity and desire for personal learning and development.

This last one, what Senge called personal mastery, relates directly to mastery as one of the three intrinsic motivators that drive us at work, as discussed in Chapter 8. The fifth discipline, systems thinking, is the one discipline that binds the other four and therefore the discipline where the focus for change needs to begin.

Systems thinking is a core construct for understanding any aspect of business. It reflects an understanding of the interrelationships, dependencies and interactions between all elements of a bounded system, or organization.

As discussed in Chapter 9 on leadership, ability to think systemically is an essential capability for leaders in understanding their organizations, and navigating change and complexity. Learning and development for any part of a business exists in a context, and cannot be effectively designed or implemented in isolation and achieve any meaningful outcome. The interrelated elements include the business strategy, needs and vision, the operating model and organizational structure, the interrelationship of different jobs and functions, the capacities and capabilities of the workforce, and even the corporate culture.

Learning organizations support and encourage their people to continually learn and expand their capabilities, to innovate but also to work collectively so that they are able to see the whole together.

Learning should be seen as everyone's responsibility – individuals having the self-awareness and curiosity to want to learn, managers and leaders to encourage and support learning, and themselves act as role models. The learning and development function is there to enable, to provide the shared resources and to understand the business needs and priorities.

A learning strategy should embrace all these elements and be considered as part of the overall people strategy which discussed in Chapter 10. Within the learning strategy, we need to understand all the different kinds of learning interventions and approaches, where and how they might be applied, and with a clear focus on the outcomes needed.

But we need to go further than just the traditional domain of learning, and into knowledge more broadly. While learning seeks to capture and structure knowledge and then deliver it in a variety of ways, most knowledge in organizations is tacit or unstructured. Figure 12.1 illustrates the point.

FIGURE 12.1 Explicit and taught knowledge vs tacit and unstructured knowledge

Explicit knowledge
- Data, information
- Structured content
- Documents, records
- Formal learning
- Known knowns

Tacit and implicit knowledge
- Experience
- Unstructured knowledge
- Good leadership
- Networks and tribal knowledge
- Intuition
- Emotional intelligence
- Known unknowns

Historically we have thought of knowledge as needing always to be codified to have real sustainable value – through policies, procedures, manuals, rules, learning programmes and content libraries. These will still be true, but many organizations operating in a fast-moving world have less reliance on this structured knowledge and rely more on collaborative working and sharing.

It is possible to understand more about how tacit knowledge flows through organizations. What became known as social network analysis (SNA) is now widespread in social media analytics, allowing a picture to be painted of how collaboration is working and where the connections are. Much more revealing than organization structures, it can show whether connections within and importantly across teams and functions are working and even who the strongest individual connectors are.

SNA pictures used to be built from surveys, asking people who they connected with and on what subjects or issues. Now it is quite possible to build this analysis from the use of collaborative tools, email flows, etc. We just have to be mindful of personal privacy concerns, be transparent and clear on how this information might be used. Another reminder of the vital importance of trust in truly collaborative cultures.

Agile learning organizations create the culture and collaborative ways of working that recognize and find the best ways to share this tacit knowledge as well as formal learning, and they work from a number of important values:

- Knowledge is shared and not seen as a source of power. Everyone needs to know.
- Transparency is a corporate mindset.
- Collaboration is a shared value, and collaborative tools and technologies encourage the dispersion of tacit knowledge.
- People are encouraged and recognized for how they collaborate and share their knowledge.
- Experimentation and innovation are seen as ways of gaining new knowledge and widely practised, reinforced by agile working principles.
- Learning from mistakes, feedback, incremental improvement and a growth mindset are the norms.

As touched on in Chapter 8, the ideas on which these principles have developed were first shown through the research and writing of Carol Dweck, a professor of psychology at Stanford University, in her powerful ideas about growth mindset.[3] These principles have been further reinforced with the insights from neuroscience and the understanding of neuroplasticity – that our brains continue to make new connections and adapt from our experiences and learnings throughout our lives.

A fixed mindset assumes that our character, intelligence and creative ability are static givens which we can't change in any meaningful way. Success and failure therefore are also seen as fixed standards, and failure something to be avoided at all costs. What Dweck showed in her research is that a growth mindset that thrives on new challenges and learning opportunities and sees failure also as learning opportunities yields very different outcomes for learning and development.

There is an apocryphal story of Thomas Watson, the driving force behind the growth of IBM from its early beginnings, that when one of his top salesmen blew a million-dollar deal everyone told him to fire the individual. But Watson's view was that he had invested a million dollars in a learning that the salesman would never forget. That person went on to become CEO of the company.

All these aspects of learning and knowledge and the importance of the underlying cultures and values should come together in a learning vision and philosophy.

Importance of a learning philosophy and vision

CIPD research on professionalizing learning and development published in 2019[4] highlighted a lack of vision and even collective understanding leaders had for learning in their organizations.

Work the CIPD has done on reshaping and redefining learning and development within organizations starts with the idea of a coherent learning philosophy. As my colleague Andy Lancaster described in his book *Driving Performance through Learning,* published in 2019,[5] a good learning philosophy should be an inspirational statement that describes the why, what, who, when, where and how.

Why is learning important and how is it seen strategically in the context of the organization? What learning is essential and desirable, and to what outcome? Who is responsible for the learning processes and interventions, and who are they aimed at? When and where is learning undertaken, formally and informally, and how is it designed and facilitated?

These are all mindset-expanding questions that we need to be asking in many contexts – and they start with why. The purpose statement again. Investments in learning and development which are not clearly aligned to purpose and expected outcome will be wasted. Purpose is the critical bedrock of a learning culture.

A learning philosophy creates the context for the shift to a learning culture. It helps to embed the rationale and mindset needed across the organization about learning and to overcome barriers discussed in Chapter 6 – making sure that the business and managers make time for learning, and really understand its importance and value to the success of the business. But it also gives confidence to the learning and development function to challenge back to the business that to get people upskilled and reskilled you have to create the right environment and support for them.

As consultant and author Ron Carucci observed in a 2019 *HBR* article,[6] learning is as much a consequence of thinking as it is teaching. 'It happens when people reflect on and choose a new behaviour. But if the work environment doesn't support that behaviour, a well-trained employee won't make a difference.' He goes on to describe the need for commitment to change. Resistance to change is anchored in that very human fear of the unknown, but as the workforce changes, and the nature of jobs evolves, a business that's averse to being adaptive and agile will definitely suffer. Learning and development goes hand in hand with change.

We then have to make sure our learning approaches are relevant, based on a strong understanding of the needs of individuals, teams and functions, and the organization as a whole. Steve Glaveski, the CEO and co-founder of Collective Campus, which helps companies and their employees to create a more meaningful impact in the world, argued in a 2019 *HBR* article[7] that training across many businesses is ineffective because not only the purpose, but also timing and content are too often flawed. 'People learn best when they have to learn. Applying what's learned to real-world situations strengthens one's focus and determination to learn,' he writes.

If we're learning something at a time when we're not about to apply any of those new skills, we're less likely to be motivated to learn because the immediate incentive to do so is not obvious. And we're probably more likely to go through the motions without properly taking new skills on board. German psychologist Hermann Ebbinghaus's pioneering work[8] on memory performed in the late 19th century posited that we forget up to 75 per cent of new information within six days if we don't apply it.

Ensuring that the content offered during training is timely, relevant and applicable is vital in translating the investment in training into enhanced productivity and performance. If the process is perceived as a rigid one-time exercise in box-ticking that's not aligned with organizational requirements or needs, then it will drag on employee morale, become an administrative headache and sap productivity and performance.

Methods of learning and how they are changing

The methods and approaches to learning have been evolving rapidly, particularly with the advances in technology in the learning and training arena. There is also now more science and evidence for how we learn, which is being used to shape learning interventions to be more effective.

As discussed in Chapter 5, the internet has led to an explosion in availability of and accessibility to content and learning. This is creating much more opportunity, and potential issues, for self-directed learning. Accessing content and learning from such expansive sources can be hugely distracting, but also requires critical thinking and ability to evaluate what might be good or not. It's the same set of steps needed for the approach to understanding good evidence that I reviewed in Chapter 9.

While self-directed learning is not new and is the way most adults learn, for the younger generations it has raised expectations about learning beyond the traditional pedagogical models of teaching. They can search anything on the internet and challenge the teacher, and question much more about the relevance of what they are being taught.

Reasons again that traditional educational models are being challenged. This was something I witnessed as a parent when my daughters were revising for exams and regularly would put aside their coursebooks or learning notes and just search the internet. Happily what they found, such as other teachers' explanations of subjects like algebra that they found more understandable, led to good outcomes.

Broadly our approaches to learning fall into three main categories, all of which exist in the modern workplace, shown in Table 12.1. Peda refers to child, andra refers to adult, and heuta refers to self-determined. Andragogy is the way in which adults learn best, and are motivated to learn, yet there is still a strong persistence of pedagogical learning in the workplace.

Each has its place, but the long historic reliance on workplace training based on pedagogy is curious given the environment of work is about motivating adults to learn. It became the safe and familiar model. However, particularly for behavioural learning and change, success has been limited. The amount spent on leadership development programmes has been disproportionate to their impact, particularly given the greatest need is in behavioural change. As discussed in Chapter 9, we need to think about leadership development differently.

TABLE 12.1 Learning models

Pedagogy	Andragogy	Heutagogy
Teacher driven	Participants as co-owners of the learning	Learner self-directed (Discovery)
Passive 'bystanders'	Transformational	Disruptive
Cognitive/theoretical	Facilitative learning	Non-linear process
Safe	Experiential and immersive	Improving learning skills themselves
Content driven	White space/reflection time	

Technical and specific job-related skills development will require more formal aspects of training. But even here the ability to learn those skills in a context of the job or role, or to embed the learning in the flow of work, is more powerful.

The essential behavioural skills discussed previously are not best approached through formal pedagogical training, although they can be enhanced through good training programmes (eg by shared learning through teamwork and problem solving).

These kinds of skills and behaviours need to be drawn out and encouraged through many different forms of learning. Mentoring and coaching is a powerful way to encourage understanding and self-awareness which are a necessary start to behavioural change. Reward and recognition systems that recognize these core skills and positive behaviours help to reinforce. Experiential learning, ie learning through work and with others, is also highly effective, and as part of individual development programmes opportunities such as working on projects or other ways of collaborative working should be encouraged.

Evolving learning effectiveness through evidence and the next generations of digital learning

Developments in neuroscience have shone a light, or more accurately a functional MRI scan, on the ways in which our brains assimilate and retain information. It is a very complex field, but there are some key findings that are helping in the design of more effective learning, and in our understanding of drivers of human behaviour.

One of the most important areas has been the understanding of neuroplasticity, and how having a growth mindset enables better learning and uptake within individuals, but also as part of wider learning culture. The CIPD pulled together insights from neuroscience in a research report, 'Neuroscience in action – applying insight to L&D practice'.[9]

While the idea of people having different learning styles (eg visual vs auditory) has been rather debunked, people do have different learning preferences and ways in which different areas of the cognitive and sensory brain interact.

These kinds of findings are providing evidence of changes needed in how we approach education and learning – more bite-sized learning, learning in the context of using the skill (learning in the flow of work and gamification), nudging and repetition, social learning, and different forms and ways of learning. And the ability to personalize learning and the learning experience, and even to engage in its development. All of which are being enabled and accelerated through the rapid growth of learning technologies.

To enable more embedded cultures of learning, a particular focus has to be how to create learning that is much more frictionless, and to support self-directed learning in particular through personalization. This is a consumer expectation in all aspects of today's world, and yet for many their experiences of accessing or being able to personalize learning in the corporate context is far from that.

Friction creates resistance. Much of that resistance comes from time pressures, need for immediate access to learning and learning content. As already noted, one of the most significant barriers to uptake in learning is often cited as managers not allowing time for their people to do training and learning.

Today, most of us instinctively go to search the internet with questions. That is also true at work, particularly if internal corporate knowledge and learning systems are not easily accessible. We need to create 'Google-like' experiences at work, and part of that is about how we can best find and curate good content and learning that we can then make readily accessible to our learners.

Learning comes from so many sources now, and the role of learning and development increasingly is about curation. Filtering and guiding learners to the best content, helping them also curate and then being able to share what they find is best which can help others. Of course, there will be specific learning content that needs to be created in every organizational context. But that also may be done through curation of experience from others and social learning as much as through creating traditional forms of content.

Then embedding learning more in the flow of work, even as part of the tasks and processes, further helps the frictionless experience. Augmented and virtual reality has tremendous application in this regard for many tasks. Gamification techniques can create highly relevant and engaging learning experiences, improving learning retention through learn, test and repeat, and through collaborative and team or social learning. All exciting and transformative developments that will shape the future of learning and learning cultures.

The evolution of learning technologies

Technology in learning, however, did not get off to a particularly auspicious start back in the 1990s. It started as eLearning, a term that was first coined by Elliott Masie, an influential and well-known consultant and writer in the learning industry for many years.

eLearning was initially constrained by the technologies available and more often than not was a straight translation of traditional learning content on to a computer, whether in book-type form or video of someone lecturing. It was too often dull and ineffectual. Sadly, there is still too much of this type of online learning around.

As technology has progressed, so has understanding of how it is best used to create the best learning outcomes. And the techniques and therefore also the learning design skills are not the same as for face-to-face training. Hence the emergence of what has been called cybergogy – facilitating and technologically enabling learner-centred autonomous and collaborative learning in a virtual environment.

Of course, these techniques and approaches are not all mutually exclusive. Indeed, what is often being shown is that hybrid or blended learning can often achieve the best outcomes, gaining the benefits of digital learning with face-to-face and social learning and interaction.

The range and variety of learning technologies is huge and growing. Organizations of all sizes are experimenting more and more with different forms of technology-enabled learning.

The report on 'Learning and skills at work 2020' referenced earlier also looked at the range of learning technologies and their current level of uptake. Figure 12.2 summarizes the findings.

The combination of the categories of 'none of these' and 'webinars and virtual classrooms' as the most used shows there is much opportunity for further investment in and benefits from learning technologies. I expect to see a significant acceleration in the coming years in the use of a much wider variety of learning technologies and collaboration tools, content curation and enablement of the self-directed learner.

The pandemic forced a huge and rapid shift to online learning for the period of lockdowns, both in the educational system and in corporate learning. As reported in *Raconteur* in September 2020, 'When the dust settles, digital education will have advanced years in months.'[10] Dr David Lefevre, director of the Edtech Lab at Imperial College Business School, said, 'Working practice has already changed and many temporary solutions will become permanent. A growth in digital education is inevitable.'

Adapting learning in these ways will blur the traditional boundaries of training, learning and development – terms that have often been confused and used interchangeably (as I have done) but which all need to work together in a true learning culture and organization.

FIGURE 12.2 Uptake of technologies supporting learning, uptake of content and collaboration

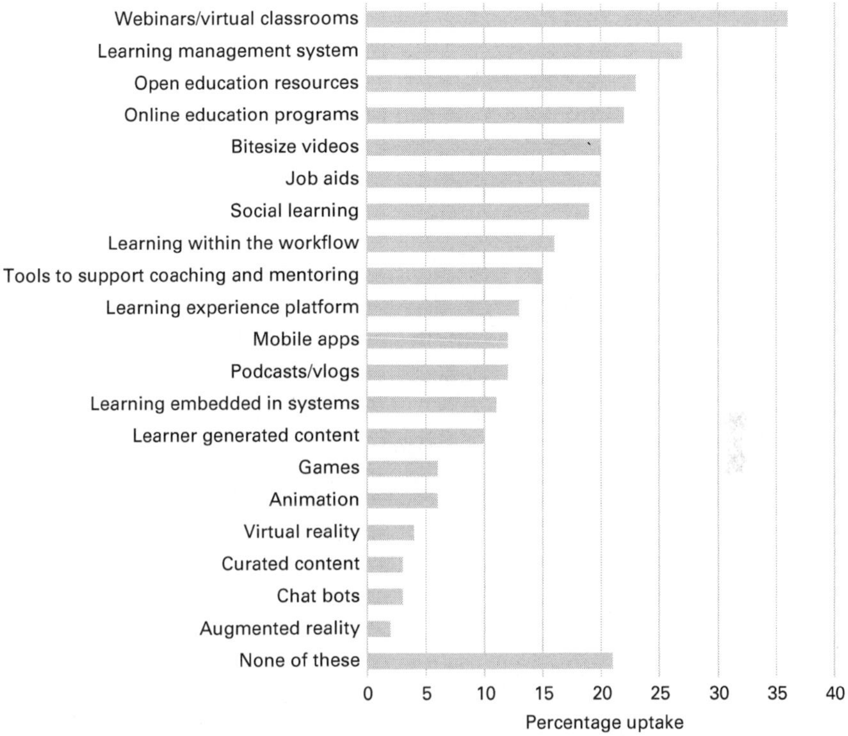

Technology	Percentage uptake
Webinars/virtual classrooms	~36
Learning management system	~27
Open education resources	~23
Online education programs	~22
Bitesize videos	~20
Job aids	~20
Social learning	~19
Learning within the workflow	~16
Tools to support coaching and mentoring	~15
Learning experience platform	~13
Mobile apps	~12
Podcasts/vlogs	~12
Learning embedded in systems	~11
Learner generated content	~10
Games	~6
Animation	~6
Virtual reality	~4
Curated content	~3
Chat bots	~3
Augmented reality	~2
None of these	~21

SOURCE Learning and Skills at Work 2020, CIPD and Accenture

Training can be defined as instructor-led, content-based interventions aimed at specific skills or behavioural change. Learning is a broader and typically self-directed formal or informal work-based process to improve competencies that lead to increased adaptive potential. Development is a longer-term or broader process, and relates more to mental and emotional maturity and how we think – impacted by a range of different means such as coaching, mentoring, formal and informal learning interventions, or planned experience. They therefore link quite closely with the learning models discussed earlier.

The outcomes of learning and how should they be measured

Estimates by Training Industry, a well-respected research body, put the total amount of spend globally on corporate training and learning at just over $370 billion.[11] In 2019, it estimated that on average 27 per cent of corporate training budgets was spent on external (outsourced) suppliers, while approximately 61 per cent of the budgets was spent on internal resources.

Generally, spend on learning is of the order of 1–5 per cent of salary costs. The national average spend per employee per year is around £300 in the UK. But as already noted, it is hard to determine how much of that spend really makes a difference and in what ways. It's also quite complex capturing all the costs, which can include facilitator costs, venue costs, and many other administrative costs, as well as the cost of time away from work for the learners.[12]

Not only have we not been good at measuring and understanding the outcome values of learning, but a lot of corporate learning was not built from good evidence and understanding of how people best learn, or from the individual and organizational needs and outcomes. Rather it appeared to be based more on the objectives of getting something out there.

To make learning efficient, it was also highly standardized and took little account of individual learning styles and needs. Sheep dipping was an oft-quoted analogy, or as American colleagues might call it, 'spray and pray'.

Much compliance training done in organizations would be good examples of this. Getting the standard training programme or course out there and having people record they have done it is taken as the proxy for the behavioural change and understanding needed. Learning outcomes and apparent success measures have as a result too often just been based on how many people did the training and what they might have thought about it.

Happy to be doing something else, particularly if it involved being somewhere else and interacting with other colleagues, often resulted in a positive bias in these 'happy sheets'. They usually bore little relation to whether or not the learning had been effective and what the value of the learning outcomes might have been.

Happy sheets emerged from the model of learning first proposed and still widely followed by Donald Kirkpatrick, a professor at the University of Wisconsin, first published in 1959. It has been updated since, and in 2016 James and Wendy Kayser Kirkpatrick revised and clarified the original theory, and introduced the New World Kirkpatrick Model.[13] One of the main additions is an emphasis on the importance of making training relevant to people's everyday jobs.

The model consists of four levels – Reaction, Learning, Behaviour and Results. Reaction is where the happy sheets came in. This level now also includes the degree to which participants felt engaged in the learning process and how relevant they thought it was. The learning level aims to measure what was actually learned, and the confidence and commitment to apply it.

Behaviour assesses how the learned skills and behaviours were actually applied on the job and the processes that reinforce that application. Results are the real end game and whether the learning objectives and outcomes were achieved.

The Kirkpatrick Model is still a widely used framework for evaluation of learning, but as we have observed, its full application is still so often missing. It could also be argued that to move away from the easy evaluations of attendance and satisfaction, the model should be turned upside down. If we can't understand the outcomes, or worse still have not even clearly defined what these should be and why they are important (back to the systems thinking point), then why are we doing the training in the first place?

So there is a range of qualitative and quantitative measures that can and should be used to evaluate training and learning. But many organizations still don't measure impact of learning. The 'Learning and skills at work 2020' report showed that still 30 per cent of organizations are not measuring the impact, and that of the range of ways in which learning can be evaluated, subjective learner feedback still dominated, as shown in Figure 12.3.

In the context of the wider learning culture, great corporate training and learning is also a strong and positive means of employee retention and attraction of new talent. It is part of the intrinsic motivator of mastery, but it is also part of the psychological contract where employees expect to be supported and developed to be able to do their jobs well. Learning can also be a tool of positive recognition, for example in

FIGURE 12.3 Measures used to assess effectiveness of learning and development initiatives

Measure	%
Learner reflection and feedback	56
General people metrics	43
Manager reflection and feedback	40
Qualitative data	36
Organizational data and metrics	30
Internal measures to compare impacts	23
Measures such as return on investment (ROI)	17
Stakeholder reflection and feedback	17
Strategic measures linked to business	14
Standard external measures to benchmark	11
Other	2
Don't know	12

SOURCE Learning and Skills at Work 2020, CIPD and Accenture

leadership development, but making it secretive can easily appear elitist and be counterproductive.

Indeed, it is very important that training and learning investment is inclusive. A learning organization applies to all who work there. And it is important to think of not just workers on employment contracts (the traditional employee), but also the increasing numbers of contractors and contingent workers that make up our organizations as discussed in Chapter 10.

Many organizations now extend their view of being a learning organization to partners, suppliers and customers, and even as part of their wider social responsibility in sharing the knowledge, experience and learning of their people with the communities they are part of, as reviewed in Chapter 8. There is engagement with schools and other centres of education to help young people understand the world of work, or to act as adjunct faculty in bringing academic learning to life.

These should also be characteristics of true learning organizations for the future.

Making training and learning inclusive

There is a lot of evidence that low-paid, low-skilled workers typically get the least amount of training, and that they have experienced the highest rate of decline in workplace training in recent years. The poorest adults with the lowest qualifications are the least likely to have access to adult training – despite being the group that has the potential to benefit most from it in terms of progression and social mobility.

Lower-skilled jobs will evidently require less training, but the decline in spend on training is concerning. Furthermore, much of the training that does occur in UK organizations is focused on health and safety and induction training. The most recent Employer Skills Survey (ESS)[14] shows that while two-thirds of organizations provided some sort of training in the previous 12 months, for a third of those organizations, between half and all of that training was either induction or health and safety related.

While it is important that organizations are compliant with health and safety legislation, and that employees are provided with support when starting in a new role, this type of training has very little impact on skill levels or tackling skills gaps and shortages.

According to UK government reports,[15] since 2011 training aimed at workers with the lowest-level qualifications (below GCSE-Level 2) has reduced by 20 per cent, which is double the average rate of decline. The evidence cited showed that 32 per cent of adults with degree-level qualifications participated in in-work training, compared to just 9 per cent of workers with no qualifications. Younger workers up to age 34 were the hardest hit of all, experiencing a 16 per cent decline in training volumes between 2011 and 2018.

CIPD research through their annual Employee Outlook survey which was run from 2009 to 2017 shows how important fair access to training and career support is. The report from 2017[16] showed that over a quarter of employees disagree that their organization provides them with enough opportunities to learn and grow. Further, almost a quarter are dissatisfied with the opportunities on offer to develop their skills in their roles. For instance, 92 per cent of employees said they find job rotation, secondment and shadowing useful, but only 6 per cent had experienced it in the last 12 months.

Research on the untapped potential within the UK workforce across a representative survey of 3,700 employees conducted by the CIPD in 2018[17] found that almost a quarter (24 per cent) of workers had undertaken no training in the past year, with older, low-wage or part-time workers and those who are self-employed the worst affected. Some 26 per cent of respondents reported a 'lack of opportunities' as the biggest barrier to progression, followed by 'lack of confidence' at 14 per cent. And the research also found that low-paid workers had much less labour market mobility or opportunity to progress. Only 12 per cent of those earning £20,000 per year or less said that they had been promoted in their current organization, compared with 45 per cent of those on £40,000 or more.

The pandemic will have further exaggerated these findings, which also go along with the higher levels of furloughing and redundancies that were faced by younger and lower-skilled workers. As discussed throughout the book, automation and AI is likely to make it even harder for those with low skills to get good jobs and to progress.

Opportunity for growth and development should be open to all employees of any responsible business. Retaining and growing a more diverse workforce is the right thing to do from many perspectives as we have discussed.

Having a workforce that reflects your customers, and the communities of which your business is part, is vital for any responsible and sustainable business. But also creating the opportunities to access diverse talent opens up recruitment pipelines and access to many different skills that businesses need and have been finding harder, as previously noted.

Organizations can help with these challenges in other ways as well. Mentoring and coaching of people struggling to find the right opportunities or to access work has immense value. People in organizations volunteering in helping others by sharing their experiences of work, or how to find the right opportunities and prepare for interviews, makes a big difference. Governments in many countries including the UK are seeking to encourage and expand these sorts of initiatives in light of the challenging job markets and fallout from the pandemic.

Volunteering work of this kind also helps to develop employees' skills and confidence in areas like communication skills, influencing skills and relationship building. Research by the UK-based charity Education and Employers released in January 2020 – 'The value of volunteering'[18] – showed strong evidence for this.

I have always been proud of the work the CIPD does in this regard, particularly through the volunteering programmes such as Steps Ahead Mentoring, which engage thousands of members often working directly through job centres to help others. They also work closely with other charities and initiatives in the UK such as Education and Employers, and the Careers and Enterprise Company, which work to bring businesses and businesspeople closer to schools and colleges, helping to inspire and prepare young people for the fast-changing world of work.

Implications for corporate learning and development functions

All these shifts and the need for a stronger focus and enablement of learning and development require learning and development professionals to develop new skills and capabilities.

The Towards Maturity report highlighted that learning and development itself is feeling overwhelmed and underequipped, particularly when it comes to technology. We need also to invest in this critical area of our business or progress will continue to be too slow.

Critical capabilities will include understanding the different learning methods and how they can best be applied and in what mix, better on analytics and value analysis, better on learning and content curation as well as creation, and working closely and collaboratively with the business.

Traditional roles of administration, L&D managers and face-to-face training facilitators still make up the majority of roles in learning and training organizations. The new roles that will support the kinds of learning capabilities we have described are still much in the minority – roles like technologist/product owner, digital asset creators and managers, learning community managers, and instructional designers who create, curate, design and support digital learning experiences. Or learning performance analysts and learning and development business partners who really can work closely with the business, aligning needs and evaluating outcomes.

As with functions like marketing and communications, technology is forcing new capabilities but also more specialized roles. As discussed in Chapter 10, every organization will have to consider how best to source these skills, whether to employ, contract or outsource. Smaller organizations will much more likely be dependent on others to bring these capabilities to them.

As the importance of learning as a more strategic capability has been recognized, so we have seen the emergence of chief learning officers (CLOs) or directors of learning and development. These roles signal the importance of learning and skills development across the organization. Jack Welch in the 1990s created the first CLO role at GE in appointing Steve Kerr, who was subsequently recruited in 2001 into Goldman Sachs in a similar role.

Their role can broadly be defined as having responsibility for maintaining a skilled and knowledgeable workforce, and for the learning strategy. This should include the organizational and cultural aspects of learning as we have discussed. The outcome is about enhancing performance, innovation, agility and confidence of the workforce to drive the organization forwards.

Some organizations have moved to creating the position of chief knowledge officer (CKO). This person's role is to manage information throughout the organization. He or she oversees the flow of information coming into the organization from across its external boundaries and assures it is directed to where it will be most useful. Most often this role is seen in intellectual capital companies, such as consulting firms, whose basic products are essentially information.

Learning and knowledge should be more seen as a continuum, across the spectrum of structured knowledge and learning to tacit knowledge and learning.

How learning and development as a function is structured and organized finds many different forms. Responsibilities for learning and development strategy and identifying learning needs is then somewhat dependent on where the function sits. As noted in Chapter 6, even with centralized learning functions, a lot of learning can still get managed and delivered via the line.

Research[19] has shown that for around half of large employers, line managers, function heads or directors have the primary responsibility for identifying learning needs. For SMEs (less than 250 employees) this rises to closer to 80 per cent. This should give a close alignment to business needs.

In larger organizations, most have the learning and development function sitting as part of HR. But there appears to be a growing trend of having learning and development as a separate, or at least adjacent, function. Most SMEs don't formally recognize a learning function at all, but there is still the need to understand skills and development requirements as part of their strategy.

As with any organization structure and design, there is never one right answer that fits all. Having a more separate learning and development function can emphasize its importance and visibility. Having closer alignment to the line functions helps connection to business needs. But a centralized capability will help to reduce overlap and ensure a more organization-wide approach in learning methods, technologies and content.

In conclusion

It is now more important than ever to recognize the strategic importance of learning and development in organizations as a core capability in agility and competitiveness. This then requires a commitment to and development of the wider learning environment and culture in your organization.

Learning needs to be reinvented using new insights on how we learn, digital capabilities to enable it differently, and engagement to involve everyone.

Learning and development strategy must align with organizational need and overall people strategy, understanding the types of skills you need and how you will source them.

It is important to approach learning for essential behavioural skills as well as technical and job-specific skills, and to recognize the differences needed in approach.

Learning outcomes need to be understood and everywhere we need to develop better analytics to understand learning impact and value, and to be able to adjust and improve as we go.

Learning cultures also require that your people managers have the knowledge, skills, behaviours and resources to support learning, and encourage them to be role models.

And finally, now is the time to increase the knowledge and capability of your learning function, particularly around analytics, curation and digital learning.

Endnotes

1. www.cipd.co.uk/Images/learning-skills-work-report-1_tcm18-79434.pdf (archived at https://perma.cc/RFR6-H2B9)
2. Senge, P (1992) *The Fifth Discipline: The art and practice of the learning organisation*, Random House Business
3. Dweck, C S (2006) *Mindset: Changing the way you think to fulfil your potential*, Random House, London
4. www.cipd.co.uk/knowledge/strategy/development/professionalising-learning-development-function (archived at https://perma.cc/FL95-C6BC)
5. Lancaster, A (2019) *Driving Performance Through Learning: Develop employees through effective workplace learning*, Kogan Page
6. https://hbr.org/2018/10/when-companies-should-invest-in-training-their-employees-and-when-they-shouldnt (archived at https://perma.cc/7RDG-J2BM)
7. https://hbr.org/2019/10/where-companies-go-wrong-with-learning-and-development (archived at https://perma.cc/R4DC-MNT9)
8. https://uwaterloo.ca/campus-wellness/curve-forgetting (archived at https://perma.cc/4BJJ-UFU6)
9. www.cipd.co.uk/Images/neuroscience-action_2014-applying-insight-LD-practice_tcm18-9714.pdf (archived at https://perma.cc/Y9TD-HQV5)
10. www.raconteur.net/digital/digital-learning-edtech/ (archived at https://perma.cc/2PQM-T54E)
11. https://trainingindustry.com/wiki/outsourcing/size-of-training-industry/ (archived at https://perma.cc/DX37-RPF3)
12. www.cipd.co.uk/knowledge/strategy/development/benchmarking-factsheet (archived at https://perma.cc/N5ME-RH4B)
13. Kirkpatrick, J D and Kirkpatrick W K (2016) *Kirkpatrick's Four Levels of Training Evaluation*, ATD Press
14. www.gov.uk/government/collections/uk-employer-skills-survey-2017 (archived at https://perma.cc/KH39-2NW9)
15. https://committees.parliament.uk/committee/203/education-committee/news/138043/mps-call-for-adult-skills-revolution-to-foster-new-culture-of-lifelong-learning/ (archived at https://perma.cc/E7PK-9VS2)
16. www.cipd.co.uk/knowledge/fundamentals/relations/engagement/employee-outlook-reports (archived at https://perma.cc/P5GB-JU3A)
17. www.cipd.co.uk/knowledge/work/skills/untapped-potential-uk-skills (archived at https://perma.cc/K56R-7MQG)
18. The value of volunteering – volunteering in education and productivity at work. Education and employers and CIPD, January 2020
19. www.cipd.co.uk/Images/learning-skills-work-report-1_tcm18-79434.pdf (archived at https://perma.cc/RFR6-H2B9)

13

Wellbeing as an outcome

The part can never be well unless the whole is well.
PLATO, ANCIENT GREEK PHILOSOPHER

I have referenced the idea of wellbeing throughout. From the notions of eudaimonia as an outcome for humanity, to healthy societies and organizations, and of wellbeing and engagement being critical components and outcomes of good work. I've also talked about compassionate management and the new era of leadership, and the importance of positive mental health.

Wellbeing is so fundamentally human. It's about how people are – physically, emotionally and mentally. Of all the constructs about the future of work, enhancing and supporting wellbeing through our work must be the most profoundly important goal for all of us.

But positive wellbeing among people and organizations also creates better economic and societal outcomes. It's a circular argument. Poor wellbeing and health, absenteeism from work or reduced productivity cost businesses and economies billions. And they cost our healthcare systems and society at large even more.

That was fundamentally understood by some of the founders of the second industrial revolution we saw in Chapter 3. But somehow, a lot of the fundamental belief in wellbeing got a bit lost over much of that last century and into the early 2000s – the obsession with financial results and getting stuff done, seeing people only as costs, and even that people's health and wellbeing were not the concern of the manager or the organization.

The 'homo economicus' view was that people are paid to turn up and work, and if they can't then they should be on sick leave. If they turn up at work with a lot of stress and anxiety, then that was their problem to deal with. For most of our lifetimes, mental health in particular was a taboo subject with great social stigma attached to it. We didn't want or know how to talk about it. Particularly at work.

This chapter, then, in exploring the different dimensions of wellbeing, the ways we can improve wellbeing, the duty of care of any responsible business, is an appropriate one to conclude on – at least before trying to pull it all together in the final chapter.

What actually is wellbeing?

As philosophers throughout the ages have observed, from Plato quoted above, wellbeing is about the whole, not just the sum of the parts. It's about external factors that impact us and our lived experiences, and the internal factors and the connections between body and mind.

At a societal level, as explored in Chapter 7, the interest in understanding wellbeing and happiness at societal levels has been growing. In the UK, the ONS has taken on the task of understanding national wellbeing and in 2011 encouraged a wider debate along the lines of the question about 'what matters most to you'.

This work has led into broad national surveys of wellbeing that recognize a wide range of factors, including the natural environment, the economy, education, personal finance, our relationships, our health, and what we do. As we will see, these are all factors that relate to general levels of stress and anxiety in people across our societies.

In general and in simpler terms at a personal level, people talk about wellbeing in terms of feeling safe, feeling loved and appreciated, and feeling fulfilled. It can be summarized as 'how are we doing'.

Diving a bit deeper, neuroscience is giving us an ever-greater understanding of how we react as humans to positive and negative stimuli and how these impact our sense of wellbeing. Science has also shown us what many of the ancient traditions such as Buddhism have espoused for a long time – that the mind and the body work together.[1] The mind and our emotions influence the body, and the body influences our mind and emotions.

We understand the action of the stress hormones like adrenaline and cortisol which are associated with threat, and may protect us in the short term but over the long term have a detrimental impact on our health.

Conversely, the so-called 'happy hormones' of serotonin, dopamine, oxytocin and endorphins are associated with reward and bring out feelings of happiness, wellbeing and even willingness to cooperate with others. We also understand how the body interacts with these – how for example exercise impacts our positive sense of wellbeing through the action of these hormones. Or how depression acts just like a physical pain on our bodies.

These hormones also drive what some neuroscientists would describe as the basic organizing principle of the brain, which is to seek to maximize reward and minimize threat. We naturally seek to optimize our wellbeing.

David Rock, co-founder and CEO of the NeuroLeadership Institute, has been one of the most effective people I know in bringing neuroscience into the practical domain. He describes this deep-rooted survival mechanism as our 'approach/avoid' response. In particular how our responses to social threat and reward can influence our behaviours as profoundly as physical threat and reward.

He developed the SCARF model,[2] which is widely referenced and covers the five domains of human social experience, all of which we see in our working environments:

- **Status** is about relative importance to others.
- **Certainty** concerns being able to predict the future.
- **Autonomy** provides a sense of control over events.
- **Relatedness** is a sense of safety with others – of friend rather than foe.
- **Fairness** is a perception of fair exchanges between people.

It is interesting to see how this understanding of how our brains work repeats much of what we have talked about in the constructs of good work and positive cultures. So the science is giving us more evidence of how to approach engagement and wellbeing in the workplace and the elements we can control to most optimize how people respond.

The science explains why we mostly seek to avoid conflict in the workplace, why we seek out others like ourselves, why some control or autonomy over our work is so important, and why status can be seen as such a threat. Therefore, as Rock describes, high levels of positive rewards in the SCARF domains link to high engagement, and conversely disengaged employees are experiencing high levels of threat in these same domains.

It has also been shown that stress hormones inhibit our learning. That has always made me think of the example of performance management sessions. For the most part both the manager and the employee are in a state of threat response for the 'difficult conversations'. Both would rather not be there, and for the employee there is unlikely to be a lot of learning going on. Good to see, then, that performance management now is moving away from these stilted meetings once or twice a year to encourage the much more regular and natural conversations about performance that should happen in the moment.

Our psychological make-up and needs, and our ability to feel positive and negative emotions, are so much of what makes us human. Wellbeing will be driven by how often and how long we experience positive or negative emotions. It is a universal construct, but it has many different contexts and understandings. Also there is a hugely bewildering range of ideas, approaches, tools and magical elixirs that we are all confronted with now about how we improve wellbeing. So it's important to talk about key principles and not delve into endless numbers of solutions.

The drivers of wellbeing in the workplace

The What Works Centre for Wellbeing, some of whose research I referenced in Chapter 7, is part of a network of centres established by the UK government in 2013 to drive more evidence-based understanding of key issues and inform government policy.

The Centre has consolidated a lot of research in the wellbeing space. It summarizes the main drivers of wellbeing in the workplace as:

- **health** – overall physical and mental health;
- **security** – work conditions and feeling safe (mentally and physically), and contractual and financial security;
- **environment** – physical and systems (facilities, working patterns) and organizational culture;
- **relationships** – line manager and others at work;
- **purpose** – engagement and job quality.

We have already talked about areas like psychological safety, sense of purpose and relationships, many of which closely relate to the research and principles behind engagement as reviewed in Chapter 11. Indeed, much of the thinking of engagement closely parallels wellbeing and they are themes which should come closer together but sometimes seem to fight for airtime – in academia and in practice.

The drivers of engagement align closely with frameworks for psychological and physical wellbeing in the workplace and we can't really talk about one without the other. Engagement contributes to wellbeing and vice versa, as an article for Engage for Success explored quite deeply.[3] Hence much of the measurement of wellbeing in the workplace comes as part of engagement surveys, also discussed in Chapter 11.

It is interesting to note how people's sense of wellbeing changes with age. Figure 13.1 from ONS data and measures covered in Chapter 7 based on the life satisfaction question shows how it varies across age groups in the UK.

The downward trend from early adulthood through middle age follows the same curve in reverse of the use of anti-depressants – another phenomenon of the modern age. Mid-life is usually the most challenging in terms of additional responsibilities at home and at work, financial worries for many, mid-career, and perhaps that nagging feeling of unfulfilment of dreams in earlier life.

This is a very important curve to understand as we think about workplace interventions. Putting more and more pressure on mid-level managers or line managers for them to support others cannot be done without also providing proper support to the managers.

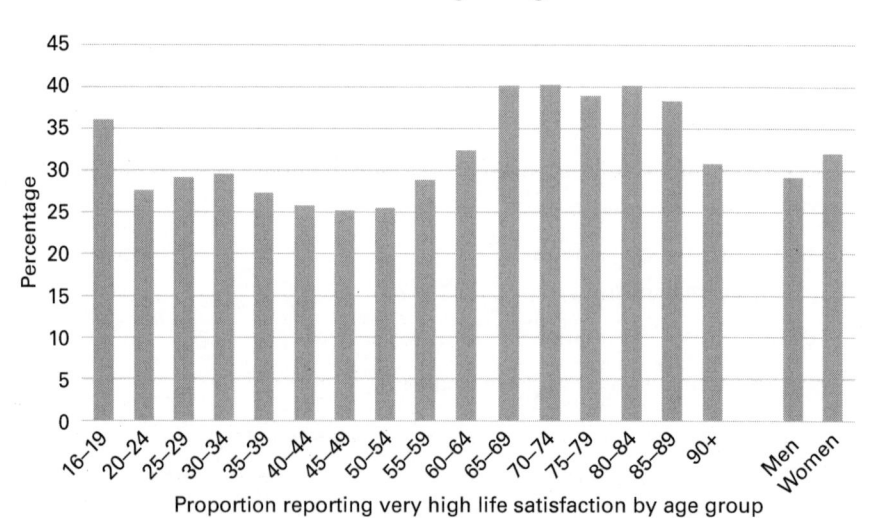

FIGURE 13.1 Variation of sense of wellbeing with age

Proportion reporting very high life satisfaction by age group

SOURCE ONS Annual Population Survey 2020, https://www.ons.gov.uk/peoplepopulationandcommunity/wellbeing/datasets/headlineestimatesofpersonalwellbeing

Physical safety and wellbeing and the outcomes of the pandemic

In understanding the different dimensions of wellbeing in the workplace, organizations have long understood the obligations and importance of physical safety. This is well enshrined in law, such as the UK's Health and Safety at Work Act which describes these obligations, including between employees, and with members of the public, and for the self-employed.

Physical safety at work, however, took on a whole new dimension during the pandemic. Those essential and frontline workers, often in the lower-paid jobs, took on new risks associated with being in their workplaces. Businesses had to rapidly respond and ensure that workers were being properly protected with PPE and the other necessary measures to ensure workplace safety.

Much of this was new ground. Protecting employees from transmissible disease is complex and uncertain. During the course of the pandemic, employers recognized they could not force people to travel to offices or places of work when they could work from home. Many employees expressed strong reservations, not just about possible exposure to the virus at work while travelling to work but also when mixing in shared office spaces.

This opened up many debates about how much employers could require people to travel to places of work, and about the legal and ethical issues of whether employees should have vaccines or be restricted from working if they do not.

Given the virus is expected to be endemic and not something we can expect to eradicate or fully control, we will have to learn to live with it. With better treatments and vaccination protections, at the time of writing the hope is that morbidity and mortality rates become more at the level of seasonal influenzas. In that case it may not require long-term policy changes either within organizations or in wider legislation, but it will certainly cause more scrutiny of a dimension of physical health that has not been of much concern within the workplace before.

For the large numbers of people who had to work at home, employers also had to focus attention on their physical wellbeing, home workplace ergonomics and technology support. These are the basics, and with the expectation that more people will work from home more often as part of the trend in flexible working that the pandemic is accelerating, employers must take a wider view of how they support and protect people's wellbeing beyond the immediate workplace.

The pandemic also accelerated awareness of mental and emotional wellbeing, even at the simple human level of social connection and looking out for each other. Mental health historically has not received enough attention, but in recent years awareness has grown steadily both in the public health domain and within organizations and workplaces.

The importance of understanding stress

According to the American Institute of Stress, 83 per cent of US workers suffer from work-related stress, costing businesses across the US economy what it estimates to be over $300 billion annually. This is an extraordinary percentage, which also begs the question about how we measure and perceive stress individually. But when you consider this price tag in relation to the cost and benefits of investing more in employee wellbeing and creating better-quality jobs, this figure is really quite astounding.

From many years of research on wellbeing in the workplace by the CIPD,[4] it has long been seen that mental ill-health and stress are the top two causes of long-term absence from work. And the biggest sources of stress at work are workload and relationship with managers. No surprises there, given much of what we have already covered.

The report published in March 2020 showed that absenteeism rates have been slightly falling over the last decade and average 5.9 days per employee per year across the UK. But this has to be offset against the growing phenomenon of presenteeism where employees still come to work even when not fully well. The research showed that presenteeism had more than tripled since 2010.[5]

But before looking more at the damaging effects of stress, it is important to balance this out with the recognition that, up to a point, stress improves performance. Something we all recognize.

Figure 13.2 shows what is known as the Yerkes-Dodson curve, named after the two psychologists who researched it back in the early 1900s.

Research has also shown that the shape of the curve varies based on the complexity and familiarity of the task.[6] For difficult or unfamiliar tasks, lower levels of arousal are needed to facilitate concentration and the top of the stress curve is reached more quickly. For tasks requiring more stamina or persistence, such as writing a book, as I have experienced, higher levels of arousal are needed to induce and increase motivation. But of course, once over the top of the curve, performance can deteriorate rapidly.

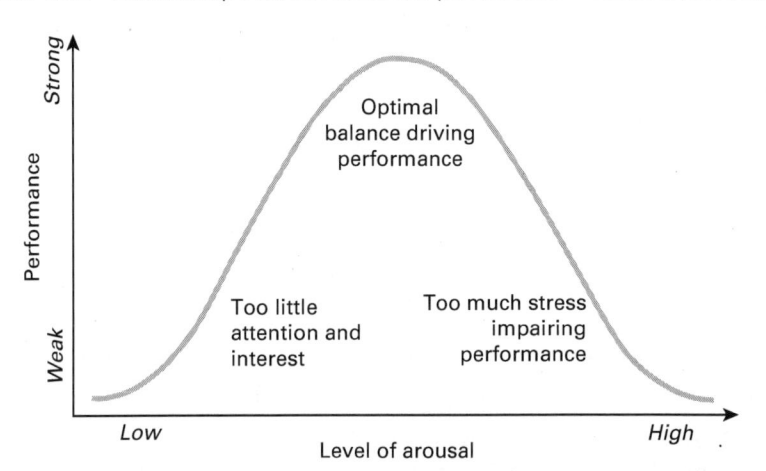

FIGURE 13.2 Relationship between stress and performance – Yerkes-Dodson law

[Graph showing an inverted U-curve with "Performance" (Weak to Strong) on the y-axis and "Level of arousal" (Low to High) on the x-axis. Labels on the curve: "Optimal balance driving performance" at the peak, "Too little attention and interest" on the left side, "Too much stress impairing performance" on the right side.]

In 1974, German-born American psychologist Herbert Freudenberger published an article in the *Journal of Social Issues* entitled 'Staff burn-out'[7] popularizing a term that would become almost emblematic of future working generations. Freudenberger implied that the caring profession was most prone to the condition – a supposition that persisted for many years and is backed up by evidence, and very concerning following the crisis of the pandemic.

In fact, research suggests that one of the first burnout epidemics materialized among air traffic controllers who were forced to perform high-risk tasks during long shifts with inadequate resources and under immense pressure.

In the US in the late 1960s, protests staged by the Professional Air Traffic Controllers Organization, known as the Patco Disputes,[8] centred around working conditions and the intolerable levels of stress that controllers were being put under. A Patco newsletter actually referenced a condition of being 'burned out' and described it as a form of severe exhaustion which manifests itself in a decline in the quality and quantity of work produced.

By the early 1970s, awareness around burnout in the profession had grown to such an extent that the Federal Aviation Administration felt compelled to commission an extensive piece of research into the phenomenon. Of the hundreds of controllers examined, the ones that were particularly likely to develop symptoms of burnout during the course of the study had displayed good psychological health at the start of the research period. They had also demonstrated a superior ability to manage anxiety and stress than those who did not develop burnout later on.

The analysis also revealed that those who were considered to be more competent at their job were more at risk of burning out. Rajvinder Samra, a lecturer at the Open University, concludes that one explanation is that it's 'likely these individuals had high internal standards and were trying to live up to these ideals but the external demands and growing complexity of work created the conditions for burnout'.[9]

The growing mental wellbeing challenge

Recognizable mental health issues prior to the Covid-19 pandemic were already being seen in one in six people. In most countries the data shows that about a quarter of people will suffer from a mental health problem at some point in their lives.[10] Many conditions are mild and tend to be short-lived, but others are far more chronic and ultimately sadly can prove fatal.

In 2019, the World Health Organization estimated that 615 million people globally suffer from anxiety and depression, costing the global workforce an estimated $1 trillion in productivity every single year.

For a 2016 paper published in the journal *Management Science*,[11] three academics from Stanford University evaluated the financial impact and effect on mortality rates of 10 different work-related stressors – unemployment, lack of health insurance, exposure to shift work, long working hours, job insecurity, work–family conflict, low job control, high job demands, low social support at work and low organizational justice.

The conclusions were startling. Stress relating to these 10 factors, the academics found, led to nearly $190 billion of spending every year, or about 8 per cent of US national healthcare outlays, and caused almost 120,000 deaths each year.

There was a strong correlation between prevalence of mental health issues and job quality. Bad jobs that, as discussed in Chapter 11, don't provide satisfaction, adequate income or security, are simply bad for your health. But even jobs that do offer those things and are fulfilling can become associated with burnout and other mental health problems, as we saw with air traffic controllers. Suicide rates within the caregiving profession are markedly higher than across the general public – by some accounts more than double – even though many doctors and nurses will say that they derive great satisfaction from their profession.

Jennifer Moss, an author and United Nations Global Happiness Council Committee Member, notes that the jobs which we are most passionate about might in fact be the ones in which mental health problems can be the most dangerous as they tend to be hardest to spot. 'You've no doubt heard the well-worn advice that "if you do what you love, you'll never work a day in your life". It's a nice idea but a total myth,' Moss writes.[12] When we equate the work we love to not actually working, she adds, it propagates a false belief that we don't need time away from work to rest and recover. As she summarized, 'This type of mentality leads to burnout, and the consequences can be both dire and hard to detect.'

Moss cites several studies to support her thesis. One, published in the *Journal of Personality* in 2010,[13] shows that purpose-driven labour – work that employees might admit to loving – is likely to breed an obsessiveness that can lead to burnout or worse. She also notes that on the Mayo Clinic's list of burnout risks,[14] two out of six are related to this sentiments: 'You identify so strongly with work that you lack balance between your work life and your personal life' and 'You work in a helping profession.'

The findings are particularly pertinent in light of the demographic trends discussed in the first half of this book. The generational cohorts that will soon make up the majority of the labour market tend to be more stressed than others that came before them, but also tend to be more purpose-driven.

A Deloitte survey on millennials published in late 2020 – the Deloitte Global Millennial Survey 2020[15] – explored the views of more than 27,000 millennials and Gen Zs, both before and after the start of the Covid-19 pandemic, on a wide range of issues, including stress.

They found that almost half of Gen Zs reported being stressed all or most of the time, and around 44 per cent of millennials. There was uneasiness, pessimism and concerns about the present and the future. These are extraordinary but also unsustainable. However, the survey also found that stress levels had improved during the course of the pandemic by 8 percentage points. Clear correlations with how so many organizations had responded with a much stronger focus on wellbeing and looking after their people.

Stress, and the challenges of mental wellbeing, are not just about work or immediate work concerns, as we observed at the beginning of the chapter. The issues that were most driving the sense of stress in the younger generations were issues from climate change, the welfare of their families, financial stability, health and long-term career prospects. But poor work–life balance and the inability to be their authentic selves also were significant issues in their minds. Important themes we have also explored earlier.

Impact of crises on mental health and wellbeing – the long shadow

Besides the obvious issues of physical health and the many challenges of protecting people during the pandemic, as noted earlier, the crisis also greatly increased issues of mental health – social isolation, anxiety and stress, blurred work–life boundaries and challenges at home, bereavement, or just being 'Zoomed' out.

Mental health issues triggered or exacerbated by a crisis can linger for years to come and long after any more tangible effects have passed. Evidence suggests that after the 9/11 attacks in New York, for example, an estimated tenth of all people living in the wider New York area likely met the full criteria for PTSD.[16]

After the 2003 outbreak of severe acute respiratory syndrome, or SARS, research indicated that among populations who had been quarantined there was a particularly high prevalence of psychological distress.[17] The considerable mental health burden of any event or development that radically alters the way we live our lives and do our jobs, even if only temporarily, simply cannot be underestimated.

In May 2020, the UK's Royal College of Psychiatrists warned that people with no history of mental illness had developed serious psychological problems as a result of the lockdown, triggered by stresses over having to socially isolate, job insecurity, relationship breakdowns and bereavement.[18] The college warned of a 'tsunami of mental illness' and said that both adults and children were experiencing psychotic episodes, mania and depression, and that many were being hospitalized.

Young men were found to have been particularly susceptible to first-time mental health issues and four in 10 psychiatrists whom the college questioned reported an increase in people needing urgent and emergency mental healthcare.

These trends were being seen everywhere. According to research conducted by the Kaiser Family Foundation, a non-profit headquartered in San Francisco, nearly half of adults in the US reported their mental health had been negatively impacted due to worry and stress over the virus.[19] Concerns around an increase in substance abuse proliferated too.

Many are worried about the longer-term effects, among those who have suffered bereavements, or from the ongoing symptoms of 'long Covid', or the anxiety of losing jobs, or for some sectors particularly in social and healthcare of PTSD from what they saw in our hospitals and care homes. These trends are of great concern, and they come on the back of the long-term growing issues of stress in people's lives and specifically at work. The Covid-19 pandemic will cast a long shadow on mental health across our communities and in our workplaces and this will significantly add to the already high levels of mental health challenges and stress already highlighted.

Managing stress and supporting wellbeing in the workplace

As we have seen, mental health and wellbeing in the workplace has been receiving a lot more attention in recent years. It's finally moving beyond the taboo to being seen as a core business issue and responsibility, particularly accelerated by the pandemic. And it needed to.

In 2016, the UK charity Business in the Community (BITC) and YouGov questioned 20,000 workers aged 16–64 across the UK on their mental health, their attitudes towards work and the extent to which they feel like their employer supports them.[20]

More than three-quarters said they had experienced symptoms of poor mental health, but more than half of the employees who disclosed their symptoms said their employers took no action. Fewer than a quarter of managers surveyed said they had had training in spotting and supporting employees who are struggling, and a shocking 63 per cent said they felt obliged to put the interests of their organization above the wellbeing of team members.

Mental health and wellbeing is a complex subject. Although it has in some ways been equated to physical first aid, it is a lot more nuanced than that. There are not simple one-size-fits-all solutions or interventions and the whole field of mental health support at work is still in its early years. Some interventions can cause more harm than good. Simplistic interventions without a wider support context will fail.

There is no doubt, however, that businesses everywhere, governments, and many charities and voluntary organizations have stepped up to the wellbeing agenda. This is happening at local, regional, national and global levels.

In January 2021, the Global Business Collaboration for Better Workplace Mental Health was launched to 'raise awareness of the importance of mental health in the workplace and facilitate the adoption of best practices'. The businesses initially backing this were BHP, Clifford Chance, Deloitte, HSBC, Salesforce and Unilever.

More evidence, however, has been needed on what really works. Not just as short-term palliatives that make bosses feel good because it looks like they are doing something, but as longer-term and sustainable solutions. It is also very important to see that employers and managers are not experts or health professionals, and the distinctions between looking after employees' wellbeing at work and trying to deal with genuine health issues.

There are now so many frameworks, guidance and 'solutions' out there that organizations and individuals are almost getting overwhelmed. Apps, websites, coaching and support programmes, training and other interventions that are aiming to help – or at least to capture our attention. Many are well intentioned and supported by credible organizations, charities as well as local and central governments. But many are jumping on a bandwagon and lack evidence of positive and sustainable impact.

In 2017, Prime Minister Theresa May commissioned a review of mental health at work. Led by Paul Farmer, the CEO of Mind, the mental health charity, and Lord Dennis Stevenson, a senior banker and business leader, the review, 'Thriving at work – the Stevenson/Farmer review of mental health and employers', set out to see how employers can better support all individuals currently in employment, including those with mental ill health or poor wellbeing, to remain in and thrive through work.

The review described the huge cost to businesses and the economy and society as a whole of poor mental health, and therefore also the payback in putting in place interventions and support to help. It highlighted academic research that showed links between good work and mental health[21] and called out this as part of a strategic vision to the future – everyone should have access to good work.

Data cited includes that 39 per cent of employees have experienced poor mental health where work was a contributing factor in the last year, 51 per cent feel comfortable talking generally in the workplace about mental health issues, and 300,000 people lose their jobs each year because of long-term mental health problems.

The review's recommendations were summarized in six 'mental health core standards' which have now been taken forward into the Mental Health at Work Commitment,[22] which encourages organizations to commit to the following.

> **MENTAL HEALTH STANDARDS FOR ORGANIZATIONS**
>
> - prioritize mental health in the workplace by developing and delivering a systematic programme of activity;
> - proactively ensure work design and organizational culture drive positive mental health outcomes;
> - promote an open culture around mental health;
> - increase organizational confidence and capability;
> - provide mental health tools and support;
> - increase transparency and accountability through internal and external reporting.

The standards were drawn from what the review found to be best practice and, as far as possible, are evidence based, but it was also acknowledged that 'there is a pressing need for more evidence'.

All these standards align to many other aspects of good business and good work we have talked about. The need for visible and engaged leadership at all levels, open and speak-up cultures, building the right capabilities and support. And certainly, the idea of greater transparency internally and externally to the awareness of wellbeing, the actions being taken and the commitment to change.

Top-down visible commitment is essential, and it is particularly impactful where leaders themselves open up to their own mental health challenges. Two leaders I have seen exemplify this are António Horta-Osório, the CEO of Lloyds Banking Group, and Bernard Looney, the CEO of BP.

Horta-Osório took time off for stress shortly after joining the bank in 2011. This was one of the first serious acknowledgements by a top business leader that they were not impervious to mental health and stress challenges. In the past, a bank's PR team may well have come up with some other excuse for his absence, not wishing to signal any 'weakness' in the top person. He talks about his challenges very openly and has encouraged open dialogue throughout the organization, and that makes a real difference.

Likewise Bernard Looney leading on the mental wellbeing agenda at BP and talking openly and personally, together with others from the senior team, about their challenges with their mental wellbeing.

Improving mental wellbeing through work

Having talked about the many issues surrounding health and wellbeing, it is also important to look at the positives and how wellbeing can be improved through having good work.

A lot of the ideas we have talked about regarding good work concern how it is good for people.

Some fascinating research by researchers from Cambridge University and Salford University looked at employment dosage and links to mental health.[23] The researchers examined how changes in working hours were linked to mental health and life satisfaction in over 70,000 UK residents between 2009 and 2018. They found that when people moved from having no job into paid work of eight hours or less a week, their risk of mental health problems reduced by an average of 30 per cent. That is very significant, particularly when they also found that there was no real further improvement beyond that equivalent of one day per week.

Having some structure to a week, doing something worthwhile with purpose, increasing the sense of self-worth and confidence were all undoubtedly contributory factors, as many studies have shown. It was interesting that it took so little time at work to gain those benefits.

The researchers acknowledged that the work needed to be of good quality to see the benefits, but they rather excitedly extrapolated these findings to suggest we should all be working shorter weeks, or have five-day weekends and longer holidays. This would also help balance out work across populations if we do end up in a future with less work because technology finally is doing what Keynes predicted all those years ago.

As the research team rightly pointed out, 'The traditional model, in which everyone works around 40 hours a week, was never based on how much work was good for people. Our research suggests that micro-jobs provide the same psychological benefits as full-time jobs.'

We will take these thoughts forward into the concluding chapter, but there is no doubt that shorter working weeks are a growing part of the debate about work today and for the future.

The importance of sleep

One of the most misunderstood areas of wellbeing and mental health historically has been sleep. As Matthew Walker observed in his bestselling book

Why We Sleep: The new science of sleep and dreams,[24] we probably sleep less now than we have throughout human history.

But all the neuroscience and research on sleep has shown just how fundamental sleep is to our wellbeing. How it allows our brains to recharge and even to retain learning and knowledge, how much poor sleep then impacts us physically, and the long-term consequences in exacerbating a whole range of human ailments, let alone the short-term consequences of basic alertness and functioning at our best.

Having met neuroscientists and sleep researchers, and in reading Walker's book, it certainly made me go to bed earlier.

Yet much of our modern work and even wider social cultures and systems have almost trivialized sleep. For decades, in many organizations, particularly in sectors like the media, financial services and professional services, there were prevailing cultures of the view that sleep was for wimps. People had to 'power on through', 'pull all-nighters' or 'work hard and play hard' and other fighting talk if they really wanted to get on. Some attribute some of these expressions to Margaret Thatcher, who was famed, or notorious doubtless among those who worked with her, for getting by on only a few hours' sleep a night.

It turns out only a very small minority of people can genuinely get by on a few hours' sleep. The rest are bluffing. Stress, anxiety and the general pressures of life are meaning more and more of us are not sleeping well.

Many health and social researchers are describing sleep disorders as having reached epidemic proportions. In 2018, the American Centers for Disease Control and Prevention (CDC) took the bold step of publicly classifying sleep disorders as a public health epidemic. It's thought that around 100 million Americans, or around 30 per cent of the population, suffer from sleep disorders, and numbers in the UK appear to be similar.[25]

Looking after your own sleep, but also encouraging good sleep behaviours across your organization, would certainly be a positive step in improving overall wellbeing.

Financial wellbeing and the issue of in-work poverty

While wellbeing is broadly our state of physical, emotional and mental health, significant external factors have been added to the umbrella of wellbeing discourse. Our state of financial security has a big impact on our wellbeing, and given the downward trends in financial security for so many, financial wellbeing is now a strong theme.

Research has shown one in four workers admitted that money worries had affected their ability to do their job, while one in ten said they had found it hard to concentrate or make decisions at work because of money worries.[26] Almost a fifth said they had lost sleep worrying about money, all of which impacts productivity.

I have talked about growing inequalities at some length in Chapter 4, and areas like living wage as part of responsible business in Chapter 8. Again, the pandemic and the economic fallout have shown up these issues further, and highlighted some of the starker differences in pay and opportunity.

Analysis by the RSA concluded that people most able to work from home 'are likely to be highly paid, and enjoy greater job stability, opportunities for progression, and generous pensions'.[27] Conversely, many gig and low-paid workers could not afford to self-isolate, effectively being forced to choose between their physical and their financial wellbeing.

A report by the Brookings Institution in the US published in April 2020 showed that 'Covid-19 has laid bare the enormous gap between the value that frontline workers [...] bring to society and the low wages—and lack of respect—many earn in return. It is long past time that low-wage workers secure a permanent income boost and earn a living wage with adequate benefits.'[28]

In the UK, the IFS estimated that one-third of the key workers were earning less than £10 an hour and that average hourly wages for this group were 8 per cent lower than for other, non-key occupations.[29]

Research by McKinsey published in mid-May 2020 showed a strong correlation between the likelihood of a worker being furloughed or laid off and that worker having previously been in a low-income job.[30] Those in part-time work as well as people under the age of 35, given their higher representation in lower-paid jobs, were also much more likely to lose out.

There were not unsurprisingly significant sector differences found in McKinsey's research. Different sectors have significantly different levels of low-paid workers. The median gross hourly pay in hospitality and food-service activities in 2019 was around £8.60. By comparison, in information and communication, a sector in which there were far fewer furloughs and job losses, it was £19.20.

More broadly, the weighted average median pay in the five hardest-hit sectors was around £10.60 per hour; for the five least affected sectors, it was around £14.60 – or nearly 40 per cent higher. In other words, if you'd been working a poorly paid role, that likely involved uncertain hours and only limited opportunities to progress, you were dramatically more likely to lose your job in the crisis.

These big differences across sectors and between types of jobs and skill levels have long been sources of inequality, but they are hard to fix. Perhaps the pandemic will provide the stimulus not only for us to better appreciate the key jobs that are so essential to us all but also how we raise basic levels of pay to ensure better financial wellbeing in work for all.

At its worst, low levels of pay have been giving rise to what is defined as in-work poverty – people in work who are not earning enough to sustain themselves or their families. Definitions can get confusing as sometimes even if only one person in a household is working, a whole household could be counted as being in in-work poverty.

In the UK, the Joseph Rowntree Foundation has long researched the field of poverty, and its reports have been showing a strong rise in in-work poverty in recent years. Its latest report[31] showed the number of workers in poverty has gone up over the last 20 years from 2.3 million in 1996/97 to 4 million in 2017/18. Of the 4 million, just under half are full-time employees, 1.4 million are part-time workers and 0.7 million are full-time self-employed workers.

As the report noted, 'Despite improvements in pay for those on the lowest wages, low pay remains endemic in the UK's economy. Once in a low-paid job it is difficult for many workers to move to a better paid one.' But the Foundation also recognized that poverty and low pay do not always go together, as the great majority of low-paid workers live in households where the income of the people they live with (such as a partner or parents) means they are not in poverty.

The IFS defines relative poverty as those living on incomes less than 60 per cent of the average.[32] This proportion hasn't changed much over the last 20 years, fluctuating between 21 per cent and 23 per cent. But the Institute agrees that the proportion of people where relative poverty has gone up are those living in working households, ie in-work poverty, which has increased from 13 per cent to 18 per cent.

The picture is not straightforward, however. The IFS cites four main reasons for this shift. They include relative income growth in pensioners which has pushed up average incomes, and the reduction in non-working households as more people access work, albeit in often low-paid and insecure work. Also, changes in tax and benefit systems have impacted, and the relative growth of higher earners versus lower earners we have described earlier.

How organizations can support the financial wellbeing of their people

Besides improving the basic levels of pay, the other significant impacts any organization can have on financial wellbeing are progression, and training and support for better financial awareness and understanding. Much of the research cited above showed that education around personal finance is a positive way to allay fears and enhance financial wellbeing, but employers could do more to provide this.

As explored in Chapter 6, too many people are coming out of education with poor numeracy skills. They may have a maths qualification that shows they understand algebra, but too many people's lack of understanding of personal finances, interest rates, mortgages and so on is troubling. They can end up in financial difficulties or huge debt from pay-day loan companies because of that lack of awareness.

These are basic life skills, and many employers are now providing training and advice to help minimize these issues. They are asking the questions of their employees in their staff surveys about financial concerns. Responsible banks are also taking more responsibility in helping to make their customers more financially savvy, and legislation is improving to protect people from unscrupulous lenders.

But with the growth of in-work poverty, there is a need for a bigger shift. The arguments come back to the ideas we have discussed throughout on stakeholder responsibilities, more fairness in distribution of wealth, and longer-term thinking versus short-term profit taking.

In Mankins and Garton's book *Time, Talent, Energy*,[33] referenced in Chapter 11, they argue that the first mistake companies make is to underpay employees as a result of a prevailing belief that investing in wages happens at the expense of customers and shareholders. But if improving wages also improves talent attraction and retention, engagement and wellbeing, and cultures of fairness, ultimately everyone benefits.

Janet Yellen, who served as chair of the US Federal Reserve from 2014 until 2018, wrote a paper[34] in 1984 arguing that higher wages motivate people to work harder, leading to lower overall turnover, an improvement in the average quality of job applicants and better morale.

Paying at least a living wage for all therefore not only has the longer-term payback but morally and ethically is the right thing to do for any responsible business.

Some business models help to enhance lower wages with shares in profit or some shared ownership of the business, where employees own shares in the company. Employees typically acquire shares through a share option plan which may be selective or open to all. Employee-owned businesses are those where all employees have a financial stake in the business. Not only does this allow a real sharing of profit and benefits across the organization, it also encourages loyalty and commitment.

The Employee Ownership Association ran a review in 2018 of the benefits of employee ownership in which I also participated. It was interesting to see the wide range of businesses that used this model and spoke of its benefits. There are over 370 employee-owned businesses across the UK, contributing around 4 per cent of UK GDP annually, but this contribution is growing. The best-known and largest example in the UK is the John Lewis Partnership.

In some cases, some business leaders have gone a whole lot further and been a bit more radical. Dan Price caused a media frenzy in 2011 when, triggered by a confrontation with a relatively low-paid worker at his Seattle-based credit card processing company Gravity Payments, he decided to establish a $70,000 minimum wage for all employees, cutting his own salary from $1.1 million to $70,000 to help fund it.

The CEO became a minor celebrity, but his company was the biggest winner. Performance soared and the company was reportedly inundated with 4,500 résumés in the first week after the announcement.[35] At the time, Gravity's workforce was only about 120 strong. I wouldn't argue that this is the approach all companies should take, but it is an interesting example of a CEO thinking way beyond conventional wisdom.

Progression for people on low pay is the other big lever. Lifting people up from lower-wage, lower-skill jobs should be part of the agenda for any responsible business. Supporting people to develop their confidence and skills to be able to progress, encouraging managers to provide more coaching and helping their people recognize and develop their talents, and having more clarity in progression routes within the organization.

Employers like the John Lewis Partnership make a point of managing and understanding progression. It is one of the company's key metrics in how its workforce is developing and its commitment to people, and it should be in every company. Far too many people in low-wage jobs see no opportunity for progression and development in their organization so they don't try or they wait until another opportunity elsewhere comes along.

Decent and fair pay and paying attention to the financial wellbeing of employees are therefore not only attributes of good work and responsible business, they quite literally pay for themselves. If we believe as we should that work should be good for people and good for their wellbeing, then financial wellbeing is a key component.

A broader understanding of wellbeing in an online world

Our increasingly online world is of itself creating other challenges around wellbeing. People are being exposed to scams, hacking and phishing attacks which can be very damaging, but also to harassment, bullying, and trolling. But there are also rising concerns about addictive-type behaviours for people who can't let go of being online.

As often reported, these can lead to great mental stresses, particularly among young people, and there appears to be no let-up. Research reported by the American Psychological Association showed how rates of mood disorders and suicide-related outcomes have increased significantly among adolescents and young adults, and that the rise of social media may be to blame.[36]

Cyber wellbeing as it could be termed is therefore also an area for attention – how to help people understand how to protect themselves, to use social media responsibly, and to deal with online bullying or trolling and other forms of harassment.

From an employer's perspective, helping to train employees on responsible use of technology as well as how to look after themselves in an online world has the significant added advantage of making them more aware of their responsibilities in protecting the organization.

With cyber security now one of the top risks and concerns for any business, and the increased reliance on technology as remote working becomes more prevalent, this is a significant corporate agenda. Training and engaging employees on understanding cyber security is critical, but if done effectively it is also good for their personal wellbeing. Too much of the training though is compliance focused for the organization and quite frankly very dry. We tick the box to say we have done it, but we remember little.

If we recognize the importance of training people to understand all the risks in the online world that impact them personally, then we get a positive double impact. Not only are we helping people to protect themselves better, and therefore also their wellbeing, but in understanding how to protect themselves, they will also understand better how the same behaviours and awareness can protect the organization. This helps to address the so-called insider threat – malicious or accidental, more often than not through people doing dumb things – which is the biggest threat to any organization's cyber security.

In conclusion

Wellbeing is perhaps the most important outcome of our future of work. Work should be good for us, and ultimately help us all achieve positive wellbeing.

We have looked at it in a variety of ways throughout this book, including physical, emotional and mental, and on to financial and even cyber wellbeing. There is little question that wellbeing is receiving more attention now than ever before, particularly with regard to mental and emotional aspects. But we need to be sure the interventions we put in place, the ways in which we talk about wellbeing and train people, are well founded in good evidence.

Healthy societies, healthy organizations and healthy individuals are all part of the same whole. But too many trends in the modern world and in the world of work have not been working to improve our wellbeing. There are many things we can positively impact in our organizations, and some which will be part of wider societal change and support.

We need to redouble our efforts. Organizations and business everywhere should commit to understanding, supporting and improving wellbeing in their workforces and even beyond into their customers and suppliers wherever they can influence that.

And they should promote the ideas of wellbeing, report on progress and be transparent. That will in turn help their own brands and reputations as organizations that care.

Combining the principles of good work with the understanding of wellbeing can help us create a better future of work, and must be at the heart of this fourth industrial revolution.

Endnotes

1. https://positivepsychology.com/body-mind-integration-attention-training/ (archived at https://perma.cc/9QDM-L93N)
2. https://neuroleadership.com/portfolio-items/scarf-a-brain-based-model-for-collaborating-with-and-influencing-others/ (archived at https://perma.cc/3CFG-FP5R)

3 https://engageforsuccess.org/wp-content/uploads/2015/12/Engagement-and-Wellbeing-Dec-15.pdf (archived at https://perma.cc/NA72-SJQP)
4 www.cipd.co.uk/Images/health-and-well-being-at-work-2019.v1_tcm18-55881.pdf (archived at https://perma.cc/V2E6-YUXC)
5 www.cipd.co.uk/Images/health-and-well-being-at-work_tcm18-40863.pdf (archived at https://perma.cc/3TVW-79BU)
6 https://hbr.org/2016/04/are-you-too-stressed-to-be-productive-or-not-stressed-enough (archived at https://perma.cc/84P9-X8ZN)
7 Freudenberger, H J (1974) Staff burn-out, *Journal of Social Issues*, 30, pp 159–65
8 Calabrese, J A (1971) The Patco dispute – a need for change in public employee labor settlements, 20, DePaul L Rev 699
9 https://thriveglobal.com/stories/why-were-wrong-about-burnout/ (archived at https://perma.cc/Z953-UGCE)
10 www.hse.gov.uk/stress/mental-health.htm (archived at https://perma.cc/587Y-FFEQ)
11 Goh, J, Pfeffer, J and Zenios, S (2016) The relationship between workplace stressors and mortality and health costs in the United States, *Management Science*, 62 (2), pp 608–28
12 https://hbr.org/2019/07/when-passion-leads-to-burnout (archived at https://perma.cc/MV57-RRQT)
13 Vallerand, R, Paquet, Y, Frederick, P and Charest, J (2010) On the role of passion for work in burnout: a process model, *Journal of Personality*, 78, pp 289–312
14 www.mayoclinic.org/healthy-lifestyle/adult-health/in-depth/burnout/art-20046642 (archived at https://perma.cc/YW36-AY99)
15 www2.deloitte.com/global/en/pages/about-deloitte/articles/millennialsurvey.html (archived at https://perma.cc/Z3P7-DT6F)
16 Marshall, R and Galea, S (2004) Science for the community: assessing mental health after 9/11, *The Journal of Clinical Psychiatry*, 65 (Suppl 1), 37–43
17 Hawryluck L, Gold W L, Robinson S, et al (2004) SARS control and psychological effects of quarantine, *Emerging Infectious Diseases*, 10 (7), DOI: 10.3201/eid1007.03070
18 www.theguardian.com/society/2020/may/16/uk-lockdown-causing-serious-mental-illness-in-first-time-patients (archived at https://perma.cc/Z2M6-HS47)
19 www.kff.org/coronavirus-covid-19/issue-brief/the-implications-of-covid-19-for-mental-health-and-substance-use/ (archived at https://perma.cc/82JM-N2FY)
20 www.theguardian.com/sustainable-business/2016/oct/04/mental-health-uk-business-employees-management-wellbeing-marks-spencer-mind (archived at https://perma.cc/T5PZ-V4E9)
21 Waddell and Burton (2006) and Marmot Review (2010) Fair Society, Healthy Lives
22 www.mentalhealthatwork.org.uk/commitment/#who (archived at https://perma.cc/Q8XH-TF9L)

23 Kamerāde, D, Wang, S, Burchell, B, Balderson, S U and Coutts, A (2019) A shorter working week for everyone: how much paid work is needed for mental health and well-being? *Journal of Social Science and Medicine*
24 Walker, M (2018) *Why We Sleep: The new science of sleep and dreams*, Penguin Books
25 www.sleepstation.org.uk/articles/sleep-science/sleep-epidemic/ (archived at https://perma.cc/SP35-DGKW)
26 www.cipd.co.uk/news-views/viewpoint/low-pay-financial-well-being (archived at https://perma.cc/99VC-YLH8)
27 www.thersa.org/blog/2020/04/low-pay-lack-homeworking (archived at https://perma.cc/86D9-GZQY)
28 www.brookings.edu/research/covid-19s-essential-workers-deserve-hazard-pay-heres-why-and-how-it-should-work/ (archived at https://perma.cc/94C9-G8G2)
29 www.ifs.org.uk/publications/14819 (archived at https://perma.cc/D9UV-C4CN)
30 www.mckinsey.com/industries/public-sector/our-insights/covid-19-in-the-united-kingdom-assessing-jobs-at-risk-and-the-impact-on-people-and-places# (archived at https://perma.cc/CUV9-C8R9)
31 www.jrf.org.uk/data/workers-poverty (archived at https://perma.cc/RR7X-GPTU)
32 www.ifs.org.uk/publications/14154 (archived at https://perma.cc/S8TD-NGDY)
33 Garton, E and Mankins, M (2017) *Time, Talent, Energy*, Harvard Business Review Press, Boston, MA
34 www.jstor.org/stable/1816355 (archived at https://perma.cc/8UVG-FSQQ)
35 www.inc.com/magazine/201511/paul-keegan/does-more-pay-mean-more-growth.html (archived at https://perma.cc/G32J-PBUT)
36 www.ajmc.com/view/mental-health-issues-on-the-rise-among-adolescents-young-adults (archived at https://perma.cc/5D9C-WG5X)

14

#WTF: What's the future?

The past is your lesson. The present is your gift.
The future is your motivation.

ANONYMOUS

Through the course of this book, a wide range of topics has been covered, from the trends that are driving the future of work to how we should respond. We are at a point of significant change and we need to be able to look around us as well as ahead. We must learn from the past, adapt and innovate in the present, to be able to shape the future.

As I set out, the intent was not to come up with the 10 or 15 or 5 inexorable laws of the future, or a set of precise predictions. Rather, it was to try to paint a picture of all the things that are already impacting the world of work, as well as point to what is emerging. There are many knowns, and just as many unknowns, but we know that unchecked, the course we are on is not sustainable.

The future has many parents, and it is not a single outcome. Change will happen in different ways, in different places and at different paces. But that also means we all have some agency, an ability to influence and shape our own piece of the jigsaw that makes up the bigger picture.

Variety will be the spice of life and the reality of the world we live in. The old models of standard practices, standard working weeks, standard ways of working, standard jobs are already starting to disappear as we enter a more flexible, personalizable, more adaptive world of work. A world of work that should be good for us all.

Pulling it all together

By covering a wide range of themes (see Figure 14.1), the aim has been to show the interconnections and to challenge how we need to think systemically.

We all live and work in a context – globalization and geopolitics, wider economy, society, political and regulatory – much of which we can't directly control but which we need to understand, and which will impact how we have to respond.

Within this context are many things that we can control – how we shape our organizations and cultures, the work and jobs we design, the people we bring in, the partnerships we develop, and the strategic choices we make about the products and services we develop and the markets we serve.

As explored in Chapter 9 on leadership, leaders need to be able to look up and out, to appreciate what is happening around them and how that will impact their decisions and actions. That hasn't always been what we have encouraged in the past, but with the pace of change now, it becomes an essential mindset and skill.

In Chapter 10 on people strategy, we looked at the importance of thinking about the workforce, organization, culture and leadership as an essential part of business strategy. Recognizing the capabilities needed for the future, what the core capabilities and competencies are, and the many options and ways in which skills, talent and resources can be accessed.

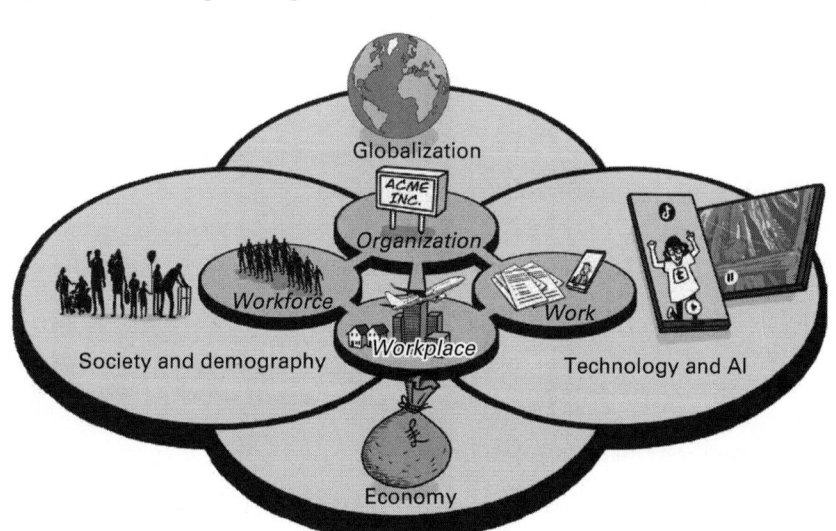

FIGURE 14.1 Pulling it all together – connection of themes

I've stressed that there is no single answer, or model, or indeed best practice. Each context for an organization is different, and it is important to innovate, to look for the evidence and to find the best-fit solutions.

And while organizations and leaders are impacted by and operate within this context, they are also part of changing and influencing the context. Business is part of society; how it changes and operates drives our economies and impacts our workforces and their livelihoods. That is why I have also stressed the principles of responsible business and good work in Chapters 8 and 11.

To the picture above must be added the crises that are shaping the future as well. The environmental crisis is a long-term problem that has been steadily building over many years. Many people denied it until the signs became incontrovertible, but it will also take many years and many different actions to address. It requires the engagement and commitment of politicians and policy makers, industries and businesses, and all of us as consumers. As measures have developed and evidence has strengthened, it has allowed businesses to be held more to account, demanding more transparency.

The Covid-19 pandemic has been a very different crisis. It hit fast and it hit hard, and it forced a rapid response and adaptations at every level. But it has also taught us a lot about how to adapt, to innovate quickly, and to challenge pre-conceptions such as whether people could work in different ways and still be productive and effective.

The ensuing economic crisis could last for some time and force significant change. The worries of inequalities and the impact on younger or older workers, lower-skilled workers and those from more disadvantaged backgrounds are all concerns that are part of the longer-term shifts in work. It may also accelerate structural changes in sectors and in rollout of technology in response.

Crises of themselves act as stimuli for change. They raise some new issues, but fundamentally they shine a light on the issues that were already with us. As the tide goes out, the rocks appear and we see who's been swimming without any clothes.

How do people view the future of work?

There is unquestionably a lot to keep us busy and thinking as we shape the future. But it's good to see that by and large, people hold a reasonably positive view of the future of work.

PwC in its report on the workforce of the future published in 2018 asked people in China, India, Germany, the UK and the US about how they felt the future of work might impact them.[1] The report showed quite a positive picture, with almost three in four having a positive view.

However, it is also true that not only is the future uncertain, but as yet we are in the early phases of what many see as a rapidly accelerating impact on jobs and roles.

Nesta, an innovation foundation in the UK, projected in 2017 that 6 million people were employed in occupations that are likely to change radically or disappear entirely by 2030,[2] and that more than two-thirds of people in those jobs think it is unlikely their jobs will be automated in that time.[3] And why would they? That's why an important part of the future will also be in providing more people careers advice and guidance throughout their working lives.

A report by the WEF in 2018 on the future of work[4] forecasted a rapid shift in jobs and levels of automation, as shown in Figure 14.3. The report concluded that half of all 'work tasks' will be capable of being carried out by machines by 2025, in the researchers' view displacing more than 75 million jobs worldwide but creating as many if not more new jobs. The challenge being that the jobs being created would require very different skill sets and would exaggerate existing inequalities.

Change happening at this pace will take a lot of managing and adjusting, and it does feel a bit of an over-estimate in the short term, but no doubt will happen in the coming years.

There have been many surveys which ask what people regard as most important for the future. These also tend to be reassuring and amplify much

FIGURE 14.2 People's views of future of work – survey of over 10,000 people in the US, the UK, Germany, India and China

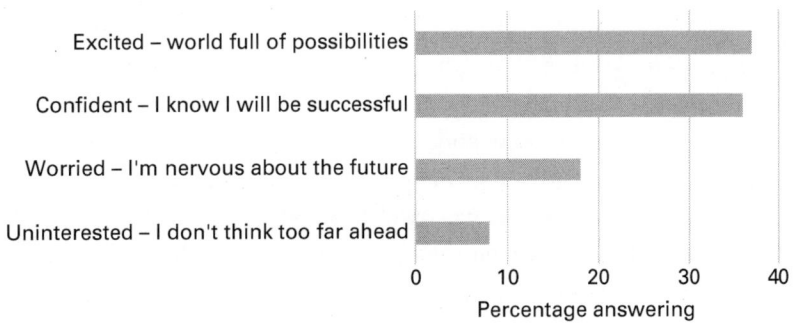

SOURCE PWC

FIGURE 14.3 Rate of automation – division of labour as share of hours spent

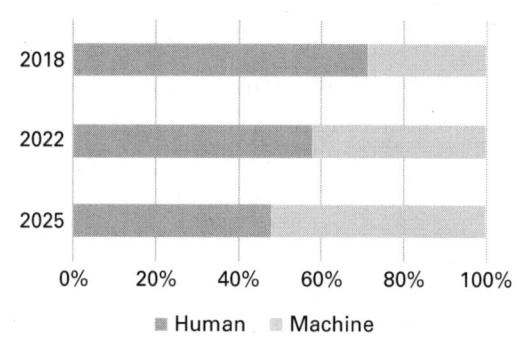

SOURCE WEF

of what we have emphasized. Deloitte's research[5] over different countries and years summarized that workers broadly agree on wellbeing, belonging and ethics at the top of their list, and that supporting these values is not achieved by rolling out a stock of best practices. Points I have made throughout.

Principles, evidence and outcomes

We have talked throughout the book about being led by principles, but also to be evidence based in approaches to seeking understanding and considering options and interventions.

A simple mantra is to be principles led, evidence based and outcomes driven.

This can apply to us individually or collectively. It is something that the CIPD has at the heart of the Profession Map, a framework for the skills and capabilities needed across the people profession.[6]

Being clear on principles, beliefs and values is the essence of integrity. It is something we look for in others, but is not often enough spoken of, and it is more and more something we look for in leaders and in organizations. Using evidence to make judgements and decisions is not only sound practice but also important in integrity and in being as fair and objective as possible. Being outcomes driven means we are clear in what we are trying to achieve and the direction we are trying to go, even if from time to time we have to course correct to get there.

Principles

Principles are usually defined as a general or basic truth on which other truths or theories can be based, a fundamental doctrine, but also a rule of conduct based on beliefs of what is right and wrong. In an uncertain world, principles set a direction and a guide for us, from which we can develop greater clarity and certainty as we progress.

I have described a number of important principles through this book that should act as our guides for the future:

- Clarity of purpose and values – defining the 'why' of our organizations and what we stand for.
- Responsible business – acting not just within the laws or rules but also ethically and morally, and guided by purpose and values. Understanding responsibility and accountability to all stakeholders.
- Transparency and measuring the right things – being open about what the organization and its leaders see as important, sharing information about trajectory and progress of travel, having clear narrative to explain what is happening.
- Putting people first – people at the heart of the business agenda, compassion and duty of care, focus on wellbeing as an outcome, but also seeing people as an essential strategic pillar to any organization.
- Good work and job quality – creating jobs that are good for people, that use technology to benefit, empower and enable.
- More flexible and agile ways of working – giving people more choice, enabling better balance of work and life, managing stress, but also creating more opportunities for more people to access work.
- Fairness, inclusion and diversity – creating organizations that reflect society, that give opportunity and are fair in how they treat people whatever their background.
- Managing the short term but investing in the long term – importance of stewardship, building for the future, understanding the difference between short-term expediency and long-term responsibility.

These would seem to be good principles which we should hold front and centre. None of them is necessarily new. But together they reflect a time of change, a shift from things we have in some cases forgotten, but which to all of us, our economies, our societies and our planet, are now essential for a positive future.

Many of these principles are embedded in various standards, charters or goals, including the UN SDGs. We should call them out and be up front about what we believe in, our 'fundamental doctrines', or our 'governing principles'. They can and should be linked to corporate values, which will also help to embed them in our corporate cultures. The more transparent we are about them, the more we can be held to account to operate to these principles, ensuring we stay true to them even when times are harder.

Evidence

We also need to better engage with real evidence. If we are in a post-truth world, we have to work much harder on understanding what is real and what is not. Critical thinking is a skill set we all need. And in the world of work, we all need more evidence, more data, more insights to be able to fairly interpret what is happening, to make decisions on as solid ground as possible. And we need the evidence to challenge pre-conceptions, our inherent biases, and to have more confidence that the actions we take and the interventions we make will lead to the right outcomes.

In Chapter 7 we talked a lot about what we should be measuring, and where the evidence was of progress. In Chapter 9 we talked about leading from evidence and the practice of evidence-based management, and defined what is evidence and where it comes from – empirical study and research, professional expertise, data, and the values and concerns of stakeholders.

Now is the time for academics and researchers, and practitioners and policy makers, to work more closely together – we need to work in Pasteur's quadrant. Make it real. The vast bodies of research on human behaviours, on cultural understanding, on leadership and management practices, on motivation and learning must more directly influence what happens in our workplaces. Without this, too much is still based on hunch, 'best practice' or just doing things to be seen to be doing things. Or worse, just virtue signalling.

Outcomes

You can't steer a ship by looking at its wake. Or as the joke goes when someone who is lost asks directions to somewhere, the reply comes back, 'Well if I was going to go there, I wouldn't start from here.'

Might be factually faultless, but it is informationally useless. However, it also makes the point that in understanding where we are going, we have to be clear on where we are. Much of the data, surveys and other insights gone through in this book are to help try to understand where we actually are. It is actually quite hard as there are many points of contradiction, but also a wide range of issues, hence continuing to stress the importance of understanding each of our own contexts, the importance of data, analytics and insights.

Being clear on what outcomes we are working towards is therefore about the clarity of direction and goals. These outcomes will come back to and be based around our principles.

For example, if we believe in creating more inclusive and diverse organizations, then it needs some definition – a mix of workforce demographics at all levels, evidence of fairness of progression and reward, feedback from all staff about whether they feel included, feedback from customers and suppliers about how they see diversity. And these ways of measuring outcomes must be embedded in the strategy and objectives throughout the organization. These measures give us evidence of progress, something leaders at all levels can be held accountable for.

With clearly expressed and measurable outcomes, we can track the interventions and actions we are taking to see how they are impacting our direction to those outcomes. There must then be the courage to course correct, to change things that are not working as expected or hoped for.

To further the ship analogy, storms will come and winds will change direction and there have to be adjustments to the course to adapt, but without losing sight of the place the ship is headed or the principles of good seamanship that get us there.

A scenario of scenarios

Since the future is hard to predict, a favourite approach of every self-respecting futurologist, think tank, consultancy, academic pundit or government policy maker is scenario planning.

Put together all the variables that are shaping the future and imagine what different scenarios might emerge. Then, if possible, give them some clever names so they become memorable. Since, as observed from the beginning of the book, there has probably never been more debate about the future of work given the perfect storm of changes happening, this is a rich time for scenario planners.

Developing scenarios is of course a helpful process because it allows thinking to be challenged, particularly when the scenarios being imagined are a bit dystopian – ie if we don't watch out, this could happen. It allows people to find the common threads, where action can be taken, pre-empting more negative outcomes and driving towards shared positive goals.

Scenarios are usually built looking at least 10 years out. So at present, there are a lot of 2030-type scenarios out there. I think 10 years is a good time frame, as much beyond that becomes more speculative, and if we want to make significant changes, then they can and need to happen at least within a 10-year time frame.

The longer-term scenarios we are being warned of today – including irreversible climate change and extinction events, or where AI could take us to the emergence of a post-human and divided world as various writers have speculated – could emerge if we don't take actions now, and certainly within the coming 10 years.

I am reminded again of Bill Gates' observation that we tend to overestimate what will happen in two years but underestimate what will happen in 10.

The pandemic has also thrown a spanner in the works of scenario planners, and will accelerate some of the changes being talked about, but also bring about some others that were less seen. The purpose here, then, is not to come up with some other broad-based scenarios but to at least review those that have been developed and look for some common themes and how they resonate with what has been covered in this book.

In reading through a lot of the scenarios envisioned from sources like the World Economic Forum, the OECD, the RSA and other research organizations and consultancies, it can be quite a depressing experience. Visions of mass unemployment, growing inequality as the rich and those with the still valuable skills win and the rest lose out, or a world of surveillance and control. Or even a polarization of the world, where 'super-economies' emerge and there is little need to move work to lower-cost locations as it has been largely automated. Or growing national protectionism to protect local labour markets where work is more scarce.

It could even be that the pandemic itself stimulates some of this protectionism, controlling movement of people for health and economic reasons for several years to come.

While the most developed economies of the world are relying on mass vaccination putting an end to the pandemic and the accompanying restrictions within 2021, the world is going to be living with the Covid pandemic for a long time. The 55-member African Union is anticipating that it will take at least three years to vaccinate 60 per cent of the continent's 1.3 billion people.[7] Unemployment rates will dominate agendas for the next few years along with what will be a variable economic recovery and likely recessionary cycle in many parts of the world.

Common themes from scenario planning

The imperatives that come through many of the scenarios that are being projected relate to much of what we have reviewed:

- The need for radical change in how skills development policy and approaches work. The surest way for people to lose out is to not have the opportunities to adapt their skills, opportunity for lifelong learning, security of transitioning between jobs and roles as they change.
- Balancing wealth and opportunity to avoid a bifurcated world of the haves and the have nots. One of the biggest challenges of all, and called out in every scenario, looked at local, regional and national levels as well as internationally and globally.
- Avoiding a direction of greater and greater protectionism and nationalism. Globalization in reverse as each seeks to look after their own in an uncertain and socially and economically more threatening world. What the WEF described as the 'workforce autarky'.[8]
- But also avoiding a world where all the people with high skills migrate away from countries with less opportunity, or those with low skills forever seeking more and more insecure work wherever they can find it because that is all that is left.
- Using data and information about people responsibly. Avoiding a world of super surveillance and control – what the RSA described as the 'precision economy'[9] or what could be described as an Orwellian future.
- Protecting the environment and the dangers of ongoing and unsustainable consumerism. How can economic growth and improving livelihoods for all be better balanced with our use of resources and impact on climate and environment?

Other scenarios talk about large-scale automation that displaces so much work that we are more consumed with how to use leisure time effectively – the Keynesian future of much-reduced working weeks, to perhaps a couple of days a week on average. And even if not going that far, reducing work-related stress, better balance of people's lives, and more choice and flexibility in how and where we work must be goals for the future.

Equality and fairness, and more balanced distribution of wealth, are dominant themes. We cannot persist with growing in-work poverty when technology could easily make this worse.

There has to be a levelling up, not least because many of the essential and often lower-paid jobs are not the ones that are most likely to be replaced by automation. We need to attract and retain more people into health and social care, and even areas of our economies like traditional trade skills – it's hard to see how jobs like plumbers, electricians, gardeners and maintenance work are going to get automated out of existence.

As considered in Chapter 4, it will require more intervention from governments, taxation and social benefit systems, and constructs like universal basic income would have to evolve as a means to spread wealth and income.

How we address the challenges of upskilling and reskilling and learning is perhaps the other really significant common issue. As noted in Chapter 6, there are already many concerns about growing skills gaps, education and learning systems that need to adapt and change. This also requires a collective and wide debate about the balance between education, publicly funded lifelong learning and privately funded investment in skills development through organizations. And how we deliver learning and skills development in very different ways.

Quite a lot of scenarios point to the dangers of unequal access to learning opportunities, which ultimately could drive further global divisions. Or it could be that globalization continues apace – access to good work can happen from anywhere, the sense of a global workforce supported by more consistent standards of learning, certification and the like. What the WEF called the 'agile adaptors' scenario.

Finally, what is also important to note in all the scenarios that are being imagined is how much of it is already happening in different ways. Not just the growing inequalities and issues of skills and environmental impacts, but also the use of surveillance and big data.

The future really is here, but it is increasingly unevenly distributed. That is what is creating more and more of our challenge.

We have to find the ways of working together more – just as the UN called out through its SDGs, or the idea of the 'empathy economy', as the RSA described it, and a 'future of responsible stewardship'.

Different forms of our economies for the future

Different ways of thinking about our economies and what drives them have been around for a while, and they have great merit. They all build on this idea of shared responsibility, for each other, for our societies and for the planet.

- **The sharing economy** – where assets or services are shared between private individuals or even organizations, either free or for a fee, typically through online platforms. Perhaps back to the future where trading isn't just about money and how much of us each individually owns but a more shared sense of common purpose where we all help each other out. Car sharing is an obvious one – if someone came back from the future or forward from the past and looked at how much money we all waste on cars, the space they take up, the cost to the environment, they would unquestionably come up with a better system of sharing.
- **The circular economy** – based on the principles of designing out waste and pollution, keeping products and materials in use, and regenerating natural systems.[10] This must surely be a platform for sustainability, and to shift the direction of unsustainable consumerism and our throwaway economies of today. A fundamental principle for all of us individually, but also for businesses to move away from in-built redundancy that drives short-term profitability, to designing for in-built reusability.
- **The inclusive economy** – embracing the idea of collective responsibility and stewardship, between individuals, business, governments and civil society, and the coming together to solve for the biggest challenges we face. As the Inclusive Economy Partnership supported by the UK government puts it, 'There's nothing more worthwhile for our country than to have all its citizens actively engaged in our economy and society so that every one of us feels included.'[11]

Similarly in the US, the Rockefeller Foundation believes that an inclusive economy is one in which there is expanded opportunity for more broadly shared prosperity, especially for those facing the greatest barriers to advancing their wellbeing.[12] The Foundation looks at the idea very broadly and calls out five interrelated characteristics: participation, equity, growth, sustainability and stability.

Some reasonable hopes and expectations for the future of work

With all that has been discussed, there are a number of outcomes that we should all anticipate and work towards. These outcomes bring together the ideas of good work and of work being good for us, but also then good for organizations, our economies and societies. In other words, our collective wellbeing.

Technology humanizes work

Technology takes out much of the routine and drudgery that have characterized work for many people for years, if not centuries. It frees people up to do the things people are best at, to be creative, to add value, and to find meaning and purpose.

Our relationship and interaction with technology is already changing rapidly, and the interactions will become more and more humanized, making the use of technology accessible to all and in almost all areas of our lives. Technologies like blockchain could take out great swathes of more administrative work of checking and cross-checking, of record keeping and basic transactional work. We will be able to move way beyond the need to standardize in order to be efficient to a world where we can personalize to best meet the needs of the individual.

This is the promise of many technologists and futurologists for the future. In Chapter 5, looking at how robotics and AI are developing, it seems like almost anything might be possible. But we must remain in control, and harness technology from a human-centric perspective.

The 'Martini' world of work – anytime, anyplace, anywhere

How we work, where we work and when we work becomes more of a choice, and we break the shackles of work routine. For those old enough to remember the famous Martini adverts of the 1970s, this is a good metaphor for how flexible work could become.

We all learned through the pandemic how much work can get done from places other than formal places of employment, or at different times and schedules. We have at last shaken up the paradigms of work, of standard hours and working weeks, and of presenteeism.

This is not the end of the workplace, but ways of using workplaces that focus more on the social connection, the camaraderie, community and sense of belonging of work, not just the routine of work. And it's about more choice and how work fits around the rest of their lives.

This needs to work also for those jobs and roles that still require physical presence and can only be done from a place of work. But as we get smarter about how we balance work demands with people's time and availability, as we automate out low-value-adding tasks, or create more opportunity to operate machines remotely, then it can be made more possible for all. If we can figure out how to do complex surgery remotely, surely we can do it for many other complex tasks.

We can also move work around to where people are. Even areas like construction are innovating more, with pre-fabrication that means so much of the work can be done away from the construction site itself. More networked, more distributed.

Less is more

The trends of stress and growing workloads are reversed. Work gets more balanced out so that people have the opportunity to work as they want and need to. Not too much, but also not too little. Output grows, enabled by technology, and everyone is able to share in these benefits fairly and equitably.

Why shouldn't the goals of a shorter working week be achievable? There is no law of nature that says humans were supposed to work five days a week, but we have also discussed some of the research that shows that even one day a week of work is good for our wellbeing.

Going back to Voltaire and his philosophy that work frees us from boredom, vice and need, the future goal isn't about no work but it is about good work and work that is good for us. And if we are going to live longer, then we need to find the best ways to work longer. Retirement becomes not a singular event but rather a glideslope into a different balance of life.

Learning to work and working to learn

Opportunities and support for learning are available to all, at the point and time of need. At the heart of education is the development of the core and essential skills that are needed for the world of work but also recognized as life skills. Lifelong learning becomes a cultural and practical norm, which is properly funded and supported. And for every job, the skills development needs become embedded in the flow of work wherever possible, allowing people to learn as they work.

Organizations invest in their people properly, not just for the short term but for the longer term as well. Learning is reinvented using digital capabilities to make it truly effective and value adding, with clear returns to the individuals as well as to organizations.

It is one of the sadder truisms of life that many never find their real talents and passions. All of us have been endowed with skills and abilities, and work should be the best means of finding and developing these. Remember the construct of 'ikigai' looked at in Chapter 11.

We need to create the systems of learning that support everyone, so no one gets left behind as the world of work evolves. This will also require good systems of career guidance and support, to help people understand and navigate the different roles, jobs and ways of working they will experience at different stages and times in their careers.

Inclusivity, equality and fairness

Organizations everywhere access, attract and retain all the diverse skills and experiences they need and have supportive workplace cultures of fairness and equality. It becomes just the norm. Transparency allows all stakeholders to see how organizations are supporting these principles and can hold leaders to account as needed.

Pay and reward are balanced more fairly and transparently to all. In-work poverty is a thing of the past. People feel psychologically safe and treated fairly wherever they work. We give people voice, they are listened to, empowered and trusted so they can contribute and give of their best.

As a result, organizations also thrive and grow. They reflect the societies they are part of, and the range of experiences and skills they draw on encourages innovation and creativity, and the ability to adapt and respond to the changes around them.

Doing well by doing good

Businesses all act responsibly and ethically. They recognize their accountabilities to all stakeholders. We build back trust into business everywhere and that in turn encourages businesses to respond positively.

Social responsibility and responsibility to all stakeholders lie at the heart of organizational thinking and are the essence of being a responsible business.

Businesses have to become clearer on their purpose and what they stand for, their values and principles. They should be able to track their impact beyond the profit and loss statements, and report on how they are fulfilling wider objectives and acting in responsible ways. In turn that attracts people to those organizations and investment in what they do. Business becomes a greater force for good and for positive change.

What work should really mean to us

All of these goals should be achievable, some within the next two to three years, but hopefully all within 10. And there are signs of positive progress and change, and many organizations that could say they are headed in the right direction.

Concluding any book is always hard. Business books often end with a summary list of things for us all to think about, but we have tried to include those as we go.

I have talked throughout about the idea that work should be good for us, and that a goal for the future must be for good work and opportunity for all.

When we retire, it's good to think that we have had a fulfilling working life and that because of that there would be many things that we would miss from work. Something that I saw a few years ago from research by the Centre for Ageing Better and Ipsos-Mori really struck me. The researchers asked a large cross-section of people who had retired what they would most miss from work. Their answers are shown in Figure 14.4.

FIGURE 14.4 Survey of 50+-year-olds on what they miss about work now they are retired

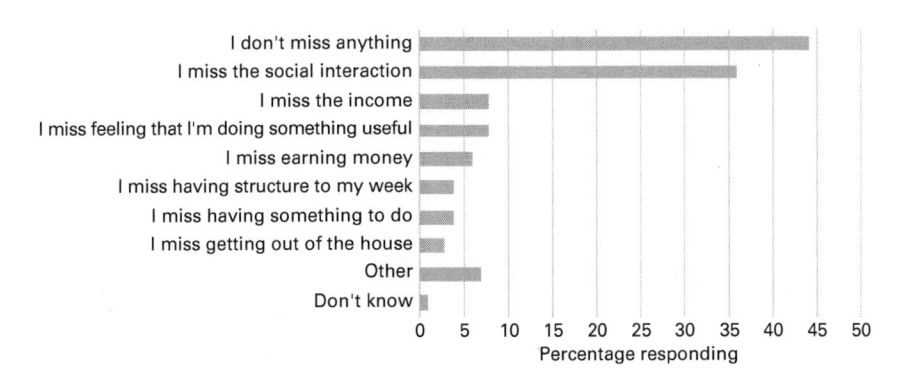

SOURCE Centre for Ageing Better, https://laterlife.ageing-better.org.uk/resources/cfab_lli_2015_survey_results.pdf

I have used this chart in lots of talks and I always ask people what they would expect were the answers. They will always come up with things like the social interaction, or a sense of purpose, or something about earning money. No one comes up with the answer of 'absolutely nothing', and it always causes some amusement when they see the results.

It is, though, perhaps a somewhat sad indictment of our working lives. If there is one way of showing we have made a difference and built a better future of work, I would like to hope that in answering a question like this in the future, the majority would say things like the sense of purpose, or the social interactions. Certainly not that they miss nothing and almost have a sense of relief as they retire that 'thank goodness that's all over'!

Endnotes

1 www.pwc.com/gx/en/services/people-organisation/workforce-of-the-future/workforce-of-the-future-the-competing-forces-shaping-2030-pwc.pdf (archived at https://perma.cc/ZXK8-KK9R)

2 www.nesta.org.uk/report/the-future-of-skills-employment-in-2030/ (archived at https://perma.cc/M2SQ-VQKZ)

3 www.nesta.org.uk/project/future-work-and-skills/ (archived at https://perma.cc/V5YW-CTUF)

4 http://reports.weforum.org/future-of-jobs-2018/ (archived at https://perma.cc/B58P-AMQW)

5 Volini, E et al (2020) Returning to work in the future of work, Deloitte Insights, 15 May

6 https://peopleprofession.cipd.org/profession-map (archived at https://perma.cc/9XEF-PLJK)

7 www.aljazeera.com/news/2021/2/4sixteen-african-nations-show-interest-in-AU-COVID-vaccine-plan (archived at https://perma.cc/3T83-73K3)

8 www3.weforum.org/docs/WEF_FOW_Eight_Futures.pdf (archived at https://perma.cc/T32Q-4NVY)

9 www.thersa.org/globalassets/pdfs/reports/rsa_four-futures-of-work.pdf (archived at https://perma.cc/D2TX-EJNT)

10 www.ellenmacarthurfoundation.org/circular-economy/what-is-the-circular-economy (archived at https://perma.cc/7DDM-285V)

11 www.inclusiveeconomypartnership.gov.uk/about-us (archived at https://perma.cc/62NR-NE8D)

12 www.rockefellerfoundation.org/blog/five-characteristics-inclusive-economy-getting-beyond-equity-growth-dichotomy/ (archived at https://perma.cc/TS2S-ZCE6)

INDEX

5G workforce 91–97
9/11 attacks 245

Accenture 203
adhocracy 236
age, and sense of wellbeing 338
ageing population 86–88, 95–96
agency staff 264–66
agile learning organization *see* learning organization
agile working 305–06
air traffic controllers 341–42
Alternative für Deutschland 60
Amazon 266, 267–68
American Psychological Association 64
Anderson, Richard G. 102
Apprenticeship Levy 145–46
apprenticeships 142–46
archetypes 62
Ardern, Jacinda 171, 228
Argenti, Paul 245
Aristotle 166–67
artificial intelligence (AI) 104–06, 118, 225, 299–300, 359
  bias in 300–02
  people strategy 261, 268–69, 273
  personification 113–14
Asian MNCs 53–55
Asilomar framework 302
Asimov's Laws of Robotics 121
Audi 74
Augar review 147
automation 50, 298–300
  humans working together with 299–300
  impact on jobs 108–10
  rate of 361, 362
  see also artificial intelligence (AI); technology
autonomy 282–83, 284

B Corp 176, 206, 208
Baby Boomers 91–92, 95, 96
balanced scorecard 235–37
Ballard, David 66
Barclays 131
Barends, Eric 233

basic skills 131, 137–38
BCG 231–32
Bean, Randy 107–08
Bebchuk, Lucian 174
Beck, Don 239
behavioural skills 129–31
Bennis, Warren 223
Bevan, S. 60
Bezos, Jeff 230–31
Bhutan 168–70
bias 300–02
Birkinshaw, Julian 236
birth rates, declining 88–89
Black Lives Matter 74, 134–35, 210
Blueprint for Better Business 176, 207
boards 186–90, 218–19
Boin, A. 70
bond yields 20
borrowing talent and skills 264–66
brand reputation 73–74
Brexit 61, 65, 90
BRICs countries 53
Briner, Rob 233
British Standards Institution 178–79
Brockman, Greg 105
Brown, Tina 30–31
Buffer 306–07
Buffett, Warren 17, 197
build-buy-borrow-bot 258–59
bull market 19–21
Burke, James 246
Burkhauser, Richard 78
burnout 341–42, 343
Business in the Community 261
business models 106–08
Business Roundtable 12

Cahen-Salvador, Colombe 65
Cameron, William Bruce 164
capabilities, leaders' 231–33
capitalism 79–80
Cappelli, Peter 97
care, ethic of 247–48
care robots 113–14
career flexibility 309–10
Careers and Enterprise Company (CEC) 263

Carnegie UK Trust 171–72
Carucci, Ron 319–20
Case, Anne 80
Center for Evidence-Based Management (CEBMa) 233–35
Chamorro-Premuzic, Tomas 297–98
Channel 4 210
chief knowledge officer (CKO) 331
chief learning officer (CLO) 331
China 53, 54–55, 61, 62–63, 89
  social credit system 118
CIPD 29, 200, 204
circular economy 369
Clarke, Nita 286–87
climate change 165–66
coaching 330
cognitive dissonance 246–47
communication 245
commitment to work 283–84
Companies Act 2006 178
compassionate management 238
competence 71–73
compliance training 326
consumerism 110, 167
core competencies 257–59
core (essential) skills 129–32, 137–38
corporate culture 198–215
  people-centric 209–15
corporate governance 175–79, 215–19
Corporate Governance Code 177–78
corporate learning and development functions 330–32
corporate reporting 175–79
corporate social responsibility (CSR) 198–202
  doing well by doing good 204–08, 372–73
corporate universities and academies 150–52
Corus 54
Covid-19 pandemic 4–5, 7, 69–70, 80, 168, 209, 360, 366–67
  economic impact 16, 18–19, 21, 29, 107
  era-defining changes 61–64
  home working 116, 303
  impact on globalization 57–58
  impact on recruitment 261–62
  impact on unemployment rates 34–35
  leadership 228–31
  school closures 138
  skills gaps 127–28
  technological attacks 120
  and wellbeing 339–40, 344–45, 350–51

Cowan, Christopher 239
creative destruction 16–19
creativity 135
crises 5, 16, 70, 168, 245, 360
  impact on mental health and wellbeing 344–45
  learning from 16–19, 227–31
crowdsourcing talent and skills 266–67
cybersecurity 120–21

Daniels, Doreetha 157
data 104–06
data protection 120–21, 301
Daugherty, Paul 299–300, 301
Davenport, Tom 107–08
De Neve, Jan-Emmanuel 78
Deaton, Angus 78, 80
DeepMind 106
degree-level education 138–42, 147, 156–57
  payback for 140–42
de-industrialization 25
demographic changes 3, 86–97, 359
  5G workforce 91–97
  impact of trends 86–89
  migration rates and ethnic diversity 89–91
developmental models of leadership 238–42
Dewey, John 134
digital badges 150
digital learning 112, 148–50, 322–25
digital skills 133–34, 135–36
discrimination legislation 81–82
diversity 184–91, 210, 243
  quotas 189–91
  regulatory reporting and 184–86
  at senior levels 186–89, 218–19
  talent sourcing and recruitment 259–61
dividend payments 22–23
doing well by doing good 204–08, 372–73
Drucker, Peter 49
Dunning-Kruger effect 241, 242
Dweck, Carol 213, 318
dystopian futures 116–20

earnings 140–42
economically inactive people 33–34
economics and the economy 15–44, 45, 359
  bull market 19–21
  creative destruction and crises 16–19
  different forms for the future 369
  economics of inequality 79–80
  employment *see* employment
  flexible working 31–32, 35–36, 302–08, 370–71

investment *see* investment
measurement 164–65
productivity *see* productivity
short-termism and the profit motive 21–23
unemployment 9–10, 21, 32–35
Edelman 71–74
Edmans, Alex 173
Edmondson, Amy C. 245
education 8, 125–61
   corporate universities 150–52
   financial wellbeing 352
   higher education 138–42, 147, 156–57
   MOOCs 148–50
   skills *see* skills
   systems and the changing world of work 134–38
   value of learning and training 154–57
   vocational education 142–48
   working with young people in towards recruitment 262–64
Education and Employers charity 263
eLearning 323–24
Elkington, John 175
employee engagement *see* engagement
employee expectations 72–73
employee ownership 353
employee surveillance 111–12, 117, 269
employment 24–36
   changing models of 30–32
   economic activities 24–27
   organization size 27–29
   participation rates 278–79
   and unemployment rates 32–35
empowerment 211–12, 272–73
Encarta 266
Engage for Success movement 286–87
engagement 79, 279–89, 337–38
   drivers of 281–84
   trends in 287–89
environment 3, 56–57, 165–66, 360
equality 372
   of opportunity 85–86
Equality Act 81
ESG reporting 175, 207, 219
Essential Digital Skills 133–34
essential skills (core skills) 129–32, 137–38
ethics 71–73, 300–02
   ethical decision-making 246–48
ethnic diversity 89–91
   senior levels 186, 187–88
ethnicity pay gaps 82, 85–86, 188
evidence 75–76, 362, 364
evidence-based management (EBM) 233–35
executive pay 191–93, 217–18

expert predictions 6
explicit knowledge 317

Fair Work Commission 293
Fair Work Convention 293
fairness 372
Festinger, Leon 246
Financial Reporting Council (FRC) 177
financial wellbeing 349–54
   supporting 352–54
first industrial revolution 47–48
First World War 49
fixed mindset 318
flexible working 31–32, 35–36, 302–10, 370–71
flexicurity 309–10
Ford, Henry 48
Ford, Martin 109–10
foreign direct investment (FDI) 52–53
fourth industrial revolution 1–3, 47, 50, 102–04, 120
Fourth Turning theory 62
Francis, Robert 248
Frankiewicz, Becky 297–98
Freudenberger, Herbert 341
Frey, Carl 109
Friedman, Milton 21, 174, 197
further education (FE) sector 147–48
future of work 358–74
   different forms of economies 369
   people's views on 360–62
   principles, evidence and outcomes 362–65
   reasonable hopes and expectations 370–73
   scenario planning 365–68

Gallie, Duncan 283–84
Galloway, Scott 201–02
Gates, Bill 104
Gatsby Charitable Foundation 263
GDP 38, 164–65, 166, 172
Gelfand, Michele 268
Gelles, David 74–75
gender diversity 82, 186–91
gender pay gaps 82, 183–86, 188–89
Generation X 91–92, 96
Generation Z 91–92, 93–94, 95, 343
generations 91–97, 343
   intergenerational tensions 95–97
gig economy 30–32, 304–05
Glaveski, Steve 320
Global Business Collaboration for Better Workplace Mental Health 345

Global Council of Corporate
    Universities 151
global financial crisis (GFC) 17–18
globalization 49–60, 359
    attitudes towards 45–46
    current trends 55–58
    evolution of 50–53
    multipolar world 53–55
    phases 49–50
    and standards of practice 58–60
glocal businesses 51
Go 106
good corporate governance
    principles 215–17
good work 276–313, 360
    engagement *see* engagement
    flexible working 31–32, 35–36, 302–10, 370–71
    job design 296, 297–300
    job quality 290–94
    skills mismatches 295–97
    values and ethics 300–02
Good Work Index 294
Google 270
graduates 156
Gravity Payments 353
Great Depression 49
Gross National Happiness 168–70
Gross National Wellbeing 168, 170–72
growth mindset 318, 322

Hamel, Gary 257–58, 271
Hamori, Monika 244
Hampton-Alexander Review 187
happiness 168–70
Harari, Yuval 119
Harbison, Neil 119
Hawking, Stephen 118, 119
Hays skills index 127–28
Hebo Logistic Technology 269
Heffernan, Margaret 227
hierarchies 270–71
higher education 138–42, 147, 156–57
holacracies 225, 271–72
holding environment 237
home working 35–36, 116, 303
Hope-Hailey, Veronica 230
hormones 335–36
Horta-Osório, António 347
Howe, Neil 62, 92
Hsieh, Tony 272
Hull, Raymond 224
human capital standards 178–79
HR 253–57

humanocracies 225, 271–72
Huxley, Aldous 117
Huxley, Julian 119

'ikigai' 290
in-work poverty 84–85, 351, 352
inclusion 210
inclusive economy 369
inclusive training and learning 328–30
inclusivity 372
income inequalities 77–79
Independent Commission on the College of
    the Future 147
India 52, 53–54
individualism 94
industrial revolutions 47–50, 101–02
    fourth 1–3, 47, 50, 102–04, 120
Industrial Strategy Council 293
inequalities 8–9, 10–11, 45–46, 76–86
    economics of inequality 79–80
    government actions and policy
        interventions 80–82
    pay gaps 82–85, 183–86, 188–89
information technology (ICT) jobs 26–27
institutional holding 237
intergenerational tensions 95–97
International Integrated Reporting Council
    (IIRC) 176
International Labour Organisation
    (ILO) 10, 278
international trade 49–50, 56–57
investment
    lack of 22, 23–24
    in skills development 152–54, 155–56
Italy 64

Jakobsdóttir, Katrin 171
Japan 88–89, 113–14
job design 296, 297–300
job losses due to automation 108–10
job quality 290–94, 342
job satisfaction 288
Jobs, Steve 241
John Lewis Partnership 353
Johnson, Kevin 229
Johnson & Johnson 200, 245–46
Jones, Laura 304
Joseph Rowntree Foundation 351
judgements 246–48

Kahn, William 280
Kahneman, Daniel 6, 78, 241
Kalanick, Travis 73
Kaplan, Robert 235

Kassoy, Andrew 208
Kastelle, Tim 271
Kennedy, John F. 5
Kennedy, Robert F. 164–65, 166
key workers 350–51
Keynes, John Maynard 110, 167
King's Fund 91
Kirkpatrick Model 326–27
knowledge 316–18
known knowns 7, 8–9
known unknowns 7, 9–11
Koyuncu, Burak 244
Krugman, Paul 36, 38
Kurzweil, Ray 118

labour market flexibility 309–10
Labour Party (UK) 65
large enterprises 27–29
Lau, Jennifer 115–16
leadership 72, 222–51, 359
　development 242–44, 321
　developmental models 238–42
　judgements and ethical decision-making 246–48
　leading from principles 237–38
　learning from crises 227–31
　and management 224–25
　measurement 233–37
　mindsets and capabilities 231–33
　open 244–46
learning 7, 368, 371–72
　from crises 16–19, 227–31
　education and 125–61
　methods 320–22
　models 321
　value of 154–57
learning organization 314–33
　corporate learning and development functions 330–32
　inclusive training and learning 328–30
　learning outcomes and their measurement 325–28
　learning philosophy and vision 319–20
　learning technologies 323–25
leavism 308
LEGO 266
Legrain, Philippe 62–63
Lewis, Paul 37
life satisfaction 79, 166–68
limited memory machines 104–05
listening cultures 213–15
literacy skills 137–38
living wage 84, 352
Lockey, Alan 305
Long Peace 46

long-term incentive plans (LTIPs) 192–93
long-termism 12–13
Looney, Bernard 347
L'Oréal 75
low-paid workers 277, 350–51, 352–53

machine learning 104–05, 106
management, leadership and 224–25
Marx, Karl 47–48, 79
massive open online courses (MOOCs) 148–50
mastery 282–83
McDonald's 151
McGregor-Smith Review 187–88, 259
McLeod, David 286–87
measurement 12, 162–96
　corporate reporting 175–79
　diversity 184–91
　economic 164–65
　environment 165–66
　leadership and 233–37
　outcomes of learning 325–28
　of people 180–93
　wellbeing 166–72
mental health 116, 340–49
　core standards 346–47
　impact of crises 344–45
Mental Health at Work Commitment 346–47
mentoring 330
mergers and acquisitions (M&A) 267–68
micro-enterprises 27–29
Mid-Staffordshire District General Hospital 248
migration 60, 89–91
Milanovic, Branko 77
Milgram experiments 247
military, the 211–12, 213
millennials 91–93, 96, 343
mindsets 231–33, 318, 322
minimum wage legislation 83–84
mission 199
mission command 211–12, 213
modern slavery 59
Moore's Law 102
MoralDNA 247
Moss, Jennifer 342–43
motivation 282–84
Muller, Vincent 121–22
multinational corporations (MNCs) 51, 52, 53–55
multipolar world 53–55
multi-stakeholder view 12, 173–74
Musk, Elon 117

National Football League 75
Neumann, Adam 202
neuroscience 322, 335–36
New Zealand 171
NHS 128, 238, 248, 264
Nicolson, Louise 307
non-conforming identity 206–07
Norman, Archie 244
Norton, David 235
numeracy skills 137–38
Nyar, Vineet 272–73

obedience, ethic of 247
OECD 136, 215–17
offshoring 57
online interactions 115–16
online learning 112, 148–50, 322–25
online world, wellbeing in 354–55
open leadership 244–46
OpenAI 105–06
opportunity
    equality of 85–86
    regulatory reporting and improving 184–86
organization design and development (OD) 254–55
organization size 27–29
organizational structure 270–72
O'Rourke, Ray 245
Orsina, Giovanni 64
Orwell, George 117
Osborne, Michael 109
outcomes 362, 364–65
    of learning and their measurement 325–28
outsourcing 51–52, 57–58
overconfidence 241–42

part-time working 35–36, 304
Patagonia 205–06
pay gaps 82–85
    reporting 183–86, 188–89
pedagogy 321–22
Peloton 202
people, measures of 180–93
    regulatory reporting 182–89
people analytics 111–12, 181, 269–70
people-centric cultures 209–15
people strategy 252–75, 359
    core competencies 257–59
    empowerment 272–73
    HR, organizational strategy and 253–57
    optimizing the organization 270–72
    productivity and performance 268–70

talent sourcing and recruitment 259–68
people's views on the future of work 360–62
performance 110–12, 268–70
performance management 336–37
performance-related pay 191–93
personal lives 112–14
personalization 323
Peter Principle 224, 242
Petriglieri, Gianpero 237
physical safety and wellbeing 339–40
Piketty, Thomas 45, 79
Pink, Daniel 282–83
politics 45–68
    era-defining changes 61–64
    eras of industrialization 47–50
    globalization see globalization
    tribalism and individual politics 64–66
populism 60–61
Powdthavee, Nattavudh 78
Prahalad, C.K. 257–58
Price, Dan 353
principles 11–13, 362, 363–64
    leading from 237–38
Prodoscore 269
productivity 36–41, 48–49, 180
    and performance 110–12, 268–70
    UK productivity puzzle 39–41
professional jobs 25, 26
profit motive 21–23
progression 353
Protect 215
protectionism 63
purpose 76, 166–68, 282
    responsible business 198–202

qualifications 146
quotas 189–91

Ramakrishnan, Venkatraman 53, 57
reactive machines 104–05
reason, ethic of 247
recruitment 115
    leaders 244
    talent sourcing and 259–68
regionalization 58
regulation
    corporate 176, 177–79
    technology 120–22
regulatory reporting 182–89
relevance 281–82
remote working 35–36, 116, 303
remuneration committees 217–18
responsible business 11–12, 173–74, 197–221, 360, 372–73

corporate culture 198–215
corporate governance 215–19
CSR 198–202, 204–08
values 202–04
retirement 373–74
Ridderstrale, Jonas 236
rigour 281–82
Rivera, Lauren 260
Robinson, Ken 135
robot carers 113–14
Rock, David 336
Rometty, Ginni 107
Rothman, Joshua 228
Rowntree, Seebohm 49, 110–11

Samra, Rajvinder 342
SCARF model 336
scenario planning 365–68
    common themes from 367–68
Schengen Agreement 51
Schumpeter, Joseph 16–17
Schwab, Klaus 1–2, 50, 102–03, 120
scientific management 48, 110–11, 226
second industrial revolution 47, 48–50
Second World War 49–50
sectors, employment by 25–27
self-aware AI 105
self-awareness 226–27
self-directed learning 320–21, 323
self-employment 30, 31–32
Senge, Peter 315–16
senior executives
    diversity 186–91, 218–19
    executive pay 191–93, 217–18
servant leadership 273
share buybacks 22–23
shared services models 256
sharing economy 369
Sharot, Tali 5
'Shift Happens' video 3–4
short-termism 12–13, 21–23, 40
Silent Generation 92
Sinek, Simon 199, 238
Singh, Manmohan 52, 53
Skidelsky, Edward 167
Skidelsky, Robert 167
skills 125–34, 367, 368
    borrowing 264–66
    corporate investments in skills
        development 152–54, 155–56
    crowdsourcing 266–67
    digital and technology skills 133–34,
        135–36
    directors and boards 218–19

essential 129–32, 137–38
gaps and mismatches 8, 40, 85, 126–28,
    295–97
upskilling programmes 156–57
sleep 348–49
small and medium-sized enterprises
    (SMEs) 27–29, 332
Smith, Ned 206–07
social care 113–14
social cohesion 76–79
social changes 3, 69–100, 359
    crisis of trust 70–76
    government actions and
        interventions 80–82
    inequalities 76–86
    see also demographic changes
social media 2, 69–70, 114–16, 121
social network anal9sis (SNA) 317
Sorenson, Arne 228–30
South Korea 88–89
Spatial 118
Solow Paradox 101–02
speak-up cultures 213–15
Spiral Dynamics model 239–40
Spotify 211
stakeholders 12, 173–74
standards 58–60, 177–79
startup failure rates 29
State Street 74
Steare, Roger 247
Stevenson/Farmer review of mental health
    and employers 346–47
Stiglitz, Joseph 167–68
Stogdill, Ralph 226
strategic workforce planning 257–59
strategy see people strategy
Strauss, William 62, 92
Streisand Effect 65–66
stress 340–42, 343
    managing 345–47
supply chain standards of practice 58–60
surveillance 111–12, 117, 269
Susskind, Daniel 109
Susskind, Richard 109
Sustainable Development Goals (SDGs) 278
Switzerland 83–84
Syed, Matthew 213
systems thinking 240, 316

T levels 146
tacit knowledge 316–18
talent sourcing and recruitment 259–68
Tata Steel 54
taxation 83

Taylor, Frederick Winslow 48, 49, 110–11, 226
Taylor review 290–91
technical skills 129–31
technology 101–24, 359, 367–68
    AI *see* artificial intelligence
    automation *see* automation
    digital skills 133–34, 135–36
    fourth industrial revolution 1–3, 47, 50, 102–04, 120
    future outcomes 116–20
    humanization of work 370
    impact on organizations and business models 106–08
    impact on real life 112–14
    lack of investment in 23–24
    learning technologies 323–25
    productivity and performance 110–12, 268–70
    regulation and education 120–22
    social media 2, 69–70, 114–16, 121
    wellbeing online 354–55
temporary staff 264–66
Tesla 20
Tetlock, Philip 6
theory of mind 105
third industrial revolution 47, 50, 101–02
Thunberg, Greta 94
time management 307–08
Timpson 261
Towards Maturity 314–15
trade tensions 56
training 324–32
    inclusive 328–30
    outcomes and their measurement 325–28
    value of 154–57
    see also education
trait theories of leadership 226
transhumanism 119
transparency 12, 75–76
tribalism 64–66, 72
trillion-valued companies 19
Triple Bottom Line 175
Trump, Donald 60–61, 73
trust 70–79, 230
    crisis of 70–76
    in governments 63–64
    undermined by increasing inequalities 76–79
tuition fees 141–42
Turing test 114
Turner, Chris 208
'turnings' 62
Tylenol 245–46

Uber 73
Ulrich, Dave 256
Umunna, Chuka 175
uncertainty 5–11, 238–39
unemployment 9–10, 21, 32–35
Unilever 59, 266
union membership 285–86
United Nations (UN) 46, 81
    Sustainable Development Goals 278
    World Happiness Reports 169
unlimited holidays 306–07
upskilling programmes 156–57
urbanization 48
Utrecht Work Engagement Scale (UWES) 282

values 202–04, 300–02
Valuing your Talent framework 180–81
Varoufakis, Yanis 79
Venzo, Andrea 65
virtue signalling 74–75
vision 199
vocational education and training (VET) 142–48
voice 272–73, 284–86
volunteering 330

wages 10, 38
Wallace-Stephens, Fabian 305
'War for Talent' 129
Ward, Robert 63
Warhurst, Chris 291
Watson, Thomas 318
Weiss Haserot, Phyllis 96
Welfare Workers' Association (WWA) 49
wellbeing 12, 334–57
    drivers of in the workplace 337–38
    financial 349–54
    measuring 166–72
    mental health 116, 340–49
    online 354–55
    physical safety and 339–40
    stress 340–42, 343, 345–47
Wells Fargo 247–48
West, Michael 238
WeWork 20, 202
What Works Centre for Wellbeing 337
whistleblowing 214–15, 285
Whole Foods 267–68
Wikipedia 266
wilful blindness 227
Wilson, James 299–300, 301
Winnicott, Donald 237
Wolf, Martin 174
women
    flexible working 304

higher education 139–40
see also gender diversity; gender pay gaps
workforce planning 252–53
  strategic 257–59
workforce scheduling 212
working hours 41, 279, 348, 371
  lost 10
working lives 277–78
Working Lives Survey 294
World Economic Forum (WEF) 61, 103, 108, 134, 135–36

World Uncertainty Index 6

Xi Jinping 61

Yerkes-Dodson curve 340–41
yogababble 201

Zanini, Michele 271
Zappos 272
zero-hours contracts 304–05
Zoom 201